W9-BJJ-848

How to Read the Bible Book by Book

Okay, you want to begin studying God's Word, but you don't know how to begin. Try the *read* and *mark* method. Find a newer version of the Bible and a pencil. Open to a manageable book, like Matthew, Philippians, or Proverbs. Ask the Lord to speak to you, then read the first paragraph. Look for something to underline, circle, or highlight. Read the next paragraph and do the same. Is there a truth to learn? A promise to claim? A prayer to echo? A command to obey?

If a verse confuses you, put a question mark by it. If it thrills you, use an exclamation mark. If you find a verse to memorize, circle it and spend time working on it, word by word. When you finish a book, go to another.

If you have a study Bible, the notes will help you understand the text. Don't grow discouraged. The more you study, the more you learn; the more you learn, the more you'll want to read—and mark.

Also by Gordon D. Fee and Douglas Stuart

How to Read the Bible for All Its Worth

Also by Gordon D. Fee and Mark L. Strauss

How to Choose a Translation for All Its Worth

From the Authors of the Bestselling
HOW TO READ THE BIBLE FOR ALL ITS WORTH

OVER 150,000 COPIES SOLD

How to Read the Bible Book by Book

A Guided Tour

Gordon D. Fee
Douglas Stuart

ZONDERVAN®

ZONDERVAN

How to Read the Bible Book by Book
Copyright © 2002 by Gordon D. Fee and Douglas Stuart

This title is also available as a Zondervan ebook.
Visit www.zondervan.com/ebooks.

Requests for information should be addressed to:
Zondervan, 3900 *Sparks Dr. SE, Grand Rapids, Michigan 49546*

This edition: ISBN 978-0-310-51808-2

The Library of Congress cataloged the original edition as follows:

Fee, Gordon D.
How to read the Bible book by book : a guided tour / Gordon D. Fee and Douglas Stuart.
p. cm.
ISBN 0-310-21118-2 (pbk.)
1. Bible—Reading. 2. Bible—Criticism, interpretation, etc.
I. Stuart, Douglas K. II. Title.
BS617 .F44 2002
220.6'1—dc21 2001006893

Scripture quotations, unless otherwise indicated, are taken from The Holy Bible, New International Version®, NIV®. Copyright © 1973, 1978, 1984, 2011 by Biblica, Inc.® Used by permission of Zondervan. All rights reserved worldwide. www.Zondervan.com The "NIV" and "New International Version" are trademarks registered in the United States Patent and Trademark Office by Biblica, Inc.®

Most New Testament Scripture quotations are taken from the New Testament edition of the Holy Bible, Today's New International Version®. TNIV®. Copyright © 2001, 2005 by Biblica Inc.® Used by permission. All rights reserved worldwide.

Scripture quotations marked NRSV are from the New Revised Standard Version Bible. Copyright © 1989 National Council of the Churches of Christ in the United States of America. Used by permission. All rights reserved.

Scripture quotations marked NEB are from the New English Bible. © Cambridge University Press and Oxford University Press 1961, 1970. All rights reserved.

Any Internet addresses (websites, blogs, etc.) and telephone numbers in this book are offered as a resource. They are not intended in any way to be or imply an endorsement by Zondervan, nor does Zondervan vouch for the content of these sites and numbers for the life of this book.

All rights reserved. No part of this publication may be reproduced, stored in a retrieval system, or transmitted in any form or by any means—electronic, mechanical, photocopy, recording, or any other—except for brief quotations in printed reviews, without the prior permission of the publisher.

Interior design: Nancy Wilson

Printed in the United States of America

19 20 21 22 23 24 25 /DCI/ 25 24 23 22 21 20 19 18 17 16 15 14 13

For Walker, Maia, and Emma
Joshua, Julia, Cherisa, Nathan, and Benjamin
Zachary and Jackson
Maricel and Annalise
and
Meriwether and Honour
and Mcaela
that they may learn to read the Story well
and love Him whose Story it is
(Psalm 71:14–18; Psalm 103:17)

ABBREVIATIONS

OLD TESTAMENT

Gen	Genesis	Song	Song of Songs
Exod	Exodus	Isa	Isaiah
Lev	Leviticus	Jer	Jeremiah
Num	Numbers	Lam	Lamentations
Deut	Deuteronomy	Ezek	Ezekiel
Josh	Joshua	Dan	Daniel
Judg	Judges	Hos	Hosea
Ruth	Ruth	Joel	Joel
1–2 Sam	1–2 Samuel	Amos	Amos
1–2 Kgs	1–2 Kings	Obad	Obadiah
1–2 Chr	1–2 Chronicles	Jonah	Jonah
Ezra	Ezra	Mic	Micah
Neh	Nehemiah	Nah	Nahum
Esth	Esther	Hab	Habakkuk
Job	Job	Zeph	Zephaniah
Ps/Pss	Psalms	Hag	Haggai
Prov	Proverbs	Zech	Zechariah
Eccl	Ecclesiastes	Mal	Malachi

NEW TESTAMENT

Matt	Matthew	1–2 Thess	1–2 Thessalonians
Mark	Mark	1–2 Tim	1–2 Timothy
Luke	Luke	Titus	Titus
John	John	Phlm	Philemon
Acts	Acts	Heb	Hebrews
Rom	Romans	Jas	James
1–2 Cor	1–2 Corinthians	1–2 Pet	1–2 Peter
Gal	Galatians	1–2–3 John	1–2–3 John
Eph	Ephesians	Jude	Jude
Phil	Philippians	Rev	Revelation
Col	Colossians		

A.D.	*anno Domini* (in the year of [our] Lord)	f(f).	and the following one(s)
B.C.	before Christ	i.e.	*id est,* that is
ca.	*circa,* about, approximately	lit.	literally
cf.	*confer,* compare	NT	New Testament
ch(s).	chapter(s)	OT	Old Testament
e.g.	*exempli gratia,* for example	p(p).	page(s)
esp.	especially	par.	parallel (textual parallels)
et al.	*et alii,* and others	v(v).	verse(s)
etc.	*et cetera,* and the rest	*x*	number of times a form occurs

Contents

THE GOSPELS AND ACTS IN THE BIBLICAL STORY ■ 267

THE EPISTLES AND REVELATION IN THE BIBLICAL STORY ■ 315

Preface

This book is intended to be a companion to *How to Read the Bible for All Its Worth*. That book was designed to help people become better readers of Scripture by taking into account the various kinds of literature that make up the Christian Bible. Through an understanding of how the various types "work," how they differ from one another, and how they raise different kinds of hermeneutical questions, we hoped that one might learn to read the Bible in a more informed way.

The success of that first book has given us the courage to try another. The aim is still the same: to help people become better *readers* of Scripture. What we hope to do here is to go a step beyond the first book: Assuming the principles of the first book, here we try to help you read—and understand—each of the biblical books on its own but especially to help you see how each one fits with the others to form the great narrative of Scripture.

But this book has undergone its own form of evolution. Some years ago we were asked to write a Bible survey textbook of the kind that many students have been exposed to over the years. For a variety of reasons, but mostly because we could never get our hearts into it, that project simply did not work out. To be sure, we hope this book will still serve the purposes of survey courses, but we have intentionally tried to write something quite different. These differences, as we perceive them, are several.

First, our goal is not simply to dispense knowledge about the various books of the Bible—the kind of knowledge that allows one to pass Bible knowledge exams without ever reading the Bible! Such books and exams usually deal with a lot of data but very often with little sense of how the various books of the Bible function as entities on their own or of how each fits into *God's story*. Our present concern is almost altogether with the latter. And in any case, the concern is with your becoming a better *reader* of Scripture; if you begin to learn some other things about each book along the way, all the better.

Second, we want to show how the separate entities—each biblical book—fit together as a whole to tell God's story. So much is this a concern that our book is introduced with a brief overview of the biblical story—what those who study narratives call the *metanarrative* of Scripture. This is the big picture, the primary story, of which all the others form a part so as to shape the whole.

Third, in coming to the various biblical books, one by one, we follow a generally consistent format that isolates questions of introduction at the beginning as "Orienting Data for ..." These kinds of issues (authorship, date, recipients, occasion, and the like) take up much of the space in most surveys. For these (sometimes important) matters there are several surveys, introductions, and Bible dictionaries for both the Old and New Testaments that you may consult. But these matters are often debatable and therefore consume a lot of time that is not always immediately relevant to the reading of the biblical text in its larger setting. Thus, we simply offer some options, or note the traditional view, or settle on one as the perspective from which this guide is written.

But a further word is needed about the matter of authorship, especially for the Old Testament books, since authors in that period did not normally attach their names to what they wrote (with the exception of letters—and there are none of these as books in the Old Testament). When individuals speak about themselves within a given book (e.g., Moses, Nehemiah, Qohelet ["Teacher" in Ecclesiastes]), we may learn something about probable or possible authorship that we wouldn't otherwise know. But for the most part, modern concerns about matters of date and authorship were not given the same attention in ancient Israel; this is made obvious by their absence from most of these books. Many books (e.g., nearly all the historical and poetical books) are entirely anonymous. And even though the source of the content of some books is given—by way of an editorial title at the beginning—and assumptions can often be made that the source also functioned as author, the concern over the book's actual author is not prominent in the book itself. As to dating, just four books—Ezekiel, Daniel, Zechariah, and Haggai—date any of their material, and of those only Haggai does so consistently. Thus we have chosen to minimize authorship in this *reading* guide, leaving it entirely alone when the biblical book itself is anonymous (one can say "unknown" only so many times!). Our interest is in your reading the biblical document in its final canonical form, not in debating the issues of dates, sources, and authorship.

Most of our energy, therefore, has gone into the three major sections of each chapter. The first, "Overview of ...," is designed to get you into the book by giving you a sense of what the whole is about. In some ways it is a brief elaboration of the "Content" sentence(s) in the "Orienting" section. The second, "Specific Advice for Reading ...," tends to elaborate the "Emphases" from the "Orienting" section. Here we offer a way of reading the text, some key themes to keep in mind as you do, or some crucial background material—all of which are designed to help you as you read the text for yourself. The final section, "A Walk through ...," then takes you by the hand, as it were, and walks you through the book, showing how its various parts work together to form the whole. Sometimes this takes more of an outline form; at other times, because we have purposely tried to keep our chapters brief, you will walk with giant steps. The books of Psalms and Proverbs were understandably the most difficult to fit into this pattern; yet even here we have tried to help you see how the collections are put together.

Above all, we have tried to write a book about the books of the Bible that will not be a substitute for reading the Bible itself. Rather, we hope it may create a desire in you to read each of the biblical books for yourself, while helping you make a fair amount of sense out of what you are reading.

NOTE WELL: The key to using this book is for you to read the first three sections of each chapter ("Orienting Data," "Overview," "Specific Advice"), and then *to read the biblical text* in conjunction with the section titled "A Walk through ..." If you read "A Walk through" on its own, it will become just more data for you to assimilate. Our intent is for you first to have some important preliminary data in hand, then truly to walk with you through your reading of the biblical book. This will, of course, be far more difficult for some of the longer books, just as it was for us to condense so much material into the brief parameters we allowed ourselves. But even here, while you may be reading over a more extended time period, we hope you will find this a helpful guide. A glossary is provided for those who need some guidance through the maze of technical terms that biblical scholars tend to use without forethought (see p. 437). We have also supplied a suggested chronological listing of the books for those who wish to read them in that order (see the appendix at the back of the book, p. 443).

We have tried to write in such a way that you will be able to follow what is said, no matter which English translation you are using, provided it is a contemporary one (see ch. 2 of *How to Read the Bible for*

All Its Worth). For the New Testament, Professor Fee regularly had Today's New International Version (TNIV) in front of him as he wrote; for the Old Testament, the New International Version (1984 edition) was used. Typically, when Bible verses are cited in this book, they are taken either from the NIV or from the New Testament edition of the TNIV.

A couple of words about presuppositions. First, while we have not assumed that the reader will already have read *How to Read the Bible for All Its Worth,* we do refer to it from time to time (as *How to 1,* with page numbers always referring to the third edition [2003] after the tenth printing of this book, all copies prior to the tenth printing refer to the second edition [1993]) so that we don't have to repeat some presuppositional things from that book (for example, sources of the Gospels). In the case of Acts and Revelation, which received individual chapters in *How to 1,* that material is reset for this book, but one will still be helped by reading those chapters as well.

Second, the authors unapologetically stand within the evangelical tradition of the church. This means, among other things, that we believe that the Holy Spirit has inspired the biblical writers (and collectors) in their task—even though most often we speak of each document in terms of what the (inspired) human author is doing.

At the same time, in most cases we have tried to be apprised of and make use of the most recent biblical scholarship—although any scholar who might venture to look at this work may well wonder whether we have consulted her or his latest work. Along with our own reading of the text, we herewith gratefully acknowledge that we have incorporated suggestions—and even language—from others too many to mention by name. Those who might recognize some of their ideas in what we have written may, we hope, take pleasure in such recognition; we trust they will also be generous to us when we have chosen to go our own way rather than to be beholden to any other scholarly endeavor.

The authors with gratitude also acknowledge the following: Regent College, whose generous sabbatical policy made it possible for Professor Fee to work on the book during spring term 1998 and winter term 2001; colleagues and friends who have read selected chapters and offered many helpful comments: Iain Provan, V. Philips Long, Rikk Watts, John Stek, Bruce Waltke, and Wendy Wilcox Glidden. Professor Fee's wife, Maudine, has taken great interest in this project by reading every word and making scores of insightful suggestions that have made it a better book. And during the month of March 2001, when Professor Fee was recuperating from surgery, she joined him in reading the entire manuscript and the entire Bible aloud—resulting in scores of changes to the book, as our ears often heard better than our eyes saw. We cannot recommend strongly enough the value of the oral reading of the Bible!

We dedicated *How to 1* to our parents, three of whom have now passed on to be with their Lord. We dedicate this present endeavor to our grandchildren—as of this writing, twelve for the Fees, the oldest of whom are now teenagers, and three for the Stuarts. Thus, in some measure, this book is our own reflection on Psalm 71:14–18.

The Biblical Story: An Overview

When the authors were boys growing up in Christian homes, one of the ways we—and our friends—were exposed to the Bible was through the daily reading of a biblical text from the Promise Box, which dutifully found its way onto our kitchen tables. Furthermore, most believers of our generation—and of several preceding ones—had learned a kind of devotional reading of the Bible that emphasized reading it only in parts and pieces, looking for a "word for the day."

While the thought behind these approaches to Scripture was salutary enough (constant exposure to the sure promises of God's Word), they also had their downside, teaching people to read texts in a way that disconnected them from the grand story of the Bible.

The concern of this book is to help you read the Bible as a whole, and even when the "whole" is narrowed to "whole books," it is important for you always to be aware of how each book fits into the larger story (on this matter, see *How to 1*, pp. 91–92). But in order to do this, you need first to have a sense of what the grand story is all about. That is what this introduction proposes to do.

First, let's be clear: The Bible is not merely some divine guidebook, nor is it a mine of propositions to be believed or a long list of commands to be obeyed. True, one does receive plenty of guidance from it, and it does indeed contain plenty of true propositions and divine directives. But the Bible is infinitely more than that.

It is no accident that the Bible comes to us primarily by way of narrative—but not just any narrative. Here we have the grandest narrative of all—God's own story. That is, it does not purport to be just one more story of humankind's search for God. No, this is *God's* story, the account of *his* search for us, a story essentially told in four chapters: Creation, Fall, Redemption, Consummation. In this story, God is the divine protagonist, Satan the antagonist, God's people the agonists (although too often also the antagonists), with redemption and reconciliation as the plot resolution.

CREATION

Since this is *God's story,* it does not begin, as do all other such stories, with a hidden God, whom people are seeking and to whom Jesus ultimately leads them. On the contrary, the biblical narrative begins with God as Creator of all that is. It tells us that "in the beginning God ...": that God is *before* all things, that he is the *cause* of all things, that he is therefore *above* all things, and that he is the *goal* of all things. He stands at the origin of all things as the sole cause of the whole universe, in all of its vastness and intricacies. And all creation—all history itself—has the eternal God, through Christ, as its final purpose and consummation.

We are further told that humanity is the crowning glory of the Creator's work—beings made in God's own likeness, with whom he could commune, and in whom he could delight; beings who would know the sheer pleasure of his presence, love, and favor. Created in God's *image,* humankind thus uniquely enjoyed the *vision* of God and lived in *fellowship* with God. We were nonetheless *created* beings and were thus intended to be dependent on the Creator for life and existence in the world. This part of the story is narrated in Genesis 1–2, but it is repeated or echoed in scores of ways throughout the whole narrative.

FALL

The second chapter in the biblical story is a long and tragic one. It begins in Genesis 3, and the dark thread runs through the whole story almost to the very end (Rev 22:11, 15). This "chapter" tells us that man and woman coveted more godlikeness and that in one awful moment in the history of our planet they chose godlikeness over against mere creatureliness, with its dependent status. They chose *in*dependence from the Creator. But we were not intended to live so, and the result was a fall—a colossal and tragic fall. (To be sure, this is not a popular part of the story today, but its rejection is part of the Fall itself and the beginning of all false theologies.)

Made to enjoy God and to be dependent on him, and to find our meaning ultimately in our very creatureliness, we now came under God's wrath and thus came to experience the terrible consequences of our rebellion. The calamity of our fallenness is threefold:

First, we lost our *vision* of God with regard to his nature and character. Guilty and hostile ourselves, we projected that guilt and hostility onto God. God is to blame: "Why have *you* made me thus?" "Why are *you* so cruel?" are the plaintive cries that run throughout the history of our race. We thus became idolaters, now creating gods in our own image; every grotesque expression of our fallenness was reconstructed into a god. Paul puts it this way: "Although they claimed to be wise, they became fools and exchanged the glory of the immortal God for images made to look like mortal human beings and birds and animals and reptiles... They exchanged the truth about God for a lie, and worshiped and served created things rather than the Creator—who is forever praised" (Rom 1:22, 24–25).

In exchanging the truth about God for a lie, we saw God as full of caprice, contradictions, hostility, lust, and retribution (all projections of our fallen selves). But God is *not* like our grotesque idolatries. Indeed, if he is hidden, Paul says, it is because we had become slaves to the god of this world, who has blinded our minds, so that we are ever seeking but never able to find him (see 2 Cor 4:4).

Second, the Fall also caused us to distort—and blur—the *divine image* in ourselves, rolling it in the dust, as it were. Instead of being loving, generous, self-giving, thoughtful, merciful—as God is—we became miserly, selfish, unloving, unforgiving, spiteful. Created to image, and thus represent, God in all that we are and do, we learned rather to bear the image of the Evil One, God's implacable enemy.

The third consequence of the Fall was our loss of the *divine presence* and with that our relationship—fellowship—with God. In place of communion with the Creator, having purpose in his creation, we became rebels, lost and cast adrift, creatures who broke God's laws, abused his creation, and suffered the awful consequences of fallenness in our brokenness, alienation, loneliness, and pain.

Under the tyranny of our sin—indeed, we are enslaved to it, Paul says, and guilty—we found ourselves unwilling and unable to come to the living God for life and restoration. And in turn we passed on our brokenness in the form of every kind of broken relationship with one another (this is writ large in Genesis 4–11).

The Bible tells us that we are fallen, that there is an awful distance between ourselves and God, and that we are like sheep going astray (Isa 53:6; 1 Pet 2:25) or like a rebellious, know-it-all son, living in a far country among the hogs, wanting to eat their food (Luke 15:11–32). In our better moments, we also know that this is the truth not only about the murderer or rapist or child abuser, but also about ourselves—the selfish, the greedy, the proud. It is no wonder people think God is hostile to us; in our better moments we know we deserve his wrath for the kind of endless stinkers we really are.

REDEMPTION

The Bible also tells us that the holy and just God, whose moral perfections burn against sin and creaturely rebellion, is in fact also a God full of mercy and love—and faithfulness. The reality is that God pitied—and loved—these creatures of his, whose rebellion and rejection of their dependent status had caused them to fall so low and thus to experience the pain, guilt, and alienation of their sinfulness.

But how to get through to us, to rescue us from ourselves with all of our wrong views about God and the despair of our tragic fallenness; how to get us to see that God is *for* us, not *against* us (see Rom 8:31); how to get the rebel not just to run up a white flag of surrender but willingly to change sides and thereby once again to discover joy and meaningfulness—that's what chapter 3 of the story is all about.

And it's the longest chapter, a chapter that tells how God set about redeeming and restoring these fallen creatures of his so that he might restore to us the lost vision of God, renew in us the divine image, and reestablish our relationship with him. But also woven throughout this chapter is that other thread—the one of our continuing resistance.

Thus we are told that God came to a man, Abraham, and made a covenant with him—to bless him and, through him, the nations (Genesis 12–50)—and with his offspring, Israel, who had become a slave people (Exodus). Through the first of his prophets, Moses, God (now known by his name *Yahweh*) freed them from their slavery and made a covenant with them at Mount Sinai—that he who had rescued them would be their Savior and Protector forever, that he would be uniquely present with them among all the peoples of the world. But they would also have to keep covenant with him, by letting themselves be reshaped into his likeness. Thus he gave them the Law as his gift to them, both to reveal what he is like and to protect them from one another while they were being reshaped (Leviticus–Deuteronomy).

But the story tells us they rebelled over and over again and looked on his gift of law as a form of taking away their freedom. As shepherds who were being brought into an agricultural land (Joshua), they were not sure their God—a God of shepherds, as they supposed—would also help the crops to grow, so they turned to the agricultural fertility gods (Baal and Ashtoreth) of the peoples who surrounded them.

So they experienced several rounds of oppression and rescue (Judges), even while some of them were truly taking on God's character (Ruth). Finally, God sent them another great prophet (Samuel), who anointed for them their ideal king (David), with whom God made another covenant, specifying that one of his offspring would rule over his people forever (1–2 Samuel). But alas, it goes bad again (1–2 Kings; 1–2 Chronicles), and God in love sends them prophets (Isaiah–Malachi), singers (Psalms), and sages (Job; Proverbs; Ecclesiastes). In the end their constant unfaithfulness is too much, so God at last judges his people with the curses promised in Leviticus 26 and Deuteronomy 28. Yet even here (see Deut 30) there is promise for the future (see, e.g., Isa 40–55; Jer 30–32; Ezek 36–37) in which there would be a new "son of David" and an outpouring of God's Spirit into people's hearts so that they would come to life and be transformed into God's likeness. This final blessing would also include people from all the nations ("the Gentiles").

Finally, just before the last scene, with its final curtain and epilogue, we are told of the greatest event of all—that the great, final "son of David" is none other than God himself, the Creator of all the cosmic greatness and grandeur, come to be present on the human scene in our own likeness. Born as the child of a peasant girl, within the fold of an oppressed people, Jesus the Son of God lived and taught among them. And finally with a horrible death, followed by a death-defeating resurrection, he grappled with and defeated the "gods"—all the powers that have stood against us—and himself bore the full weight of the guilt and punishment of the creatures' rebellion.

Here is the heart of the story: A loving, redeeming God in his incarnation restored our lost *vision* of God (took off the wraps, as it were, so that we could plainly see what God is truly like), by his crucifixion and resurrection made possible our being restored to the *image* of God (see Rom 8:29; 2 Cor 3:18), and through the gift of the Spirit became *present* with us in constant fellowship. Marvelous—well nigh incredible—that revelation, that redemption.

The genius of the biblical story is what it tells us about God himself: a God who sacrifices himself in death out of love for his enemies; a God who would rather experience the death we deserved than to be apart from the people he created for his pleasure; a God who himself bore our likeness, experienced our creatureliness, and carried our sins so that he might provide pardon and reconciliation; a God who would not let us go, but who would pursue us—all of us, even the worst of us—so that he might restore us into joyful fellowship with himself; a God who in Christ Jesus has so forever identified with his beloved creatures that he came to be known and praised as "the God and Father of our Lord Jesus Christ" (1 Pet 1:3).

This is *God's* story, the story of his unfathomable love and grace, mercy and forgiveness—and that is how it also becomes *our* story. The story tells us that we deserve nothing but get everything; that we deserve hell but get heaven; that we deserve to be wiped out, obliterated, but we get his tender embrace; that we deserve rejection and judgment but get to become his children, to bear his likeness, to call him Father. This is the story of the Bible, *God's story,* which at the same time is also our own. Indeed, he even let his human creatures have a part in writing it!

CONSUMMATION

Because the story has not yet ended, the final chapter is still being written—even though we know from what has been written how the final chapter turns out. What God has already set in motion, we are told, through the incarnation, death, and resurrection of Jesus Christ and the gift of the Holy Spirit is finally going to be fully realized.

Thus the one thing that makes this story so different from all other such stories is that ours is filled with hope. There is an End—a glorious conclusion to the present story. It is Jesus, standing at the tomb of his friend Lazarus, telling Lazarus's sister Martha that Jesus himself was her hope for life now and for the life to come: "I am the resurrection and the life," he told her, "anyone who believes in me will live, even though they die"—because Jesus is the *resurrection.* And because he is also the *life,* he went on: "and whoever lives and believes in me will never die" (John 11:25–26). And then he proceeded to validate what he had said by raising Lazarus from the grave.

Jesus himself became the final verification of those words by his own resurrection from the dead. The wicked and the religious killed him. They could not tolerate his presence among them, because he stood in utter contradiction to all their petty forms of religion and authority, based on their own fallenness—and he then had the gall to tell them that he was the *only* way to the Father (see John 14:6). So they killed him. But since he himself *was* Life—and the author of life for all others—the grave couldn't hold him. And his resurrection not only validated his own claims and vindicated his own life on our planet, it also spelled the beginning of the end for death itself and became the guarantee of those who are his—both now and forever.

This is what the final episode (the Revelation) is all about—God's final wrap-up of the story, when his justice brings an end to the great Antagonist and all who continue to bear his image (see Rev 20) and when God in love restores the creation (Eden) as a new heaven and a new earth (see Rev 21–22).

This, then, is the metanarrative, the grand story, of which the various books of the Bible are a part. While we have regularly tried to point out how each book fits in, as you read the various books, you will want to think for yourself how they fit into the larger story. We hope you will also ask yourself how you fit into it as well.

The Narrative of Israel (Including the Law) in the Biblical Story

We should begin by noting that the arrangement of the Old Testament books in the Hebrew Bible is a bit different from that in our English Bibles. Ours comes to us by way of the second-century B.C. Greek translation known as *the Septuagint.* The Hebrew Bible is divided into three parts: *the Law* (the Pentateuch, or "five books of Moses"), *the Prophets* (the Former Prophets, including Joshua through Kings [minus Ruth], and the Latter Prophets, including Isaiah, Jeremiah, Ezekiel, and the Book of the Twelve [the so-called Minor Prophets]), and *the Writings* (the Psalms [including Lamentations], the Wisdom books [Job, Proverbs, Ecclesiastes, Song of Songs], Daniel, and the four narrative books of Ruth, Esther, Ezra-Nehemiah, and Chronicles). In this book we will follow the English order, except for Lamentations in the Old Testament, which is placed among the Writings, and Acts in the New Testament, which properly belongs with the Gospel of Luke.

As noted in *How to 1* (p. 22), despite the way many of God's good people handle the Bible, it is, in fact, no mere collection of propositions to be believed and imperatives to be obeyed. Rather, the essential character of the Bible, the whole Bible, is *narrative,* a narrative in which both the propositions and the imperatives are deeply embedded as an essential part. And so the Bible begins with a series of narrative books—which is true even of Leviticus and Deuteronomy, which may appear otherwise because they are composed largely of laws, but which, in fact, cannot be properly understood apart from the narrative structure in which they are placed.

Thus the beginning of the biblical story takes root in the lengthy narrative that tells the story of God's chosen people, Israel. The first of the five books of Moses (Genesis) relates the beginnings of everything (Creation and Fall) and then focuses especially on God's call and covenant with Abraham and his seed, promising both to make them a numerous people and to give them the land of Canaan. After rescuing the people from slavery in Egypt (the exodus), God meets with them at Mount Sinai in the vast Sinai wilderness. Here he makes a second covenant with Israel that takes the form of "the law," which includes the building of a tabernacle (Exodus), the place where God will dwell among his people and where they are to worship him with proper offerings and sacrifices (Leviticus) as a part of the way they uphold their end of the covenant.

As the people prepare to leave Sinai and make their way to the promised land, the number of men twenty years old and older are counted (those who will be Israel's warriors) and placed around the tabernacle in battle formation (Numbers). Thus they are prepared to take their place in the holy war by which they are to gain the land God had promised to their fathers—Abraham, Isaac, and Jacob. Before they embark on this conquest, Moses gives them a review of this history, another overview of the law, and the blessings and curses (promises and threats) of a kind that accompany ancient covenants; in their case, disobedience to God's covenant meant exile, but with a promised, even more glorious restoration in the form of a new exodus (Deuteronomy).

After the story of the initial conquest and occupation of the land (Joshua) come stories of their failures to keep covenant with God, their true King (Judges). In this latter story (including Ruth), we are prepared for the next major turn in the main story line—that God will rule Israel through an earthly king. The books of Samuel thus tell the story of David, with whom God makes another covenant—that one of his sons will never fail to sit on the throne in Israel, as long as they keep covenant with God. As in many ancient kingships, David himself was also understood to embody the people, a key element in many of the psalms and in the final unfolding of the story of Jesus of Nazareth. But alas, the story of Israel repeats itself, as one king after another leads Israel astray to pursue other gods (1–2 Kings). Indeed, within two generations David's kingdom is divided into two parts. The northern kingdom (Israel; sometimes called Ephraim by the psalmists and prophets) falls to the Assyrians in 722 B.C. and for all practical purposes ceases to exist as a distinct entity. The southern kingdom (Judah) falls to the Babylonians in 586 B.C. In this case, the leading people carried into exile in Babylon thus form part of the remnant through whom God will still work out his redemptive plans.

The exile brought untold misery and trauma to God's people, since they lost their promised land and their temple—the primary evidence of God's special presence and of their being his people. Especially through the prophetic ministry of Ezekiel, the exiles were held together. Many, though by no means the majority, were finally restored to their land under the Persians and rebuilt the temple (Ezra 1–6); about a century later, Ezra and Nehemiah led a further return of exiles and were instrumental in bringing about a significant reform (Ezra 7–10; Nehemiah). During this same overall restoration period, the story of Judah is retold from a more positive perspective (1–2 Chronicles), while Esther tells the story of the Jewish exiles throughout the Persian Empire being saved from annihilation.

As you read through the books in this section of the Bible, you will find various threads that hold the larger narrative together: God's *covenants* with his people; God's *faithfulness* to them despite their repeated unfaithfulness to him; God's choice of the *lesser* and the *unfavored* ones (his choosing the "weak to shame the strong" [1 Cor 1:27]); God's *redeeming* his people from slavery to make them his own; God's *dwelling* among them in tabernacle and temple as the gift of his renewed presence on earth (lost in the Fall); God's gift of the *law* in order to reshape them into his own likeness; God's provision of a *sacrificial system*—the "red thread" of blood poured out for the life of another—as his way of offering forgiveness; God's choice of a *king* from Judah who would represent him on earth and thus prepare the way for his own coming in the person of Jesus. These are the matters that make the whole story hold together as one story. Be watching for them as you read.

Genesis

ORIENTING DATA FOR GENESIS

- **Content:** the story of the creation, of human disobedience and its tragic consequences, and of God's choosing Abraham and his offspring—the beginning of the story of redemption
- **Historical coverage:** from creation to the death of Joseph in Egypt (ca. 1600 B.C.?)
- **Emphases:** God as the Creator of all that is; God's creation of human beings in his image; the nature and consequences of human disobedience; the beginning of the divine covenants; God's choice of a people through whom he will bless the nations

OVERVIEW OF GENESIS

For modern readers Genesis might appear to be a strange book, beginning as it does with God and creation, and ending with Joseph in a coffin in Egypt! But that strangeness is evidence that even though it has integrity as a book in its own right (careful structure and organization), it is at the same time intended to set the whole biblical story in motion. Indeed, its opening word (*Bereshith* = "in [the] beginning") both serves as its title and is suggestive as to what the book is about. Thus it tells of the beginning of God's story—creation, human disobedience, and divine redemption—while it also begins the Pentateuch, the story of God's choosing and making a covenant with a people through whom he would bless all peoples (Gen 12:2–3).

The narrative of Genesis itself comes in two basic parts: a "prehistory" (chs. 1–11), the stories of creation, human origins, the fall of humanity, and the relentless progress of evil—all against the backdrop of God's enduring patience and love—and the story of the beginning of redemption through Abraham and his seed (chs. 12–50), with focus on the stories of Abraham (11:27–25:11), Jacob (25:12–37:1), and Joseph (chs. 37–50). These stories are structured in part around a phrase that occurs ten times: "This is the account [genealogy/family history] of," a term which can refer both to "genealogies" proper (as with Shem, Ishmael, and Esau) and to "family stories." You will see that the major stories of Abraham, Jacob, and Joseph in each case come under the family story of the father (Terah, Isaac, and Jacob).

The overall narrative of Genesis thus begins immediately after the prologue (1:1–2:3) with the first human family in the Garden of Eden and works successively from Adam's family through Noah and Shem to Terah and Abraham and finally through Isaac to Jacob (Israel) and thus to Joseph. At the same time, the family lines of the rejected sons (Cain, Ishmael, Esau) are also given so that the "chosen seed" and the "rejected brother" are set off in contrast (the one has a story, the other only a genealogy). Finally, watch for one further framing device that holds the major part of the book together: God's use of Noah to preserve human life during the great deluge (chs. 6–9) and of Joseph to preserve human life during the great drought (chs. 37–50).

SPECIFIC ADVICE FOR READING GENESIS

As you read this first book in the Bible, besides being aware of how the narrative unfolds according to the family stories, also be watching for both the major plot and several subplots that help to shape the larger family story, the story of the people of God.

The *major plot* has to do with God's intervening in the history of human fallenness by choosing ("electing") a man and his family. For even though the families of Abraham, Isaac, and Jacob are the major players, you are never allowed to forget that God is the ultimate Protagonist—as is true in all the biblical narratives. Above all else, it is his story. God speaks and thereby creates the world and a people. It becomes their story (and ours) only as God has brought this family into being and made promises to them and covenanted with them to be their God. So keep looking for the way the major plot unfolds and for how the primary players become part of God's ultimate narrative.

At the same time, keep your eyes open for several subplots that are crucial to the larger story of the Old Testament people of God—and in some cases of the people constituted by the *new* covenant as well. Six of these are worthy of special attention.

The first of these—crucial to the whole biblical story—is the occurrence of the first two covenants between God and his people. The first covenant is with all of humankind through Noah and his sons, promising that God will never again cut off life from the earth (9:8–17). The second covenant is with Abraham, promising two things especially—the gift of "seed" who will become a great nation to bless the nations, and the gift of land (12:2–7; 15:1–21; cf. 17:3–8, where the covenant is ratified by the identifying mark of circumcision). The second covenant is repeated to Isaac (26:3–5) and Jacob (28:13–15) and in turn serves as the basis for the next two Old Testament covenants: the gift of law (Exod 20–24) and the gift of kingship (2 Sam 7).

The second subplot is a bit subtle in Genesis itself, but is important to the later unfolding of the theme of *holy war* (see glossary) in the biblical story. It begins with God's curse on the serpent, that God "will put enmity between you and the woman, and between your offspring [seed] and hers" (3:14–15). The crucial term here is "offspring" (seed), picked up again in 12:7 with regard to the chosen people. This curse anticipates the holy-war motif that is accented in Exodus in particular (between Moses and Pharaoh, thus between God and the gods of Egypt; see Exod 15:1–18), is carried on further in the conquest of Canaan and its gods (which explains the curse of Canaan in Gen 9:25–27), and climaxes in the New Testament (in the story of Jesus Christ, and especially in the Revelation). Although in Genesis this motif does not take the form of holy war as such, you can nonetheless see it especially in the strife between brothers, between the ungodly and godly seed (Cain/Abel; Ishmael/Isaac; Esau/Jacob), where the elder persecutes the younger through whom God has chosen to work (see Gal 4:29).

God's choice of the younger (or weaker, or most unlikely) to bear the righteous seed is a third subplot that begins in Genesis. Here it takes two forms in particular that are then repeated throughout the biblical story. First, God regularly bypasses the firstborn son in carrying out his purposes (a considerable breach of the cultural rules on the part of God): not Cain but Seth, not Ishmael but Isaac, not Esau but Jacob, not Reuben but Judah. Second, the godly seed is frequently born of an otherwise barren woman (Sarah, 18:11–12; Rebekah, 25:21; Rachel, 29:31). As you read through the whole biblical story, you will want to be on the lookout for this recurring motif (see, e.g., 1 Sam 1:1–2:11; Luke 1).

Related to this theme is the fact that the chosen ones are not chosen because of their own goodness; indeed, their flaws are faithfully narrated (Abraham in Gen 12:10–20; Isaac in 26:1–11; Jacob throughout [note how dysfunctional the family is in ch. 37!]; Judah in 38:1–30). God does not choose them because of their inherent character; what makes them the godly seed is that in the end they trusted God and his promise that they would be his people—an exceedingly numerous people—and that they would inherit the land to which they first came as aliens.

A fourth subplot emerges later in the story, where Judah takes the leading role among the brothers in the long Joseph narrative (chs. 37–50). He emerges first in chapter 38, where his weaknesses and sinfulness are exposed. But his primary role begins in 43:8–9, where he guarantees the safety of his brother Benjamin, and it climaxes in his willingness to take the place of Benjamin in 44:18–34. All of this anticipates Jacob's blessing in 49:8–12, that the "scepter will not depart from Judah" (pointing to the Davidic kingdom and, beyond that, to Jesus Christ).

A fifth subplot is found in the anticipation of the next "chapter" in the story—slavery in Egypt. Interest in Egypt begins with the genealogy of Ham (10:13–14; *Mizraim* is Hebrew for "Egypt"). The basic family narrative (Abraham to Joseph) begins with a famine that sends Abraham to Egypt (12:10–20) and concludes with another famine that causes Jacob and the entire family to settle in Egypt, whereas Isaac, while on his way toward Egypt during another famine, is expressly told *not* to go there (26:1–5).

Finally, the interest in detailing the origins of Israel's near neighbors, who become thorns in their sides throughout the Old Testament story, forms a sixth subplot. Besides the major players, Egypt and Canaan (10:13–19), note, in turn, Moab and Ammon (19:30–38) and Edom (25:23; 27:39–40; 36:1–43), as well as the lesser role of Ishmael (39:1; cf. Ps 83:6).

A WALK THROUGH GENESIS

□ 1:1–2:3 *Prologue*

Although written as prose, there is also a clearly poetic dimension to this creational prologue. Part of the poetry is the careful structure of this first "week," where day 1 corresponds to day 4, day 2 to day 5, and day 3 to day 6. Notice how the two sets of days respond to the earth's being "formless and empty" (1:2): Days 1–3 give "form" to the earth (light, sky, dry land), while days 4–6 fill the form with content. Thus:

Day 1 (1:3–5)	Light
Day 2 (1:6–8)	Sky and seas
Day 3 (1:9–13)	Dry land/plant life
Day 4 (1:14–19)	Sun, moon, stars
Day 5 (1:20–23)	Sky and sea animals
Day 6 (1:24–31)	Land animals eat plant life
Day 7 (2:2–3)	God rests from this work

Watch for several emphases as you read, some of which are picked up later in the biblical story—that God speaks everything into existence (cf. Ps 33:6; John 1:1–3); that God blessed what he created, including the material world, calling it all "good"; that human beings, male and female, are created in God's own image and are given regency over the rest of creation; that God rested on the seventh day and set it aside as holy (thus setting the pattern of six days of work and one for rest; cf. Exod 20:8–11, God's great gift of rest to former slaves).

☐ 2:4–4:26 *The Account of Human Beginnings*

This is the first of the six "accounts" that make up the prehistory of Genesis 1–11. It falls into three clearly discernible parts, following present chapter divisions. It begins (2:4–25) with human beings created and placed in Eden, with its centerpiece of the two trees (of life; of the knowledge of good and evil—both reflecting God's own being); included are the warning not to eat from the tree of the knowledge of good and evil, and the creation of Eve from Adam's side, with emphasis on their mutuality and partnership. Note how the story descends rapidly from there. The serpent beguiles them into disobedience (3:1–13), followed by God's cursing the serpent and the land and judging the woman and the man (3:14–19) and, after a momentary alleviation (3:21), by their punishment—the loss of God's presence (3:22–24). It is important to be reminded here that Eden is seen as restored in the final vision of the Revelation (Rev 22:1–5)!

The descent is completed with the story of Cain's murder of his brother, Abel, and Cain's further banishment from God's presence (4:1–

18), concluding on the twin notes of the arrogance of Cain's descendants (4:19–24) and of the birth of Seth, with the hopeful note that "at that time people began to call on the name of the LORD" (4:25–26).

☐ 5:1–6:8 *The Account of Adam's Family Line*

This genealogy stands in contrast to Cain's line (compare the difference between the two Lamechs at the end of each). Note two important things about this genealogy: First, it begins (5:3) and ends (5:29) with echoes from the prologue (Seth is in Adam's likeness; Noah will bring comfort from the curse). Second, one man in this lineage, Enoch (5:21–24), continues to experience God's presence. Despite some puzzling details, don't miss the point of 6:1–8: The utter degeneration of the human race leads God to act in judgment (6:6–7); mercifully, however, "Noah found favor in the eyes of the LORD" (6:8).

☐ 6:9–9:29 *The Account of Noah*

This narrative is so well known that you could easily miss its significant features. Note at the beginning how Noah's righteousness echoes Enoch's "walking with God" (6:9). Observe also how the story echoes the original creation story, so that in effect it becomes a "second creation" narrative: The flood returns the world to its state of being "formless and empty" (1:2), but Noah and the animals provide a link with the old while yet starting something new. The covenant with Noah is full of echoes from Genesis 1–2—the reestablishment of the seasonal cycles (8:22; cf. 1:14); the command to multiply (9:1, 7; cf. 1:28); humankind in God's image (9:6; cf. 1:27). Here God is starting over, and thus he makes a covenant never to destroy the whole earth in such a fashion again. Alas, the story ends on a sour note (9:20–23)—a "fall" again, leading to the curse of Ham's seed, Canaan—but it concludes with the blessing of Shem (from whose seed redemption will emerge).

☐ 10:1–11:9 *The Account of Shem, Ham, and Japheth*

Here you find the development of human civilization into the three basic people groups known to the Israelites. Singled out in particular are Mizraim (Hebrew for "Egypt") and Canaan (10:13–20). Capping these accounts is the story of Babel, which leads directly to the Abraham narrative, as the story returns from the scattered nations to one man who will found a new nation through whom all the nations will be blessed.

☐ 11:10–26 *The Account of Shem*

This list of names isn't riveting reading, but it gets you from Noah's son Shem to Abram (Abraham), and thus to the "father" of the chosen people.

☐ 11:27–25:11 *The Account of Terah*

You can hardly miss seeing that Terah's son, Abraham, dominates this family story. Here you can watch how skillfully the narrative is presented. It introduces Abraham's family, who have moved partway to Canaan (11:27–32), with a special note about Sarah's barrenness (11:30). The key moments are in 12:1–9, where God calls Abraham to leave Haran and "go to the land I will show you" (12:1) and promises to make him "into a great nation" and to bless "all peoples on earth" through him (vv. 2–3). After obediently traveling to the land inhabited by Canaanites (vv. 4–5), Abraham traverses the whole land and then is promised, "To your offspring [seed] I will give this land" (vv. 6–7), whereupon "he built an altar there to the LORD and called on the name of the LORD" (vv. 8–9). In the rest of the narrative, you will see these several themes played out in one form or another: The *promised land* will be given to the *promised seed,* who will become *a great nation* and thus a *blessing to the nations*—even though the Canaanites now possess the land and Sarah is barren!—and so Abraham *trusts* and *worships* the God who has promised this.

Thus the first narrative, which is about Abram's failure in Egypt (12:10–20), has to do with God's protecting the *promised seed.* The first Lot cycle (chs. 13–14) focuses on *great nation* and *promised land* while introducing Sodom and Gomorrah, and indicating Abraham's considerable significance in the land. The back-to-back narratives of chapters 15–16 come back to the *promised seed* from a *barren woman,* while the centerpiece narrative of chapter 17 focuses on all the themes together. The next narrative focuses again on the promised seed from a barren woman (18:1–15), which is picked up again in the series of three narratives in chapters 20 and 21 (Abimelech, the birth of Isaac, the expulsion of Ishmael). These narratives bookend the second Lot cycle (18:16–19:38), which begins with the great nation that will be a blessing on the nations (18:18). Here the destruction of Sodom and Gomorrah and the incestuous conception of Moab and Ammon stand in contrast to Abraham's trust in God for the promised land, a theme picked up again in 21:22–34.

Four crucial narratives then conclude the family story of Terah. First comes the testing of Abraham as to whether he would be willing to give up to God his firstborn son (ch. 22). In this crucial narrative, be sure to note

(1) the renewal of the promises (vv. 15–18),
(2) Abraham's obedience and implicit trust in God throughout,
(3) God's provision of a sacrifice in place of Isaac.

Taken together, the deaths of Sarah (ch. 23) and of Abraham (25:7–11) complete the promised-land motif—a piece of the future promised land is purchased so that their bodies can rest there, waiting for the future to be fulfilled! These enclose the story of Isaac's marriage, which is included in the Abraham series because it continues the promised-seed motif, as does the introduction to the narrative of Abraham's death (25:1–6).

Note finally that unwise choices made in moments of shaky faith do not thwart God's purposes (the Pharaoh and Abimelech stories in chs. 12 and 20, and Hagar in ch. 16), while Abraham in his turn "believed the LORD, and [the LORD] credited it to him as righteousness" (15:6, a text that becomes especially important in Paul's letters). Thus Abraham's regular response to God is *worship* and *obedience* (12:7–8; 13:4, 18; 14:17–20; 22:1–19).

□ 25:12–18 *The Account of Ishmael*

This, the briefest of the origin stories, confirms that God fulfilled his promise (16:10) to make Ishmael, not just Isaac, into a great twelve-tribe nation.

□ 25:19–35:29 *The Account of Isaac*

The Isaac story is mainly about Jacob, who represents the chosen lineage. Note how the promises made to Abraham are repeated for both Isaac (26:3–5) and Jacob (28:13–15). Again, following prayer, the promised seed is born to a barren woman (25:21–26). Esau's despising his firstborn right (25:29–34) shows his character (cf. Heb 12:16) and by implication that of his descendants, the Edomites—perennial enemies of Israel (see the book of Obadiah). In chapter 26 Isaac repeats Abraham's failure (chs. 12, 20) and, as before, God intervenes to protect the promised seed. In chapters 27–28, despite Jacob's cheating Esau out of his father's blessing (and thus living up to his name, "he deceives"), note that God renews the Abrahamic covenant with him (28:10–22). This event also marks the beginning of a change in Jacob's character, evidenced in the events surrounding his reconciliation with Esau (chs. 32–33; note especially the narrative where his name is changed from Jacob to Israel).

In chapters 29–31 you begin to follow the expansion of the nation of Israel. The chosen family now numbers twelve sons whose offspring will form the twelve tribes, a concept reflected later in the tribal districts of the land and later still in Jesus' choosing twelve disciples, and even in the final architecture of the new Jerusalem that comes down out of heaven (Rev 21:12, 14, 21). Unfortunately, Jacob's sons (ch. 34) reflect the character of the younger Jacob, a factor that plays a huge role at the beginning (37:12–36) of the final family story in Genesis (chs. 37–50).

☐ 36:1–37:1 *The Account of Esau*

Esau's lineage, the Edomites, became a great nation as promised but are also another of the neighbors who continually threaten the chosen people and their security in the promised land.

☐ 37:2–50:26 *The Account of Jacob*

The final family story is primarily about Joseph, whom God uses to rescue Israel (and the nations, thus blessing them, 12:2–3) from famine so that the promised seed can be preserved. You will find reading this story to be a different experience from what has gone before, since it is a single cohesive narrative (the longest of its kind in the Bible), with just three interruptions (the story of Judah in ch. 38, the genealogy in 46:8–27, and Jacob's "blessing" in ch. 49). Note how it begins and ends on the same note—his brothers bowing to him (37:5–7; 50:18; cf. 42:6). Look for the various themes that hold the story together: God overturns the brothers' evil against Joseph; he allows Joseph to languish in prison (which came about because of Joseph's refusal to sin) but finally rescues him and elevates him through his divinely given ability to interpret dreams (note the repeated "the LORD was with Joseph," 39:2, 3, 21, 23)—again, God works through a younger, despised son. Note also at the end (ch. 48), Jacob's blessing of Joseph's two sons continues the pattern of God's choosing the younger (the unfavored one).

Finally, you will want to observe the role Judah plays in the narrative. Although his beginnings are anything but salutary (ch. 38), Judah later shows a repentant heart for his past role in the story (44:18–34). And eventually he is blessed as "the lion" through whose lineage will come the Davidic king (49:8–12) and eventually the messianic king himself, Christ Jesus.

Although the narrative ends with Joseph in a coffin in Egypt (50:26), this too anticipates the next part of the narrative, the book of Exodus, where special note is made that the Israelites took the bones of Joseph with them because he had made them swear an oath, "God will surely come to your aid" (Exod 13:19).

Genesis begins the biblical story with God as Creator, human beings as created in God's image but fallen, and God's response through a redemptive creation of a chosen people—and doing so through all kinds of circumstances(good and ill) and despite their faults.

Exodus

ORIENTING DATA FOR EXODUS

- **Content:** Israel's deliverance from Egypt, her constitution as a people through covenant law, and instructions for and construction of the tabernacle—the place of God's presence
- **Historical coverage:** from Joseph's death (ca. 1600 B.C.?) to Israel's encampment at Sinai (either 1440 or 1260 B.C.)
- **Emphases:** God's miraculous rescue of Israel from Egypt through Moses; covenant law given at Mount Sinai; the tabernacle as the place of God's presence and Israel's proper worship; God's revelation of himself and his character; Israel's tendency to complain and rebel against God; God's judgment and mercy toward his people when they rebel

OVERVIEW OF EXODUS

You may find Exodus a bit more difficult than Genesis to read all the way through. The first half (chs. 1–20) is easy enough, since it continues the narrative that began in Genesis 12, but after that you get a series of laws (chs. 21–24), followed by detailed instructions about the materials and furnishings for the tabernacle (chs. 25–31). The narrative then returns for three chapters (chs. 32–34), only to be followed (chs. 35–40) by a repetition of chapters 25–31, as the tabernacle and its furnishings are constructed exactly per instructions. Both the details and repetitious nature of chapters 25–31 and 35–40 can serve to derail you unless you keep them in the context of the big picture, both of Exodus itself and of the larger story found in the Pentateuch as a whole.

The narrative portion begins with Israel's enslavement in Egypt (ch. 1), followed by the birth of Moses, his flight and subsequent call (where Yahweh's name is revealed), and his return to Egypt (chs. 2–4). This is followed by the exodus itself (5:1–15:21), including Israel's forced labor, Yahweh's conflict with Pharaoh in the holy war by way of the ten plagues, the Red Sea miracle, and a hymn celebrating God the Divine Warrior's victory over Pharaoh. The rest of the narrative (15:22–19:25) gets Israel to Sinai in preparation for the giving of the covenant law (chs. 20–23) and its ratification (ch. 24). Part of this narrative is Israel's constant complaining to God, which in chapters 32–34 becomes full-blown idolatrous rebellion, followed by judgment and renewal of the covenant.

The book concludes with a final moment of narrative (40:34–38) in which God's glory (his presence) fills the tabernacle, the last essential act of preparation, thus making the people ready for their pilgrimage to the promised land. Note especially how the two parts of this short scene anticipate the next two books of the Pentateuch: The glory of the Lord filling the tabernacle/Tent of Meeting leads directly into Leviticus, where God speaks to Moses (and thus to the people) from the Tent of Meeting and gives instructions on the uses of the tabernacle (Lev 1:1; "Tent of Meeting" and "tabernacle" are used interchangeably thereafter), and the cloud reappears in the narrative early in Numbers, to give guidance when Israel finally breaks camp and sets out toward the promised land (Num 9:15–23).

The parts of the law enclosed in the Exodus narrative include the Ten Commandments (ch. 20), the Book of the Covenant (chs. 21–23)—various laws dealing mostly with relationships among the people—and the instructions regarding the tabernacle (chs. 25–31), followed by its construction and implementation (35:1–40:33).

SPECIFIC ADVICE FOR READING EXODUS

Any sense of confusion as you read this book may be lessened greatly if you have a sense of the why of its overall structure. Why especially the instructions about and construction of the tabernacle in *this* narrative? Why not wait until Leviticus, where it would seem to fit better? The answer is that Exodus narrates the crucial matters that define Israel as a people in relationship to their God, Yahweh. As you read, therefore, watch especially for the three absolutely defining moments in Israel's history, which cause this narrative with its embedding of portions of the law to make sense: (1) God's miraculous deliverance of his people from slavery, (2) the return of the presence of God as distinguishing his people from all other peoples on the earth, and (3) the gift of the law as the means of establishing his covenant with them.

First, the crucial defining moment, and the one referred to over and again throughout both the Old Testament and the New, is the exodus itself. Israel is repeatedly reminded that "it was because the LORD loved you and kept the oath he swore to your forefathers that he brought you out with a mighty hand and redeemed you from the land of slavery, from the power of Pharaoh" (Deut 7:8); Israel itself repeatedly affirms, "The LORD brought us out of Egypt with a mighty hand and an outstretched arm" (Deut 26:8).

Watch for the ways the narrative highlights this event—that the story of Moses is given solely with his role in the exodus in view; that Israel's desperately hopeless situation is overcome by God's miraculous intervention on their behalf; that this is God's victory above all else, over both Pharaoh and the gods he represents; that God's victory is commemorated with the first of two celebratory hymns in the Pentateuch (15:1–21; cf. Deut 31:30–32:43), emphasizing his unrivaled greatness and his triumph in the holy war. Yahweh here "adopts" Israel as his *firstborn son,* who is to be set free so that "he may worship me" (Exod 4:22–23). Notice finally in this regard how the narrative is interrupted twice, on either side of the actual exodus (12:1–28; 12:43–13:16), in order to give instructions for the Passover (the annual celebration of the exodus) and for the consecration of the firstborn male (as a reminder of God's rescue of them as his firstborn while protecting their own firstborn).

Second, the divine presence, lost in Eden, is now restored as the central feature of Israel's existence. This theme begins with the call of Moses at "the mountain of God" (3:1), where he did not dare "look at God" (3:6). It is picked up again in chapter 19, where the people encamp "in front of the mountain" (19:2) and experience a spectacular theophany (a visible manifestation of God), accompanied by warnings against touching the mountain. The awesome nature of this encounter with the living God is further highlighted by the ascending and descending of Moses "up to God" (19:3, 8, 20) and "down to the people" (19:7, 14, 25).

The pivotal nature of this motif can be seen especially in chapters 25–40 and helps to explain the repetition about the tabernacle on either side of chapters 32–34. For the tabernacle was to assume the role of "the Tent of Meeting" (40:6) and was thus to function as the place where Israel's God would dwell in their midst (after he "left" the mountain, as it were). Thus the debacle in the desert (ch. 32) is followed by Moses' pleading for Yahweh not to abandon them, for "if your *Presence* does not go with us ... what else will distinguish me and your people from all the other people on the face of the earth?" (33:15–16, emphasis added; later identified in Isa 63:7–14 as the Holy Spirit). Notice, finally, that Exodus concludes with God's glory covering the tabernacle/Tent of Meeting, which means the Israelites are now ready for their journey to the promised land. At the same time, these final chapters (25–40) prepare the way especially for the regulations for worship and sacrifice that appear in the next book, Leviticus.

Third, there is the giving of the law with its centerpiece of the Ten Commandments (ch. 20), followed by the Book of the Covenant (chs. 21–24). These laws together focus on Israel's relationship with God and with one another, the latter as an expression of their living out God's character in those relationships. This first expression of the law in the narrative of Exodus thus prepares the way for its further elaboration in the final three books of the Pentateuch. On the nature of these laws and how they function in Israel, see *How to 1*, pp. 169–75.

It is also important to note here that these laws are patterned after ancient covenants known as "suzerainty treaties," where a conqueror made a treaty with the conquered in which he benefited them with his protection and care as long as they would abide by the treaty stipulations. There are six parts to such covenants:

1. Preamble, which identifies the giver of the covenant ("the LORD your God," 20:2)
2. Prologue, which serves as a reminder of the relationship of the suzerain to the people ("who brought you out of Egypt," 20:2)
3. Stipulations, which are various laws/obligations on the part of the people (20:3–23:19; 25:1–31:18)
4. Document clause, which provides for periodic reading and relearning of the covenant
5. Sanctions, which describe the blessings and curses as incentives for obedience
6. List of witnesses to the covenant

You will note that only the first three of these six covenant ingredients are found in Exodus. It is only the first portion of the full covenant that continues on in Leviticus and Numbers and finally concludes at the end of Deuteronomy. Nevertheless, already in Exodus the key elements of the covenant are evident—(1) the revelation of who God is and what he wants from his people, and (2) the enumeration of obedience as the path of covenant loyalty and thus of maintaining its blessings.

A WALK THROUGH EXODUS

☐ 1:1–2:25 *The Setting: Growth and Oppression of Israel in Egypt*

Here you find the two primary narratives that comprise the setting for the exodus: (1) the multiplication and subjection of the Israelites under Pharaoh, including infanticide in a vain attempt to control their population (ch. 1); (2) enter Moses, an Israelite who grows up as a privileged Egyptian but sides with his own people (2:1–15). Years later, as an escaped elderly outlaw settled in Sinai (vv. 16–22), he is a most unlikely candidate for the role of deliverer of Israel (vv. 23–25), picking up a central motif from Genesis.

☐ 3:1–6:27 *The Call and Commission of Moses*

Watch for several important features in this narrative: God's revelation of himself to the unsuspecting Moses, including the disclosure of his name (Yahweh, "the one who causes to exist"; translated in small capitals [Lord] in most English versions); God's repeated announcement that he has seen the misery of his people in Egypt and intends to deliver them by his mighty power; Moses' fourfold "thanks but no thanks" response to the call; and his first encounter with Pharaoh, which leads to increased oppression and Israel's rejection of Moses. The startling episode in 4:24–26 reminds us that Moses as an Israelite father had not even circumcised his own son, so poorly was he prepared for this task.

☐ 6:28–15:21 *The Miraculous Deliverance from Bondage*

This narrative is in four parts, each blending into the next. Watch for them as you read. First is the confrontation with Pharaoh (6:28–11:10), which begins with Aaron's staff becoming a serpent and swallowing those of the Egyptian sorcerers (perhaps echoing the curse of the serpent in Eden), followed by nine plagues and the announcement of the tenth; each of these strikes at the heart of Egyptian idolatry and arrogance.

The second part (12:1–30) is a careful weaving together of the institution of the Passover and the actual narrative of the tenth plague. The reason for the instruction here is that the Passover meal is to be an annual celebration in which the momentous event of deliverance is recounted. Notice also the foreshadowing of redemption through the shedding of blood, which in the New Testament happens when God's "firstborn" sheds his blood (Col 1:15–20), as he assumes the role of the lamb and thus lives out this narrative in reverse.

Part 3 is the account of the exodus itself (12:31–14:31). Note especially how reminders of the first two parts are carefully woven into this narrative: It begins with additional Passover regulations and the law of the firstborn; the actual crossing of the Red Sea involves one final confrontation with Pharaoh—and ends with the demise of his whole army. Here also you are introduced to the *grumbling* motif (14:10–12; cf. 5:21) that will become the main theme of the next section of narrative.

Part 4 is the celebratory song of Moses, Israel, and Miriam (15:1–21). Note that it begins as a celebration of the triumph of God the Warrior over Pharaoh and his gods (vv. 1–12) and concludes by anticipating the same victory in the conquest of Canaan (vv. 13–16) and Yahweh's future settled presence on Zion (vv. 17–18; cf. Ps 68). It may be helpful to note how often this aspect of God's victory continued to be celebrated in Israel's hymns (Neh 9:9–11; Pss 66:5–7; 78:12–13; 106:8–12; 114:3, 5; 136:10–15).

☐ **15:22–18:27** ***The Journey to Mount Sinai***

The first thing you meet after Israel's great deliverance is a series of three episodes in the desert in which the people grumble against Moses and thus test God (15:22–17:7); these episodes foreshadow many such moments throughout the rest of the story. This is followed by their first encounter with opposition along the way (17:8–16), which also anticipates future encounters of this kind, as well as the future leadership of Joshua. The story of Moses as he takes Jethro's advice about shared leadership, especially for judging (ch. 18), not only prepares for the later organization of the tribes but also for many of the laws in the Book of the Covenant (21:1–23:19; e.g., 21:6, 22; 22:8–9).

□ 19:1–24:11 *The Covenant at Sinai*

The prelude (ch. 19) is especially significant to the narrative. Note how it begins (vv. 3–6). Here God combines his deliverance of Israel "on eagles' wings" (v. 4) with the call to obedience and his adoption of them as his own treasured possession (much of the language in these verses is picked up by New Testament writers with reference to the church). The rest takes the form of a great theophany, with the reminder of the awful distance between the holy and living God and his people.

Note also that God speaks the Ten Commandments (the "Ten Words," 20:1–17) directly to the people (20:18–21)—a sign of their primacy. Here fundamental responsibilities to both God and neighbor are addressed in proper order (first "vertical," then "horizontal"). When the people plead for indirect communication with God, the first order of business is to repeat the injunction against idolatry (20:22–26).

The Book of the Covenant (chs. 21–23) gives specifics as to what the Ten Words mean in practice. Note that they primarily cover various aspects of societal living—treatment of slaves/servants (standing first in order and in stark contrast to their conditions in Egypt), compensations and penalties for injuries, property law, rape, fairness in dealings with others, and worship. They conclude with a promise of divine guidance and the eventual conquest of Canaan, predicated on the people's obedience to the covenant (23:20–33). The covenant is ratified by Israel's consent, the sprinkling of blood, and a theophanic meal for Israel's elders in the presence of God (24:1–11).

□ 24:12–31:18 *Instructions regarding the Tabernacle*

As you read these instructions, keep in mind the reason for their many and very precise details—that the tabernacle will be the place of God's presence among them. This not only is said expressly (25:8, 22; cf. Lev 16:2), but it also accounts for the order of the instructions. The ark, where Yahweh dwells between the cherubim (25:22; cf. Lev 16:2), stands in first place, followed by the table on which will sit "the bread of the Presence" (25:30). All the rest of the furnishings, including the bronze altar and the priests' attire, are predicated on the primary reality that Yahweh has chosen to dwell here on earth in the midst of his people. Note, for example, that the reason for the priests' attire is "to give him/them dignity and honor" (28:2, 40). And when you come to Leviticus, you will see that the reason for the bronze altar is for sacrifices, so that the priests may approach Yahweh on behalf of the people. Note how this section ends with a renewal of the Sabbath commandment, which is related especially to Yahweh's "rest" (repeated here because this is God's gift to former slaves who worked all day, every day of the week).

☐ 32:1–34:35 *Rebellion, Covenant Breaking, Covenant Renewal*

Note the contrast: While Moses is atop Sinai receiving instructions for the place of Yahweh's dwelling among them, his brother is below, leading the people in constructing and worshiping idols (32:1–26)—although note that they are allegedly worshiping Yahweh (v. 5). Punishment (32:27–29) is followed by Moses' intercession for the people, thus securing God's promise that his own Presence will accompany them and thus distinguish them from all other peoples (32:30–33:23). This is the significance of including here the brief narratives about the Tent of Meeting (33:7–11) and the (foretaste) vision of God's glory (33:18–23). In chapter 34, the covenant is renewed (vv. 1–28; a brief condensation of the Book of the Covenant [chs. 21–23] is included) in the context of another significant theophany. The language of Yahweh's self-revelation in verses 4–7 is one of the more important moments in the biblical story and is appealed to throughout the rest of the Old Testament. The concluding narrative—having to do with Moses emerging from the Tent of Meeting with a face that radiates God's glory (34:29–35; cf. 2 Cor 3)—anticipates the glory that will descend on the tabernacle when it is finished (40:34–38).

☐ 35:1–39:43 *The Construction of the Tabernacle and Its Furnishings*

This lengthy repetition of the matters from chapters 25–31 serves further to highlight the significance of the tabernacle as the place of Yahweh's presence. Note that the order changes slightly so that the tabernacle will be in place before the symbol of the Presence (namely, the ark) is constructed. But it begins with the Sabbath command (35:1–3). Even something as important as the construction of the tabernacle must not supersede the gift of Sabbath.

□ 40:1–38 *The Tabernacle Is Set Up and the Glory Descends*

Note how this final event in Exodus follows the preceding pattern: Instructions on setting up the tabernacle (vv. 1–16), followed by the implementation (vv. 17–33). All of this so that the glory of Yahweh—the same glory that had so impressed the Israelites when it was seen on Mount Sinai—might fill the tabernacle (v. 34; cf. 1 Kgs 8:10–11), taking the form of a pillar of cloud by day and fire by night (v. 38), a constant visible reminder of God's presence with his people.

Exodus plays an especially important role in the rest of the biblical story, since it tells the basic story of God's saving his people from bondage and of his giving them the law so that they will become the people of his presence. Exodus also serves as a pattern for the promised "second exodus" in Isaiah (esp. chs. 40–66) and thus for Jesus' own "departure" (exodus) that would be accomplished in Jerusalem (Luke 9:30, spoken in the presence of Moses[!] and Elijah).

Leviticus

ORIENTING DATA FOR LEVITICUS

- **Content:** various laws having to do with holiness before God and with love of neighbor, including sacrifices, ritual cleanness, and social obligations, as well as laws for the Levites regarding their priestly duties.
- **Emphases:** getting it right with regard to worship, for both people and priests; institution of the priesthood under Aaron; laws protecting ritual cleanness, including atonement for sins (the Day of Atonement); laws regulating sexual relations, family life, punishments for major crimes, festivals, and special years (sabbaths and jubilees)

OVERVIEW OF LEVITICUS

The title of this book (by way of Latin from the Greek *levitikon*) means "pertaining to the Levites," which not only aptly describes its basic contents but also gives a clue as to why it is so often unappealing to contemporary readers—not to mention that it has so little narrative (chs. 8–10; 24:10–23 are the exceptions). But with a little help, you can come to a basic understanding of both its contents and its place in the narrative of the Pentateuch—even if the nature of, and reason for, some of the laws themselves may escape you (for this you may wish to consult a good commentary; e.g., Gordon J. Wenham, *The Book of Leviticus* [see *How to 1,* p. 268]).

It is important to note that Leviticus picks up precisely where Exodus left off—with the Lord speaking to Moses "from the Tent of Meeting" and saying, "Speak to the Israelites and say ..." From that point on, the movement from one section to another is signaled by the phrase, "The Lord said to Moses" (4:1; 5:14; 6:1, 8; and so forth). It will be no surprise, then, to discover that the first main part of the book (chs. 1–16, commonly known as the Levitical Code) has primarily to do with regulations for the people and the priests related directly to the tabernacle, which appeared toward the end of Exodus (chs. 25–31; 35–40).

This code outlines easily. It begins with offerings by the people (1:1–6:7), followed by instructions for the priests (6:8–7:38). These are followed (logically) by the institution of the Aaronic priesthood (chs. 8–9) and the judgment on two of Aaron's sons who thought they could do it their own way (10:1–7), with further instructions for the priests (10:8–20). The next section (chs. 11–15) then begins with a new rubric, "The LORD said to Moses *and Aaron*" (11:1, emphasis added; see also 13:1; 14:33; 15:1, but nowhere else in Leviticus). Here you find laws that deal especially with ritual cleanness (purity)—with a view to avoiding what happened to Aaron's two sons. Here also appears for the first time the very important injunction, "Be holy, because I am holy" (11:44, 45). This is followed, appropriately, by the institution of the Day of Atonement (ch. 16).

What follows (chs. 17–25) is commonly known as the Holiness Code, which is governed by the repeated charge to "be holy, because I am holy" (beginning in 19:2 and throughout). But now a significant part of being holy is to "love your neighbor as yourself" (19:18). Thus the section is a collection of various laws dealing with one's relationship both to God and to others. At the end are requirements for the sabbath and jubilee years (ch. 25), while the book concludes with covenant blessings and curses (ch. 26) that provide a formal conclusion to the covenant structure that began in Exodus 20. The book itself concludes with an appendix on vows and tithes (Lev 27).

SPECIFIC ADVICE FOR READING LEVITICUS

In order to get the most out of your reading, you need to remind yourself of two things: (1) These laws are part of God's covenant with Israel, and therefore they are not just religious rites but have to do with *relationships*, and (2) Leviticus is *part of the larger narrative* of the Pentateuch and must be understood in light of what has preceded and what follows.

To pick up the second point first: Just as the legal portions of Exodus make good sense when you see their place in the larger narrative, so you need to see Leviticus as a longer expression of the same before the narrative resumes in Numbers. Crucial here is the fact that Israel is still camped at the foot of Sinai—a wilderness area—where they will spend a full year being molded into a people before God will lead them toward the conquest of Canaan. Here they will need double protection—from diseases of various kinds and from one another! Therefore, in order for these individuals who grew up in slavery to be formed into God's people, there is great need for them to get two sets of relationships in order, namely, with God and with one another. Note, then, that Leviticus continues with the same ordering of things found in the Ten Commandments (first vertical, then horizontal).

The covenantal aspect of these various laws is their most important feature. Recall the parts of the covenant noted in our Exodus chapter (p. 37). God has sovereignly delivered these people from slavery and has brought them to Sinai; here he has promised to make them his own "treasured possession" out of all the nations on earth (Exod 19:5), who will also therefore be for him "a kingdom of priests and a holy nation" (v. 6). That is, their role as a "kingdom" is to serve as God's priests for the world, and to do so they must bear his likeness ("be holy, because I am holy"). Thus, God covenants with them on his part to bless them (Lev 26:1–13); what he requires on their part is that, even though they are his treasured possession, they maintain a holy awe and obedience toward him. So note in this regard how often, especially in chapters 18–26, the requirement is punctuated with the words, "I am the LORD [Yahweh]" or "I am the LORD your God."

Thus the first set of laws in Leviticus has to do with their "getting it right" when they come to God with various sacrifices. You will note that they are not told what the sacrifices mean (which they already knew), but how to do them properly—although we can infer some things about their meaning from these descriptions. The covenantal nature of these sacrifices appears in three ways: First, the sacrifice constitutes a *gift* on the part of the worshipers to their covenant Lord; second, some of the sacrifices imply *fellowship* on the part of the worshiper with God; third, sacrifice sometimes functions as a way of healing a break in the relationship—a form of *atonement*.

So also with the laws of purity. Here the concern again is that the people have a proper sense of what it means for God to be present among them (see 15:31). At issue here is who may be in the camp, where God himself dwells at the center, and who must remain outside (because they are unclean). Included is the separating out of certain animals and insects that are clean or unclean. At the heart of all of this is the fact that "God is holy" and therefore his people also must be holy.

But holiness does not deal simply with rites and being clean. God's holiness is especially seen in his loving compassion that made the Israelites his people. Therefore, the laws—particularly in the Holiness Code—demand that God's people bear God's likeness in this regard. Since the Israelites are thrown together (in a very orderly way, of course!) in this very tight camp where God dwells in the midst of them, they must display his character in their dealings with one another. Thus, even though this code also contains further "relationship with God" laws, it is especially concerned with how people in community treat one another. And it includes treating them justly and mercifully, which is why the collection ends with the sabbath and jubilee years, so that the land also may "rest," and a time to "proclaim liberty to all" may occur on the sabbath of the sabbath years (25:10).

If you look for these covenantal moments as you read these laws, you may find it to be a far more interesting experience than you might have expected.

A WALK THROUGH LEVITICUS

☐ 1:1–7:38 *Instructions for the Five Offerings*

You need to know that Israel's offerings (sacrifices) were regularly crucial elements in symbolic meals. A portion of the sacrifice was burnt on the altar as God's part, but the rest was eaten by the worshipers and priests as a fellowship meal—a meal at God's house, in God's presence (see Deut 14:22–29), with God as the host (see Ps 23:5–6; cf. "the *Lord's* table" in 1 Cor 10:21). This is especially important in your reading these laws about offerings, since what is described is not their function or meaning but only their proper preparation. Not all were sacrifices for sins. Some offerings were for fellowship and had different covenantal functions altogether.

Note that only the burnt offering (ch. 1) was dedicated entirely to God and thus burned entirely as an atonement for sin. Again, the principle was this: If you are to live, something must die in your place (see Exod 12:1–30). Leviticus 2 describes the grain offering (various options for oil and flour ingredients within a balanced meal). Chapter 3 addresses the fellowship offering (sometimes translated "peace offering"), which was an animal offering with the general purpose of keeping one in fellowship with God. The sin (also "purification") offering (4:1–5:13) provided atonement for accidental sin, since "transgression" is not limited to intentional disobedience. Finally, the guilt (sometimes "reparation") offering in 5:14–6:7 provided a means for making amends for the transgression. The rest of the section (6:8–7:38) reviews the role of the priests in supervising the five offerings, as well as prescribing their share of the sacrificed animal.

☐ 8:1–10:20 *Priesthood Begins*

Since priests specially represented God to the people and the people to God, Aaron and his sons were ordained to their assignments (chs. 8–9), and Aaron's first official sacrifices are listed. Note that his sons failed to follow clear rules and so died, showing the importance God placed on proper worship, further emphasized in various commands from Moses (ch. 10).

☐ 11:1–16:34 *On Cleanness and Uncleanness*

You need to know that *clean* here means acceptable to God in worship. *Unclean* means unacceptable to God and banned from the tabernacle, or sometimes (in the case of skin diseases) from the encampment itself. This mixture of food, health, sanitation, and ritual laws is thus aimed at helping the covenant people to show that they belong to God and reflect his purity (holiness, 11:44–45). The laws seem to be partly a matter of simple hygiene and partly symbolic obedience, but always in light of the divine presence (15:31).

Thus certain animals, for reasons not given, are unclean (ch. 11). Childbirth (ch. 12) and some diseases (ch. 13) require ritual cleansing (ch. 14) before one is restored to purity. The Israelites were to regard any bodily discharges as unclean (ch. 15, perhaps because in general these are unsanitary). The Day of Atonement (ch. 16) was a special solemn day of forgiveness that not only cleansed the people of their sin but also purified the tabernacle itself and kept it a holy place for worship.

☐ 17:1–25:55 *The Holiness Code*

Notice that the first part (17:1–20:27) concentrates on personal and social holiness in daily life. It begins with prohibitions regarding nonregulated sacrifices and drinking blood (17:1–16), aimed especially at countering Canaanite practices (idolatry and drinking blood in an attempt to capture its life force; cf. Acts 15:20, 29; 21:25), followed by rules for sexual behavior (Lev 18) and for neighborliness, which means truly caring for others, not just for those who live near you (ch. 19). Here occurs for the first time the second love command, "love your neighbor as yourself" (19:18), picked up by Jesus (Mk 12:28–34 and par.) and his followers (e.g., Rom 13:8–10). Note how the punishments for serious crimes in Leviticus 20 respond directly to the prohibitions in chapter 18.

With chapter 21, note the shift back to holiness in matters of religious observance—rules for priests (ch. 21); for the proper offering and eating of sacrifices (ch. 22); for observing the religious festivals, both weekly (sabbath) and annual (ch. 23); and for lamp oil and offering bread at the tabernacle (24:1–9).

Finally in 24:10–23 you come to another narrative—about punishment for blasphemy (cursing God)—that is used to introduce prescriptions for various crimes. At the end of Leviticus are laws concerning the seventh (sabbath) and fiftieth (jubilee) years, which provided liberation for those indebted or enslaved (ch. 25), and a sabbath for the land as well.

☐ 26:1–46 *Covenant Sanctions*

These sanctions (blessings and curses as incentives to keep the covenant) both conclude the Sinaitic covenant and anticipate the conclusion of the covenant in Deuteronomy 27–28.

☐ 27:1–34 *Redemption Laws*

This appendix deals with the cost of redeeming persons who have been promised to God and of redeeming tithes (material goods belonging to God).

Leviticus is the part of God's story where the Israelites are given instructions on how to be holy, on how to be truly acceptable to God and in good relationship with one another—which they could not achieve without his special provision.

Numbers

ORIENTING DATA FOR NUMBERS

- **Content:** the Israelites' long stay in the desert as they journey from Mount Sinai to the plains of Moab, with supplemental covenant laws
- **Historical coverage:** forty years, a period within which the generation that left Egypt died off
- **Emphases:** preparation for military conquest of the promised land; God's covenant loyalty toward Israel with regard to the land; Israel's repeated failure to keep covenant with God; God's leadership of his people and affirmation of Moses' leadership; preparations for entering and worshiping in the promised land; conquest and settlement of the land east of the Jordan River

OVERVIEW OF NUMBERS

If Leviticus tends to be an unappealing book to contemporary readers, then Numbers must be one of the most difficult in terms of "what in the world is going on?" The problem for us is that it is such a mixture of things—narrative, additional laws, census lists, oracles from a pagan prophet, the well-known Aaronic blessing—and it is not easy to see how it all fits together.

Numbers primarily records the pilgrimage of Israel through the desert from the foot of Mount Sinai to its encampment in the plains of Moab (on the east bank of the Jordan River), poised for conquest. But it is the second generation that ends up on the east bank—because the exodus generation refused to enter by way of the more direct southern route (at Kadesh) and so were judged by God as unworthy to enter at all. The basic travel narratives are found in 9:15–14:45 (from Sinai to Kadesh, including the refusal to enter and the declaration of God's judgment) and 20:1–22:1 (from Kadesh to the plains of Moab along the Jordan).

There are four other major sections of narrative that have slightly different functions: (1) 7:1–9:14 records the preparations for the journey; (2) chapters 16–17 speak to the issue of Moses' and Aaron's God-given (and recognized) leadership; (3) the Balaam cycle (22:2–24:25) and the seduction at Shittim with the Baal of Peor (ch. 25) anticipate both the fulfillment of God's giving them the land and their own capacity nonetheless to be seduced by Canaanite idolatry; (4) chapters 31–36 narrate events on the east bank as they prepare for conquest.

Interspersed among these narratives, but at the same time adding meaning to them, are two census lists (chs. 1–2; 26–27), plus a genealogy/account of Aaron's family and of the Levites (chs. 3–4), as well as several collections of laws (chs. 5–6; 15; 18–19; 28–30), most of them picking up items from the Levitical Code (Lev 1–16; 21–22).

This, then, is what Numbers is all about: the journey to the edge of the promised land and further laws pertaining to proper worship. The question is, Can one make sense of its arrangement as narrative?

SPECIFIC ADVICE FOR READING NUMBERS

In order to appreciate how the narrative of Numbers works (both the journey and the various surrounding matters), you need to recall several items from Genesis and Exodus.

First, the primary driving force behind everything is God's promise/covenant with Abraham that his seed would inherit the land of Canaan. This is what keeps the narrative going in all of its parts. And God will bring about the fulfillment of that covenant promise, even in the face of Israel's reluctance and disobedience.

Second, the conquest of the land involves the second stage of the holy war. The first stage—against Pharaoh in Exodus—even though led by Moses, was carried out by God the Divine Warrior through miraculous intervention. In this second stage, God intends his own people to be involved. He rescued them from slavery in order to make them his own people and place them in the land, but they must take ownership of the actual conquest of the land. This accounts for the two census lists, which count the men who can fight and put the tribes in battle formation around the tabernacle. The list at the beginning (from which Numbers derives its name) prepares the first generation for conquest by way of Kadesh; the second prepares the second generation for conquest by way of the Transjordan. This motif also accounts for the various narratives at the end, including the succession of Joshua (27:12–23) and the various matters in chapters 31–36 that anticipate the conquest.

Third, recall that in Genesis 12:7, immediately following the promise of the land, Abraham built an altar to the Lord. As you now read the various law portions interspersed within this narrative, you will find that they focus primarily on the Israelites' relationship with their God. Thus both the central role of the tabernacle and the priestly matters in Numbers continue to focus on two previous concerns in the Pentateuch to this point: the *presence* of God in the midst of his people—both his being with them and his guiding their journey—and the proper *worship* of God once they are settled in the land.

Finally, God's people themselves do not come off well in Numbers. You can hardly miss the relentless nature of their complaints and disobedience. In fact, apart from the future blessing that God speaks through a pagan prophet, there is hardly a good word about them in the entire narrative. The same complaints against God and his chosen leader Moses that began in Exodus 15:22–17:7—and then some—are repeated here (Num 11–12; 14; 16–17; 20:1–13; 21:4–9). This is simply not fun reading. In the New Testament, the Israelites' disobedience serves as warning for us (1 Cor 10:1–13; cf. Heb 3:7–13); in the Old Testament, even though their sins are expressly remembered, so also is God's "great compassion" on them (Neh 9:16–21; cf. Pss 78:14–39; 106:24–33, 44–46; see also the invitation and warning in Ps 95).

Thus, even though the narrative has some abrupt shifts of focus, Numbers carries on the burden of the Pentateuch in grand style. You are not allowed to forget that, despite Israel's waffling, this is *God's story* above all, and God will keep his part of the covenant with Abraham regarding his seed inheriting the land. At issue is whether Israel will keep covenant with God—and Numbers reminds you over and again that the divine provision for them to do so is always ready at hand.

A WALK THROUGH NUMBERS

□ 1:1–2:34 *The Census at Sinai*

This introduction to Numbers is in two parts: (1) the census and (2) the arrangement of the tribes around the Tent of Meeting (the place of God's presence). Note that the census is for those "twenty years old or more who were able to serve in the army" (1:3) and that the arrangement of the tribes concludes in each case, "All the men assigned to the camp of ..." These are preparations for their engagement in the holy war; former slaves are being transformed into an army.

☐ 3:1–4:49 *The Account of the Levites*

Observe how this section begins with the narrative theme formula of Genesis ("This is the account of ..."). As you read, recall two things from before: (1) the central role of the Tent of Meeting with its ark of the covenant, the place of God's presence, for the journey to Canaan—and beyond—and (2) in making covenant with Israel at Sinai (where they still are), Yahweh adopted them as a "kingdom of priests and a holy nation" (Exod 19:6). Hence the reason for this material: This is part of what makes them a "kingdom of priests," a nation set apart for God.

☐ 5:1–6:27 *Cleansing the Camp*

Note how this section is structured around the rubric of Leviticus: "The LORD said to Moses" (Num 5:1, 5, 11; 6:1, 22), who in turn is to instruct the people. Remember also their calling to be a "holy nation." Thus the narrative about purifying the camp (5:1–4) is followed by three sets of laws: (1) the restitution of wrongs (5:5–10, they must be in accord with one another); (2) purity/faithfulness in marriage (5:11–31, thus keeping the holy "seed" pure); (3) the Nazirites, laypeople who dedicate themselves to God's service, as special illustrations of Israel's holy calling (6:1–21). The section concludes with the Aaronic blessing (6:22–27), a reaffirmation of God's covenant promise as the Israelites look toward the promised land.

☐ 7:1–9:14 *Final Preparations for Departure*

Notice how 7:1 picks up from Exodus 40:2, so that each part of this section deals with final preparations for their journey. Everything now centers on the tabernacle, the place of sacrifice (worship) and of God's presence. Thus the narrative proceeds from the twelve-day dedication of the altar (Num 7:1–89), through setting up the lamps (8:1–4) and the purification of the Levites (8:5–26), to the celebration of the Passover as they set out (9:1–14; cf. Exod 12).

☐ 9:15–14:45 *From Sinai to Kadesh*

Israel is now ready to go, so observe how this narrative begins: with the reminder from Exodus 40:34–38 of God's presence, symbolized especially by the cloud that would lead them (Num 9:15–23), and with the blowing of the trumpets (10:1–10). And so they take off in battle formation (10:11–28). See also how each day ends: with a call for God the Divine Warrior to lead in battle and to return to Israel (10:35–36).

You can hardly miss the emphasis in the rest of the narrative (11:1–14:45): Israel complains to God and rejects Moses' leadership. Note how much of this recalls Exodus 15:22–18:27 and 32:1–34:35, where Israel complains rather than offers praise and gratitude to God and where God gives them what they need but also judges them; Moses' intercession for the people (in Num 14:18, recalling the very words of Exod 34:6–7); the seventy elders, who now also anticipate Spirit-empowered prophecy in Israel; God's reaffirmation of Moses' leadership. Note also the crucial roles of Joshua and Caleb (from Ephraim [the northern kingdom] and Judah [the southern kingdom]). Their stories will continue (Num 27:12–23; the book of Joshua; Judg 1:1–26), as will the roles of the two tribes they represent (1–2 Kgs).

☐ 15:1–41 *Supplemental Laws*

Since the next generation *will* enter the promised land, this section records God's giving his people laws in anticipation of that time. Note that it includes provisions even for unintentional sins, no matter how the failure occurs. Note also how the death of a Sabbath violator (15:32–36) carries forward the theme of covenant obedience both from the beginning of the whole story (Gen 2:1–3) and from the beginning of the covenant (Exod 20:8–11).

☐ 16:1–19:22 *The Crisis over Leadership and Priesthood*

The narrative portion of this section (chs. 16–17) has to do with Moses as God's chosen leader and with Aaron as God's chosen high priest. This second matter explains the placement here of the law portion as well (chs. 18–19).

☐ 20:1–25:17 *From Kadesh to the Plains of Moab*

As you read this next portion of the journey narrative, look for several narrative clues: (1) The deaths of Miriam and Aaron (20:1, 22–29) indicate that the forty years are coming to an end and the transition to the next generation is beginning. (2) The refusal of Edom (descendants of Esau, Jacob/Israel's brother) to let Israel pass through their lands marks the beginning of a long history of enmity (see the book of Obadiah). (3) The defeats of the Canaanite king of Arad (21:1–3) and the Amorite kings (21:21–35) mark the beginning of Israel's victories in the holy war and anticipate the book of Joshua; it is of some importance that the first victory (Arad, 21:1–3) eliminates a foe that had defeated them a generation earlier (Num 14:45; cf. Josh 12:14). (4) The Balaam cycle (chs. 22–24) and its sequel—the cultic immorality with the Baal of Peor (Num 25)—both recapitulate the story to this point and anticipate the rest of the Old Testament story. Note especially how the Balaam cycle is told with mockery—and a touch of humor (an ass speaks and Balaam thinks it reasonable to talk back!) and irony, as God uses a pagan prophet(!) to announce God's certain fulfillment of his covenant, even as many in Israel fall prey to cultic prostitution and thus to idolatry.

☐ 26:1–36:13 *In Moab: Preparations for Entry into the Land*

Again, watch for the various narrative clues that give significance to this section and anticipate the actual possession of the land: (1) The second census (ch. 26) reaffirms God's promise that the new generation will indeed enter the promised land, as does the repetition of the stages of the journey in 33:1–49. (2) Various succession and inheritance issues (chs. 27; 32; 34–36) reaffirm God's promise of a long stay in the land, as do (3) the repetition (and enhancement) of the annual cycle of worship festivals (chs. 28–29). (4) The vengeance on the Midianites (ch. 31) anticipates the long story of success and failure in Judges (cf. Num 33:50–56). (5) The sanctity of people and of the land must be preserved (ch. 35), because it is "the land ... where I dwell, for I, the LORD [Yahweh], dwell among the Israelites" (v. 34).

The significant part of Israel's story we find recorded in Numbers had a long history in Israel's memory (Deut 1–4; Neh 9; Pss 78; 105; 106; 135; Acts 7), stressing God's faithfulness to his people despite their many failures, and the story continues to be sung in the Christian church ("Guide Me, O Thou Great Jehovah").

Deuteronomy

ORIENTING DATA FOR DEUTERONOMY

- **Content:** rehearsal of the covenant for a new generation of Israelites just before the conquest
- **Historical coverage:** during the final weeks east of the Jordan
- **Emphases:** the oneness and uniqueness of Yahweh, the God of Israel, over against all other gods; Yahweh's covenant love for Israel in making them his people; Yahweh's universal sovereignty over all peoples; Israel as Yahweh's model for the nations; the significance of the central sanctuary where Yahweh is to be worshiped; Yahweh's concern for justice—that his people reflect his character; the blessings of obedience and the dangers of disobedience

OVERVIEW OF DEUTERONOMY

As with Genesis, two kinds of structure are evident in Deuteronomy at the same time. First, there is a concentric (chiastic) structure to the book, which looks backward at the beginning and forward at the end. Thus:

A The Outer Frame: A Look Backward (chs. 1–3)
 B The Inner Frame: The Great Exhortation (chs. 4–11)
  C The Central Core: The Stipulations of the Covenant (chs. 12–26)
 B* The Inner Frame: The Covenant Ceremony (chs. 27–30)
A* The Outer Frame: A Look Forward (chs. 31–34)

Note how easily you could read each of the two parts of both framing sections as continuous narrative: chapters 1–3 and 31–34; chapters 4–11 and 27–30. The first part of the outer frame (A) repeats the essential narrative of Numbers, up to where Moses is forbidden to enter the land; the second part (A*) picks it up right at that point and concludes with the appointment of Joshua, Moses' song, his blessing, and his death. The inner frame (B), which calls Israel to absolute devotion to God, concludes with the *announcement* that God is setting before them "a blessing and a curse" (11:26); the second part (B*) picks up right at that point by offering the *content* of the curses and blessings.

This insight into how Deuteronomy works also highlights its second structural feature—that Deuteronomy presents this restatement of God's covenant (for the new generation) in the style of an ancient Near Eastern suzerainty treaty-covenant (see "Specific Advice for Reading Exodus," p. 37), with preamble, prologue, stipulations, document clause, sanctions, and witnesses. These last three items both supplement and reiterate the final three elements of the covenant of Exodus 20–Leviticus 27.

Thus, as a restatement of the covenant, Deuteronomy begins with a *preamble* and *historical prologue* (chs. 1–4), which look both to the past and to the future. God has been faithful in the past, rewarding Israel for their faithfulness and likewise punishing them for unfaithfulness. Now they must again commit to being his people. The *stipulations* (chs. 5–26) begin with a restatement of the Ten Commandments, while the laws in chapters 12–26 tend to follow their vertical/horizontal order, having first to do with an individual's relationship with God and then with one another. The *document clauses,* reminders of the terms of the covenant, are found mainly in chapters 27 and 31, joined immediately by a long list of blessings and curses (prose in chs. 28–29 and poetry in 32–33), which serve as the *sanctions* of the covenant. Finally, there are three kinds of *witnesses* to the covenant: "heaven and earth" (4:26; 30:19–20), the song of Moses (31:19; 31:30–32:43), and the words of the law itself (31:26).

On this reading, Moses' death and Joshua's succession to leadership (ch. 34) form a kind of epilogue—not part of the covenant per se, but a narrative that connects Deuteronomy to the book of Joshua that follows.

SPECIFIC ADVICE FOR READING DEUTERONOMY

Deuteronomy has perhaps had more influence on the rest of the biblical story (both Old and New Testaments) than any other book of the Bible. The continuation of Israel's history (Joshua–Kings) is written mostly from its perspective, so that this history portion has come to be called the Deuteronomic History. Deuteronomy likewise had considerable influence on Israel's and Judah's prophets, especially Isaiah and

Jeremiah, and through them deeply influenced the major figures of the New Testament (especially Jesus and Paul).

As you read, you will discover what drives Deuteronomy from beginning to end—an uncompromising monotheism coupled with an equally deep concern for Israel's uncompromising loyalty to Yahweh ("the LORD") their God. This comes out in any number of ways, but its primary moment is in the Shema (6:4–5), which became the distinguishing mark of Judaism and is identified by Jesus as "the first commandment": "Hear, O Israel: The LORD our God, the LORD is one. Love the LORD your God with all your heart and with all your soul and with all your strength." The reason they are to love Yahweh in this way is that he first loved them—when they were slaves and counted for little: "The LORD did not set his affection on you and choose you because you were more numerous than other peoples.... But it was because the LORD loved you and kept the oath he swore to your forefathers that he ... redeemed you from the land of slavery" (7:7–8; cf. 4:37). Thus, everything is predicated on Yahweh's love and faithfulness and his actions that flow out of that love and faithfulness.

This concern in turn accounts for the other distinctive features in the book, three in particular that are closely allied with this first one. Watch for the following:

1. The constant reminder that Israel is about to possess "the land" (a word that occurs more than one hundred times in Deuteronomy). God in his love is about to fulfill the oath he made with Abraham. But the land is currently under the control of the Canaanites.
2. The relentless demand that, when entering the land, Israel not only avoid idolatry but that they completely destroy the places of Canaanite worship as well as the Canaanite peoples. If they do not, Canaanite idolatry will destroy Israel's reason for being. This motif begins in the historical prologue (2:34; 3:6) and continues as a divine demand throughout (7:1–6, 23–26; 12:1–3; 13:6–18; 16:21–17:7; 20:16–18; cf. 31:3). The only hope for Israel to bless the nations (4:6) is for them to obliterate all forms of idolatry and to walk in the ways of the God who redeemed them to be his people (5:32–33).
3. The requirement that they regularly worship at one central sanctuary, "the place the LORD your God will choose as a dwelling for his Name" (12:11). You will recognize this as carrying over the

theme of the presence of God in the tabernacle into their new setting in the promised land. Note how often this theme, which begins in 12:5, is repeated thereafter (12:11, 14, 18, 26; 14:23–25; 15:20; 16:2–16; 17:8–10; 26:2). Yahweh, the one and only God, will dwell among his one people in one place; he is not like the many pagan gods who can be worshiped at many high places throughout the land.

Why are these matters so important? Because the whole biblical story depends on them. At issue is not simply a choice between Yahweh and a Baal—although that too is involved—but syncretism, i.e., thinking that Yahweh can be worshiped in the form of, or alongside, Baal and Ashtoreth (Asherah), the Canaanite fertility gods. Since Yahweh is *one* Lord, not many—as are the pagan gods—he must not be worshiped at the high places where Baal and Ashtoreth were worshiped, and since Yahweh made human beings alone to bear his image (Gen 1:26–27) and does not have "form" as such (the second commandment), they must not think that he can be given form in some way by human beings (see especially Deut 4:15–20). You will notice how this issue recurs throughout the rest of the story, right through 2 Kings, and continues as a predominant feature in the prophets.

Two final items: God's love for his people in redeeming them and in making them his own, and then in giving them "this good land" (9:6), also lies behind the special nature of the Law Code in Deuteronomy (12:1–26:19). Be watching for how the code follows the pattern of the Ten Commandments, beginning with requirements that have to do with loving God (chs. 12–13) and continuing with various laws that have to do with sacred days and with loving neighbor (chs. 14–26). But note especially how often God's people are required to include "the poor and needy" (see 15:11; 24:14), which in Deuteronomy specifically takes the form of "the alien, the fatherless and the widow," and sometimes includes "the Levite" (26:13). Their common denominator is that they do not own land among a people who will become agrarian in culture. As you read, observe how often these laws are tied either to God's character or to the redemption of Israel.

Finally, don't lose sight of one other important characteristic of Deuteronomy, namely, its forward-looking thrust throughout. This includes not only the immediate generation, which is poised to take possession of the land, but also future generations (4:9, 40). This motif in particular creates tension throughout the book between God's goodness in bringing them into "this good land" and God's awareness that Israel will fail nonetheless. Thus at both the beginning and the end, there are prophecies that the curses will eventually come upon them; their failure to keep covenant will result in loss of the land and in exile (4:25–28; 30:1; see 29:19–28 and 32:15–25), but God's enduring love will result in their being restored to the land through a "second exodus" (4:29–31; 30:2–10; 32:26–27, 36–43). As you read on from here in both the Old Testament and New, you will see how often this theme recurs.

A WALK THROUGH DEUTERONOMY

☐ 1:1–3:29 *Historical Prologue*

You will recognize that most of this prologue is a succinct, carefully designed retelling of the narrative portions of Numbers. Note how the preamble (1:1–5) introduces you to the format of Deuteronomy—a speech of Moses by which God speaks to his people.

The story is recounted in three parts, each with an eye toward the rest of the book: (1) The appointment of leaders, because Moses is not going to enter the land (1:6–18), (2) a reminder of wasted opportunity and rebellion at Kadesh (1:19–46), and (3) a reminder of God's being with them nonetheless and bringing them to where they are now (2:1–3:29).

☐ 4:1–43 *Introduction to the Great Exhortation*

Note how this introduction sets forth the emphases of the rest of the book: God's speaking his covenant directly to the people in the form of the Ten Commandments (vv. 12–14); God's uniqueness, both as to his character and over against idols, which cannot speak or hear (vv. 15–31); God's choice of Israel to be his unique people (vv. 32–38); the prophecy of Israel's eventual failure and restoration (vv. 25–31).

☐ 4:44–11:32 *The Great Exhortation*

Watch now as the themes introduced in 4:1–43 are developed in this eloquent speech. It opens with the Ten Commandments (5:1–21), for this is the code that will be spelled out in chapters 12–26. This is followed by a reminder of Moses' mediatorial role at Horeb/Sinai (5:22–33), but even here the emphasis is on God and his longing for the Israelites' obedience. Then comes the primary commandment of all, namely, that they should love Yahweh their God totally (6:1–25), with emphasis on (1) Yahweh's being the only God there is, (2) his redeeming them so as to make them his people, and (3) his gracious gift of the bountiful land. Next comes the Israelites' need to destroy the pagan peoples who now inhabit their promised land so that Israel will not succumb to syncretistic idolatry (7:1–26), followed by Moses' urging them not to forget God in the midst of their plenty (8:1–20), accompanied by the reminder that the gift of the bountiful land had nothing to do with their own righteousness (9:1–6). Indeed, Israel has a history of stubbornness (9:7–29). The final section (10:1–11:32) anticipates what comes next, reminding the people of the central role of the ark of the covenant and urging that they fear and obey God. The choice is theirs with regard to whether it will be blessing or curse (11:26–32).

☐ 12:1–26:19 *The Deuteronomic Code*

This second giving of the law (*deutero-nomos* = "second law") is the heart of the book of Deuteronomy. Toward the end it is called "this Book of the Law" (28:61; 29:21; 30:10; 31:26), a term picked up five times in Joshua to refer to Deuteronomy (as the covenant-renewal ceremony at Mount Ebal in Josh 8:30–35, with its references to Deut 11:29–30 and 27:12–13, makes clear).

Laws Governing Worship (12:1–16:17). Note how the specific law code of Deuteronomy begins: with the future replacement of the tabernacle by a central sanctuary as the place where God will choose to put his Name (12:4–32, eventually Jerusalem). This is surrounded by reminders to destroy the idolatrous high places (12:1–3) and to avoid every vestige of idolatry (13:1–14:2). These are followed by the clean and unclean statutes (14:3–21; cf. Lev 11), in this case limited to what the people eat, since this also set Israel apart from surrounding nations. These laws lead to regulations about the tithe of the field's produce and the firstborn of the animals, which are to be eaten at the central sanctuary and shared with the Levites (Deut 14:22–29; 15:19–23). These latter two laws surround statutes related to caring for the poor (15:1–18), which were to be constant reminders of their own deliverance from slavery. Worship includes the annual cycle of feasts, whose regulations also include reminders of the Israelites' redemption and of their need to care for the poor (16:1–17).

Laws Governing Leadership (16:18–18:22). Note that most of the next series of laws pick up the theme of "leadership after Moses" from the prologue (1:9–18). In turn these laws deal with judges (16:18–20, 17:8–13, which surround another prohibition of idolatry in 16:21–17:7), kings (17:14–20), priests and Levites (18:1–8), and prophets (18:14–22), the latter two also surrounding yet another prohibition of idolatrous practices in 18:9–13. Note especially the emphasis on social justice on the part of the leaders, who are thus pivotal for the two crucial matters of the people's obedience to God, namely, detesting idolatry and promoting social justice (cf. Isaiah; Hosea; Amos; Micah).

Laws Governing Community Life (19:1–25:19). Be sure to notice here that most of the rest of the code deals with matters from the second half of the Ten Commandments and focuses especially on personal and community relationships. Note also how various themes keep reappearing. For example, the laws governing war (20:1–20) show special care for men and their families (vv. 5–10) and even for trees (vv. 19–20), while at the same time repeating the command to destroy idolatrous nations (vv. 10–18). Be sure to observe the recurrent concern about social justice, especially caring for the poor and needy.

Conclusion (26:1–19). Observe how the specific laws of Deuteronomy end, with reminders of the Israelites' need always to put their God first (firstfruits and tithes, vv. 1–15) and with a final injunction to obedience.

□ 27:1–30:20 *The Covenant Ceremony*

As Deuteronomy now returns to the inner frame, recall what was said above (and in Exodus) about suzerainty treaties. Here in sequence you find the *document clause* (27:1–8), a picture of how Israel is to preserve the laws for the future, and its *sanctions* in the form of curses and blessings (27:9–28:68). The final part of the covenant ceremony contains a concluding charge from Moses, which anticipates Israel's future rebellion and exile, as well as God's restoring them once again to the land (chs. 29–30).

□ 31:1–34:12 *The Look Forward*

The conclusion of the outer frame of Deuteronomy is full of anticipations about the future. The larger section (chs. 32–33, where you find the poetic expression of covenant sanctions) offers the song of Moses—a prophetic word about future rebellion and restoration—and Moses' blessing of the twelve tribes (cf. Joseph in Gen 49). These are enclosed within the two essential transitional matters: (1) the succession of Joshua, including another prediction of future rebellion (Deut 31), and (2) the death of Moses, with a concluding eulogy (ch. 34). Note Yahweh's charge to Joshua, "Be strong and courageous" (31:23), which is then how the book of Joshua begins (Josh 1:6, 7, 9, 18).

Deuteronomy brings the Pentateuch to a conclusion with its constant reminders of God's love and faithfulness despite his people's constant rebellion, but the final word is one of hope that God will ultimately prevail with his people.

Joshua

ORIENTING DATA FOR JOSHUA

- **Content:** the partial conquest, distribution, and settlement of the promised land
- **Historical coverage:** from the beginning of the conquest to the death of Joshua
- **Emphases:** the engagement of the holy war, as God through his people repeatedly defeats the idolatrous Canaanites; the gift of the land to God's people, thus fulfilling his covenant promise to the patriarchs; Israel's need for continuing covenant faithfulness to the one true God

OVERVIEW OF JOSHUA

Following the five books of Moses, the book of Joshua begins the second large section of the Hebrew Bible known as the Former Prophets (Joshua—2 Kings, apart from Ruth). Later scholarship has called the same group of books the Deuteronomic History. Both designations are full of insight. This section of the Old Testament is intended to be prophetic, in the sense that it records Israel's history with the purpose of instructing and explaining from the divine perspective how and why things went the way they did; they are Deuteronomic in that they tell the story from the very decided point of view of Deuteronomy. Thus, for example, Joshua's farewell speech in chapter 23 repeats language from Moses' farewell exhortation in Deuteronomy 7, but now from the perspective after the conquest; at the same time Joshua calls for obedience to "the Book of the Law of Moses" (Josh 8:31), a term that occurs only in Deuteronomy in the Pentateuch—and will appear again at the end of the Former Prophets in 2 Kings (2 Kgs 14:6; 22:8, 11; cf. 23:2).

Joshua itself tells the story of how a second generation of former slaves succeeded in invading and possessing Canaan, thus inheriting the land that God had promised to Abraham and his seed hundreds of years earlier (Gen 12 and 15). The story is told in four parts:

Chapters 1:1–5:12 focus on Israel's *entrance* into the land (with several echoes of the account of Israel's exit from the land of Egypt). After some crucial preparatory matters, the Jordan River is crossed. Accounts of circumcision and the celebration of the Passover (recall Exod 12) bring closure to this part of the story.

Chapters 5:13–12:24 tell the story of the (partial) *conquest* of the land. Featured here are the divine overthrow of Jericho (ch. 6) and the defeat at Ai (ch. 7), which are told in detail and serve as the paradigm for what follows—that this is God's holy war, not theirs, and everything is predicated on obedience and loyalty to the covenant with Yahweh. Hence the covenant renewal ceremony (8:30–35) immediately follows the taking of Ai (8:1–29). Following the Gibeonite deception (ch. 9), which serves as grounds for victory in the south (ch. 10), the rest of the conquest is briefly summarized (chs. 11–12).

Chapters 13–21 narrate the *distribution* of the land, setting out the administrative organization of Yahweh's earthly kingdom. After repeating the settlement of the eastern tribes (ch. 13; cf. Num 32), the focus is on the tribes that will play the leading roles in the history that follows (Judah, Ephraim; Josh 14–17); Benjamin (from whom the first king comes) leads the summation of the rest of the tribes (ch. 18–19). It concludes with provision for those who kill unintentionally (ch. 20) and for the Levites, who otherwise do not inherit land (ch. 21).

Chapters 22–24 are concerned primarily with Israel's continued loyalty to Yahweh and thus conclude with the *renewing of the covenant* at Shechem (cf. 8:30–35).

SPECIFIC ADVICE FOR READING JOSHUA

You will notice that the story in Joshua is told from the perspective of a later time, as the narrator repeatedly mentions certain kinds of memorials that "are there to this day" (4:9; 5:9; 7:26; 8:28–29; 10:27), as are many of the Canaanite peoples (13:13; 15:63; 16:10). The former serve as reminders of God's faithfulness in the past, the latter as reminders of what had not been done.

Both the structure of the book and God's opening words to Joshua (1:2–9) reveal the three major concerns. First, there is the engagement in the holy war. Notice how the emphasis is always on God's initiative and participation ("I will be with you," 1:5). Thus the opening battle (Jericho) is God's alone; after that, the Israelites are themselves militarily involved, but always with God fighting for them (8:1; 10:14; 23:10); as David would put it later, "the battle is the LORD's" (1 Sam 17:47). This is God's holy war, not just to give Israel the land, but especially to rid the land of idolatry (false gods)—all of this so that Yahweh will dwell as King among a people who are to reflect his likeness and follow his ways. In this regard be watching also for the several instances when the author speaks of the gift of "rest" following the holy war (Josh 1:13, 15; 14:15; 21:44; 22:4; 23:1), a theme picked up negatively in Psalm 95:11 regarding the wilderness generation and then in Hebrews 4:1–11 as warning and assurance.

Second, even though chapters 13–21 are not a good read as such, they are profoundly important to the story, for here at last is the fulfilling of God's promise to Abraham and to his seed that they would one day inherit this very land. It was to be their special territory precisely so that here God could develop a people who, by honoring and serving Yahweh, would bless the nations.

Third, and most important, everything has to do with the Israelites' covenant loyalty to the one God. This is the key element in the opening address to Joshua ("Do not let this Book of the Law depart from your mouth; meditate on it day and night, so that you may be careful to do everything written in it," 1:8). This is the central factor in the defeat at Ai (7:11, 15). It also accounts for the early insertion of the covenant renewal at Mount Ebal (8:30–35) and for the final covenant renewal at Shechem with which the narrative concludes (24:1–27).

You will readily see how much all of this picks up and carries on the concerns of Deuteronomy: God's war against false gods; God's promise of the land; and the concern for loyalty to the one true God against all forms of idolatry.

Two further things might help you to read Joshua well. First, read with helpful maps in hand (such as those found in Marten Woudstra's commentary on Joshua [see *How to 1*, p. 269]). This will give you a good sense of the geography mentioned throughout.

Second, it may help you to know that, at the time of Israel's invasion, Canaan was not occupied by a superpower, as it had been earlier by the Egyptians and Hittites. Thus, Israel did not have to face that kind of powerful opposition. Rather, the land was organized in the form of city-states, so that each major city and its surrounding villages had its own king, each of whom was politically independent. Such an arrangement meant that the Israelites, though a small people themselves, could fight each state or small grouping of states (9:1–2; 10:5–27; 11:1–9) separately and thus gradually possess much of the land.

A WALK THROUGH JOSHUA

☐ 1:1–18 *Introduction*

This chapter introduces all the main themes: God as the protagonist of the story; the call of Joshua and recognition of his role as true successor to Moses; that Joshua would lead the people to inherit the land God had promised to their ancestors; and the central concern for covenant loyalty. Note Yahweh's repeated exhortation to Joshua to "be strong and courageous" (vv. 6, 7, 9), repeated at the end of the chapter by the people (v. 18) and by Joshua to the army at the beginning of the southern campaign (10:25). Note also the beginning of the theme of "rest" (1:13, 15).

☐ 2:1–5:12 *Preparation for and Entrance into the Promised Land*

Look for the ways the several narratives of these chapters describe the preparation of the people for the conquest of the land. The first is military (ch. 2): sending spies to Jericho, who, protected by Rahab, learn of the dread their previous victories (Num 21:21–35) have aroused in the people. The second is the miraculous crossing of the Jordan (Josh 3–4), which echoes the previous crossing of the Red Sea during the exodus. The final two are spiritual: the renewal of the rite of circumcision and the celebration of the Passover. Israel can only possess the land as a circumcised people (recall Gen 17:9–14), with the "reproach of Egypt" removed (Josh 5:9), and Passover can now be celebrated again (after a hiatus of 39 years; see Exod 12:25 and Num 9:1–14) as the gift of manna ceases (Josh 5:10–12).

Take note also of the significant role that Gilgal will play in the rest of the conquest (5:9; 9:6; ch. 10); later it becomes one of Israel's sacred sites (1 Sam 7:16; 11:14) and eventually a place of syncretistic idolatry (Hos 4:15; 9:15; 12:11; Amos 4:4; 5:5).

☐ 5:13–8:35 *Jericho and Ai*

Note especially how the conquest begins—with Joshua's encounter with "the commander of the LORD's army" (Josh 5:13–15). Already on the scene to take charge of the conquest, he is Joshua's (and Israel's) assurance that Yahweh's heavenly army is committed to the conquest—a conquest of which Joshua and his army are the earthly contingent. This item is full of echoes of—and significant contrasts with—Moses' encounter with Yahweh in the burning bush (Exod 3:1–4:17).

Observe how closely linked the two stories of Jericho and Ai are, both in the present narrative and beyond (Josh 9:3; 10:1). Together they disclose the conditions under which Israel can conquer and then retain possession of the land. Don't miss the important features of the well-known account of the fall of Jericho—that it is God's victory altogether; that, except for the trumpets, the role of Israel's army is quite nonmilitary; that it is the firstfruits of victory, and therefore everything in the city belongs to God (the city itself is burned as a thing "devoted ... to the LORD," 6:21; its precious stones and metals will go into the Lord's house); and that Rahab and her family are spared because she had confessed that the future belongs to Yahweh (2:8–13).

The first part of the Ai story (ch. 7) picks up the theme of the "devoted things" from chapter 6, focusing on Israel's defeat because of one man's covenant disobedience (7:11, 15; cf. 22:18–20). Note the significance of Achan, a man from Judah whose story may be read against the background of the account of Rahab the harlot (Achan and his family lose all inheritance in the land, while Rahab the foreigner and her family gain inheritance).

The second part of the Ai story (ch. 8) then narrates how God enabled Israel through a shrewd military stratagem to defeat and destroy Ai. These two decisive victories at the point of entry, one miraculous and one through human instrumentality—and told in detail as they are—suggest to the reader how to understand the rest of the stories that are not told in detail. So at this point the narrator includes the covenant renewal at Mount Ebal (8:30–35; see Deut 27:4–8).

□ 9:1–10:43 *The Gibeonite Ruse and Its Consequences*

The first account after the covenant-renewal ceremony is another breach of the covenant, this time by Joshua himself, who "did not inquire of the LORD" (9:14); note that the Gibeonites are Hivites (9:7; 11:19), who are one of the seven Canaanite people groups who are to be utterly destroyed (9:1; cf. Deut 7:1–2). Nonetheless, their deception leads directly to the defeat of the five "kings of the Amorites," who intend to subdue Gibeon but are themselves then defeated (Josh 10:1–28). This in turn leads to the narrative of the conquest of the southern city-states (vv. 29–43); note that the army immediately heads for the cities of the kings who have been killed.

□ 11:1–12:24 *The Northern Conquest and Summary of Defeated Kings*

Here as before, the defeat of the southern kings leads in turn to the defeat of many in the north (ch. 11). Then chapter 12 summarizes all the kings and their city-states that were destroyed.

□ 13:1–21:45 *The Distribution of the Land*

Although this part of Joshua is not exciting reading, you need to be aware of its importance for the rest of the biblical story. For here is the actual fulfillment of the gift of the land made to Abraham and his seed. But observe especially the importance given to certain parts of the narrative—both by placement and by the amount of space devoted to them.

The account begins with a reminder of what still needs to be done (13:1–7), which becomes important for reading both Judges and 2 Samuel 5 and 8, where David finally succeeds in subduing these peoples. After repeating the allotment given to Gad, Reuben, and half of Manasseh (13:8–32; cf. Num 32), the focus is first of all on Caleb and the tribe of Judah (chs. 14–15) and then on the two tribes of Joseph (Ephraim and half of Manasseh, Josh 16–17). Note that a clear break (18:1–2), highlighted by the appearance of the Tent of Meeting at Shiloh, separates these allotments from the rest that follow (18:3–19:48); observe further that these latter begin with Benjamin, which includes Jerusalem (18:28), even though it has not yet been conquered. The distribution narrative itself concludes with Joshua's allotment (19:49–51) so that Caleb and Joshua bookend this narrative (see comments on Num 9:15–14:45, p. 53).

Appended to the distribution narrative are two other very important land matters: provision for unintentional killing (ch. 20) and for the Levites (ch. 21). Note how these repeat Numbers 35, but in reverse order and by condensing the one and expanding the other.

□ 22:1–24:33 *Epilogue*

The three chapters that conclude Joshua have loyalty to God and the covenant as their common denominator. The near outbreak of war over an altar built by the eastern tribes had to do with fear that they had broken faith with the God of Israel (22:16). The two farewell addresses by Joshua have covenant loyalty as their singular theme. Observe how much these speeches reemphasize the concerns of Deuteronomy.

The book concludes on the encouraging note that not only Joshua and Eleazar are buried in the promised land, but that the bones of Joseph, first buried in Egypt (Gen 50:26; cf. Exod 13:19), are also reinterred at Shechem, in the tribal lands of Joseph's son Ephraim. And so God keeps covenant with his people! Unfortunately, the next chapter in the story (Judges) tells of Israel repeatedly breaking covenant with God.

Joshua contributes to God's story of redemption by bringing closure to the covenant promise of the land made in Genesis (and throughout the Pentateuch), thus setting the stage for the next phases of the story.

Judges

ORIENTING DATA FOR JUDGES

- **Content:** the cyclical narrative of the time of the judges, with emphasis on Israel's repeated lack of covenant loyalty
- **Historical coverage:** from the death of Joshua to the beginning of the monarchy
- **Emphases:** the tenuous results of the conquest; God's constant rescue of his people, despite their habitual failure to keep covenant with him; the desperate conditions and overall downward spiral during this period; the need for a good king

OVERVIEW OF JUDGES

The book of Judges, which tells the story of Israel between Joshua and the beginning of the kingship (1 Samuel), is a carefully composed narrative in three essential parts:

1:1–3:6	Introduction: An "overture" setting forth the main themes
3:7–16:31	Main Narrative Cycle: A series of "variations" on the themes
17:1–21:25	Epilogue: A "coda" illustrating the primary theme

As you read, be looking for the ways these various parts interplay with each other so that the whole narrative presents a vivid picture of the times, concluding with the repeated refrain that much of this is related to Israel's not having a king.

The introduction is in two parts. Part 1 (1:1–2:5), which picks up and enhances some of the conquest narrative from Joshua, has two emphases, both found in the conclusion (2:1–5)—(1) that God did not break covenant with Israel, but that they broke covenant with him by not driving out the Canaanites (1:21, 27–36), and (2) that God will no longer come to their aid in this cause; instead, the Canaanites "will be thorns in your sides and their gods will be a snare to you" (2:3). Thus this part gives the basic reason for what follows.

Part 2 (2:6–3:6) rehearses in summary form how the narrative will unfold. Here the basic Deuteronomic cycle is introduced:

1. Israel does evil in the eyes of Yahweh by serving the Canaanite Baals (2:11–13).
2. They experience Yahweh's anger in the form of failure in battle and oppression by their enemies (vv. 14–15).
3. The people cry out in their distress, and God rescues them by sending a judge-deliverer (vv. 16, 18).
4. When the judge dies, the cycle begins all over again (vv. 17, 19–23).

You will notice that the epilogue is also in two parts, giving in gruesome detail case studies of Israel's syncretism and failure to keep covenant with their God.

Between these two framing sections lies the main narrative itself, in which the cycle is repeated again and again, but with the emphasis on the stories of deliverance. Common to these stories is that God stands behind all deliverance, even though the deliverers themselves are seldom shining examples of devotion to Yahweh!

This central series appears to be carefully constructed, presenting twelve "judges" corresponding to the number of Israelite tribes. It begins with Othniel, whose story is told only in summary and as a pattern for the rest. This is followed by the exploits of five judges (Ehud, Deborah/Barak, Gideon/Abimelech, Jephthah, and Samson), interspersed with what amounts to a list of other such judge-deliverers (Shamgar, Tola, Jair, Ibzan, Elon, Abdon). This series is framed by accounts of two loners (Ehud, a Benjamite; Samson, a Danite). In the inner frame of stories (Deborah/Barak, Jephthah) deliverance is dependent on a woman and an outcast/outlaw. At the center is the account of Gideon and his son Abimelech (whose name means "father of the king"), and here surface the two central issues in the narrative: Who is the true God? Who is Israel's king? The narratives of Samuel and Kings pick it up from there.

SPECIFIC ADVICE FOR READING JUDGES

So that you keep focused as you read Judges, you need to know three things in advance. First, the word traditionally translated "judges" (*shophetim*) does not in this book refer primarily to judicial officials (although the word does carry that sense; see, e.g., Exod 18:13). Rather they were military leaders and clan chieftains whom God used to deliver Israel from enemies who threatened parts of Israel over a long period of time. Hence the NIV compromises by translating the noun in the traditional way, but uses "lead/led" for the verb.

Second, even though such terms as "led Israel" and "the Israelites" regularly appear, you should not imagine that each (or any) of these judges was the leader of all Israel in the same sense that Moses and Joshua were. In fact, as the stories unfold, you will recognize that part of the concern of the narrator is that precisely the opposite is true—that one or several tribes are oppressed and call on other tribes for help, which sometimes comes and sometimes doesn't, often resulting in intertribal strife. The irony of the narrative is that only at the end, in a case of intertribal disciplinary warfare, are all twelve tribes "united," as it were. Note, for example, the stinging words in Deborah's song about Reuben (5:15–16), who in a time of crisis and after "much searching of heart" stayed home "to hear the whistling for the flocks."

Third, and related to this, is the matter of overall chronology. You will note that chronological language is frequently employed ("after the time of ..." and "the land had peace for ... years") and that the overall scheme reflects the history of the times, beginning with sporadic oppression (Moab in the east) and concluding with Philistine oppression, which is where the Samuel narrative picks up. Even so, you should not think of all of this as happening in chronological order. Peace in one place does not mean peace in another. And the parenthetical note in 20:27–28 sets that story very early on in the period (the priest at Bethel is Aaron's grandson). The point is that the narrator is not as interested in a time line as such, as in the overall picture of the times he is portraying.

But the one chronological matter that is crucial to his narrative is the gradual but unrelenting deterioration of things in Israel down to the time of Samuel. This is portrayed first of all by the structure itself, with its concluding stories in chapters 17–21. It is also reflected in the portrayal of the six major judges. The portrayals of Othniel, Ehud, and Deborah are basically positive, despite some subterfuge on the part of Ehud and Jael (4:18–21). But beginning with Gideon, things begin to tilt. The Gideon story begins well, but turns out badly in the form of an idolatrous ephod (8:24–27) and a murderous son, Abimelech (ch. 9). The Jephthah and Samson stories paint a picture of God's Spirit using less than exemplary leaders. Another way this theme is carried through is the use of "in the eyes of." Watch how each of the cycle stories begins: "Again the Israelites did evil in the eyes of the LORD." At the end we are told what this means: "In those days there was no king in Israel; all the people did what was right in their own eyes" (17:6; 21:25 [NRSV]). The hinge point of this theme is an idiom that is usually expressed differently in English translation, where Samson rebelliously desires a young Philistine as his wife because (literally) "she is right in my eyes" (14:3, 7).

Yet despite all this, God's care for his people holds the story together. This is especially discernible in the repeated notice that "the Spirit of the LORD [Yahweh]"—mentioned in the opening Othniel story but absent in the Ehud and Deborah episodes—does come upon Gideon (6:34), Jephthah (11:29), and Samson (13:25; 14:6, 19; 15:14). Even so, what is noticeably absent from Judges is any mention of, or even any sense of, the presence of the Lord in the midst of his people. The Tent of Meeting that Joshua set up at Shiloh (Josh 18:1) reappears there in 1 Samuel 2:22. In Judges we are told that the idolatry of the tribe of Dan continues "all the time the house of God was in Shiloh" (18:31), but Israel never consults with Yahweh there to hear from him. Israel is a people who have lost their way and their primary identity, and only God in mercy can bring order to this chaos.

A WALK THROUGH JUDGES

□ 1:1–2:5 *The Basic Problem: Failure to Destroy the Canaanites*

Watch for the narrator's purposes to unfold. After a review of some victories in the south, led by Judah (1:1–18), he notes Israel's failure to dislodge all the Canaanites (1:19–21). The same thing happens again in the north—victory at Bethel (1:22–26), but mostly failure (1:27–36). This failure is then denounced as an act of disobedience (2:1–5), so God will now leave Canaanites in the land as thorns in Israel's sides. And this means that the Canaanite gods "will be a snare" to them (2:3).

☐ 2:6–3:6 *The Pattern Established*

In 2:6–19 you encounter the Deuteronomic cycle, which sets the pattern for the rest of the book: The people stop serving Yahweh; he abandons them to their enemies; they suffer subjugation; they pray for help; God's Spirit comes on a person who leads them to defeat their enemies; they then become complacent and repeat the cycle. Note that the rest of this introduction (2:20–3:6) picks up the theme from 2:1–5, but now indicating that God himself has left the hostile nations within and on the outskirts of the promised land to trouble the Israelites.

☐ 3:7–11 *Othniel (from Judah/against the Arameans)*

Note that in this initial judge episode, the cycle (2:6–19) is fully represented: Israel abandons God (v. 7), incurring his anger and their subjugation to the Arameans (v. 8); this results eventually in prayers for help that cause God to send a deliverer (v. 9). The "Spirit of the LORD" then gives Othniel the wisdom to lead, so that "the land had peace" (v. 11).

☐ 3:12–31 *Ehud (from Benjamin/against the Moabites) and Shamgar*

"Once again the Israelites did evil in the eyes of the LORD," which leads to their subjugation to a (very fat) Moabite king. Note how his obesity and Ehud's being left-handed are the intrigue on which the story turns. Although this is basically the story of a loner, Ehud nonetheless prepares the way for an Israelite victory (vv. 26–30). The Spirit is not mentioned here, but "the LORD" is nonetheless responsible for the victory (3:28). The appended report about Shamgar (3:31) introduces the Philistines, who later become Israel's worst foreign foe.

☐ 4:1–5:31 *Deborah (from Ephraim/against Northern Canaanites)*

The intrigue of this story is its focus on two women, Deborah and Jael, who overshadow the actual "deliverer," Barak. Note that Deborah initiates the action in the name of the Lord, and that Barak's refusal to go to battle without her leads to the prophecy that the Lord will hand over Sisera to a woman—but the woman turns out not to be Deborah but Jael! Deborah's song (see 5:7, also sung by Barak, 5:1) retells the story with some added detail, while it praises God and shames the tribes that did not help.

☐ 6:1–10:5 *Gideon (from Benjamin/against the Midianites and Amalekites) and Tola and Jair*

Notice how in this case the narrator fills out the various parts of the cycle in more detail than before. As always it begins with, "Again the Israelites did evil in the eyes of the LORD" (6:1). The oppression is from hordes of easterners, led by Midian and Amalek, and is particularly desperate (6:2–6) so that Israel cries out to God, who again reminds them that they have broken covenant with him (6:7–10). But the greatest elaboration is with the deliverer and the tale of victory. As you read, watch for signs of the book's downward-spiral motif within the narrative itself.

Gideon is portrayed as fearful and diffident (6:11–19), obedient but doubting (6:20–40). He starts well—by tearing down the altar of Baal (6:24–32) and "leading" a decisive, God-orchestrated victory over Midian (ch. 7). But then a quite different Gideon pursues Zebah and Zalmunna (8:1–18); nonetheless, even though his zeal represents something of a personal vendetta over the death of his brothers (8:19–21), he is still pictured as carrying on the holy war. But he ends up making an ephod that becomes idolatrous, and his son Abimelech is thoroughly degenerate.

Key to this episode is the demand of the Israelites that Gideon rule over them (8:22), which he rejects—a rejection that includes his sons—in favor of the rule of Yahweh (v. 23). Note how the story hits a low point with Gideon's son, Abimelech, who makes himself a king after killing all but one of his seventy brothers. But also note the irony: An unnamed woman kills him with a dropped millstone (9:50–53). Israel is thus delivered from one of her own! The notices about Tola (10:1–2) and Jair (vv. 3–5), who represent Issachar (and Ephraim) and Gilead (eastern Manasseh), conclude the Gideon cycle and prepare the way for Jephthah. By so briefly mentioning Tola and Jair, the narrator reminds you that his stories are purposely selective rather than exhaustive accounts of all that transpired.

☐ 10:6–12:14 *Jephthah (from Eastern Manasseh/against the Ammonites) and Ibzan, Elon, and Abdon*

The downward spiral continues. Jephthah is something of a successful outlaw (11:3–6) at the time his fellow Gileadites appeal to him for help against the Ammonites. He is pictured as rash and self-centered, a man for whom a vow is more important than a daughter. He is successful in battle because the Spirit of the Lord was upon him (11:29), but he is also responsible for the deaths of thousands of Israelites (12:1–6). The accounts of Ibzan, Elon, and Abdon (12:8–15) are apparently the author's brief reminders that God continued to work through judges in various locales.

□ 13:1–16:31 *Samson (from Dan/against the Philistines)*

This final cycle story is the most tragic—and ambiguous—of all. Samson in his own person represents all that is wrong in Israel during the period of the judges: born of a barren woman, dedicated to be Yahweh's special servant from birth (ch. 13), unbeatable when the Spirit of Yahweh is with him—but he breaks his vows (see comments on Num 5:1–6:27, p. 52) by getting honey from a dead (Philistine) lion, by marrying a foreigner (Judg 14), and by dallying with a prostitute (ch. 16). Note how all of these mirror Israel's own story of prostitution with the Baals and Ashtoreths. Nonetheless the Spirit of God continues to come on him to defeat small groups of Philistines. Blind and imprisoned, Samson is enabled by God to kill a temple full of Philistines, as he himself dies in the process (16:23–30). This narrative also sets the stage for the long struggle with the Philistines that marks the Saul and David stories that are to come, but more immediately it serves as a transition from the sins of Israel as a people to the sins of individuals narrated in chapters 17–21.

□ 17:1–21:25 *Two Stories Illustrating Israel's Degeneracy*

Note how this conclusion is carefully crafted around the phrase, "In those days Israel had no king; everyone did as [they] saw fit [what was right in their own eyes]" (17:6; 21:25; cf. 18:1; 19:1). With these words the narrator gives you the perspective from which the whole story has been told: Israel is in disarray; it has no central leadership—and no accepted central sanctuary, as had been commanded in Deuteronomy.

Thus, the first episode (ch. 17) in the first story illustrates Israel's syncretism (Micah's mother consecrates her silver to Yahweh for her son to make an idol), while the second (ch. 18) illustrates both the Danite context out of which Samson came and the unsettled conditions in Israel due to the failure of conquest with which the book began. Both episodes illustrate the failure of true worship in Israel.

The gruesome nature of the second story (chs. 19–21) illustrates both the depth of Israel's remembered moral decay (see Hos 9:9–10) and the reality that she teeters regularly on the brink of intertribal war. Israel needs God's appointed king.

The tragic pattern in Judges points to the next phase of God's great story of redemption, which will begin to move forward considerably through the stories of Ruth and of her great-grandson David.

Ruth

ORIENTING DATA FOR RUTH

- **Content:** a story of loyalty to Yahweh during the period of the judges, in which Naomi's fortunes mirror Israel's during this period (while also providing the lineage of King David)
- **Historical coverage:** a few years around 1100 B.C.
- **Emphases:** life in a village that remains loyal to Yahweh during the time of the judges; the welcoming of a foreign woman under Yahweh's wings; God's superintending care that provides Israel with its great king

OVERVIEW OF RUTH

What a relief to find Ruth after Judges! Indeed, here in bold relief is another story from the same period, about one good man and two good women, not to mention a whole community, who are portrayed as faithful to the covenant. Although the book of Ruth (along with Esther) appears among the Writings in the Hebrew canon, in the Greek Bible—used by the Christian tradition—Ruth was placed between Judges and 1 Samuel, almost certainly because of the way it begins ("In the days when the judges ruled") and ends ("Obed [was] the father of Jesse, and Jesse the father of David"). You will see how perceptive that move was.

The book of Ruth is sometimes treated as a love story—and in some ways it is indeed a love story, but not a romance. Yahweh's love for Israel here finds expression in Ruth's and Boaz's loving concern for Naomi, and in Boaz's for Naomi and Ruth. Although the heart of the story features the actions of Ruth and Boaz, the central figure throughout is Naomi, as the prologue (1:1–5) and epilogue (4:13–17) make clear. The narrative plot deals with Naomi's moving from "emptiness" in a foreign land to "fullness" back home in Bethlehem in Judah, from a form of barrenness (widowhood with no male heir) to full inheritance through

Boaz's assuming the responsibilities of kinsman-redeemer and, through his marriage to Ruth, providing her with a male heir—and what an heir he turned out to be!

The story is told in four scenes, each employing an opening thematic sentence and each, except for the last, containing a closing sentence that sets up the reader for the next scene. In turn the scenes depict Naomi's emptiness (1:6–22), her awakened hope (ch. 2), the progress toward fulfillment (ch. 3), and fullness realized in the birth of an heir (ch. 4).

And how does fullness come? Through Ruth, a young Moabite widow, and Boaz, the established, wealthy, upstanding man of Judah—extremes on the sociological scale—who both act toward the needy one (Naomi) in the way that is open to them and without considering their own benefit, and both risking all to do so. Indeed, the role played by their two foils (Orpah and the other kinsman) highlights the risk factor for each.

SPECIFIC ADVICE FOR READING RUTH

In telling this story as he does, the narrator probably intends the reader to see here a comparison with Israel as a whole during the time of the judges (1:1). In a time of famine, the family of Elimelech seeks life away from Yahweh's promised land in the land of Moab, only to find death and emptiness. By returning home—to Bethlehem, the "house of bread" with its abundant harvest—the one whose name means "sweet" but calls herself "bitter" (1:20) starts on a journey from hope to fulfillment, to having a "son" who will serve as her ultimate kinsman-redeemer. And in so doing, she sets in motion events that will lead to Israel's receiving their foremost king. You can hardly miss the final blessing of Naomi by the women of Bethlehem in 4:14: "May he become famous throughout Israel!" Indeed!

In this regard it is important that you also watch how both the town of Bethlehem in general and the three main characters in particular are portrayed as loyal to Yahweh and the covenant, and thus experience the covenant blessings (see esp. Deut 28:3–6) during "the days when the judges ruled" (1:1). This comes out in a variety of ways: Ruth's determination to follow Yahweh because of her relationship with Naomi (1:16–18); the greetings of Boaz and the harvesters, reflecting God's presence and blessing (2:4); Boaz's welcoming of Ruth, who has chosen to take refuge under the wings of Yahweh (2:12); Boaz's own generosity and largeheartedness (2:8–9, 14–18); and Naomi's "blessing" of Boaz (2:20).

But this theme is especially evident in the way the narrator weaves into the story indications of their obedience to the covenant law—gleanings left for an alien; the kinsman-redeemer; inheritance through the covenant marriage-inheritance laws. The narrator assumes his readers will recognize all these covenantal factors. These are not people who need to be portrayed as consulting the law for guidance on what to do; rather they are simply demonstrating their covenant loyalty to Yahweh by the way they live and treat people. The author seems concerned in the end to show that David's forebears were themselves faithful Yahwists in a time when much of Israel was not.

Note finally how Ruth herself becomes an example of the blessing of Abraham working out in practice (Gen 12:3, "all peoples on earth will be blessed through you"). She is an alien from a hated foreign nation (Deut 23:3). Yet she chooses to follow Israel's God and thus becomes part of his people (Ruth 1:16–17); as such she herself loves Naomi (4:15) by showing Yahweh's kindness (2:11–12) to one who has experienced exile and bitterness (1:19–21). In turn she is blessed by Boaz as one who has chosen to come under Yahweh's care and blessing (2:12); and at the end Yahweh thus "enabled her to conceive" (4:13). Though a foreigner without the covenant history enjoyed by the other Israelites, she nonetheless shows covenant love and loyalty in a way that most Israelites did not at this time in history. She, a non-Israelite, is used as an example to Yahweh's own "firstborn" (see Exod 4:22). Thus she is one of four Gentile women included in Matthew's genealogy (Matt 1:5b; cf. vv. 3, 5a, 6), which in his Gospel anticipates the gospel as good news for "all nations" (Matt 28:19).

A WALK THROUGH RUTH

☐ 1:1–5 *Prologue*

Note how the narrator sets up the whole story with this prologue. Because of famine, Elimelech and Naomi and sons leave Yahweh's land for Moab; Naomi ends up in exile in a foreign land, destitute, without husband or sons.

☐ 1:6–22 *Scene 1: Naomi and Ruth—Grief, Loyalty, and Conversion*

With the opening sentence (v. 6), the narrator sets the stage for this first scene: Naomi's determination to go back to Bethlehem. You will recognize that the heart of this opening scene is Ruth's determination to remain loyal to her mother-in-law and thus to convert and become a true Yahwist herself. Note how the final sentence (v. 22) sets the stage for the next scene.

☐ 2:1–23 *Scene 2: Ruth, Boaz, and Naomi—Surprising Kindness*

Watch for the buildup of anticipation as this chapter unfolds. You are introduced to Boaz (v. 1) and to Ruth's initiative (v. 2), who "as it turned out" [!] gleans in Boaz's fields (v. 3). Then it is Boaz's turn to show kindness (vv. 4–17): He blesses Ruth in Yahweh's name for her kindness to Naomi (v. 12), she works and eats with the harvesters under his protection (vv. 9, 14), and her gleanings become greater by design (vv. 15–16). Notice also how toward the end Naomi blesses Boaz (vv. 19–20) for his kindness to Ruth, and through Ruth to herself. With a final sentence (v. 23) the narrator moves on to the end of harvest to set you up for what happens next.

☐ 3:1–18 *Scene 3: Naomi, Ruth, and Boaz—Ruth Petitions Marriage*

Naomi now takes the lead—on the obvious, and correct, assumption of Boaz's goodness—while Ruth carries out the plan (vv. 1–9). Her action in verse 9 invites Boaz to become Naomi's kinsman-redeemer and thus to take Ruth as his wife. Boaz accepts, but the law requires that he offer her first to one who is more qualified (vv. 10–12). Note how carefully the author portrays Boaz as a man of moral nobility, just as he did with Ruth in the former scene. Again, the last sentence (v. 18) sets up the final scene.

☐ 4:1–22 *Scene 4: Boaz, Ruth, and Naomi ... and David—Marriage and a Son*

Following ancient custom in Israelite towns, the matter is decided between Boaz and his kin in the presence of the town elders at the town gate. Boaz risks, as Ruth had risked earlier. So Boaz marries Ruth; Naomi has an heir—"bitter" becomes "sweet" again (see comment on p. 79)—and eventually Israel gets her premier king.

The book of Ruth tells the story of God's faithfulness to his people in a specific case, as a Moabite woman becomes part of his story of redemption.

1 and 2 Samuel

ORIENTING DATA FOR 1 AND 2 SAMUEL

- **Content:** the transition from the last judge, Samuel, to the first king, Saul; the rise and reign of David
- **Historical coverage:** from Samuel's birth (ca. 1100 B.C.) to the end of David's kingship (970 B.C.)
- **Emphases:** the beginning of kingship in Israel; the concern over kingship and covenant loyalty; the ark of the covenant as representing God's presence; the choice of Jerusalem as "the City of David"; the Davidic covenant with its messianic overtones; David's adultery and its consequences

OVERVIEW OF 1 AND 2 SAMUEL

The books of Samuel and Kings together form a continuous history of the Israelite monarchy from the time of Samuel to its demise in 587/6 B.C. It is important as you read them to remember that in the Hebrew Bible they belong to the Former Prophets. Like the books of the Latter Prophets, these books present God's perspective on the history of his people; although they concentrate on Israel's kings, prophets play an important role as well.

The book of Samuel tells the story from the beginnings of kingship to the declining years of David's reign. The story centers on three key people: *Samuel,* the last of the judges and the prophet who anoints the first two kings; *Saul,* Israel's first king; and *David,* Israel's most important king. The book itself is in four basic parts, related to these three men.

Part 1 is about Samuel alone (1 Sam 1–7). Essential here are the birth, call, and early career of Samuel (1:1–4:1a) and the loss and return of the ark of the covenant (4:1b–7:1), followed eventually by a great victory over the Philistines (7:2–14).

In part 2 (1 Sam 8–15), Samuel and Saul overlap. Two matters are essential here: (1) Yahweh's affirmations of and warnings about the monarchy (chs. 8–12; cf. Deut 17:14–20) and (2) the beginning of Saul's reign and Yahweh's rejection of him as king (1 Sam 13–15).

In part 3 (1 Sam 16–31), Saul and David overlap. Its essential story is told at the beginning and the end: the anointing of David to replace Saul as king (16:1–13) and the death of Saul and his heir apparent, Jonathan (ch. 31). Thus it is all about David's rise and Saul's decline, as well as Saul's constant pursuit of David in order to kill the upstart rival to his dynasty.

Part 4 (2 Samuel) concentrates on David—although concern over Saul continues (chs. 1–4; 9; 21)—while Nathan (chs. 7, 12) and Gad (ch. 24) now don the prophetic mantle of Samuel. Chapters 1–9 set out the basic story of David's reign, the most significant part of which is the covenant in chapter 7 that establishes David's dynasty "forever" (vv. 15–16). Chapters 10–20 narrate David's sin with Bathsheba that becomes a catalyst to expose the internal weaknesses in David's family and the tenuous nature of the united kingdom. Chapters 21–24 are a kind of reflective appendix to the story of David.

SPECIFIC ADVICE FOR READING 1 AND 2 SAMUEL

The book of Samuel is full of many intriguing and riveting individual stories. But this very fact, which makes reading Samuel so interesting, can also cause you to miss some significant things with regard to the bigger picture of the story of Israel. To read Samuel well, you need to be aware of a few of these, especially some Deuteronomic themes that pervade the whole.

The history itself takes place roughly over the eleventh century B.C., a time when no superpower is a major player in Palestine (see "Specific Advice for Reading Joshua," p. 65). Thus the time was ripe for a strong local power to arise and subdue the others, which was precisely what David did (see 2 Sam 8). The major obstacle to such a program came not from the Canaanites but from the Philistines, whom you first meet in the book of Judges (Shamgar, Samson). They were sea peoples who had settled on the Mediterranean coast and held sway over the coastal area (and often further inland) from their five major cities (Gaza, Ashdod, Ashkelon, Gath, and Ekron). It is their influence that pushes the Israelite tribes toward the unification and protection afforded by the monarchy, and it is their presence that lies behind so much of the story of the book of Samuel, until David defeats them "in the course of time" (2 Sam 8:1).

The book of Samuel, therefore, is especially the story of transitions—from the periodic, partial rule of judges to an institutionalized, hereditary monarchy; from a king who looks like the typical Near Eastern king (warned about by Samuel as a prophet, 1 Sam 8:10–18) to one who is loyal to Yahweh; from no central place where God's Name dwells to a new center in Jerusalem. All of this is marvelously told—with wit, irony, suspense, wordplays—but above all with an eye to what God is doing with and among his people, even as he gives them a king.

One of the central (Deuteronomic) concerns of the book, evident in the structure itself, is the true worship of God at the place of his dwelling (his presence). This theme begins with a prophecy against the house of Eli because they "scorn my sacrifice and offering that I prescribed for my dwelling" (1 Sam 2:29). Then chapters 4–7 focus on the ark of the covenant, whose capture meant "the glory has departed from Israel" (4:22). Later, a central feature of David's reign is his bringing the ark to Jerusalem (2 Sam 6), where he desires to build a temple for it, but is forbidden (ch. 7). And the book ends with David's building an altar on the threshing floor of Araunah (24:18–25), which the intended reader would know is the precise place where the temple will eventually stand.

Linked to this is another theme that is a central feature of the narrative, namely, the tension between monarchy and covenant loyalty. You will see how this is set up near the beginning—in the contrasting sentiments between Samuel and the people in 1 Samuel 8–12. As the story proceeds, you are regularly reminded that even divinely appointed kings can, and do, act like other kings (as warned about in Deut 17:14–20). Yet David's essential loyalty to Yahweh lies at the heart of the story, and God covenants with him that his dynasty will endure forever (2 Sam 7)—a covenant that becomes a central feature in much of the rest of God's story.

Note how this tension lies at the heart of the contrasting stories of Saul and David (1 Sam 16–31). At issue in the end for our narrator is not *whether* Israel has a king, but *what kind of king* they will have. Key to this is whether the king will both be *faithful* to Yahweh and display Yahweh's *character,* since whatever else is true about Israel's king, he is to be the earthly representative of Yahweh's own kingship over Israel. Thus, even though Saul is anointed by Samuel and appears to begin well, there are deep flaws in his character, many of which are already subtly present at the beginning. At the end he is rejected because he thinks like any other king—that he is above the law and can act autonomously. Moreover, the prophetic tradition in Israel, represented by Samuel and Nathan, serves as a constant reminder that kings were *not* autonomous. Israel may indeed have rejected theocracy (the direct rule by God) for monarchy (1 Sam 8), but the role of her king was to mediate Yahweh's rule in Israel and thus to *lead God's people in obedience* to Yahweh.

A similar ambivalence pervades the story of David's reign as well (2 Sam 5–20). The fact that David's *kingly* exploits are merely summarized in 2 Samuel 8 while the story of his *sin* and the evil it let loose in the kingdom is narrated in considerable detail (chs. 10–20) should get our attention! Thus the narrator reminds us in various ways of David's genuine loyalty to Yahweh, not least by his placing the two great poems of David's devotion and praise to the Lord (22:1–23:7) as the centerpiece of his summarizing appendix (chs. 21–24). Yet this picture of "the man of faith" (21:15–17; 23:13–17) is set in the context of "the man of weakness" (24:1–17)—but who, when confronted with his sin, repents by means of prayer and sacrifice.

You will also want to watch for two parts of a subplot from Genesis (see "Specific Advice for Reading Genesis, p. 26) that mark this story as well: (1) the barren-woman motif that begins the story of Samuel (echoed in a variety of ways in Luke 1) and (2) God's choice of the "lesser" to fulfill his covenant purposes (David the shepherd boy).

There is one other important matter to keep in mind as you read, which leads to how this narrative fits into the metanarrative of the biblical story. In the ancient Near East the king was considered both the embodiment of his people (that is, he stood in for them at all times as their representative) and the representative of the deity for the people (cf. Ps 2:7, where the Davidic king is called "God's Son"). This is why Samuel and Kings tell the story of Israel almost exclusively as the story of their kings—and why the king speaks for the people in the Psalter. But this also explains why kingship was such a frightening prospect in Israel. At the same time, however, the role of David in the biblical story is affirmed, for in the end it is David's greater Son who comes as the true *embodiment* of Israel while also, as the true Son of God, *representing* God to Israel. This is why Jesus' kingship plays such an important role in the New Testament telling of his story.

A WALK THROUGH 1 AND 2 SAMUEL

The Story of Samuel (1 Samuel 1–7)

The narrator intends for you to admire Samuel, who serves as Israel's last judge and next great prophet after Moses. He is also the one who will anoint Israel's first two kings.

☐ **1 Samuel 1:1–4:1a** ***The Birth and Call of Samuel***

Note the decisive role that Hannah plays in this story: a barren woman praying for a son (1:1–20), dedicating him to God (1:21–28), and rejoicing in the Lord (2:1–11). Note also how her prayer anticipates at least two motifs of the story—(1) God blesses the weak, not the strong, and (2) God will give strength to his king. Samuel's origins are then set in contrast to the wickedness of Eli's sons (2:12–36), followed by Samuel's call (3:1–18) and a concluding summary of his ministry (3:19–4:1a). Note how Eli's acceptance of Yahweh's rejection of him as priest (3:18) serves as a foil for Saul's later refusal to accept Yahweh's rejection of him as king.

☐ **1 Samuel 4:1b–7:17** ***The Loss and Return of the Ark***

Note how this section is dominated by the loss and return of the glory of God, associated with the ark, where God "is enthroned between the cherubim" (4:4). The ark is not a talisman for Israel to use at a whim (4:1b–22), but neither are the Philistines to think that they have conquered Israel's God (ch. 5), so it is returned partway toward its final resting place (6:1–7:1). Some twenty years later, Samuel calls for national repentance, which results in God's aid in defeating the Philistines (7:2–13, echoes of Judges). Note how the concluding section summarizes Samuel's ministry, even though there is more to say about him (cf. the role of 1 Sam 15:34–35 in the Saul narrative).

The Story of Samuel and Saul (1 Samuel 8–15)

Here watch for the tension between kingship in Israel and covenant loyalty; Samuel warns of this three times, and the first king then comes to represent covenant disloyalty.

☐ **1 Samuel 8:1–12:25** ***Saul Anointed King***

You might want to read this section in light of Deuteronomy 16:18–17:20. Note how it starts (8:1–3) with echoes from Deuteronomy

16:18–20 (judges who pervert justice and show partiality). The rest of this section is bookended by two warnings about the potential evils of monarchy, including statements about the people's rejection of Yahweh's kingship (8:4–22 and 11:14–12:25). These frame the narratives about Saul's becoming king—first, his anointing by Samuel (9:1–10:8), which emphasizes Saul's humble beginnings, and second, his being presented to the people and their confirmation of him (10:9–11:13), emphasizing his continuity with the prophetic tradition, his timid nature, and his military success (the holy war).

☐ 1 Samuel 13:1–15:35 *The Failure of Saul's Kingship*

Here Saul's entire reign (13:1) is reduced to three incidents that occurred well into his reign. Two framing narratives demonstrate his covenant disloyalty—offering his own sacrifice (13:2–15) and violating the covenantal holy-war rules (15:1–35; cf. Achan's sin in Josh 7). The central narrative (13:16–14:48) demonstrates his weakness of character and personal failure in engaging the holy war. Each of these is symptomatic of his general disobedience and provides evidence of his lack of true faith in Yahweh. Thus Yahweh rejects him as Israel's king (encapsulated in 15:22–23). Note how, despite the fact that Saul lives on until chapter 31, his reign comes to its effective end at 15:35, where he is rejected (though mourned) by Samuel and by Yahweh.

The Story of Saul and David (1 Samuel 16–31)

As you read this part of the story, look for the interweaving of David's rise to power, even though a fugitive, and Saul's decline. You need to be aware that the author's interest at the beginning is not so much with the chronology of events as with their significance for the story as a whole.

☐ 1 Samuel 16:1–17:58 *The Rise of David*

Notice how the opening story of David's anointing as future king (16:1–13) concludes on the twin notes that the Spirit of Yahweh came on David (v. 13) but had departed from Saul (v. 14). The first two scenes (16:14–23; 17:1–58) set up the program: David's initial positive relationship with Saul; David's first exploit—a shepherd boy who trusts Yahweh ("the battle is the LORD's [Yahweh's]," 17:47) slays the Philistine champion Goliath (thus success in the holy war).

☐ 1 Samuel 18:1–31:13 *The Decline and Death of Saul*

This section begins with a story illustrating its central theme: Saul's jealousy of David and his attempts to kill him (ch. 18). Note how the rest of the section is dominated by Saul's pursuit of David, while David in turn has two opportunities to kill Saul, but will not lift his hand against "the LORD's anointed" (chs. 24 and 26, which encircle his being saved from his own anger by Abigail).

Interwoven into this theme are (1) other accounts of Saul's downward spiral, in the end consulting a medium (ch. 28) and finishing in shame (ch. 31); (2) accounts of David's existence as the fugitive head of a band of guerrillas; (3) evidence of David's obedience to Yahweh and consideration of his character (e.g., his largeheartedness toward Saul and Jonathan)—note especially how Abigail's speech in 25:26–31 not only saves David from vengeful wrongdoing but in effect allows the narrator to express his theme for these chapters; and (4) David's frequent, temporary stays in enemy territory, where God protected him from harm and covenant disloyalty under conditions that could have produced either result.

The Story of David (2 Samuel)

You will observe that the first part of the story is dominated by the theme of David's covenant loyalty, which leads to the Davidic covenant, yet one particular moment of covenant disloyalty sets up much of what goes wrong with the rest of the story (1 and 2 Kings).

☐ 2 Samuel 1:1–4:12 *The Story of David as King of Judah*

This section presents the aftermath of Saul's death; note how it emphasizes David's *non*role in the civil war that followed. Thus he laments over Saul and Jonathan (ch. 1). Following the account of his becoming king of Judah (ch. 2), he is notably exonerated in all the tragedies that follow (chs. 3–4). Keep your eyes open for the rift between north and south, which is picked up again in chapters 19–20 and becomes final in 1 and 2 Kings.

☐ 2 Samuel 5:1–9:13 *The Story of David as King over All Israel*

Following David's assuming the kingship over all Israel (5:1–5) is a sequence of four narratives (5:6–7:29) that are especially crucial: (1) David's conquest of Jerusalem, (2) the conquest of the Philistines,

(3) bringing the ark to Jerusalem, and, above all, (4) God's covenant with David that "your house and your kingdom will endure forever before me" (7:1–16), to which David responds in an outpouring of praise and gratitude (7:18–29).

The importance of the preceding narratives is highlighted by the brevity of chapter 8, which serves to bring the conquest to a conclusion (see Joshua). Here you find David's many years as king condensed into two brief summaries. And because our narrator is ultimately concerned not with David's kingly exploits but with his character, he concludes with another narrative of David's kindness to the house of Saul (ch. 9), where the "lame" enter the palace—despite the saying in 5:8! But note how this scene sits in contrast to the unfortunate story that follows.

☐ 2 Samuel 10:1–20:26 *David's Sin and Its Consequences*

Note how the account of David's sin against Bathsheba and Uriah is told in detail. It is set up in chapter 10, recounted in chapter 11, and condemned in chapter 12. And watch for the irony in chapter 11—the faithful foreigner Uriah honors an unfaithful Israelite king; the foreigner retains sexual purity during war, while the Israelite king dallies with his wife; the king, who has not gone into battle himself, sends the faithful soldier to his death in battle. The king is portrayed throughout as one who is accountable to God for his actions (note how crucial ch. 12 is to the Israelite view of kingship), but in contrast to Saul, David repents—and is then filled with remorse over the dying child, the result of his sin.

This event sets in motion the rest of the story (chs. 13–20) in two ways. First, watch how illicit sexuality, murder, and intrigue are multiplied in David's family, as Nathan's prediction (12:10–12) is fulfilled. In turn there is rape, fratricide, treachery, rebellion, seizure of David's concubines, and civil war, and the fissures between north and south portrayed in 19:8b–20:26 anticipate the unbridgeable chasm related in 1 Kings 12. And second, observe how this whole series of events is related to the question later raised by Bathsheba in 1 Kings 1:20: "Who will sit on the throne of my lord the king after him?"

☐ 2 Samuel 21:1–24:25 *Final Reflections on David and His Reign*

Notice how the narrator also summarizes David, as he did Samuel and Saul, before David's story is actually over (cf. 1 Sam 7:15–17;

15:34–35). But in this case it is a purposeful arrangement (in a concentric, nonchronological pattern) of two narratives, two accounts of David's mighty warriors, and two poems. The two poems (2 Sam 22:1–51 [a version of Ps 18] and 23:1–7) review, first, God's mighty acts for and through David and, second, God's covenant promise of an enduring throne. Note especially how both poems ascribe glory to God at every point. If David is "the lamp of Israel" (21:17), *God* is in fact David's lamp (22:29).

The inner frame for these affirmations comprises two accounts of David's mighty warriors (21:15–22; 23:8–39), reminding you of God's role both in battle and in times of David's humanity and vulnerability. Significantly, the famine and plague stories (3 years/3 days) that frame the whole (21:1–14; 24:1–25) end with obedience and sacrifice. Again watch for the irony: Following the two poems and the list of David's mighty men, 2 Samuel concludes with the story of David counting his fighting men, in violation of holy-war law, to begin preparations for further conquests, and to establish his own importance (24:1–17). At the same time, the sacrifice on the site of the future temple (24:18–25) prepares the way for 1 and 2 Kings.

The book of Samuel takes God's story into the monarchy, especially by means of the story of King David, a man of faith even while a man of weakness. God's covenant with David is the basis for Jewish messianism, fulfilled finally in the ultimate Son of David, Jesus of Nazareth.

1 and 2 Kings

ORIENTING DATA FOR 1 AND 2 KINGS

- **Content:** starting with the reign of Solomon, the story of the decline and eventual dissolution of the monarchy in Israel and the expulsion of God's people from the land
- **Historical coverage:** from the death of David (970 B.C.) to the sixth-century exile of Judah (586)
- **Emphases:** the evaluation of the monarchy on the basis of covenant loyalty; the fateful national consequences of disloyalty to Yahweh, resulting finally in expulsion from the land; the schism and civil wars between north and south; the rise of superpowers that, under the direction of God, subjugated Israel and Judah; the role of prophets who speak for God in Israel's national life

OVERVIEW OF 1 AND 2 KINGS

As with Samuel, the book of Kings was divided to fit on two scrolls. The title tells the story of its content, but it is also important to remember that in the Hebrew Bible, Kings concludes the Former Prophets, as a description of God's verdict of judgment on Israel's history. And you will hardly be able to miss the important role of the prophets in this book.

Kings covers the story of the monarchy from Solomon through its subsequent division into two kingdoms, to its demise in the north (Israel) and the exile of the final king in the south (Judah). This pretty well describes its "parts" also: 1 Kings 1–11 give an abbreviated account of Solomon's reign. Four things are important to the narrator: (1) how Solomon came to the throne, (2) his renown for wisdom, (3) the building of the temple and his palace, and (4) his demise and the reasons for it. The events surrounding the schism are narrated in 1 Kings 12–14.

Crucial here is the reign of Jeroboam I, who, with echoes of Aaron and the golden calf, declares his golden calves in Dan and Bethel to be "your gods ... who brought you up out of Egypt" (12:28; Exod 32:4). This is then followed by alternating accounts of the northern and southern kings as their reigns overlap (1 Kgs 15–2 Kgs 17), where each northern king in turn is judged by God for "walking in the ways of Jeroboam and in his sin" (e.g., 1 Kgs 15:26, 34). Here the narrative is dominated by prophetic activity in the north, especially of Elijah and Elisha (1 Kgs 17–2 Kgs 13), until the capture and destruction of Samaria, the northern capital.

The rest of the book (2 Kgs 18–25) tells the story of another 150 years of Judah's kings, until the fall of Jerusalem in 587/6 B.C. Over half of this last section concentrates on two notably good kings (Hezekiah, chs. 18–20; Josiah, chs. 22–23) and includes the prophetic activity of Isaiah (chs. 19–20).

SPECIFIC ADVICE FOR READING 1 AND 2 KINGS

Whereas all history is written from a point of view, not all historians reveal their point of view as clearly as this narrator does (note his own summary of the history after the fall of Samaria, 2 Kgs 17:7–23). The Deuteronomic perspective on Israel's history that began with Joshua is especially pronounced in this telling of the story, both by its clear echoes of Deuteronomic themes and by the way the story is structured. Therefore, it is not surprising—since all the northern kings and the majority of those in the south evidenced disloyalty—that the story has distinct echoes of Judges with its spiral downward, as the promised curses of Deuteronomy 28:15–68 come to their inevitable fulfillment.

The key to everything is whether a given king has been loyal to the covenant with Yahweh. In Kings this is expressed in Deuteronomic terms—his attitude toward the central sanctuary (the temple in Jerusalem) and whether or not he advocated syncretism (e.g., Jeroboam's golden calves; see 2 Kgs 17:41) or rival gods altogether, especially Canaanite Baal worship (note how these distinctions are assumed in 1 Kgs 16:31–32 and 2 Kgs 10:28–29). This "program" is set up by the narrative of Solomon, whose long and prosperous reign is finally reduced to two matters. His one significant deed is the *building of the temple* in Jerusalem, which is filled with the glory of God (God's presence, 1 Kgs 8:10–11), precisely as with the tabernacle in Exodus 40:34–35. But he is finally judged for *going the way of all kings* (see Deut 17:16–17; 1 Sam 8:11–18) and for *promoting idolatry* through his many foreign wives (1 Kgs 11:1–13). These two items sit side by side in 1 Kings 8 and 9—in Solomon's prayer and Yahweh's response. The former emphasizes the significance of the temple for Israel's loyalty to Yahweh; the latter repeats the Deuteronomic blessings and curses, especially outlining the nature of the latter: "I will cut Israel off *from the land* I have given them" (9:7, emphasis added), "because they have forsaken the LORD [Yahweh] their God ... and have embraced other gods" (v. 9). For our narrator, this foretells the story he will proceed to unfold.

This view of things is also accented by several structural matters. First, all the kings are placed within the story by means of a common regnal formula:

1. when a king came to reign (in Israel or Judah) in relation to another king
2. how long he reigned and in what capital
3. (for Judean kings) the name of his mother
4. his religious policy: for the northern kings this consistently takes the form of following in "the sins of Jeroboam son of Nebat"; for Judah the issue was whether the king followed Yahweh and whether or not he removed "the high places"
5. often the source for further information about the king
6. at the end, information about his death/burial and who succeeded him

Items 4 and 5 are especially telling. Item 4 is the only basis on which a given king is judged—no matter how long he ruled or what his other exploits or accomplishments might have been; item 5, therefore, tells the reader where the other kinds of materials might be found, e.g., in "the book of the annals of the kings of ..."

The second structural matter may be especially trying for those who might want a different kind of history. Many of the kings have almost nothing said about them beyond the regnal formula itself. And what is narrated about those who get more press, apart from accounts of civil war, has almost altogether to do with their loyalty or disloyalty to Yahweh. This results in purposeful disproportions of major kinds: the overlapping reigns of Jeroboam II of Israel (forty-one years in Samaria) and Azariah (Uzziah) of Judah (fifty-two years in Jerusalem) are merely skimmed in seven verses each (2 Kgs 14:23–29; 15:1–7), while the twenty-two-year reign of Ahab and twenty-nine-year reign of Hezekiah cover several chapters each.

Third, this also accounts for the disproportionate space given to the prophets Elijah and Elisha. They become God's agents in the holy war, but now over against the northern kings themselves and the foreign-born Baalist Jezebel. Through them God demonstrates that he is still Lord over all the earth (creation, nature; the nations; Israel). And thus the Deuteronomic cycle brings the story to its crashing end in the north; eventually the same thing happened in the south in terms of promised exile.

Finally, note that in contrast to the book of Samuel this story is eventually told in the context of major superpowers that have arisen—Assyria, then Babylon and Egypt. They become the instruments of God's judgment that drive his people from the land, but they do so because Yahweh is the God of the nations and has brought them into power for this very purpose (Deut 28:49–52).

A WALK THROUGH 1 AND 2 KINGS

☐ 1 Kings 1:1–2:46 *Solomon Becomes King*

This opening section tells of Solomon's succeeding David (1:1–53) and David's charge to him (2:1–12), which is then followed by Solomon's consolidating his position by disposing of Adonijah and his co-conspirators Joab and Abiathar (2:13–46). Note the question about succession that is being answered (1:20): How did it happen that David was succeeded by Solomon, who was not first in line? (1:6; 2:22; cf. the narratives of Gen 12–50). The answer lies with an oath made to Bathsheba. Note also how the section concludes in 1 Kgs 2:46 ("The kingdom was now firmly established in Solomon's hands"), which sets up what follows.

☐ 1 Kings 3:1–11:43 *The Reign of Solomon*

You need to be alert to two important things about this narrative: (1) The narrator signals that (a) with the reign of Solomon, the promise to Abraham of vast population increase has been fulfilled (4:20; see Gen 22:17; 32:12) and (b) with the construction of the temple, the exodus is now completed, as Yahweh gets his permanent dwelling place in

Jerusalem (1 Kgs 6:1). Thus, (2) the centerpiece of this section is the temple narrative (5:1–9:9), which is told in some detail while the many long years of Solomon's reign are merely summarized on either side of it. Indeed, a careful reading makes it clear that Solomon's relationship to the temple is the one thing that "saves" him, as it were.

Otherwise the narrator shows considerable ambivalence toward Solomon. As you read, note, for example, how much of 3:1–4:34 and 9:10–11:43 fulfill Samuel's prophecy (1 Sam 8:11–18). The narrator recognizes that Solomon's wisdom and splendor are a gift from God, and at the heart of it all is the fact that Solomon is David's son (1 Kgs 3:3, 7, 14; 8:15–26; 9:4–5). Yet he also knows that the seeds of future decline and schism are being sown (heavy taxation and slave labor, 4:27–28; 5:13–18; cf. 12:4; note the contrast with Joash's repairing the temple, 2 Kgs 12:4–16 [freewill offerings and paid workers!]). God's judgment on Solomon sets the tone for the rest of the story ("You have not kept my covenant and my decrees, which I commanded you," 1 Kgs 11:11, 33). Thus despite all of Solomon's greatness, wisdom, and splendor and the construction of the temple, and despite the fact that God appeared to him twice (11:9; cf. 3:5–15; 9:2–9), in the end he abandoned God in order to worship idols (11:1–10) and thereby split the nation, incurring God's wrath (11:11–40).

☐ 1 Kings 12:1–16:20 *The Kingdom Divides (931–885 B.C.)*

Chapters 12–14 describe the nation's dissolution into politically unstable and religiously rebellious Israel (ten northern tribes) and the somewhat more orthodox and stable Judah (sometimes plus Benjamin, 12:20–23). Note four emphases: (1) the dominant role of prophets, who both reveal God's plans and call the northern kings to account (12:22–24; 13:1–4; 14:1–18; 16:1–4; cf. 11:29–39); (2) civil war that pits north against south with foreign alliances (15:6–7, 16–22); (3) God's commitment to Judah for the sake of David (14:8; 15:4–5, 11; note especially the echo of 2 Sam 21:17 that David is the "lamp of Israel"; cf. 2 Kgs 8:19); (4) "succession" in the north is by treachery and power politics (1 Kgs 16:9–13), not by the will of God.

The story of Jeroboam I is especially important to the rest of the narrative. Watch how the narrator tells Jeroboam's story in two parts: His beginning echoes similarities to Moses (chosen by God, he comes out of Egypt to deliver a people laboring under a "heavy yoke"; 12:1–4; cf.

Exod 6:6–7), but in the end he resembles Aaron (Exod 32), making golden calves and repeating Aaron's words verbatim: "Here are your gods, O Israel, who brought you up out of Egypt" (1 Kgs 12:28). This repetition of the rebellion at Sinai marks all the rest of the kings of Israel, who walked in the ways of Jeroboam (e.g., 15:26, 34). But note carefully that this is a form of syncretism (Yahweh in the form of an Egyptian deity), not Baalism, as 2 Kings 10:28–29 and 17:41 make clear.

□ 1 Kings 16:21–2 Kings 10:36 *The Divided Kingdom: The Omri Dynasty (885–841 B.C.)*

With Omri comes another dynasty that neither descended from David nor worshiped at Jerusalem. Omri's son Ahab outstrips even Jeroboam in his sin, marrying a Baal worshiper and thus adding Baal worship to that of the golden calves. Note how this brings on the holy war, as the prophet Elijah contests for Yahweh against the prophets of Baal. Note also that for all his sins, it is when Ahab seizes the vineyard of Naboth by treachery and murder (thus breaking the covenant law in several ways; cf. Deut 19:14) that God's judgment comes on him and Jezebel (1 Kgs 21:17–24). And even though Ahab himself dies in accord with the prophetic judgment (22:37–38), we wait until 2 Kings 9–10 before the rest of the prophecy is fulfilled against Jezebel and against Ahab's house. Thus judgment is held in suspense while Elisha succeeds Elijah and performs Elijah-like miracles, and Ahab is succeeded by two sons. The execution is carried out by an ardent (but bloody) Yahwist, Jehu, who destroys Baal worship, but not the golden calves at Dan and Bethel. Be aware also in this section that outside pressure is still coming only from neighboring local kingdoms (Aram/Damascus), but all of that will change in the next section, as the superpower Assyria looms on the horizon (2 Kgs 15:19).

Note finally how this part of the story concentrates on affairs in Israel; the Judean exceptions are brief summaries of Jehoshaphat (1 Kgs 22:41–50, a "good" king) and of Jehoram and Ahaziah (2 Kgs 8:16–29), evil kings who walked in the ways of the kings of Israel. The intrigue of their stories is that Jehoram marries into the house of Omri; Athaliah, a daughter of Ahab and Jezebel, turns out to be like her mother and nearly succeeds in wiping out the Davidic dynasty (2 Kgs 11).

☐ 2 Kings 11:1–17:41 *The Divided Kingdom: Jehu to the Fall of Samaria (841–722 B.C.)*

From here on the story begins to shift back again to the kings of Judah. Note how Israel's kings are merely summarized, as one story of covenant unfaithfulness follows another, until Samaria is conquered and Israel is annexed to the Assyrian Empire. Notice how the author's summary in 17:7–23 tells the story in the way he has expected you to read it. The Assyrian resettlement of the land (vv. 24–41) sets in motion the many difficulties that will be faced in Ezra and Nehemiah—including northerners of mixed ethnicity, whom you will meet again as the Samaritans in the New Testament Gospels.

Three kings of Judah are featured in this section, highlighting concerns you've met earlier in the narrative. The story of Joash (chs. 11–12) is important for two reasons: (1) He represents God's commitment to keep "a lamp for David" (8:19); having been protected by his aunt, he is proclaimed king while the usurper Athaliah of Samaria cries "treason" but is killed (11:14–16). (2) He repairs the temple—and does so with the freewill offerings of the people (12:4–5)!

Amaziah (14:1–22), another "good" king, continues his father Joash's policies, but he is noted mostly for continuing the civil war with the north. And obviously everything is not well in Jerusalem, as both his father and he are assassinated by unnamed officials.

Ahaz (ch. 16), unlike David his father, "did not do what was right in the eyes of the LORD his God." He is remembered primarily for bringing Judah under Assyrian influence and, in contrast to Joash, who repaired the temple, for reconfiguring the temple on the basis of foreign influence.

☐ 2 Kings 18:1–25:30 *Judah's Final Years: The Babylonian Exile (722–560 B.C.)*

In contrast to the story of Israel, where the narrative concentrates on the gross evil of the worst of the kings (as judged by Deuteronomic criteria), the story of Judah tends to concentrate on the good kings. Note how this is especially so in this final episode, where only two kings, Hezekiah (chs. 18–20) and Josiah (chs. 22–23), do what is right in the eyes of Yahweh. And again they are judged on the basis of covenant loyalty (18:5–6; 22:11; 23:1–3). In the case of Hezekiah, his loyalty to Yahweh is the reason for his escaping Assyrian conquest, but some of his actions actually forecast the Babylonian exile (20:12–21). And despite Josiah's reforms and devotion to Yahweh, the die has been cast by the idolatrous reign of Manasseh (23:24–27), so the story from there heads inexorably toward exile. Kings ends with Judah in exile, but the release of Jehoiachin presents the reader with a ray of hope regarding "the lamp of David," even at the end.

The book of Kings is ultimately answering the question, "In light of God's covenant with Abraham [the land] and with David [an everlasting throne], how did all of this happen to us?" The answer: God has not failed his people; his people, led by their kings, have failed their God. The covenants, after all, have the contingency of Israel's faithfulness written into them. But the covenant also promises return from exile for those who return to Yahweh (Deut 30:1–10).

1 and 2 Chronicles

ORIENTING DATA FOR 1 AND 2 CHRONICLES

- **Content:** a postexilic, positive history of Judah's kings, with emphasis on the temple and its worship
- **Historical coverage:** an opening genealogy goes back to Adam; the narrative itself covers the kingdom of Judah from David (ca. 1000 B.C.) to the decree of Cyrus (539/8)
- **Emphases:** the continuity of the people of Judah (and others) through the exile and beyond; David's and Solomon's covenant loyalty as models for the time of restoration; the central role of the temple and worship for the restoration; true worship as a matter of the heart and full of joy and song; divine blessing and rest for obedience, and retribution for disobedience

OVERVIEW OF 1 AND 2 CHRONICLES

The book of Chronicles is the final book in the Hebrew Bible, taking its place at the end of the Writings. Its present place and division into two books come from the Greek Bible, where it was (perceptively) placed after Kings and followed by Ezra-Nehemiah. Using Samuel and Kings as his basic narrative, the Chronicler adds other materials—genealogies, lists, psalms, speeches—to present the continuous story of Israel (especially Judah) from Adam to the decree of Cyrus, which brought the exile to its official end.

The story itself is in three parts. It begins with the infamous *genealogies* (1 Chr 1–9), which is what has made it one of the more neglected books in the Old Testament. What is crucial here is that the Chronicler takes the line of descent all the way back to Adam, while concentrating finally on Judah and the Levites (which is where his narrative interests lie).

Part 2 (1 Chr 10–2 Chr 9) tells the story of the *united monarchy* under David and Solomon, a section that is longer by some pages than the whole rest of the story from Rehoboam to the end of the exile. Concentrating only on the positive dimensions of their lives, the author also deliberately overlaps their stories. Thus 1 Chronicles 10–21 tells the story of David alone, 1 Chronicles 22–29 introduces Solomon into David's story, whom David prepares for the construction of the temple, and 2 Chronicles 1–9 then picks up the story of Solomon alone, who constructs the temple. The temple and correct worship is the obvious focus of this section. More than half of David's story is concerned with preparations (1 Chr 22–26; 28–29) and over two-thirds of Solomon's with its construction and dedication (2 Chr 2–7).

These same concerns carry over to part 3 (2 Chr 10–36), which relates the story of Judah (only) during the period of the *divided monarchy.* But here you will note a further pattern as well: Success in battle and material prosperity are related directly to obedience to Yahweh, while failure is due to unfaithfulness or lack of trust. The story includes the exile, ending with the edict of Cyrus, king of Persia, who in fulfillment of the prophecy of Jeremiah was "appointed" by Yahweh "to build a temple for him at Jerusalem," and thus he invites the people to go up (2 Chr 36:22–23).

SPECIFIC ADVICE FOR READING 1 AND 2 CHRONICLES

To read Chronicles well, it will help you to have a sense of the times in which the Chronicler wrote. His era was that of the restoration, a period that began limply at the end of the sixth century B.C. with the repeatedly postponed, yet finally completed, temple project (see "Specific Advice for Reading Haggai," p. 253; "Zechariah," pp. 257–58; Ezra 1–6, p. 111), which picked up real steam only with the systematic reforms of Ezra and Nehemiah in the middle of the fifth century. The Chronicler most likely wrote somewhere within this period—a time of identity crisis in the Persian province of Judah. The restoration thus far had been a far cry from the glorious "second exodus" envisioned by Isaiah (e.g., Isa 35:1–10; 40:1–11; 44:1–5). Cyrus had technically inaugurated the new era, which included the initial token rebuilding of Jerusalem and the temple (Isa 44:28–45:5, 13). But in fact only a relative handful of Jews had returned to their "promised land," and the second temple was neither of the grandeur of Solomon's (Hag 2:3) nor had it yet attained its promised glory (Hag 2:6–9)—while Jerusalem itself lay in general decay with few inhabitants (Neh 1; 11). So a time of general spiritual malaise had settled in, including, increasingly, a great deal of intermarriage (Ezra 9–10, a sure way to lose national identity).

Into this context stepped Haggai and Zechariah to urge on the work of a priest (Jeshua) and a governor (Zerubbabel). A generation later it was a priest (Ezra) and a governor (Nehemiah) who themselves stepped in with their reform movement—and with greater results. Into the same overall context also steps the Chronicler, with a brilliant retelling of the story of Judah intended to give the present generation a sense of continuity with its great past and to focus on the temple and its worship as the place where that continuity could now be maintained.

As you read, you will note that several emphases stand out: The Chronicler is interested altogether in the Davidic dynasty, and in the northern kingdom only as she is in allegiance with Judah. About Judah his interest focuses on two concerns: the Davidic dynasty (David and Solomon) and the temple in Jerusalem. About the temple his interest focuses altogether on the nature and purity of the worship (over 60 percent of the story). Combine these emphases with the fact that the book ends with Cyrus's edict that the temple be rebuilt, and you can see where our author thinks the hope for the future lies, namely, in getting it right this time around with regard to the temple.

But getting it right for the Chronicler is not a matter of mere ritual. Be watching for his repeated emphasis on devoting "your heart and soul to seeking the Lord [Yahweh] your God" (1 Chr 22:19; cf. 29:17; 2 Chr 6:38; 7:10; 15:12), plus an accent on singing "joyful songs" (1 Chr 15:16), which is where the emphasis on the Levites comes out. The book abounds with the language of praise, thanksgiving, and joy in God's goodness and love. Note especially the thrice-repeated "He is good; his love endures forever"—(1) when the ark is brought into Jerusalem and then (2) into the temple, and (3) when the temple is consecrated (1 Chr 16:34; 2 Chr 5:13; 7:3). The presence of God (from the exodus) is thus renewed in Israel.

The Chronicler's focus on the southern kingdom, however, is not over against the north as such; rather he tells the story of the north only in terms of its failure to worship at the place of God's choosing, namely, the temple in Jerusalem. For example, the Chronicler regularly uses the expression "all Israel," by which he means north and south together in allegiance to temple worship in Jerusalem. In this regard you will see how his two main themes (the authenticity of the Davidic dynasty and the temple in Jerusalem) merge in Abijah's speech in 2 Chronicles 13:4–12 as the real point of condemnation against Jeroboam and his successors. And watch further for Hezekiah's invitation—and acceptance by some—to the north (now no longer functioning as a nation) to join once more in the worship in Jerusalem, after he had purified the temple (2 Chr 30:1–31:1).

It is also in this regard that you should understand the Chronicler's presentation of David and Solomon. What may appear to some as a kind of whitewash job on their lives is best understood as his concentrating only on those dimensions of their stories that serve as ideals both for the people as a whole (when they no longer have a king) and for the appropriate emphases as they live for the future (proper worship at the temple). The Chronicler knows that his readers are well aware of the faults of these kings (see Neh 13:26). His interest is in how their positive accomplishments can inspire hope for a new day.

This is also how you should understand the emphases in the narrative of the divided kingdom—that God blesses those who obey and punishes those who do not. Although life is not quite that simple, the Chronicler knows that this is a biblical pattern established from the beginning. And so he retells the story to encourage such loyalty in a new generation who live in and around Jerusalem (1 Chr 9).

Finally, you should also note the Chronicler's interest in the role of "the nations." In the midst of his readers' present sense of insignificance, he reminds them that not only are the nations ultimately under the control of Yahweh (e.g., Shishak king of Egypt, 2 Chr 12:5–9; Cyrus king of Persia, 2 Chr 36:22–23), but by placing Psalm 105 in the midst of the narrative of David (1 Chr 16:8–36), he emphasizes that God's goodness to Israel will be the source of making Yahweh known among the nations (recall the blessing of Abraham, Gen 12:3).

A WALK THROUGH 1 AND 2 CHRONICLES

□ 1 Chronicles 1–9 *The Genealogies*

There are several important things for you to notice as you look through these genealogies. First, the fact that the Chronicler begins his narrative this way says something about what he wants the postexilic community to understand—that they have continuity with a divinely ordained past that ultimately goes back to the creation of the world.

Second, note that both the focus and the larger amount of space are devoted to the tribes of Judah, Benjamin, and Levi. These are the surviving tribes of the southern kingdom who also represent in turn the Davidic dynasty, Jerusalem, and proper worship in the temple; they also led the original return from Babylon (Ezra 1:5). Thus the first set of genealogies (1:1–4:23) go through to the sons of Israel (2:1–2) only then to concentrate primarily on Judah (2:3–4:23), with the Davidic dynasty as its centerpiece (3:1–16) and including the royal line after the exile (3:17–24)—the time of our author.

Notice how the genealogies of the remaining tribes (4:24–7:40) then have the Levites as their centerpiece (ch. 6), with special emphasis on the temple musicians (vv. 31–47). Finally, the genealogy of Benjamin is expanded in chapter 8 (see 7:6–12).

Chapter 9 is not a genealogy but a list of Babylonian exiles who had returned, with special emphasis on the Levites who ministered in the temple. Note that in 9:35–44, the last part of the Benjamite genealogy (8:29–38) is repeated in order to introduce Saul at the beginning of the narrative proper.

☐ 1 Chronicles 10–21 *The United Monarchy: The Story of David*

Watch for the Chronicler's concerns as they emerge in this section, noting his arrangement and emphases. He begins (ch. 10) with the death of the failed king (Saul) in order to introduce the great king (David) by way of contrast. Then in chapters 11–12, he selects and arranges various materials from 2 Samuel (5:1–3, 6–10; 23:8–39) and other sources to emphasize that "all Israel" came together to make David king (1 Chr 11:1, 4, 10; 12:38).

The next section (chs. 13–16) tells the story of bringing "the ark of the covenant of the LORD [Yahweh]" (15:25) into Jerusalem. Note (1) how it continues the theme of "all Israel" (13:1–4); thereafter the author considerably expands 2 Samuel 6 by breaking apart its two phases (1 Chr 13:1–14; 15:1–16:6) so that, in contrast to Uzzah's death, he can focus especially on the role of the Levites with their joyful songs (15:2–24); (2) how it climaxes with a marvelous collage of portions of three psalms (1 Chr 16:8–36 = Pss 105:1–15; 96:1–13; 106:1, 47–48), extolling God's greatness in all the earth and over the nations, and especially his goodness toward his people; and (3) how the psalm ends with a cry to God to "deliver us from the nations" (1 Chr 16:35–36), to which all the people said, "Amen" and "Praise the LORD" (thus reflecting the author's own situation).

This is followed by the Davidic covenant (ch. 17), with its emphasis now on Solomon as the one who will build "God's house," which is followed in turn (chs. 18–21) by a collage from 2 Samuel 8–21 of David's wars. You'll want to especially note two points here: (1) The significance of this section is to explain why David himself could not build the temple—he was a man of war (1 Chr 22:8), while his son Solomon (whose name means "peace") is a "man of peace and rest" (v. 9), and (2) it concludes with the only negative story about David (21:1–22:1), necessary to relate because Araunah's threshing floor, which David refuses as a gift but instead purchases, is to be the site of the temple (22:1).

□ 1 Chronicles 22–29 *The United Monarchy: David and Solomon*

The material in this section serves for what is essential to the transition between David and Solomon. Note how the Chronicler's concerns are highlighted by the structure itself. The larger central section (chs. 23–27) deals with David's preparations of the Levites for worship in the temple. These are framed by three speeches of David (chs. 22; 28; 29), which get at the heart of the author's concerns. The first one (22:5–16) is addressed to Solomon himself and repeats the essence of the Davidic covenant (17:10b–14), focusing especially on his calling to build the temple; the second (28:2–10) repeats the essence of this to all the officials of Israel; while the third (29:1–5) calls for them to follow David's own example of generous giving toward the project. It then ends with a Davidic blessing and thanksgiving (vv. 10–19). Thus the overall intent is (1) to designate Solomon as the divinely appointed builder of the temple and (2) to secure the support of "all Israel" for his kingship and for the erection of the temple. So the section concludes with Solomon's being acknowledged as king by all Israel (vv. 21–25) and with David's death (vv. 26–30).

□ 2 Chronicles 1–9 *The United Monarchy: The Story of Solomon*

Note two things in particular as you read this section. First, all of the ambiguity toward Solomon found in 2 Kings has been removed, since he serves for our author as exhibit A of devotion to Yahweh at the one essential point—faithfulness to the temple as the place of true worship. Therefore, second, the bulk of this section is its centerpiece (2 Chr 2–7)—the preparations for and the building and dedication of the temple. Two additions to the 1 Kings narrative reflect the Chronicler's concerns: (1) The twice-repeated theme from David's psalm (1 Chr 16:34) in 2 Chronicles 5:13 and 7:3—when the ark of God's presence rests in the temple that is dedicated to him—emphasizes *God's goodness* to his people; (2) the best known passage from this book—the addition to God's response to Solomon's prayer (7:13–16)—seems especially included for the sake of the author's own readers.

□ 2 Chronicles 10–36 *The Divided Monarchy: The Davidic Dynasty*

The rest of the story is about the kings who succeed Solomon. Besides continuing all the themes of the narrative to this point ("all Israel"; the Davidic dynasty; the central place of the temple), here the Chronicler also puts special emphasis on God's direct intervention for blessing and judgment on the basis either of the kings' "seeking" or "humbling themselves before" Yahweh or of their "abandoning" or "forsaking" Yahweh.

Chapters 10–12. Three things to note in the Chronicler's account of Rehoboam: (1) The divided kingdom is Yahweh's doing (11:2–4); (2) nonetheless it is immediately followed by the theme of all Israel coming to Jerusalem to sacrifice (11:5–17); and (3) the new theme of judgment for abandoning Yahweh begins with Rehoboam and Israel's leaders (12:2–5).

Chapter 13. Note how the author uses a speech by Abijah to Jeroboam and Israel (13:4–12) to set forth his own emphases: Yahweh has given the kingship to David and his descendants forever (v. 5), and true worship occurs only in Jerusalem at the temple (vv. 10–12). Thereafter the northern tribes are included when they join Judah in Jerusalem (15:9–15) or are invited to do so (29:1–31:1). Note also that it was when the people cried out to Yahweh that "God routed Jeroboam" (13:14–15).

Chapters 14–16. In this longer account of Asa, watch for two emphases: (1) that Asa "called to the LORD his God" (14:11), to which God responds by striking down the Cushites (v. 12), and (2) that in response to a prophetic word, Asa institutes a reform with respect to the temple and proper worship (ch. 15). But note also that his long reign ends on something of a sour note due to failure to rely on Yahweh (16:1–9, 11–12) and oppression of some of the people (16:10).

Chapters 17–20. In the still longer account of Jehoshaphat, note that he is praised because in his early years he "walked in the ways that his father David had followed" (17:3–6), which found expression in the Levites' instructing the people through the law (17:7–9; 19:4–11). The centerpiece of his narrative is the defeat of Moab and Ammon (20:1–30), which is punctuated by a speech at the temple (vv. 4–19) and thanksgiving, song, and praise by the troops (vv. 20–26). But this narrative is sandwiched by an unholy alliance with Israel (18:1–19:3; 20:31–37), which leads to his downturn at the end.

Chapters 21–24. Next come two evil kings, Jehoram and Ahaziah, who aligned with Ahab (21:1–22:9). Note that Ahaziah "did evil in the eyes of the LORD" (22:4); therefore "God brought about Ahaziah's downfall" (v. 7). Even so, the dynasty continues because of Yahweh's covenant with David (21:7; cf. 23:18). The account of Joash concentrates on two of the themes: the divine rescue of the Davidic dynasty (22:10–23:21) and the repairing of the temple (24:1–16). Note that both of these highlight the ministry of the high priest Jehoiada, after whose death Joash comes under the influence of officials who abandon Yahweh (24:17–27), even to the point of murdering Jehoiada's son. Unfortunately, Joash's son then follows in these later steps.

Chapters 25–28. Joash is followed by two kings (Amaziah and Uzziah) toward whom the Chronicler shows considerable ambiguity. They in turn are followed by one who is praised (Jotham) and one who is condemned (Ahaz). Note how thoroughgoing the theme is here of blessing or judgment based on the kings' loyalty or disloyalty to Yahweh. Observe especially that this series ends with Ahaz's shutting the doors of Yahweh's temple (28:24).

Chapters 29–32. Then comes Hezekiah, whose story concentrates on the temple purification; this is also where you find all the themes noted above in the introductory paragraph on 2 Chronicles 10–36 (p. 105) brought together in this good king.

Chapters 33–36. Finally, after Manasseh, an evil king who repents at the end, and his son Amon, who does not, comes the story of Josiah. Note that the Chronicler again concentrates on a great renewal of the

Passover, calling attention especially to the central role of the priests and Levites (35:1 – 19). With Josiah's death the book moves quickly through the final four kings to the fall of Jerusalem, but given the Chronicler's emphasis, it is no surprise that the final words in the book remind you of Cyrus's decree that the temple be rebuilt (36:23).

By this retelling of the story of God's people, Chronicles reminds us of the central role of worship; for the readers of the New Testament, it also points forward to the one whose own "cleansing" of the temple and death and resurrection replace the temple as the place of God's presence (John 2:19 – 22).

Ezra-Nehemiah

ORIENTING DATA FOR EZRA-NEHEMIAH

- **Content:** rebuilding and reform in postexilic Judah through the latter half of the fifth century B.C.
- **Historical coverage:** from the first return (539/8 B.C.) to the end of the fifth century, but especially from 458 to 430, during the reign of Artaxerxes of Persia
- **Emphases:** successful completion of the second temple despite opposition; successful rebuilding of the walls of Jerusalem despite opposition; the crisis of intermarriage and national identity; concern for covenant renewal and reform, based on the law, among the exiles who had returned to Jerusalem

OVERVIEW OF EZRA-NEHEMIAH

Just as with Samuel, Kings, and Chronicles, the books of Ezra and Nehemiah, which appear in our English Bibles as separate books, originally formed one book in the Hebrew Bible. They were not separated until well into the Christian era. You will do well to read them together, since they do in fact tell one story, not two.

Using the memoirs (journals?) of Ezra and Nehemiah (noticeable for their use of "I"), plus archival letters and lists of various kinds, the author-compiler of this book (conceivably Nehemiah himself) records the story of Jewish reform between 458 and 430 B.C. The reform includes the building of the walls around Jerusalem (thus giving definition again to "the place I have chosen as a dwelling for my Name," Neh 1:9; cf. Deut 12:5, 11), repentance over intermarriage, and a covenant-renewal ceremony with the reading from the Book of the Law as its center point. In so doing, the author provides us with the most important source for the history of Judah in the postexilic period.

By watching for the shift between first-person and third-person narratives, you can easily track the flow of the narrative. It begins (Ezra 1–6) with a historical review of events some seventy years earlier—the building of the second temple (538/7 to 516 B.C.). Based on several archival records, this review emphasizes the Persian kings' role in seeing that the temple was, in fact, completed. At the same time the author inserts by way of digression (4:6–23) a much later opposition to rebuilding the walls, which is the more immediate problem of Ezra-Nehemiah. With this literary stroke he ties the two events together as having the same sorts of difficulties from similar sources.

The Ezra memoirs (Ezra 7–10) first locate him in the lineage of Aaron, thus of priestly descent, and then report his return along with others (in 458 B.C.) under the auspices of Artaxerxes. Here the main focus is on rebuilding the religious community in and around Jerusalem in the midst of a conflict surrounding intermarriage, which is recognized as a main source of going astray after other gods.

The first of Nehemiah's memoirs (Neh 1–7) tells the story of the rebuilding of the walls of Jerusalem despite intense opposition by various groups, including even some Jews who had resettled or remained in the land (and were quite syncretistic); it concludes (7:6–73) by repeating the list of returnees found at the beginning of the book (Ezra 2).

This is followed by the high point of the narrative (Neh 8–10)—a covenant-renewal ceremony, which begins with a reinstitution of the Feast of Tabernacles and continues for twenty-four days (ch. 8), climaxing in a great national confession (ch. 9) and a community document signed by the leaders, committing themselves to obedience to specific aspects of "the Law of God given through Moses" (ch. 10).

After two more lists (of the repopulation of Jerusalem and its environs and of the priests and Levites, 11:1–12:26) the book concludes with the second part of Nehemiah's memoirs (12:27–13:31). These describe the consecration of the wall (12:27–47) and some final reforms (ch. 13).

SPECIFIC ADVICE FOR READING EZRA-NEHEMIAH

Before reading Ezra-Nehemiah, you may wish to review what was said about this historical period in "Specific Advice for Reading 1 and 2 Chronicles" (pp. 100–101), since the same basic historical and religious background lies behind this book as well. You should be looking for several emphases in the narrative that offer keys to making sense of things as you read.

Most important, and in keeping with all that has preceded him thus far, our author (reflecting his main sources, Ezra and Nehemiah) is intensely concerned with the purity of faith in Yahweh, the God of Israel. This purity is to be found in keeping the commandments in the "Book of the Law of God." All the reforms mentioned in the book are based on the Law, and the repentance in Ezra 10 and Nehemiah 9–10 is in both cases solely in light of what is said in the Law. This also accounts for the emphasis on the priests and Levites (as in Chronicles), because of their role both in teaching the Law and in maintaining purity of worship.

Crucial to this reform is the crisis over national identity: Who constitutes the true remnant of the people of God and thus is in genuine continuity with the past? It is in this context that you can best understand the urgent concern over intermarriage (Ezra 9–10; Neh 9:2; 10:28–30; 13:23–28). Thus the suggestion that Ezra-Nehemiah is mostly about community building is not far off the mark; it is indeed about rebuilding the community of God, based on the religious realities of the past.

This crisis over national identity is also the context in which to understand the passion for building the walls of Jerusalem. Walls do not simply keep unwanted people out; in ancient times they set boundaries and therefore gave *identity* to a city and its people. Nehemiah lived in a time when Jerusalem, the City of David and the place where God had chosen that his Name should dwell, had become the ultimate symbol of Israel's national and religious identity (a theme that pervades the book of Psalms and is crucial to the Revelation of John).

Finally, this concern over a pure people of God worshiping in a purified temple in a newly consecrated city (the word translated "dedicated" in Neh 3:1 is used most often for "consecrating" holy things) is also the context in which to understand the (somewhat ambivalent) attitude toward the Persian kings. On the one hand, the people, even those who have returned, are regularly referred to as "the exiles" (see esp. Ezra 10)—and they smart from their general lack of independent status as a people ("slaves," Ezra 9:9; Neh 9:36). On the other hand, they know full well that both their temple and the wall around Jerusalem are possible only because of the decree and protection of their Persian overlords—which gives them a margin of safety from local opposition. This is a primary reason for the recounting of the building of the temple in Ezra 1–6, since its construction under the decree of Cyrus serves as an introduction to the main project of Ezra-Nehemiah, namely, the building of the walls—this time on the basis of official letters from Artaxerxes (Neh 2:7–9).

A WALK THROUGH EZRA-NEHEMIAH

☐ Ezra 1–6 *A Review of the Rebuilding of the Temple (538–516 B.C.)*

Watch for the narrative art of the author-compiler as you read this introduction to his book. Except for 4:6–23, he basically reviews the events surrounding the building of the temple, begun under Cyrus in 538/7 and completed under Darius in 516. In turn he describes Cyrus's decree (cf. 2 Chr 36:22–23) and his beneficence toward the project (Ezra 1); the list of the exiles who returned at that time (ch. 2), focusing especially on the priests and Levites (the interest is in the temple, after all!); the successful beginnings of the project, starting with the altar and then the foundations of the temple itself (ch. 3; don't miss the repetition in v. 11 of the theme from Chronicles); the opposition to the project that brought the rebuilding to a halt (4:1–5, 24) down to the time of Haggai and Zechariah (you might want to read at least the book of Haggai in connection with this part of Ezra); the renewed opposition in 520 that brought about the exchange of official letters (Ezra 5:1–6:12) and cleared the way for its completion (6:13–18), followed by a Passover celebration (6:19–22). What doesn't fit into this review chronologically, of course, is the insertion of the later opposition to an apparently abortive attempt to rebuild the walls (4:6–23 [ca. 448]), which is included here for literary purposes, anticipating the later opposition endured by Nehemiah.

☐ Ezra 7–8 *The Return of Ezra and Others to Jerusalem (458 B.C.)*

Note how the author begins this section with an introduction to Ezra and his return, emphasizing his being a priest and a teacher of the Law of Moses given by Yahweh (7:1–10). This is followed by Ezra's own memoirs (7:11–8:36, note the shift to the first-person pronoun in 7:27–28), which tell of the circumstances of his leaving Babylon (7:11–28, note especially the role of the Persian king), those who accompanied him (8:1–14), and the circumstances of the return itself (8:15–36).

☐ **Ezra 9–10** ***The Crisis of Intermarriage***

With this section you come to the first major threat for our author, namely, that the returnees—even many priests and Levites (10:18–24)—"have mingled the holy race with the peoples around them" (9:2) by intermarrying with them. Note how Ezra's prayer (9:6–15) sets forth the main issues (and includes the tension between their present "slavery" and the kindness of the kings of Persia). Chapter 10 then describes the reform itself. Note also that all of this is from Ezra's memoirs.

☐ **Nehemiah 1–7** ***Rebuilding the Walls under Nehemiah's Governorship (444 B.C.)***

Using Nehemiah's memoirs, the narrator describes in some detail the circumstances surrounding the rebuilding of the wall. He begins with how Nehemiah, a prominent court figure, secured the king's permission and authority to return to Jerusalem (as governor, you learn in 5:14) to rebuild the walls (chs. 1–2). Chapter 3 describes in detail the who and the where of the participants in the project, while chapter 4 describes the opposition (thus recalling Ezra 4:6–23) and their rebuff. Note here also the surfacing of the holy-war theme (Neh 4:20). The interlude of chapter 5 relates Nehemiah's handling a conflict related to Jerusalem's poor—by reinstituting the "no usury" clause from the Mosaic Law (Exod 22:25; Deut 23:19–20). Further opposition and the completion of the project are recounted in Nehemiah 6:1–7:3. But note here the narrator's skill. Instead of going on to the dedication, which appears in 12:27–43, he brings this first long section of his narrative (Ezra 1–Neh 7) to completion by a nearly verbatim repeating of the list of returnees from Ezra 2. This enclosure, which also holds the narrative in suspension, is his way of calling special attention to the two events that follow.

☐ **Nehemiah 8–10** ***The Renewal of the Covenant***

With this account you come to the first of the two climactic moments in our author's narrative. Before the repopulation of Jerusalem and the dedication of its walls (chs. 11–12) comes the ceremony of primary significance for him—a time of national renewal of the covenant. It begins with a long celebratory reading of the Law (7:73b–8:12) and includes the great celebratory Feast of Tabernacles (8:13–18). This is followed by a time of community confession (ch. 9) in which the long history of disobedience is recounted (cf. Ps 106), and by the corporate signing of the renewal agreement (Neh 10).

☐ Nehemiah 11–12 *The Resettlement and Dedication of the Wall*

Note the narrative insight that puts this event *after* the covenant-renewal ceremony. Once covenant loyalty on the part of the renewed community is in place, then in turn are listed the new population (ch. 11) and the priestly community (12:1–26). With that the walls that give them definition and protection are dedicated (12:27–43)—in great ceremonial pageantry and with much music and praise (the reason for the Levites!).

☐ Nehemiah 13 *The Conclusion: Community Purity Reinforced*

Note that the final concern in the book is the one you have met throughout—that the renewed community of faith be pure with regard to the faith. Singled out are the exclusion of Ammonites from the sacred places (vv. 1–14), the purity of the Sabbath (vv. 15–22), and (not surprisingly) intermarriage (vv. 23–29).

Ezra-Nehemiah advances the biblical story by describing how the necessary reforms in Jerusalem were set in motion, which were later to serve as the basis for the Judaism out of which Jesus and the early church emerge.

Esther

ORIENTING DATA FOR ESTHER

- **Content:** the story of God's providential preservation of Jews throughout the Persian Empire through Mordecai and his niece, Esther
- **Historical coverage:** most of the story takes place during a single year during the reign of Xerxes (486–465 B.C.), a generation before the events recorded in Ezra-Nehemiah
- **Emphases:** God's providential care of the Jews in a context of a pogrom against them; Jewish remembrance of their survival through the feast of Purim

OVERVIEW OF ESTHER

As with the book of Ruth, Esther appears among the Writings in the Hebrew Bible, but in the Septuagint it was placed in its basic historical setting, although after Ezra-Nehemiah. With a marvelous display of wit and irony, and with obvious literary skill, the author tells the story of how Jews in the Persian Empire were saved from genocide instigated by a member of the royal court, who may himself have been a non-Persian—possibly an Amalekite who carried with him their ancient hatred for God's people.

The story revolves around the actions of its four main characters: (1) the Persian king Xerxes (mentioned by name 29*x*), an arrogant Eastern despot who serves as God's foil in the story; (2) the villain Haman (48*x*), a foreigner who has been elevated to the highest place in the empire, next to Xerxes himself—who is even more arrogant than Xerxes, and full of hatred for the Jews; (3) the Jewish hero Mordecai (54*x*), a lesser court official who uncovers a plot that saves the king's life, but whose refusal to bow to Haman sets in motion the basic intrigue of the plot—a plan to kill all Jews in the empire, which ultimately backfires on

Haman; and (4) the heroine, Mordecai's younger cousin, Hadassah, given the Persian name Esther (48*x*), who by winning a beauty contest becomes Xerxes' queen and the one responsible for unraveling Haman's plot, thus saving the Jews from annihilation.

The story line itself is easy to follow. It begins with a lavish feast given by Xerxes and the deposal of his queen Vashti, who had refused to come and be put on display; this leads in turn to Esther's becoming queen (1:1–2:18). The basic plot of the story, with its various intrigues, unfolds in the central section (2:19–7:10), which climaxes at two private feasts that Esther holds for Xerxes and Haman. The rest of the story primarily has to do with the Jewish defeat of their enemies (the holy war again) and their celebration that eventually becomes the feast of Purim (chs. 8–9). Inside this basic plot is the story of Mordecai, who represents God's favor toward his people, so that the book concludes with Mordecai's exaltation to Haman's position, where he achieved much good for the Jewish people (ch. 10; cf. Daniel's role the century before).

SPECIFIC ADVICE FOR READING ESTHER

As you read this story of Jewish survival, you will want to be looking for two factors that help make the story work. The first is *literary*. The author is a master storyteller, evidenced not only by the way he unfolds the characters and plot but especially by his inclusion of details that provide humor and irony. Who wouldn't smile at the thought of a king whose response to his wife's defiance is an empirewide decree that "every man should be ruler over his own household" (1:22)—as though that would solve the king's own problem! After all, he had been advised that, on the basis of this decree, "all the women will respect their husbands, from the least to the greatest" (1:20)!

You will hardly be able to miss other, although less humorous, touches of irony: Haman, who intends to destroy the Jews, ends up destroying himself and his family; the gallows erected for Mordecai are those on which Haman himself is hanged; Haman's edict was intended to plunder the wealth of the Jews—instead his own estate falls into Jewish hands; Haman, in writing the script for his own honor and recognition, in fact writes the script for Mordecai, and instead of receiving honor Haman must lead Mordecai through the streets of Susa on horseback. And these are not all of them, so be looking for other such moments as you read.

The second factor is *religious*. Although the book of Esther is known for the fact that God is never mentioned in the book (cf. Song of Songs), the author nonetheless expects his intended readers to see God at work at every turn in the story. First, Xerxes himself is portrayed as God's foil: He who displayed "the vast wealth of his kingdom and the splendor and glory of his majesty" (Esth 1:4) turns out to be something of a puppet, manipulated at will by those around him—while the reader knows that the God of eternal glory and majesty is behind everything that happens in the story. Thus, what the unschooled reader might regard as "just happening" is to be recognized instead as God's own sovereignty lying behind, for example, Esther's being chosen as queen (2:15–18), the king's sleepless night in which he discovers that he had failed to honor Mordecai (6:1–3), the fact that after a three-day fast Esther receives the gold scepter when she approaches the king unbidden (4:11; 5:1–2), and so on throughout the book.

The other religious factor you will want to watch for is the author's recognition that the action of Mordecai and Esther—and the Jews who are spared from annihilation—is an expression of the holy war. This comes out first in the conflict between Haman and Mordecai, who carry on the centuries-old conflict between the Israelites and the Amalekites. As the first to attack Israel after her deliverance from Egypt (Exod 17:8–16), the Amalekites came to be viewed as the epitome of the surrounding nations that stood against her. But especially this story needs to be read against the background of 1 Samuel 15. It is probably not incidental to this story that Haman is regularly called an Agagite (an intentional link to the Amalekite king in 1 Sam 15 whom Saul refused to slay?), whereas Mordecai—as Saul was—is a Benjamite who also belongs to the line of another Kish (1 Sam 9:1–2). This "son of Kish" (Esth 2:5) does indeed land the telling blow on this "Agag."

This is how you are also to understand the narrative in chapters 8–10. In a way similar to the narrative of Joshua, the Jews assemble in all the cities of the empire and "no one could stand against them" (9:2). That they saw this as a continuation of the holy war is highlighted by the author in his repeated notation that they would not touch the plunder (9:10, 15, 16; cf. Saul's action in 1 Sam 15:7–9), even though the king had decreed that they should have it (Esth 8:11). In the holy war the firstfruits of the plunder belong to God (cf. Deut 13:16).

A WALK THROUGH ESTHER

☐ 1:1–2:18 *The Setting: Xerxes, Vashti, Mordecai, and Esther*

The story begins in the palace complex at Susa, where Xerxes gives a great state banquet as a display of his wealth and splendor, while his queen, Vashti, is giving a banquet for the women. Her refusal to also be put on display leads to her being deposed as queen, which sets the stage for Esther. Enter the hero and heroine (2:5–7). Mordecai's—and Esther's—actions in this matter are not without their ethical flaws, but both Esther's beauty and her keeping her origins quiet are crucial to the story that follows. Note how this first section ends with yet another banquet, this time in Esther's honor—but especially as a way for the king to show off his new queen.

☐ 2:19–3:15 *The Plot Thickens: Mordecai and Haman*

Observe how this section begins by repeating Esther's readiness to follow her cousin's instructions. The plot itself begins with Mordecai using Esther's position as his way of warning the king about an assassination plot. Enter the villain (3:1), who is elevated to his high position and thus demands homage of all others, but Mordecai will not bow down or pay him honor. With his pride pricked, Haman sets in motion the plot to exterminate Mordecai and his people from the empire. Note how this "chapter" concludes with the king and Haman sitting down to drink (in contrast to the Jews, who will proclaim a fast).

☐ 4:1–7:10 *The Plot Unfolds: Mordecai and Esther, Haman and Xerxes*

Again Mordecai turns to Esther for help, this time urging that she has "come to royal position for such a time as this" (4:14). Note especially the literary skill of the author in chapters 5–7, where he encloses the irony of Mordecai's and Haman's reversals, including Xerxes' sleepless night and the recall of the matter in 2:21–23, within the framework of Esther's two banquets. At the end of the second banquet, the ultimate irony is narrated: Haman is hanged on the gallows he had prepared for Mordecai!

☐ 8:1–17 *Xerxes' Edict in Behalf of the Jews*

Since Xerxes cannot repeal his former edict, he does the next best thing: Mordecai assists in framing a new decree in which the Jews are allowed to defend themselves against all attacks on the day of the *pur* (the day "the lot" fell for the extermination of the Jews; see 3:7). Notice how the decree is sent to all the provinces in their own languages and that the end result is the conversion of many Gentiles (further fulfilling the Abrahamic covenant, Gen 12:3).

□ 9:1–10:3 *The Triumph of the Jews*

Here you will see the three ways the story is wrapped up: (1) The Jews engage in the holy war and slay many of their enemies, (2) the final feast in the book is narrated—the feast of Purim that will be celebrated annually on the fourteenth and fifteenth days of Adar—and (3) Mordecai is promoted to a position where he is able directly (not through the less certain means of the queen) to benefit the Jews.

The book of Esther tells the story of God's providential protection of his people during a bleak moment in the Persian Empire, thus preserving them for the future gift of the Messiah.

The Writings of Israel in the Biblical Story

The books known as the Writings in the Jewish tradition stand in the final position in the Hebrew Bible, after the Law and the Prophets. In the Writings the Psalter is in first position, followed by the four books that belong to the Wisdom tradition plus Ruth—Job, Proverbs, Ruth, Song of Songs, and Ecclesiastes—concluding with Lamentations, Esther, Daniel, Ezra-Nehemiah, and Chronicles. But when the Greek translations of the biblical books were brought together into one collection (the Septuagint), the Writings were rearranged into what seems to be a mostly chronological and/or authorial order, to which then our English Bibles fell heir. Thus, in the current arrangement, only five of these books remain together, even though the traditional Jewish order has much to commend it.

These diverse books play an important role in the biblical story. For here, in a variety of forms, you find inspired human responses to the words and deeds of God that are recorded in the Law and the Prophets. Thus, even though many instructional moments appear in the psalms, for the most part they are prayers addressed to God, with the primary traditions in the biblical story (the promises, the exodus, the giving of the law, etc.) as the bedrock foundation from which these prayers are made—and thereafter recited and sung in the believing community. So one of the things you will regularly want to look for as you read the psalms are the various moments that echo the biblical story—both the revelation of God and his character, and the story of Israel. The same is true of Lamentations, which we have placed in this section so that you will read it in light of what is here said about the book of Psalms.

The Wisdom tradition, on the other hand, is quite different. These books contain few references to these primary traditions. Instead, here are writings whose authors or compilers are wrestling with many of the issues found in the wisdom traditions of *other* cultures. Thus, even though their content assumes Israel's God and story as the basis for their reflections, their method is very similar to what one finds in these other traditions. By and large, Wisdom concentrates on human conduct in society before God. And the assumed reader is "my son," which could refer, of course, to the teacher's own progeny or student but could also refer to anyone in the next generation who needs this instruction.

What makes the biblical books essentially different from the other traditions is their fundamental assumption that "the fear of the LORD [Yahweh] is the beginning of wisdom" (Prov 1:7 and throughout). While this is said less often in the two books that belong to the "speculative" Wisdom tradition (Job and Ecclesiastes), God and his story are nonetheless foundational for their wrestling with the larger questions of life—how to understand the undeserved suffering of the innocent (Job) and how one should live the brief span of years (mere "vapor," as it were) God has given (Ecclesiastes). And at the heart of both of these books is the reminder that true wisdom has to do with the fear of God (Job 28:28; Eccl 12:13–14).

The "odd book out" in all of this is Song of Songs, which does not even mention God and which reflects the Wisdom tradition in a much more specialized way. Nonetheless, even here, where the emphasis is on the delight of monogamous love and human sexuality, the presupposition of the story is Genesis 1–2, where God created man and woman to be precisely like this in their married relationships.

Thus, rather than wonder why God would have included books that speak to us "from our own level," as it were, you can find wonder precisely in the fact that he did so. The delight of these books is that they constantly remind us that God's love and faithfulness, which lie at the heart of the story, demand responses of various kinds from his people—the rich variety of these books both eliciting and guiding your own responses to this love and faithfulness.

Job

ORIENTING DATA FOR JOB

- **Content:** a brilliant wrestling with the issue of the suffering of the righteous and the justice of God, while also speaking to the larger question, "Where is wisdom found?"
- **Date:** the story takes place in the period of the patriarchs; various suggestions have been offered regarding the composition itself
- **Emphases:** wisdom is ultimately found in God alone; human wisdom cannot on its own fathom the ways of God; undeserved suffering has no easy answer; God is not obligated to fallen human beings to explain all things; the fear of the Lord is the path to true wisdom

OVERVIEW OF JOB

The book of Job is one of the literary treasures of the world. The central issue is the struggle over the ways of God, especially his justice when the godly suffer not from human hands but from "acts of God." At the same time, the author raises the question, "Where is wisdom found?" which in the end is powerfully answered in terms of God alone, as each of the participants—the three friends, the younger Elihu, and Job himself—in turn is silenced before the ultimate wisdom of God.

The structure of the book, important to the author's purposes, is easily discernible. The two larger parts (chs. 3–27; 29–42:6) consist of three sets of speeches. Part 1 is a series of *dialogues*. Framed by Job's lament (ch. 3) and closing discourse (ch. 27), the dialogues are also arranged in a three-cycle pattern—speeches by Eliphaz, Bildad, and Zophar, with a response to each by Job. The dialogue cycle gets shorter by a third each time—as they run out of anything new to say and as they all become increasingly blunt in disagreement. Part 2 consists of three *monologues:* by Job (chs. 29–31), Elihu (chs. 32–37), and God (chs. 38–41)—who has the last word. All of this, except for the narrative framework, is expressed in superb poetry.

The poems are skillfully framed by their narrative setting (chs. 1–2; 42:7–17), which gives the reader an access to what's going on that is not given the participants themselves: Job's suffering is the result of a contest in the heavenly court, where Satan has argued that people are righteous only if they get "paid" for it—the crucial theological issue being put to the test. A second framing device can be found in the central position of the author's own wisdom discourse (ch. 28), which anticipates the answers given in the speeches by God at the end, with respect to "where is wisdom found?" Thus:

chapters 1–2	prologue
chapters 4–27	the three dialogue-disputes
chapter 28	the discourse on "Where does wisdom come from?"
chapters 29–41	the three monologues
chapter 42	epilogue

The four who dispute with Job all express a stark form of conventional wisdom—that a just God would not allow the righteous to suffer unjustly and that Job's suffering, therefore, is the direct result of specific sin. Job knows better, but in the end he has protested too many other things as well. So God speaks out of the storm and calls him—and the whole world—to a humble recognition that human wisdom amounts to nothing before God.

SPECIFIC ADVICE FOR READING JOB

Crucial for your reading of Job is to understand what the author is ultimately about, through both his arrangement of things and the content of the various speeches. His concern lies at two points: (1) the challenge to God by Satan (1:9): "Will [a person] fear God for nothing?" and (2) the question the author himself asks (28:12, 20): "Where can wisdom be found?" The issues are two: As creatures wholly dependent on God for well-being, will the godly love God for himself or only for his benefits? As creatures endowed with creaturely wisdom, are the godly willing to live within the bounds of creaturely wisdom (which is to be one who "fears God and shuns evil," 1:8; 2:3; 28:28), or will they demand to participate as equals in God's wisdom? Thus creaturely *dependence* and creaturely *wisdom* are the points at issue. What will bring these questions to the fore—and will dominate most of the human speeches—is the question of *theodicy,* namely, how to reconcile *undeserved* suffering with a God who is both almighty and just. Each of the participants has a significant role to play in this divine-human drama.

Satan plays the crucial role of putting God on trial, as it were, about the basic relationship between God and his human creatures—whether their reciprocal joy in each other is only the result of what the human creature gets out of it. *Job's wife* plays Satan's role on earth by urging Job to "curse God and die!" (2:9). You can imagine Satan whispering, "Do it, do it!" At issue is whether human beings love God, not for his own sake, but for what they get out of the relationship—which puts them in the driver's seat. But whatever else Job does or says, he will not curse God, as God in his wisdom knows.

Eliphaz, Bildad, and *Zophar* play the (likewise) crucial role of one form of "conventional wisdom"—the unbending, have-it-all-together theologians who believe their wisdom sufficient to understand the ways of God in the world: God is both almighty and just; suffering is the result of human sin; therefore, there is no such thing as undeserved suffering, and Job should own up and confess his (hidden) sins so that he will be restored.

Elihu plays the role of the overconfidence of youth, who think they really are wiser than their elders. At the same time, ironically, he does in fact have an additional point to make that the other three do not—that beyond Job's obviously deserved punishment there is a chastening value to such punishment that Job ought to be willing to accept.

Job plays the central role. For him it is all a frustrating enigma. He believes that his calamities ultimately come from God, yet there is no clear cause-and-effect correlation. But that is also his problem, since at issue for him is his integrity—recognized by God in the opening narrative. He is thus both the innocent sufferer and the one for whom the easy answers do not work anymore. Although he knows that no one is without sin (9:2), nonetheless, in his case, there is no correlation between the enormity of what has happened to him and his sin, and to confess sins not actually committed would be to lose his integrity—and thus take from him something far more than life itself. So he continually seeks an explanation for his suffering, and many of his speeches are pleas for the right to defend himself before God.

Yahweh, of course, plays the ultimate role. As the initiator of the story, he is thus in charge from the beginning, including getting Satan to think about Job—not the other way around. In the end, the tables are completely turned: (1) The question of where wisdom is found is answered not only in terms of God alone but also by silencing all human voices that would insist that God must explain himself to them, and (2) the question of whether one will serve God without receiving benefits is answered with a resounding *yes!*—the crucial role Job will play in the story. The brilliance of this book lies in the fact that although it looks as though it were a theodicy (human beings putting God on trial, insisting on explanations for his actions), it turns out in fact to be a theology (God putting human beings on trial as to whether they will trust him not only when they receive no immediate benefits but also when he does not give them the explanations they demand—and thus as to whether they will live within the bounds of creaturely wisdom). The whole point of the final speeches to Job is that God's wisdom evidenced in the created order is both visible to the eye and yet beyond human understanding (with no explanations given). If that be so, then Job should trust God and his wisdom in the matter of his suffering as well—to which Job offers the ultimate response of humility and repentance.

One final matter. With regard to the long speeches by the five disputants (including Job), we need to be reminded that these are *not* to be thought of as a word from God. Even though Job is more on target than the others (42:8), they all say things that carry enough truth to be dangerous. But their speeches are not God's words; he speaks only at the end, when all human voices have been silenced. Your concern as you read these dialogues is to be aware of their measure of truth, but also of their false suppositions.

You might try reading the poetry aloud. It is much too good for you to let your eye skip over it lightly. The speakers are wrestling with deep issues, and they also have a sense of the power of words, so they often both phrase and rephrase their thoughts. Note, for example, how often a point of comparison is made and then elaborated considerably, even though the elaboration is not strictly required to make the point at hand. Thus, in complaining that his friends are of no help (6:14–23), Job likens them to intermittent streams (v. 15), which he then elaborates richly and eloquently for several lines before returning to their non-help (v. 21). All of it is a wonderful read, even in the midst of so much pain and anguish.

A WALK THROUGH JOB

☐ 1:1–2:13 *Prologue*

This opening narrative is *not* the point of the book; it is rather the essential framework within which you are to understand the speeches that follow. Note that it has four parts (marked off by the NIV headings): 1:1–5 gives the essential information that makes the story work; Job is then tested as to whether he will serve God if his possessions are stripped from him (vv. 6–22); when Satan loses that round, he tries again (2:1–10)—and loses, even though Job's wife sides with Satan; the visit by the three friends (vv. 11–13) then sets the stage for the dialogues.

☐ 3:1–26 *Job's Lament*

Job finally breaks his silence with a curse against both the day and night of his birth (vv. 3–10); note how the whys in the following lament (vv. 11–26) tie it closely to the curse. Job may wish he had not been born, but neither will he take his own life. Thus pain is his only option.

☐ 4:1–14:22 *First Cycle of Speeches*

Job's lament launches the first cycle of speeches, in which each friend speaks in turn and in turn hears Job's response. Note that Eliphaz's speech is the longest of the three, while Job's speeches increase in length as Bildad's and Zophar's get shorter.

Chapters 4–5. *Eliphaz* begins the dialogue with an eloquent recital of the basic theology of "the wise." Not yet accusatory (see 4:1–6), this speech prepares the way for the rest. Divine retribution is certain (4:7–11), since no one is innocent before God (4:12–21). Job should therefore appeal to God for help (5:1–16); he is further urged to recognize his calamity as correction and to seek God for his benefits (5:17–26)—thus siding with Satan! Note Eliphaz's supreme confidence in his own wisdom (5:27).

Chapters 6–7. *Job* responds by defending his opening lament (6:1–13), accusing his friends of being no comfort to him (vv. 14–23), protesting his innocence (vs. 24–30), and finally appealing directly to God for the comfort lacking in his friends (7:1–21), concluding again with "whys."

Chapter 8. *Bildad* takes up Eliphaz's position, arguing that God is just, and thus calamity is punishment for wrongdoing (vv. 1–7), basing it on traditional teaching (vv. 8–10) and the laws of nature (vv. 11–22). Note how verse 20 states his basic position: Good and evil are clearly defined by what happens to people.

Chapters 9–10. Job's friends are no help, so *Job* agonizes over bringing his case before God, because he is unsure of its outcome (ch. 9); thus he bursts into lament (ch. 10). Note in passing that much of 9:1–10 anticipates chapters 38–39.

Chapter 11. The truth that *Zophar* finally speaks about forgiveness (vv. 13–20) unfortunately follows from his assumption that Job's calamity must be the result of Job's sin (vv. 1–12). How harsh the "righteous" can sometimes be!

Chapters 12–14. *Job* has been stung (12:1–3); to follow their advice (which continually sides with Satan) means to cash in his own integrity. So after defending his skill in wisdom equal to theirs (12:4–13:12), he mulls over bringing a legal case before God, which is his only hope (13:13–14:22), but again it is an agonizing alternative.

□ 15:1–21:34 *Second Cycle of Speeches*

In this second round of speeches, the three accusers all play variations on a single theme—the present torment and final fate of the wicked. Job's responses show faint glimpses of hope, which are dashed by the others, so he points out finally that the wicked do not always suffer.

Chapter 15. *Eliphaz* appeals once more to their traditional wisdom: It is the wicked who suffer torment, so Job must be wicked, and his own mouth condemns him automatically when he questions his suffering.

Chapters 16–17. *Job* agrees that his affliction is from God, but he is also at a loss as to why. His only hope lies in a heavenly advocate (16:18–21).

Chapter 18. *Bildad* can hardly take it (vv. 1–4), so he picks up from Eliphaz by pointing out the terrible fate of the wicked—like Job!—and thus God will not hear him (vv. 5–21).

Chapter 19. *Job* complains about his friends (vv. 1–6) and about God's treating him as an enemy (vv. 7–12) with the result that his alienation is total (vv. 13–20). His plea for help is accompanied by another note of hope (vv. 21–27) before warning his friends (vv. 28–29).

Chapter 20. *Zophar* rejects Job's note of hope, repeating the refrain about the fate of evildoers.

Chapter 21. *Job* now calls into question his counselors' insistence on God's speedy retribution of the wicked (vv. 7–33), complaining about his friends on either side (vv. 1–6, 34).

□ 22:1–26:14 *Third Cycle of Speeches*

The debate is now winding down. Note (1) that this final cycle is a third the length of the first one, (2) that there is no speech from Zophar, and (3) how much repetition there is of former arguments.

Chapter 22. Note *Eliphaz's* false accusations against Job (vv. 6–9; cf. 31:13–23), assumed to be true because Eliphaz's theology demands it; so after instructing Job on God's ways once more (22:12–20), he again calls him to repentance (vv. 21–30).

Chapters 23–24. *Job* again expresses a desire to plead his case before God (23:1–7), indicating both hesitant confidence (vv. 8–12) and trembling fear (vv. 13–17). In any case, Eliphaz is simply wrong. The world is full of injustice (24:1–17); may the wicked be cursed (24:18–25).

Chapter 25. *Bildad* utters the counselors' final word: God is too great for Job to question him.

Chapter 26. *Job* agrees about God's majesty, but (in what follows) not the implications they draw from it.

□ 27:1–23 *Job's Closing Discourse*

Note the introductory formula (v. 1), indicating that these verses will serve (with ch. 3) to bookend the discourses. After arguing that integrity demands that he protest his innocence (27:1–6), Job then turns the tables on his friends, who have become his enemies (vv. 7–12), finally—and ironically—reminding them of the fate of the wicked (vv. 13–23)!

□ 28:1–28 *Raising the Question of True Wisdom*

Read this pivotal chapter carefully. Here the author—not Job or his "friends"—raises the essential questions: Where can wisdom be found (v. 12)? Where does it come from, and where does it dwell (v. 20)? The answer of course is "in God" (vv. 23–27), and human wisdom is to be found in the fear of the Lord (v. 28). This insertion between the two sets of discourses clearly anticipates the final answer of chapters 38–41.

☐ 29:1–31:40 *Job's Call for Vindication*

In this first of the series of three monologues, Job presents his final case before God. He points out first his past honor and blessing (ch. 29) and then his present dishonor and suffering (ch. 30) before turning to a specific listing of his uprightness with regard to truth and marriage (31:1–12). He concludes with deeds on behalf of the people God himself cares for—widows and orphans (vv. 13–34; over against Eliphaz's accusation in 22:6–9)—before making his final appeal (31:35–40).

☐ 32:1–37:24 *The Elihu Speeches*

After an introduction (32:1–5), Elihu speaks (overconfidently) for the young, making four speeches whose basic point is found in the first one (chs. 32–33, esp. ch. 33)—that rather than protest his innocence, Job should learn about the disciplinary nature of suffering. With this insight, Elihu advances several steps beyond Eliphaz, Bildad, and Zophar, acknowledging at least that the righteous do sometimes suffer. But in his second speech (ch. 34), he agrees with his three elders that God governs a fair universe without exception; so in the third speech (ch. 35), he points out the uselessness of Job's appeals of innocence. In the fourth (chs. 36–37), he concludes by returning to the theme of his first speech (36:6–26) before extolling the majesty of God (ch. 37), which (ironically) prepares Job for what comes next.

☐ 38:1–42:6 *God Speaks and Job Responds*

Here you come to the climax of the book. God speaks out of the storm, breaking silence in fulfillment of Job's deep yearnings. But rather than vindicate Job (as Job had hoped) or reprove him (as his friends expected), God simply calls human wisdom into account, powerfully demonstrating over and over again from creation—both its origins and his care for it—that wisdom lies with him alone.

In the first speech (chs. 38–39), God begins with the basic question for all human wisdom: "Who is this that darkens my counsel with words without knowledge?" (38:2). The rest is a litany of questions about creation intended to give Job (and his friends) perspective: "Where were you when all of this was set in place and carefully watched over?" At the end Job properly responds with shame and silence (40:3–5).

The second speech (40:6–41:34) recounts God's mighty powers and then challenges Job to demonstrate his own prowess—as if he could—

by defeating the two beasts, behemoth and leviathan. The great issue raised by the book finds its answer in Job's twofold response (42:1–6), namely, his admission that he has spoken without understanding, and his repentance once he has truly "seen" Yahweh! And this, of course, is what the author intends that others should do as well.

□ 42:7–17 *Epilogue*

Note that the epilogue is in two parts: First (vv. 7–9), God pronounces his verdict in favor of Job over against his friends; second (vv. 10–17), God finally vindicates Job—who has maintained trust in God whether he receives benefits or not—with a double portion of everything.

The book of Job has an important place in the biblical story, not only by calling us to total trust in God even in the most trying of situations but also by preparing the way for Jesus Christ, who as the incarnate God gives the ultimate answer to Job's question by assuming the role of innocent sufferer—only in his case to bear the sins of the entire world.

Psalms

ORIENTING DATA FOR PSALMS

- **Content:** 150 psalms of rich diversity, which in their present arrangement served as the "hymnbook" for postexilic (Second Temple) Judaism
- **Date of composition:** the psalms themselves date from the early monarchy to a time after the exile (ca. 1000 to 400 B.C.); the collection in its present form may be part of the reform movement reflected in Chronicles and Ezra-Nehemiah
- **Emphases:** trust in and praise to Yahweh for his goodness; lament over wickedness and injustices; Yahweh as king of the universe and the nations; Israel's king as Yahweh's representative in Israel; Israel (and individual Israelites) as God's covenant people; Zion (and its temple) as the special place of Yahweh's presence on earth

OVERVIEW OF PSALMS

The 150 pieces that make up the book of Psalms were originally 147 different psalms (one occurs twice—14 and 53; two are broken into two—9 and 10, 42 and 43). Each was originally composed independently; thus each has integrity and meaning on its own. But the psalms were not randomly collected; rather they have been ordered and grouped in such a way that the whole together carries meaning that further enhances the affirmations each makes on its own. Therefore in the Psalter you can look for meaning both in the individual psalms and in their ordered relationship with each other. The latter is what we especially emphasize in this chapter and encourage you to be aware of as you read.

Although the present arrangement of the Psalter comes from the postexilic period, it also maintains the integrity of smaller collections that were already in use as part of Israel's ongoing history. Besides three collections of Davidic psalms (3–41; 51–70; 138–145), there are also two collections of "Asaph/sons of Korah" psalms (42–50; 73–88), plus four topical collections (God's kingship, 93–100; psalms of praise, 103–107; songs of ascent [pilgrimage songs], 120–134; and Hallelujah psalms, 111–113 and 146–150).

The collection in its present form was brought together as five books, probably with the Pentateuch in view (thus "David" corresponds to "Moses"):

Book 1 Psalms 1–41: All but 1, 2, and 33 titled "of David"

Book 2 Psalms 42–72: Psalms 42–50 "of the sons of Korah" or "of Asaph"; Psalms 51–70 "of David"; concluding with one "of Solomon" (72; note that 71 is untitled), with a coda at the end, "This concludes the prayers of David son of Jesse"

Book 3 Psalms 73–89: All titled, mostly "of Asaph" or "of the sons of Korah"

Book 4 Psalms 90–106: Mostly untitled, except for 101 and 103 ("of David")

Book 5 Psalms 107–150: Mostly untitled, but fifteen are "of David," including Psalms 138–145; also includes fifteen "songs of ascent" (120–134) and concludes with five "Hallelujah" psalms (146–150)

You will note that each book concludes with a similar doxology (41:13; 72:18–19; 89:52; 106:48; and the whole of 150). In the first four instances these are not a part of the original psalm; rather they are the work of the final compiler, and they function to conclude the books themselves. It is also important to observe that, although the vast majority of the psalms are addressed to God, within many of them there are words that address the people themselves (thus assuming a corporate setting), while some of the psalms function primarily as instruction (especially the Torah-Wisdom psalms; e.g., 1; 33; 37). In this regard, compare Colossians 3:16 and Ephesians 5:19 (hymns about Christ sung in thanksgiving to God also function to instruct the people).

SPECIFIC ADVICE FOR READING PSALMS

The psalms were written first of all to be sung—one by one and not necessarily in their canonical order; this is also how they are most often read—as songs. Since chapter 11 in *How to 1* is intended to help you read them this way, the contents of that chapter will be presupposed throughout this discussion, especially the information about the various kinds and forms of psalms and the nature of Hebrew poetry. The present concern is twofold: (1) to help you make some sense of the canonical arrangement of the Psalter and (2) to offer a minimal guide to reading the psalms as part of the biblical story. At the same time you should be constantly watching for their basic theological assumptions, viewed in terms of how the psalms fit into the story. (The analogy would be a Christian hymnbook, which is not intended to be read through, but is in fact carefully arranged, usually along theological/church-year lines.)

It is important to be aware that, even though the majority of the psalms are themselves preexilic, the collection as we have it was the hymnbook of Second Temple (postexilic) Judaism. When you recall the emphasis in Chronicles and Ezra-Nehemiah on the musicians associated with the temple, you can easily imagine the present Psalter taking shape during that period and that the arrangement itself had meaning for them.

The five books are carefully arranged so that they mirror the story of Israel from the time of David until after the exile. Books 1 and 2 basically assume the time of the early monarchy, as David speaks words of lament and praise, both for himself and for the people, based on Yahweh's unending goodness and righteousness. Together they are bookended by two coronation psalms (2 and 72) that extol the king as Yahweh's anointed one for the sake of his people. In book 2, especially in the Korahite collection inserted at the beginning, you also find a goodly number of royal and Zion hymns, which focus on the king but now especially emphasize Jerusalem and its temple as the place of God's presence and reign. Thus both books concentrate on David as king under Yahweh's ultimate kingship.

Book 3, on the other hand, has only one Davidic psalm; instead, by the presence of some prominent exilic and postexilic laments, it assumes the fall of Jerusalem. Picking up the mournful note of Psalm 44, the psalmists repeatedly ask "Why?" and "How long?" regarding Yahweh's rejecting them. This book thus begins with a Wisdom psalm that wonders aloud about the "prosperity of the wicked" (73:3); it ends first with the "darkest" psalm in the Psalter (Ps 88), whose only note of hope is the opening address ("the God who saves me"), and then with a poignant lament over the present (apparent) demise of the Davidic covenant (Ps 89).

In response book 4 begins by going back to Moses with a psalm that reminds Israel that God has been her dwelling place throughout all generations. Then, after two psalms of trust and thanksgiving (91–92), comes the collection of Yahweh's kingship (93–100). Despite the present state of the Davidic monarchy, Yahweh reigns! This book then ends with psalms of praise (101–106), whose last word is an appeal for Yahweh to gather the exiles (106:47).

Book 5 begins with a psalm of praise that assumes the gathering of the exiles (107:2–3), followed by Psalm 108, which acclaims God's rule over all the nations. The rest of this book, more heterogeneous than the others, looks forward in a variety of ways to God's great future for his people. Included are some royal psalms (110; 118) that were used in anticipation of the coming of the great future king, so one is not surprised by the significant role that these psalms played in the earliest Christians' understanding of Christ. Likewise, the psalms of ascent would have been used for present (and in anticipation of future) pilgrimages of God's people to Zion—while the final five "Hallelujahs" (146–150) remind them of God's ultimate sovereignty over all things. Thus in the final arrangement of things, the first three books contain predominantly laments, while the final two are predominantly praise and thanksgiving.

In light of this overall arrangement, you will want to read with an awareness of the undergirding *theological* bases on which these poems (songs, prayers, and teachings) were written. First, even though many of them are individual laments or hymns of praise, the collection itself assumes that even these have a "people of God" dimension to them: The individual is always aware of being part of the people who together belong to God in covenant relationship and who share the same story.

As elsewhere, Yahweh is the center of everything, and the psalmists are fully aware that their own lives are predicated on their covenant relationship to Yahweh. Thus their songs regularly remind those who sing them that Yahweh is the Creator of all that is and therefore Lord of all the earth, including all the nations—reminders that usually also affirm Yahweh's character, especially his love and faithfulness (cf. Exod 34:4–6), but also his mercy, goodness, and righteousness. At the same time they repeatedly echo the significant moments in their sacred history as God's people. Indeed several psalms relate the larger story itself, either in part or in whole, and for different reasons (Pss 78; 105–106; 136). So as you read, be looking for these affirmations about God (including the marvelous metaphors) and for the echoes of the story itself: creation, election, deliverance, the holy war, inheritance of the land, the role of Zion/Jerusalem as the place of God's presence and the abode of his vice-regent the king, and Israel's role in blessing the nations.

Finally, it is important to note that Psalms 1 and 2, which are untitled and framed by the expression "Blessed are …" (1:1; 2:12), serve to introduce the whole Psalter. Psalm 1 (a Torah-Wisdom psalm) has pride of place because it sets out the basic theological presupposition on which everything else rests, namely, that God blesses those who delight in the law and thus commit themselves to covenant loyalty, while the opposite prevails for the wicked. This serves as grounds for most of the laments, as well as for the songs of praise and thanksgiving, since it is true even when one's experience suggests otherwise. Psalm 2 then introduces the role of the king, who as God's "Anointed One" and "Son" (Israel as Yahweh's son [Exod 4:22–23] now focuses on its king) is Yahweh's protector of his people. Psalm 2 thus serves as the basis not only for the Zion and kingship dimensions of the Psalter—not to mention the agony of Psalm 89—but eventually becomes the key to New Testament messianism as these psalms are recognized as fulfilled in Jesus Christ.

A WALK THROUGH THE PSALMS

Book I (Psalms 1 to 41)

☐ Psalms 1–2 *Introduction to the Psalter*

Even though these two psalms introduce the whole Psalter (see above), Psalm 1 also introduces the main thrust of book 1 in particular, while Psalm 2 introduces the main concerns of book 2.

☐ Psalms 3–7 *Five Laments (Pleas for Help)*

Since book 1 is predominantly lament, it is fitting that three statements of evening and morning trust (3:5; 4:8; 5:3) stand at the beginning of the collection. Typically, these laments combine prayer to Yahweh with affirmations about and trust in Yahweh, also the subject of the address to others in Psalm 4:2–5 (cf. 6:8–9). Psalms 3, 5, and 7 plead for deliverance from foes, while 4 pleads for relief in time of drought and 6 for healing. Note also the theological presuppositions (God's role in the holy war; Yahweh's presence on Zion [3:4; 4:5; 5:7]; God's character [merciful, righteous]) and that each of them presupposes the basic assumptions of Psalm 1.

☐ Psalm 8 *Praise to the Creator*

This hymn revels in Yahweh and his majesty as Creator, and it marvels at his condescension toward humanity and their role in the created order, thus echoing Genesis 1 and 2.

☐ Psalm 9–13 *Lament for Deliverance of the "Righteous Poor"*

Together these five (or four) psalms are of exactly equal length to the first five laments (3–7). Psalms 9 and 10 together form an acrostic prayer for deliverance, each line beginning with successive letters of the Hebrew alphabet (see Ps 119). The first half (Ps 9) is a plea for deliverance from wicked nations; the second (Ps 10) assumes the stance of the righteous poor, the helpless person who is the recipient of social injustice (see Exod 22:22–27; Amos; Isaiah; and Micah). After an affirmation of trust in Yahweh's righteous rule (Ps 11), two further laments appeal for help and deliverance (12; 13). As you read, watch for the various expressed and assumed affirmations about God that mark these psalms.

☐ Psalm 14 *The Folly of Humankind (see Psalm 53)*

Note how this psalm serves to conclude this second set of laments, as Psalm 8 did the first, by pointing out the utter folly and wickedness of humanity that does not acknowledge God (thus echoing Genesis 3), while affirming the righteous poor.

☐ Psalms 15–24 *On Access to the Temple*

Together this series of psalms forms a chiastic pattern. In the outer frame, Psalms 15 and 24 ask the same basic question: Who has access to the temple of Yahweh (15:1; 24:3)? The answer, of course, is those who are righteous in keeping with Psalm 1 (note how each affirms different aspects of the law). In the next frame, Psalms 16 and 23 express trust in Yahweh, both concluding on a note of joy for being in Yahweh's presence (16:11; 23:6). Psalms 17 and 22 are then pleas for deliverance, which especially express trust in Yahweh. In the inner frame, Psalms 18 and 20–21 together express prayer and praise for the king's deliverance from his enemies (hence picking up on Ps 2). The centerpiece in this group is Psalm 19, which glories in creation (Ps 8)—especially the summer sun as it moves across the sky—and the law (Ps 1). Again, as you read, be looking for the basic theological affirmations (Yahweh's love, Yahweh as Divine Warrior, etc.) and the echoes of Israel's story (the Law, inheritance of the land, election [the point of 22:22–31], their role among the nations, etc.).

☐ **Psalms 25–33** ***Prayer, Praise, and Trust in the King of Creation***

As with the prior grouping, one can detect a chiastic pattern here as well. In the outer frame (both acrostics), Psalm 25 offers prayer and praise for Yahweh's covenant mercies, while (the untitled) Psalm 33 is a hymn of praise for Yahweh's gracious rule. In the next frame, Psalm 26 is the prayer of one who is "blameless" before Yahweh's covenant law, while Psalm 32 expresses the blessedness of the one whom Yahweh has forgiven. Psalms 27 and 31 both appeal to Yahweh against false accusers (note how they conclude with nearly identical admonitions: "Be strong and take heart"). In the next frame, Psalm 28 is the prayer of one going "down to the pit" (v. 2), while Psalm 30 is praise from one spared from "going down into the pit" (v. 3). As with the preceding group, the centerpiece (Ps 29) praises the King of creation, this time in light of a thunderstorm. Again, mark the various theological affirmations expressed in these hymns.

☐ **Psalms 34–37** ***Instruction in Godly Wisdom and Appeals against the Wicked***

This group of four psalms also forms a chiasm. Psalms 34 and 37 are alphabetic acrostics, both of which teach godly wisdom (again reflecting Ps 1), while the enclosed psalms appeal to Yahweh as Divine Warrior against malicious slanderers (35) and against the godless wicked (36, which has its own chiastic pattern: vv. 1–4, 5–9, 10–12). Note that in keeping with the Wisdom tradition (see "Overview of Proverbs," p. 145), the "fear of the LORD" lies at the heart of Psalm 34 (see vv. 7, 9, 11), while this is exactly what the godless lack (36:1).

☐ **Psalms 38–41** ***Four Laments: Prayer and Confession of Sin***

These final laments in book 1 have a fourfold common denominator: (1) The psalmist is in deep trouble (illness in three cases), which he perceives as the result of sin (again, Ps 1); (2) he is mocked by enemies; (3) while appealing for mercy he confesses his sin; and (4) the appeal is based on his trust in Yahweh. It is of some interest that in the original Davidic collection, Psalm 51 would be the next in order, which carries on the theme of confession of sin.

Book 2 (Psalms 42–72)

This book features Zion, the temple, and the king—all of them in relation to Yahweh, who dwells in the temple on Zion and whose kingship over Israel is represented by the human king—although you will note in this book that the generic name "God" *(Elohim)* occurs with greater frequency than Yahweh ("LORD"). It begins and ends with a series of three prayers followed by a royal psalm (42–44 and 45; 69–71 and 72), whose inner frame is a collection of Zion psalms (46–48) and the marvelous psalm celebrating Yahweh's own enthronement in the temple on Zion (68).

☐ Psalms 42–45 *Three Prayers and a Royal Psalm*

You will observe that Psalms 42 and 43 belong together as one (note the thrice-repeated refrain in 42:5; 42:11; 43:5). Their place at the head of book 2 lies with the psalmist's longing to join in the pilgrimage to Zion (42:4; 43:3–4), while Psalm 44 anticipates book 3 by mourning over a national defeat of considerable proportions (but with no mention of the devastation of Jerusalem as in Ps 74). Note especially the appeals to Israel's history and covenant loyalty. The royal psalm that comes next (45) was composed to celebrate the king's wedding.

☐ Psalms 46–48 *In Celebration of Zion*

This trio of Zion psalms is central to book 2, celebrating the people's security in Zion (46 and 48) and Yahweh's kingship over all the earth (47). No matter how they may have felt about the Davidic dynasty, the singers of Israel well remembered that the real "palace" on Zion was the temple of Yahweh Almighty.

☐ Psalms 49–53 *On the Proper Stance before God*

Watch for the echoes of Yahweh's rule from Zion in this group of psalms (50:1–15; 51:18–19; 52:8–9; 53:6), even as they focus on other matters. As a group they contrast proper and improper approaches to

God—not to trust in wealth (49), but to bring sacrifices based on covenant loyalty (50), especially a penitent spirit (51), because God rejects the wicked (52) and exposes their folly (53).

☐ Psalms 54–59 *Six Laments: Prayers for Help*

Note what is common to these laments, namely, that they assume the king's presence in Jerusalem, that they assume Yahweh's presence in Jerusalem, that they are all complaints against enemies, and that the chief weapon of their attacks is the mouth (slander, lies, etc.).

☐ Psalms 60–64 *Five Prayers with Common Themes*

These five psalms are enclosed by a community lament (60) and an individual lament against enemies (64). Watch how they all continue some of the previous themes: They are spoken by the king; Yahweh's presence on Zion lies at the heart of both prayer and praise; they look to Yahweh for protection or deliverance from enemies.

☐ Psalms 65–68 *In Praise of God's Awesome Deeds and Presence*

The main theme of book 2 comes into full focus with this group of hymns and thanksgivings that exalt Yahweh's kingship by recalling his "awesome" deeds, first on behalf of the whole earth (65 and 67) and then on behalf of Israel (66 and 68). Psalm 68 is especially crucial, both to book 2 and to the whole Psalter, as it celebrates Yahweh's enthronement on Zion—note how he has moved from Sinai to Zion, and thus is King over Israel and the nations, not to mention the whole earth. Psalm 72, which concludes book 2, must be read in light of this psalm.

☐ Psalms 69–72 *Three Prayers and a Royal Psalm*

Book 2 now concludes in a way similar to how it began—with three pleas for help that conclude with a royal psalm. Note how the plea in Psalm 69 especially assumes David's role as king in relation to the people. Note further that Psalms 70 and 71 rework/restate portions of Psalms 40:13–17 and 31:1–5. The final psalm (72) is crucial to the larger concerns of the Psalter: An enthronement psalm attributed to David's son, Solomon, it functions with Psalm 2 to frame the royal dimension of books 1 and 2; at the same time, it stands in bold relief to the conclusion of book 3 (89), which mourns the present demise of the Davidic dynasty.

Book 3 (Psalms 73–89)

The several prominent exilic and postexilic laments in this collection (including several community laments) reflect the time after Zion had been laid waste, the temple desecrated, and the Davidic dynasty, with its "everlasting covenant" (see 2 Sam 7:14–16), was now without a king. Thus, even the several preexilic psalms (e.g., 76; 78; 83; 84; 87) are best understood in this light; namely, that they contain the memory that the surrounding psalms now lament.

☐ **Psalms 73–78** ***On Rejection and Hope for Zion***

As in book 1, a Wisdom psalm opens book 3, pondering the puzzle of the prosperity of the wicked and thus setting the tone for what follows. Along with Psalm 78 (another Wisdom psalm), it frames two prayers (74; 77) that cry out the basic question of book 3 (Why have you rejected us?/Will the Lord reject us forever?). These in turn frame a thanksgiving and a Zion psalm (75/76), which highlight the reasons for the laments. Note that Psalm 78 is one of four psalms that retell Israel's story in some detail (cf. 105; 106; 136), in this case recalling past rebellions and their dire consequences as a warning to what could—and did—happen again, on an even larger scale.

☐ **Psalms 79–83** ***On Rejection and Hope for Zion, Again***

This group of five is framed by two sets of psalms that again express the basic theme of book 3. Although Psalms 79 and 80 reflect two different times (after and before the fall of Jerusalem), they have in common the basic question "How long?" (79:5; 80:4). Likewise Psalms 82 and 83 have in common the plea that concludes the first one (82:8) and begins the second (83:1): "Rise up" and "do not keep silent." Together these enclose an exhortation to Israel that suggests the reason for her fall (81).

☐ **Psalms 84–89** ***In Celebration of Zion, and Lament over Its Demise***

This final group is in two sets of three, each set having a similar pattern. They begin (84) with a celebration of, and yearning for, the courts of Yahweh. This is followed by another psalm that asks the theme question ("Will you be angry with us forever?" 85:5), which is followed in turn by the only Davidic psalm in book 3 (Ps 86)—a plea for mercy based on the great revelation of Yahweh on Sinai, that he is a "compassionate and gracious God, slow to anger, abounding in love and faithfulness" (v. 15; cf. Exod 34:4–6).

The second set follows the same pattern—beginning with a celebration of Zion (Ps 87), followed by the dark lament of Psalm 88, and concluding with a three-part psalm (89) that echoes concerns from Psalm 86. The first part (89:1–18) celebrates Yahweh's love and faithfulness to his people, especially evidenced by the covenant with David (vv. 19–37); together these become the basis for the lament over the present demise of the Davidic dynasty (vv. 38–51). Note that the concluding section of Psalm 89 contains the theme question: "How long, O LORD?" (v. 46).

Book 4 (Psalms 90–106)

In direct response to the devastation of Jerusalem and the present void in the Davidic dynasty, book 4 begins with the reminder that Yahweh has been Israel's "dwelling place" throughout all generations. The heart of this collection, therefore, is the series of psalms that celebrate Yahweh's kingship—over both Israel and all the nations. The book ends with a series of responses to Yahweh's reign, concluding with two that retell Israel's story from two different perspectives.

☐ Psalms 90–92 *Yahweh Our Dwelling Place*

Reaching back to the one psalm that is titled "of Moses," the collector placed this psalm at the head of book 4, with its opening assurance that God has been Israel's "dwelling place throughout all generations." This is followed by a psalm of trust, which has making "the Most High your dwelling" as its centerpiece (91:9), and by a psalm of praise to "O Most High" (92:1) for his many benefits, including the defeat of adversaries.

☐ Psalms 93–99 *Yahweh Reigns, Let the People Rejoice*

The common theme of this group of psalms is their celebration—in a variety of ways and for a variety of reasons—that Yahweh reigns over Israel, the nations, and the whole earth. The one apparent exception (94) nonetheless assumes Yahweh's reign as it calls for justice on those who reject Yahweh's law. Note also the inherent warning in 95:7–11, which picks up the concerns of Psalm 78 and anticipates the concluding psalm of this book (106), and is the basis for the exhortation in Hebrews 3:7–4:11.

☐ Psalms 100–106 *In Praise of Yahweh and in Hope of Restoration*

This final group in book 4 forms a kind of mini-Psalter, as these psalms reflect various responses to Yahweh's reign: celebration (100); a pledge to live faithfully (101); a prayer for the future rebuilding of Zion (102; note especially v. 12, which assumes Yahweh's reign but pleads for him also to return to Zion); praise for Yahweh's great love (103); and praise of Yahweh as Creator (104). The concluding two psalms retell Israel's story from two points of view: a call to remember all his mercies in that story (105) and a warning not to repeat the rebellion side of the story (106). Note how book 4 ends with a prayer of deliverance from exile (106:47, reflecting Deut 30:1–10).

Book 5 (Psalms 107–150)

This final book in the Psalter is much more varied, both in form and content, than the first four. It begins with a thanksgiving psalm that opens (107:1–3) in direct response to the prayer in Psalm 106:47; it ends with the five Hallelujah psalms. Besides the central role of Psalm 119, which echoes the concerns of Psalm 1, the major part is composed of three sets of psalms: (1) 110–118, which begin and end with psalms that, in this setting at least, look forward to the renewal of the Davidic kingship; (2) 120–134, the songs of ascent—now sung in the context of the second temple, but also with a future orientation; and (3) 138–145, a Davidic collection that functions as a kind of reprise, looking back to books 1 and 2, and concluding on the note of the eternal nature of God's kingdom and his faithfulness to his promises (145:11–13). Thus, on the whole, this book contains psalms that reflect the current situation and the future longings of postexilic Judaism.

☐ Psalms 107–109 *In Praise of God's Rescue of His People, and Two Davidic Laments*

Although not written with the return of the exiled community in mind, the opening hymn of thanksgiving for deliverance begins with the "gathering" motif (107:1–3) and thus serves to introduce book 5. Note how readily Psalm 108 responds to this, combining praise (vv. 1–5) with an appeal for Yahweh to give aid against Israel's enemies (vv. 6–13)—a psalm constructed from 57:7–11 and 60:5–12—while Psalm 109 picks up that plea, spelling out the enemy's sins in great detail and asking the divine Judge for justice in kind.

☐ Psalms 110–118 *The Coming King, and Festival Psalms*

This group of psalms is framed by two royal psalms (110; 118) that in postexilic Judaism were recognized as messianic, which explains why together they played such an important role in Jesus' own ministry (Mark 11:4–12:12, 35–37) and in the early church (Ps 110 in particular; Acts 2:34–35; Rom 8:34; 1 Cor 15:25; Col 3:1; Heb 1:13). They enclose a series of psalms (excepting 114) that either begin or end with "Hallelujah," which were used in Israel's great festivals. Psalm 114 is one of Israel's great celebrations of the exodus—with marvelous imagery (the sea "looked and fled," Mount Sinai "skipped like rams").

☐ Psalm 119 *In Celebration of the Law, Yahweh's Faithful Word*

This great poem in celebration of the Law forms the centerpiece of book 5, thus taking us back to the introductory Psalm 1. An alphabetic acrostic (eight lines of poetry for each letter of the Hebrew alphabet), it was composed by someone who recognized the benefits of, and gloried in, God's covenantal gift to his people.

☐ Psalms 120–134 *Songs of Ascent*

This collection, all titled, belongs to the tradition of making the pilgrimage to Zion for the three annual feasts. In the setting of postexilic Judaism, they almost certainly also carry a forward-looking dimension. Be looking for the many different theological and "story of Israel" themes that are found in these psalms.

☐ Psalms 135–137 *In Response to the Ascents*

Psalms 135 and 136, as different as they are, both assume the pilgrims' arrival at Yahweh's sanctuary for worship. Note how the first one praises him for creation and election (over against those whose gods are idols), and the second is another retelling of Israel's story, with antiphonal response. The final one (137) bemoans the reality of the exile when pilgrimage was not possible.

☐ Psalms 138–145 *The Final Davidic Collection*

The main body of the Psalter appropriately concludes with a final collection of psalms attributed to David. They begin with praise (138), move to an acknowledgment of Yahweh's greatness as the all-knowing, ever-present God—expressed in wonder, not fear (139)—followed by five prayers for deliverance (140–144). They conclude with another alphabetic acrostic (145) praising Yahweh for his awesome works and his character (goodness, compassion, faithfulness, righteousness). Note especially verses 11–13, which anticipate God's everlasting kingdom.

☐ Psalms 146–150 *Fivefold Hallelujah*

These concluding "Hallelujahs" punctuate the main point of the Psalter: God is to be praised—for his being the Helper of the helpless (146); as Creator and Restorer of his people (147; note how these two themes are interwoven); from heaven above and earth below (148); with dancing, with the mouth, and with sword in hand (149); and with calls to praise with all manner of music and dancing (150). This last psalm seems to have been composed deliberately to conclude both book 5 and the entire Psalter. We do well to heed this call on a continuing basis. God is worthy. Hallelujah!

The collection of psalms, which is the voice of Yahweh's people singing to him in praise and prayer, functions also to remind them—and us—of the central role of worship in the biblical story, worship that focuses on the living God by recalling his essential goodness and love and his wondrous deeds on their behalf.

Proverbs

ORIENTING DATA FOR PROVERBS

- **Content:** a series of opening poems praising wisdom and warning against folly, followed by several collections of proverbs from sages who taught wisdom to Israel, starting with Solomon
- **Author(s):** collections of proverbs originating with Solomon, various wise men, Agur, and Lemuel's mother—gathered and arranged for later generations by someone otherwise unknown
- **Emphases:** wisdom begins with the fear of and trust in Yahweh; at the practical level, it consists of making wise choices between good and evil behavior; such wisdom is to be desired above all else in order to live a full and godly life

OVERVIEW OF PROVERBS

The larger part of the book of Proverbs is made up of six collections of proverbs/aphorisms, that is, wisdom sayings, mostly couplets (two-liners) that offer guidance to the young—although their value is by no means limited to any age group—on how to live morally and beneficially in the world. On either side of these collections is a prologue of several poems (1:8–9:18) that stress the importance of listening to the sages, and an epilogue of one poem (31:10–31) that idealizes a wife who is characterized by wisdom. A preamble (1:1–7) sets forth the book's title, purpose, and theme.

The groupings of proverbs and aphorisms are all identified within the book itself:

Proverbs of Solomon I (10:1–22:16)
Sayings of the Wise I (22:17–24:22)
Sayings of the Wise II (24:23–34)

Proverbs of Solomon II (25:1–29:27)
Sayings of Agur (30:1–33)
Sayings of Lemuel (31:1–31)

All of these are intended to be read and studied in light of the prologue, with its emphasis on the need to attain wisdom and to reject folly (to walk in righteousness and to shun evil). Here you also find the book's fundamental theological perspective: "The fear of the LORD is the beginning of wisdom, and knowledge of the Holy One is understanding" (9:10; cf. 1:7). For even though many of the proverbs are common to other cultures, these have been especially tailored for life in the covenant community of Israel. They presuppose not only the covenant of law (6:16–19)—indeed, to fear Yahweh is to hate evil (8:13)—but also the life of the people of God in their promised land (2:21–22; cf. 10:27–30).

SPECIFIC ADVICE FOR READING PROVERBS

As with the book of Psalms, reading through the book of Proverbs is not the ordinary way of handling the proverbs (who would read a collection of familiar quotations?). On the other hand, the preamble, the prologue, and the macrostructure of the whole indicate a rather careful overall arrangement, probably intended to be memorized by the young (see 3:3; 4:21; 7:3; 22:17–18). So two matters are of importance in order for you to read the book well.

First, some observations about *structure.* The preamble (1:1–7) prepares you for reading the book as a whole, setting forth its theme (v. 2, attaining wisdom), its purpose (vv. 3–5), the basic contrasts between wisdom and folly (v. 7), and its theological foundation (v. 7). At the same time verse 6 offers an outline of the book, according to its main "authors" (proverbs belonging to Solomon and the sayings of the wise).

It is important to observe that the contrast between wisdom and folly is also a contrast (primarily) between righteousness and wickedness. These contrasts become the predominant theme in the poems of the prologue (1:8–9:18), where the two main illustrative themes are *easy money* (money taken by corrupt means) and *easy sex* (being seduced by another man's wife). At the end of the prologue, wisdom and folly are personified as women calling the young men to follow them. It is therefore no surprise that the central section of these poems (chs. 5–7) admonishes the young man to a lifelong love of his wife (5:15–19) and not to be tempted by a wayward wife, which in turn also serve as analogies for loving wisdom rather than folly (chs. 8–9). This also helps to make sense of the acrostic poem with which the entire collection ends (31:10–31), where the idealized wife is a model of wisdom, while serving as an analogue for Lady Wisdom. It is also not surprising that these poems are primarily in the form of admonitions.

These contrasts between wisdom and folly carry through the first half of Solomon I (10:1–15:29), now with mostly antithetical couplets (the second line in sharp contrast to the first) rather than with admonitions. Here wisdom/righteousness means diligence in work and care of the land, prudent use of money (resources), caring relationships with neighbor and in family, proper use of the tongue, and proper attitudes and actions (being humble, avoiding anger, etc.); while folly is pictured as its opposites. The second half of Solomon I (15:30–22:16) continues these themes, now using predominantly synthetic couplets (the second line completes or builds on the first), with the noteworthy addition of several proverbs that focus on the king and his court.

Second, a few comments about proverbs themselves and what makes them work. First, their *form* is that of poetry. But the poetry is *Hebrew* poetry, which means that some things translate into English, and some do not. Think about how difficult it might be to put the following English aphorisms into another language: “A stitch in time saves nine,” or “A penny saved is a penny earned,” or “An apple a day keeps the doctor away.” Common to these are their rhythmic nature and “sound alike” pattern, which are what makes them memorable. Another language cannot always capture these qualities, even though the gist of the proverb may be plain. So it is with these Hebrew proverbs, which are pithy (typically only three or four Hebrew words to a line) and full of alliterations, catchwords, poetic meter, etc.—not to mention allusions and metaphors that belong to their cultural setting, not all of which are easily captured in English.

Their *function* is to offer practical instruction for the young, with the focus on how to live uprightly and well in a society that understands itself to be under God. It is important to remember that these proverbs functioned primarily in the home to reinforce the benefits of living prudently and well in everyday life; they are not religious instruction as such. Nonetheless, their goal is to mold the character of the young in ways that conform to the law, even if the law itself is not mentioned.

Their *method* is the same as with proverbs universally—to express important truths for practical living in ways that are memorable and thus repeatable. This is done by overstatement, by "all or none" kinds of phrases, or by catchphrases that are not intended to be analyzed for their precision. Sometimes it is the overstatement—which speaks truth but not the whole truth—that makes the point. Take, for example, the American proverb, "A penny saved is a penny earned." While true, its point is thrift, *not* that one should never spend. Or take its reverse, "A fool and his money are soon parted," which reminds one of the need for thrift in a different way. The latter has an earlier counterpart in Proverbs 17:16, "Of what use is money in the hand of a fool, since he has no desire to get wisdom?" Thus what is at stake for you in reading the proverbs is to determine their point by looking carefully at their content and poetic form, but to be careful also not to make them "walk on all fours"—and not to ignore counterproverbs, which also speak truth. (See *How to 1*, pp. 231–41.)

A WALK THROUGH PROVERBS

The Preamble (1:1–7)

Several important matters for reading the whole collection are presented here. The proverbs originate with Solomon, who is significantly noted as the son of David, king of Israel (v. 1); their purpose is given (vv. 2–5)—to attain a prudent life that is also righteous and just; they are addressed to the young and "simple" (v. 4, the latter word meaning something like "gullible"—those who are easily led astray); their content is anticipated (v. 6); and their basic perspective and basic contrasts are spelled out (v. 7).

The Prologue (1:8–9:18)

To understand the collection of proverbs that begins in 10:1, it is important for you to pay close attention to this prologue. You will see that it comes as a series of ten lessons from a father to his son(s), especially picking up the antitheses set out in 1:7; you will also see that most of this material comes as admonition. Each new lesson begins with an introduction of several couplets ("Listen, my son, to your father's instruction," etc.), followed by the lesson itself. The lessons themselves are carefully structured and arranged, building toward the climax of chapter 9, where wisdom and folly make their final appeals.

☐ 1:8–33 *Lesson 1 (and Interlude 1): Warning and Rebuke*

Note that this first introduction (vv. 8–9) includes both the father and mother (cf. the beginning of the collection at 10:1). You will see that this lesson is a strong warning against the enticements of wicked men (vv. 10–19) who plot evil against others for easy money ("ill-gotten gain").

You will also see that in the interlude (vv. 20–33), personified wisdom speaks, rebuking not the "son" but the "simple ones" and "mockers," those who would entice the son away from his parents' wisdom. Her rebuke basically describes the just end of such people.

☐ 2:1–22 *Lesson 2: Safeguard against the Wicked*

Watch for the four distinct parts of this lesson. A longer introduction urges the son to seek wisdom (vv. 1–4); then he will "understand the fear of the LORD and find the knowledge of God" (vv. 5–6), which in turn will protect his way (vv. 7–8) and enter his heart to guard him (vv. 9–11). What follows, then, are the two main ways in the prologue the son needs protection: (1) from "wicked men" (vv. 12–15) and (2) from the "wayward wife" (vv. 16–19). Verses 20–22 then return to his walking in the paths of the righteous.

☐ 3:1–35 *Lessons 3 and 4: The Value of Wisdom*

Lesson 3 (verses 1–10) sets forth God's promises and the son's obligations: love and faithfulness = favor with God and people (vv. 3–4); trust in the Lord = straight paths (vv. 5–6); humility = good health (vv. 7–8); tithes and offerings = abundant crops (vv. 9–10).

Lesson 4 (verses 13–26) presents three poems that highlight the value of wisdom (note the 6–2–6 couplet arrangement)—its blessings and value (vv. 13–18; note the "blessed" at the beginning and end); its role in creation (vv. 19–20), picking up on "the tree of life" from verse 18; and its blessings again (vv. 21–26), now picking up especially the theme of peace and prosperity from verse 2.

Now watch how verses 27–35 at the end of lesson 4 correspond to lesson 3 by offering negative admonitions and warnings.

☐ 4:1–27 *Lesson 5–7: The Supremacy of Wisdom*

The first of these three lessons (vv. 1–9) emphasizes the family's heritage of wisdom and thus urges the sons to continue in it. Lesson 6 then urges the son to stay off the wrong way, the way of wickedness (vv. 10–19), while lesson 7 urges him not to swerve off the right way, the way of righteousness (vv. 20–27).

☐ 5:1–6:19 *Lesson 8: Warnings against Adultery, Folly, and Wickedness*

Picking up from 2:16–19, this lesson warns against adultery (5:3–14, 20), which also includes an admonition to marital fidelity (vv. 15–19); this is followed by a further warning against the wicked (vv. 21–23) and against two kinds of folly (securing strangers, 6:1–5; sloth, vv. 6–11). It concludes with the final warning in the prologue against the wicked (6:12–19).

☐ 6:20–35 *Lesson 9: Further Warning against Adultery*

Note how this introduction begins as the others did (vv. 20–23), but concludes on the warning note (vv. 24–25) that will then be elaborated. With a threefold series of couplets (vv. 26–29, 30–33, and 34–35), the lesson points out the fearful consequences of adultery (punishment, disgrace, a vengeful husband).

☐ 7:1–8:36 *Lesson 10 (and Interlude 2): The Unfaithful Wife, and Wisdom's Call*

This final lesson corresponds to lesson 8, focusing now on the seductive tactics of the unfaithful, adulterous wife. Note that she will also serve as an analogue for the invitation of Folly at the end of the prologue (9:13–18; cf. 9:18 with 7:27; and 9:14 with 5:8).

Notice how the second interlude (8:1–36) corresponds to the first one (1:20–33), which followed the warning against the "wicked men." This time Wisdom offers self-praise to the "simple" and "foolish" (v. 5) to recognize her value both to kings and the prosperous (vv. 12–21), not to mention to Yahweh himself (vv. 22–31). And at the end (vv. 32–36), she steps into the father's shoes and invites the sons to watch daily at her doorway (vis-à-vis the seductress).

☐ 9:1–18 *Epilogue: Rival Banquets of Wisdom and Folly*

Note how this final series begins and ends with rival invitations to "all who are simple" to banquet at the houses of Wisdom and Folly (vv. 1–6; 13–18), and note especially how Folly both mimics Wisdom and echoes the seductions of the unfaithful wife. Between the two final invitations you will find two brief lessons (vv. 7–9, 10–12) contrasting the wise and mockers—all of this to lead you into reading the proverbs themselves with diligence and thoughtfulness.

Proverbs of Solomon I (10:1–22:16)

□ 10:1–15:29 *Solomon I, Part I*

Our division of Solomon I into two parts is intended to highlight the fact that most of the couplets in this section are antithetical, thus following hard on the antitheses of the prologue. But in contrast to the prologue, there is scarcely an admonition among them. They begin with a couplet (10:1) that not only picks up the "instruction" of the young from the prologue, but also puts both parents in the picture, along with the contrast between the wise and foolish child.

As you read through this collection, note how certain themes characterizing wisdom/folly and righteousness/wickedness are replayed over and over in different ways and with different images. Scholars are only recently discovering various patterns that hold smaller groupings together, often in relationship to groupings that precede and follow. But many of these are difficult to trace in English translation. So two things may help you here as you set out to read through the proverbs.

First, be aware of the many educative proverbs that look very much like the introductions to the lessons in the prologue (e.g., 10:17; 12:1; 13:13). These usually mark "seams" in the collection, so you should look more closely at the smaller groupings before and after these educative proverbs.

Second, you might find it helpful to use a set of colored pencils and mark out some of the recurring themes. Along with the more generic wise/foolish and righteous/wicked themes, note the frequency of themes such as wealth/poverty, work/sloth, speech (truth/lying, etc.), relationships (neighbors, family, king), and attitudes (anger, love/hatred, etc.).

For example, the following may be marked out among the thirty-two couplets in chapter 10: Contrasts between the righteous and the wicked (either expressly or implied) occur 18*x*, both generically (10*x*, where this is the point of the proverb [vv. 3, 6–7, 9, 24–25, 27–30]) and in conjunction with other themes (8*x*, vv. 2, 11, 16, 20–21, 23, 31–32); contrasts between wisdom and folly occur 2*x* generically (vv. 1, 23) and 8*x* in conjunction with other themes (vv. 5, 8, 13–14, 18–19, 21, 31); contrasts between proper and improper speech occur 11*x* (vv. 8, 10–11,

13–14, 18–21, 31–32) and constitute the main theme in most of their occurrences; contrasts between work and sloth are the subject 3*x* (vv. 4–5, 26); and contrasts between wealth and poverty occur 3*x* (vv. 15–16, 22), occurring in conjunction with work/sloth in verse 4. The only proverb in this chapter that does not belong to these concerns is verse 17, which deals with discipline (cf. also v. 13). The fact that many of these are related and grouped suggests that the arrangement is not simply haphazard. You may wish to try this for yourself on other small groupings that emerge as you read.

☐ 15:30–22:16 *Solomon I, Part 2*

While this section of Solomon I continues the themes and emphases of part 1, they are noticeably different in two ways. First, you will see that, even though antithetical couplets still occur, the majority of couplets are now synthetic, so that both lines add up to one point. Second, there is an increase in couplets that reflect the king and his court (and other forms of "vertical" relationships, which began at 14:28, 35 in part 1).

The Sayings of the Wise (22:17–24:34)

☐ 22:17–24:22 *First Collection of the Sayings of the Wise*

Two things mark this collection to distinguish it from Solomon I: (1) The verses are not uniform, having from two to several lines each, and (2) they return to the admonitions that marked the prologue. Note also that they are introduced and numbered as "thirty" (22:20), which probably includes the introduction (22:17–21) as the first of these. Watch for the interesting and broad range of topics covered here.

☐ 24:23–34 *Second Collection of the Sayings of the Wise*

This collection is separate, because "thirty sayings" (22:20) sets limits to the preceding collection. The five sayings of this second collection are diverse both in form and content, dealing with relationships with neighbors and diligence in work.

Proverbs of Solomon II (25:1–29:27)

Observe how this collection of Solomonic proverbs moves away from the admonitory style that has just preceded it. These were collected by

Hezekiah's "men." Two collections are in evidence (chs. 25–27; 28–29), while the whole is less uniform in style than Solomon I.

☐ 25:1–27:27 *Solomon II, Part 1*

You will find that in this first part the proverbs are more vivid and diverse in nature, with explicit comparisons becoming more frequent (note the number of verses that begin with "like"). The collection begins with a series relating to the king's court (25:2–8), which also sets a pattern for several longer units (sometimes called "proverb poems": 25:16–17, 21–22; 26:23–26; 27:23–27). Otherwise most of them repeat themes found in the first collection.

☐ 28:1–29:27 *Solomon II, Part 2*

This second collection is a series of fifty-five (mostly antithetical) couplets that focus primarily on the wicked and the righteous. Note how the first, middle, and final couplets make this theme explicit (28:1, 28; 29:27; but see also 28:12; 29:2, 7, 16), and that they frame couplets that are basically concerned with rulers, teaching, and justice for the poor.

More Sayings of the Wise (30:1–31:31)

☐ 30:1–33 *Sayings of Agur*

This diverse collection is full of interest, in terms of both form and content. Note especially the following: how verses 2–4 echo material in Job 38:5–11; the prayer in verses 7–9 (the only one in Proverbs); the four classes of wrongdoers singled out in verses 11–14; and the numerical sayings/riddles in verses 15–31, which seem to contain simply various kinds of observations about life as opposed to specific moral teaching.

☐ 31:1–9 *Sayings of Lemuel*

This final collection is unique in that it relates sayings of a king taught to him by the queen mother. Both parts of this concluding chapter, therefore, offer examples of wise women—thus serving to bookend the instruction of Lady Wisdom in chapters 1–9.

☐ 31:10–31 *Epilogue: A Wise/Ideal Wife*

This final, idealistic portrait of "a wife of noble character" is probably to be understood as another saying that Lemuel's mother taught him. It is an acrostic poem (each verse begins with a succeeding letter of the twenty-two-letter Hebrew alphabet). Note how it idealizes the wife in terms of the values that have been taught throughout the book—a fitting conclusion to the collection.

The book of Proverbs fits into the biblical story by giving practical instruction to the young (and all others listening in) in order to help them follow in the ways of the Lord and have a beneficial, fruitful life on earth.

Ecclesiastes

ORIENTING DATA FOR ECCLESIASTES

- **Content:** the ponderings of a Wisdom teacher who wrestles with life's realities; what is to be gained by achieving wealth or wisdom when in the end death claims both rich and poor, wise and foolish; but specially set in a context of knowing the fear of God
- **Date of composition:** unknown; scholarly guesses cover a broad range
- **Emphases:** the transitory nature of present life; how to live wisely in a world where the only certainty is death and judgment; the futility of human pursuits that do not take the fear of God into account

OVERVIEW OF ECCLESIASTES

Ecclesiastes comes to us from an editor (12:9–14) who has compiled the teachings and proverbs of an Israelite king who calls himself Qohelet ("assembler"), a title that alludes to his role as a teacher of wisdom in an assembly—presumably of God's people (12:9). A prologue (1:1–11) sets forth the basic concern that drives Qohelet's whole enterprise, namely, the *hebel* (= "breath," "vapor"; NIV, "meaningless") nature of human life in a world that continues as it was before and after anyone's own life span. The book concludes with the words of the editor-compiler, who encourages contemplation of Qohelet's words as goads for the young, but also warns that there is a proper limit to such speculation (12:12)—and in the end he makes sure that all is placed within the ultimate setting of biblical wisdom: Fearing God by keeping his commandments gives meaning to human life.

The words of Qohelet himself are enclosed (1:2; 12:8) by the melancholy refrain: *Hebel, hebel!* says Qohelet; *Hebel* of *hebel!* Everything is *hebel.* The rest is an inquiry into how one should live in such a world, since reality isn't as neat as some expressions of traditional wisdom might lead one to think. And the structure of the book mirrors its content, for there is no immediately apparent order to it. What the author does is to play and replay certain themes, all the while moving toward his concluding advice to the young (11:9–12:7): to enjoy life while they are young, but to do so remembering their Creator. If Qohelet's material can be divided into coherent subdivisions at all, they would seem to be 1:12–6:12 and 7:1–12:7, the first playing and replaying Qohelet's primary concerns, the second, while keeping these themes alive, sounding much more like proverbial wisdom.

SPECIFIC ADVICE FOR READING ECCLESIASTES

Traditionally, no other book in the Bible has been such a difficult read. This is because of (1) the somewhat rambling nature of many of Qohelet's observations—at least to the Western mind—(2) some strikingly antithetical statements existing together in the same book, and (3) the negative side of some of these statements, which seem so contradictory to the rest of the Bible. But if you try to read the book from the editor-compiler's perspective—that of a teacher of wisdom who, living before the full revelation of resurrection, recognized the value of Qohelet's assertion that life in the present world doesn't always add up—then you will be able to see that the final message of the book is not at all the hedonist or fatalist tract that some have made it out to be. Crucial to understanding this is to appreciate Qohelet's own context(s).

First, whatever else, Qohelet was written within Israel's Wisdom tradition (see the introduction to the Writings, p. 120), a tradition that was not trying to speak for God in the same way the prophets did, but one that was musing carefully on life in order to teach the young how to live well before God. And somewhat like the author of Job, but in contrast to the way some might mechanistically apply the book of Proverbs, Qohelet is convinced that the ways of the Creator are past finding out. Although he maintains a sturdy trust in God throughout (2:24; 3:11–14; 5:7b, 19; 9:7) and believes God to be just (3:17; 8:12–13), he nonetheless finds the real world not nearly as predictable as, for example, Job's "comforters" do, who see a sure cause and effect to everything and thus represent a kind of "wisdom" that Qohelet is likewise reacting strongly against.

Four realities dominate Qohelet's overall perspective: (1) God is the single indisputable reality, the Creator of all and the one from whom all life comes as gift (e.g., 3:12–14), including its—for Qohelet—usually burdensome nature. (2) God's ways are not always, if ever, understandable (3:11; 8:17). (3) On the human side, what is "done under the sun" (2:17) simply is not tidy; indeed, much of it doesn't add up right at all. The way things should be (the righteous get the good, the wicked get the bad) is not in fact the way things are—at least not consistently in this present life. (4) The great equalizer is death, which happens to rich and poor, wise and foolish alike. Given Qohelet's lack of hope in a resurrection, then once you're dead that's it—without memory, forgotten, no matter what your life may once have meant (9:5–6). And it is this reality that makes life seem *hebel* (a word that occurs thirty-seven times, just over half of its seventy-three OT occurrences).

At issue is what this word means for Qohelet, since it literally means "wisp of air" or "vapor." Most of the time he uses it as a metaphor for the nature of human existence. But what metaphorical freight does it carry? A tradition that goes back to the Septuagint translates it "emptiness" (cf. the KJV, "vanity," that is, "in vain"), pointing to the "vaporous" nature of our human lives (along with its companion, "chasing after the wind"). Another tradition, followed by the NIV, goes for "meaningless." While either of these work fine in some instances, they do not help in others. In most cases the sense seems to be the passing/transitory or unsubstantial nature of things, like vapor itself. This seems especially to be its sense in the prologue, where human life, in contrast to the constancy and "oldness" of the world, e*vapor*ates very quickly. Moreover, the "vapor" that is our life is also elusive, lying outside our own control; it is like "chasing after the wind" (an ironic play on *hebel* = "wisp of air").

So what should one make of such a "vapor," these "few and *hebel* days" we pass through like a shadow (6:12; cf. 2:3; 5:18), especially in light of life's inequalities and, for the one who lives apart from God ("the fool"), its utter meaninglessness? Qohelet's answer is not, as some have accused him, "milk it for all you can, because you only go around once" (a misunderstanding of his repetition of the "eat and drink" theme, 2:24; 3:13; 5:18; 8:15; 9:7). Rather, his point seems to be that, even if one knows so little except the certainty of the grave, one should live life, *hebel* as it usually is, as a gift from God. This is because, in the end, joy and pleasure come not in "getting" (securing "profit" from what one does)—because that will evaporate—but in the journey itself, the life God has given. Death comes to all alike, but not all live alike; in such a world, joy and satisfaction are to be found in living the rhythms of life without trying to be in control or to "make gain" of what is itself merely transitory.

Even read from this perspective, Qohelet's wisdom is not altogether comforting. But overall it is an orthodox book. If one misses any mention of the great events of Jewish history, that is quite in keeping with the Wisdom tradition, and if one feels squeamish about great but contradictory realities being set side by side, that is probably because we too, like Job's "comforters," prefer things to be tidier than they are. But in the end even Qohelet does not leave the young dangling. One way is clearly to be preferred to the other, and the so-called contradictions serve to highlight that fact. The Christian believer, who now reads from the perspective of joyous hope in the resurrection and the certainty of divine judgment, should all the more be prepared to appreciate Qohelet's embracing of life in the present, despite its *hebel* nature.

A WALK THROUGH ECCLESIASTES

☐ 1:1–11 *Introduction to the Theme*

After the heading, where Qohelet is identified as a Davidic king (yet purposely not named), verses 2–11 introduce the main themes of the book: Everything is like a vapor; nothing human is permanent or new. The basic question to be answered comes up front (v. 3): What, then, is the profit of human toil? The reason for this is verse 4: Human beings come and go, but the earth is permanent—which is then illustrated in several ways (vv. 5–7), before concluding on the note of human finitude in the face of the massive reality of history (vv. 8–11).

☐ 1:12–2:26 *Various Ways of Trying to Gain from Labor*

From the perspective of his role as king (who should have profited most in life), Qohelet picks up the question from verse 3 about "gain/profit" from human toil. He starts with his special concern, namely, wisdom (1:12–18). Useful as it is, it only brings more sorrow, because one now understands the *hebel* nature of things. He then moves to the pursuit of pleasure (2:1–3) and the accumulation of wealth and possessions (2:4–11), but these too are ephemeral, and thus of no gain, since the same fate—death—overtakes all (2:12–16). The fact that one's gain must be left to someone else spoils everything (2:17–23)—unless one is prepared to make some adjustments, namely, to enjoy the gift of life as from God rather than to use it to make gain (2:24–26).

□ 3:1–22 *A Time for Everything*

Qohelet now lyrically describes the nature of the reality that his reader should appreciate: The world God has made has its rhythms and seasons (vv. 1–8) that put it outside the reach of profit (v. 9), but bring joy when one adjusts to it (vv. 10–22). Note Qohelet's insistence that this is a gift from God (vv. 11–14) and that he takes this position even though he lives in a world that has no certainty about the future of the individual (v. 21). At the same time, he returns to earlier themes (human wickedness; death as the great leveler).

□ 4:1–16 *Success, Oppression, and Solitariness*

Picking up the theme of wickedness (3:16–17), Qohelet notes that the desire for gain results in oppression of others, which is such a sorry sight for him that nonexistence would actually be better (4:1–3); labor and achievement (success), he goes on, spring from envy (vv. 4–6). Such striving is antineighbor and thus lonely (vv. 7–8); the better alternative is to live in community (vv. 9–12). Using an illustration from kingship (vv. 13–16), he concludes that poverty with wisdom is better than success with folly: The youthful "successor" to an old king eventually suffers the same fate as the one he succeeded.

□ 5:1–7 *On Approaching God*

Qohelet breaks into his litany against gain and oppression by urging a proper stance toward the worship of God—being a listener whose speech is brief and correct, as one who stands in awe of God.

□ 5:8–6:12 *Wealth and Oppression*

Returning to the theme of oppression and the quest for and hoarding of wealth, Qohelet focuses now on the love of money itself (5:8–13); in the same vein, he ponders wealth that is lost through misfortune, thus leaving no inheritance (5:14–17; cf. 1 Tim 6:6–10, where Paul reflects on this passage), before returning again to God-given contentment (Eccl 5:18–20). Then, typically, Qohelet acknowledges how few have received this gift (6:1–2), the example of which—in that culture—is the enormously blessed man who does not receive proper burial (6:3–6), the madness of which is summed up in verse 7. The first half of the book is then summarized in 6:8–12.

☐ 7:1–29 *The Advantage of Wisdom*

In 12:9 Qohelet is called a collector of proverbs; here at last is such a collection—of "better than" proverbs that echo previous concerns. Note how he steers a middle path regarding wisdom, neither idolizing nor hating it, but living in full light of it, since even in our transient existence, wisdom is better than folly—and this includes embracing the reality of death (vv. 2–4). At the heart of things is the contentment argued for earlier (vv. 7–24). But even if wisdom per se is still elusive (vv. 23–25), some wise things can be learned, such as the need to avoid the woman who sets a snare (v. 26; cf. Prov 2:16–19; 5:1–23) and the reality that human beings have gone astray, despite how they were created (vv. 27–29).

☐ 8:1–17 *Dealing with an Unjust World*

Note how Qohelet "explains" the question of verse 1 as referring to the wise man in the king's court (vv. 2–6), who will withdraw rather than confront the king. This observation is then applied to the wise person, who cannot change things as they are (vv. 7–8). In verses 9–15, he returns to the theme of wickedness and injustice, insisting that it is better to fear God and enjoy the life he has given, but concluding on the enigma of life (vv. 16–17).

☐ 9:1–12 *Living in the Face of Death*

Note how many previous themes are picked up once again: the certainty of death for all (vv. 1–6); that meaning lies in enjoying whatever life God has given (vv. 7–10), even though the outcome is unpredictable and often unpleasant (vv. 11–12).

☐ 9:13–10:20 *The Way of Wisdom*

Here Qohelet once more ponders the advantages of the way of wisdom over against folly; note especially the repetition of "better than" in 9:13–18, while most of chapter 10 reaffirms this with a collection of proverbial material, especially on how to survive bad government.

□ 11:1–8 *On Not Understanding the Ways of God*

Once more Qohelet returns to a former theme, this time emphasizing our lack of control of the times, based on our limited understanding (vv. 1–6), and concluding on the reality of life as bittersweet (vv. 7–8).

□ 11:9–12:8 *A Final Word to the Young*

Having repeatedly advocated the enjoyment of this brief life to the extent possible and while it lasts, Qohelet concludes by focusing on the young man (the wise man's son, 12:12). The brevity of youth gives him an even shorter time in which to make the most of his opportunities. He is thus urged to live life to the full (11:9–10) in light of the slow but steady intrusion of death into life as people age (12:1–7). This is what it means to "remember your Creator" (12:1, 6). Note how verse 8 serves to enclose the whole book (1:2): Life is transitory and elusive.

□ 12:9–14 *Epilogue: Qohelet As a Wise Man*

The compiler, whose voice was heard previously in 1:1–2 and 7:27, now adds an epilogue, highlighting the value of Qohelet's arguments but summarizing his own orthodox perspective in verses 13–14 (cf. Qohelet's in 8:12–13). Qohelet's musings are quite true; life's emptiness *without* the fear of God and keeping his commandments should impel the truly wise to think on these "just the right words" (12:10).

The book of Ecclesiastes fits into the biblical story as a constant reminder of the brevity of human life in light of eternity, emphasizing our need to fear God while also paving the way for the greater revelation of our certain resurrection through Jesus Christ.

Song of Songs

ORIENTING DATA FOR SONG OF SONGS

- **Content:** a love poem of several episodes, celebrating the sexual love between a woman and a man
- **Date of composition:** unknown; scholarly guesses cover a broad range
- **Emphases:** the proper love of a woman and a man for one another; the unquenchable nature of pure love; the delight in and longing for each other that pure love engenders

OVERVIEW OF SONG OF SONGS

Song of Songs is a unique biblical book. Without mention of God and written in marvelous poetry, full of evocative and vivid images, it is a celebration of sexual love—and marital fidelity—between a woman and a man. Although it may have originated as several separate love poems, its title, Song of Songs (singular), indicates that in its canonical form it is intended to be read as several episodes/scenes of one poem, thus a "narrative" only in the sense that such poetry is trying to create a picture.

SPECIFIC ADVICE FOR READING SONG OF SONGS

Crucial for a good reading of the Song is to recognize that it comes to us basically in three voices: the woman, who plays the leading role throughout; the man, who especially celebrates the beauty of, and his love for, the woman; and the woman's companions, called the "daughters of Jerusalem." (The NIV headings "Lover" [the man], "Beloved" [the woman], and "Friends" [the woman's companions] are not in the Hebrew text; they are an attempt to help you see when there is a change of speakers.) Other characters are present basically as helpful props (the shepherds, 1:7–8; the city watchmen, 3:3; 5:7; the woman's brothers, 1:6; 8:8–9).

What is most difficult to determine is the role of Solomon. While it is possible to read 3:6–11 as suggesting that the man in the poem is Solomon himself and that this paragraph presents him as the bridegroom, it is not necessary to hold this view to appreciate the message of the Song. Indeed, there is little else that supports such a view, other than the possibility that "Shulammite," the woman's title in 6:13, means something like "Mrs. Solomon." The superscription (1:1) is quite ambiguous in Hebrew, since the preposition *l*[e] could be either possessive (as NIV) or a form of dedication to Solomon as the original commissioner of the Song for one of his weddings—but with the intention that it could be used to encourage pure love in any marriage. At the same time 3:6–11 is unique to the poem—a third-person description of a named person—and the allusion to his harem in 6:8 and 8:11–12 looks like an intentional contrast between Solomon's "vineyard" being let out to tenants (8:11) while the woman's "vineyard" is her own to give (8:12).

This ambiguity has created several different readings of the text; the one offered here assumes an intended contrast, suggesting that the Song was never intended to apply only to Solomon, but to make every married couple who share pure love each other's "king" and "queen." That is, the "Lover" in most of the Song is not specifically Solomon, who as an oriental king might not invite love but take it as the privilege of position—and it is harder to imagine the primary role of the woman as taking place if she were part of his harem. On the other hand, such factors as the explicit association with Solomon and the proverbial nature of the conclusion (8:6–7) brought about its inclusion in the Jewish Wisdom tradition.

The constant shift of speakers and the richness of the poetry can make the structure difficult to discern. The clues seem to lie with some repeated refrains that conclude several of the scenes (e.g., the charge to the daughters of Jerusalem, 2:7; 3:5; 8:4). The poetry itself is full of rich and powerful images intended to evoke the imagination. They cover a large range of human activity—the world of nature (gardens, mountains, forests, animals, plants, spices, etc.), architecture (towers, walls, cities, etc.), clothing/jewelry, and warfare. The woman, whose body and love are described three times as the lover speaks to her (4:1–15; 6:4–7; 7:1–9), is especially seen in terms of a garden and vineyard full of precious spices and wine for the man's pleasure. The man's body is described but once—by the woman to the daughters of Jerusalem—with a whole range of images (5:10–16).

The forthrightness and evocative nature of these descriptions has historically been a point of difficulty for many, especially male readers/interpreters, both Jewish and Christian. The result has usually been to allegorize it—so much so that an early church council (A.D. 550) forbade any interpretation that was not allegorical! But such a reading seems to be a capitulation to human fallenness and to the way sexual love has often been twisted so as to become exploitative, manipulative, and destructive—up to the present day. This poem should be read in light of Genesis 1 and 2. Following the command to "be fruitful and increase in number" (Gen 1:28), God plants a *garden* (2:8) in which he placed the man and woman he created in his own image. The narrative concludes with the words: "A man will ... be united to his wife, and they will become one flesh. The man and his wife were both naked, and *they felt no shame*" (2:24–25, emphasis added). The picture of sexual love in this book recaptures that scene, where the woman and the man take utter delight and pleasure in each other's bodies and do so without shame. This is thus God's way of recapturing both the fidelity and the unity and intimacy of marriage, which the enemy has tried to take away from God's people by making it seem either titillating outside of marriage or something shameful and unmentionable within marriage. This inspired author has a different view.

A WALK THROUGH SONG OF SONGS

□ 1:1–6 *The Lovers Presented*

Note that, typical within the book, the woman takes the lead role, so that in this opening scene where each is introduced, she sets the stage for the rest—her desire for and delight in him, with an invitation to be taken away by him. If "the king" is literal, then Solomon is intended; otherwise it is a metaphor, using royal imagery to evoke love's grandeur.

□ 1:7–2:7 *First Scene: The Lovers Together*

As you read this first scene, note that verse 8 could just as easily be the man's own response to the beloved's question. That would mean that the whole scene is an exchange between the two lovers. She first searches for him among the shepherds (vv. 7–8), followed by an interchange of description (vv. 9–11, 12–14) and of delight in each other (vv. 15–16), before turning to a description of the scene of love (v. 17, a forest). She then evokes the imagery of flowers (2:1–2), while he is an "apple tree" in whose shade she rests and whose fruit she enjoys (vv. 3–6). Her last words are to the daughters of Jerusalem to let love take its own course (v. 7).

☐ 2:8–3:5 *Second Scene: Hope, Invitation, and Dream*

This scene is characterized by longing; he is a gazelle leaping across mountains, then gazing through the window (2:8–9). She then recites his words of invitation—it's spring, the time for love (vv. 10–13). He calls her out of hiding (vv. 14–15) and for the "foxes" (those who would oppose their love) to be caught so as not to ruin the "vineyards" (their bodies; cf. 1:6, 14) that are in bloom. With the total mutuality and exclusive fidelity of love (2:16), her lover then "browses among the lilies," but is (apparently) sent away at the close of day (v. 17). That leads to what is probably a dream scene (3:1–4) in which she seeks and finds her lover, concluding again with the admonition to the daughters of Jerusalem (v. 5). Note also the minor, passive role of the watchmen.

☐ 3:6–11 *Solomon's Wealth and Extravagance*

This enigmatic section may be intended to provide contrast to the woman's lover, since the descriptions of him thus far have been from nature, not from pomp and circumstance; otherwise Solomon is the lover and the section introduces their lovemaking in the next scene. Note that it is the only thing that borders on narration in the entire poem, and the picture educed is one of wealth, power, and opulence (thus echoing 1 Kgs 10:14–11:6).

☐ 4:1–5:1 *Third Scene: Admiration and Invitation*

This is the first scene in which the man takes the lead. He begins with a description of the beloved's body from head to breasts (4:1–5). Picking up her language from 2:17, he will go to the mountain of myrrh (vv. 6–7, echoing 1:13). He then describes her as a lover, a garden of delights and spices (vv. 8–15). Her response is to invite the winds to enhance her fragrance and thus to invite him into the garden (v. 16), to which his response after love (5:1) echoes language from the preceding description (myrrh and spice [4:14], honeycomb and honey [4:11], wine [4:10] and milk [4:11]). To this the daughters of Jerusalem respond by encouraging them to eat and drink their fill (5:1c).

☐ 5:2–6:3 *Fourth Scene: Dream and Search*

The woman is again in the lead. In what appears to be another dream scene, her lover comes and beckons her and then disappears (5:2–6); again she searches for him, but this time the watchmen abuse her (v. 7). In response to the short dialogue with the daughters of Jerusalem (vv. 8–9), she gives her only description of him (vv. 10–16), moving from head to legs, but concluding, as at the beginning (1:2) by recalling his kisses. To their second question (6:1), she answers first (v. 2) by echoing language from the preceding love scene and then (v. 3) by repeating the word of mutuality and exclusive fidelity (cf. 2:16).

☐ 6:4–8:4 *Fifth Scene: The Delights of Love*

Note that in this scene the man and woman both speak at length. The scene begins with him in the lead, describing the beauty of her head (6:4–7)—in contrast to the king's wives and concubines (vv. 8–9b), who also admire her (vv. 9c–10). After an interchange with them (vv. 11–13), he then launches into his final description of her body, this time from feet to hair (7:1–6), before returning to her breasts and mouth (vv. 7–9a). She then picks up the imagery of her mouth as wine, urging that it go straight to him who desires her, with further invitation to lovemaking (vv. 9b–13). Her love for him is such that she would gladly express it in public, against all cultural norms (8:1–2a); her desire again echoes previous language (vv. 2b–3) before she concludes with the refrain to the daughters of Jerusalem (v. 4).

☐ 8:5–14 *Conclusion(s): Love Strong As Death*

The poem concludes with a series of brief sketches that suggest the unquenchable nature of their love (8:5–7), despite opposition (vv. 8–9, 10–12), concluding with their final interchange of invitation (vv. 13–14).

Song of Songs fits into God's story as a reminder that the sexual love he created is good and should be embraced with godly fidelity and delight.

Lamentations

ORIENTING DATA FOR LAMENTATIONS

- **Content:** a series of five laments over the fall of Jerusalem
- **Date of composition:** unknown, probably soon after the fall of Jerusalem (586 B.C.)
- **Emphases:** the deep personal suffering and spiritual agony experienced at the fall of Jerusalem; the justice of God in carrying out the overthrow of Zion; hope lies finally in God's character alone

OVERVIEW OF LAMENTATIONS

Lamentations consists of five laments written in response to the fall of Jerusalem in 586 B.C. The laments, which correspond to the five chapters, are carefully composed pieces of literature, similar in form and content to Psalms 74 and 79 (cf. Ps 89). Together they express deep anguish over Zion's desolation and Israel's exile—recognized to be well deserved—and mourn the sorry plight of those who were left in the now desolate and dangerous city, while raising some larger questions about justice and the future. The whole is written basically from the perspective of those who have been left behind.

At least three voices can be identified: the narrator-author, Zion (personified Jerusalem), and the people of Zion (Yahweh himself never speaks). In the first two (closely related) poems, the narrator and Zion are the speakers; they mourn over the fall of the city itself, recognizing that it happened because of her sins, so that Yahweh himself had become her enemy. In the final two (again closely related) poems, the speakers are the narrator and the people of Zion, who agonize for the people in occupied Jerusalem. In the central poem (ch. 3) Jerusalem is essentially personified, that is, the only identifiable speaker is the author, whose personal agony is so closely tied to that of Jerusalem that in various ways they become one; here you also find the single expression of hope, as well as a brief discussion of the meaning of suffering.

SPECIFIC ADVICE FOR READING LAMENTATIONS

In order to read Lamentations well, you need to be aware of its basic literary features, as well as its historical background and theological perspective. The most striking literary feature of these poems is that they are a series of acrostics (cf. Pss 34; 119), where the first letter of each verse starts with a succeeding letter of the (twenty-two-letter) Hebrew alphabet. The first two poems thus have twenty-two stanzas of three lines each, the first line in each case being the acrostic. The third poem also has twenty-two stanzas, but in this case all three lines in each stanza begin with the same letter. The fourth poem returns to the form of the first two, but now with stanzas of two lines each, while the fifth, although not an acrostic, is nonetheless composed of twenty-two lines. Thus the pattern builds to the agonizing climactic descriptions of chapter 3, then diminishes somewhat in chapter 4, and ends with a whimper in chapter 5, a pattern that mirrors the city's destruction and its aftermath. While not all these features can be carried over into English, the acrostic pattern does affect verse numbering (22, 22, 66, 22, 22) and to some degree explains why these poems contain some abrupt shifts of topic (the alphabet often controls what may be said at any point). But throughout the whole, the lament form itself (see *How to 1*, pp. 212, 215–218) implicitly encourages hope—though nothing is guaranteed—in the midst of suffering.

As to its historical and theological perspective, it is hard for us at our point in history to appreciate the utter devastation of the fall of Jerusalem for the people of Judah. First, there was the terrible suffering of the historical event itself, narrated in 2 Kings 25. The siege lasted for two years, as tens of thousands huddled in Jerusalem, hoping that Yahweh would intervene. Instead, the Babylonian troops finally breached her walls, raped her women, and slaughtered many of her inhabitants. In light of subsequent conditions in Jerusalem, our author wonders rhetorically whether death might not have been the better option. All of these horrible realities—famine, thirst, cannibalism, rape, slaughter—are echoed in these poems.

But beyond that there was the larger question of Israel's calling and role as the people of God. Here was a people whose history was singularly bound up with the God who had redeemed them from slavery in Egypt, created them as a people for his Name, made covenant with them at Sinai, and eventually fulfilled his promise that Abraham's offspring would inherit the land. At the heart of their self-understanding was the fact that their God—who was God alone, the living God, and Creator of all that is—had chosen to dwell personally in their midst, first in the tabernacle in the desert and finally in the place he chose "as a dwelling for his Name" (Deut 12:11; Neh 1:9), Jerusalem itself. Thus both the land and the city held a significance for Israel in terms of identity unlike most other peoples in history. Indeed, because of this, many wrongly thought Zion inviolable (cf. Jer 7; 26; 28; Ezek 13–14). It is this total identification of the people with their city as God's own dwelling place that lies behind the utter anguish of these poems and that makes the appeals over the present plight of her people so poignant. And even though the author is fully aware that their punishment is just, his agonized descriptions indicate how hard it was to handle the reality and enormity of the desolation and suffering (e.g., Lam 2:20–22).

At the same time, however, the author wrestles with the issues also raised by Habakkuk and Obadiah, for example. What about Israel's enemies, who were equally deserving of God's anger? This is what lies behind the frequent imprecations (Lam 1:21–22; 3:61–66; 4:21–22). And in the end, even though Moses and the prophets foretold such disaster as a result of unfaithfulness to the covenant, our author struggles with it right up to the last words, where the promised future is only a distant shadow. But in the crucial central poem he also holds out the one all-important ray of hope—the character of Yahweh himself, who has revealed himself to Moses on Sinai as full of love and faithfulness (Exod 34:5–7; cf. the appeal in Ps 89).

A WALK THROUGH LAMENTATIONS

□ 1:1–22 *First Lament: Zion Laments over Her Destruction*

In the first part of this poem (vv. 1–11b), the narrator sets out the basic matters, which are repeated throughout: Zion and her temple have been laid waste, her people taken into exile; during the siege her friends deserted her, while her enemies mocked and her foes are now her masters. Those who remain, both priests and people, are in dire straits, the pilgrimage feasts a thing of the past; for them there is only weeping and groaning. And all of this is because of Judah's many sins.

Toward the end of this first part, Zion herself calls out to Yahweh to look on her affliction (v. 9c), which is then repeated at the beginning of her own lament (vv. 11c–22). Calling out to any "who pass by" (v. 12), she basically repeats the matters from verses 1–11, but now in more detail and with increased pain and distress, concluding with an imprecation against her enemies (vv. 21–22). Note especially the role that Yahweh played in her destruction; note also that her lament is momentarily relieved halfway through by the poet's own voice (v. 17).

☐ 2:1–22 *Second Lament: Zion's Lament and Appeal*

With still further intensification, the poet speaks again, spelling out in great detail the ultimate cause of Jerusalem's destruction, namely, Yahweh's anger. The Divine Warrior, who in the past had fought *for* Israel, had now become their enemy—city, land, leaders, and people alike (vv. 1–9). The poet then concentrates on those left behind (vv. 10–17). Note here how he speaks in the first person (vv. 11, 13), and finally calls on Zion herself to call out to Yahweh (vv. 18–19), which she does in the poignant words of verses 20–22, reminding Yahweh of both the famine and the subsequent slaughter (of priest and prophet, young and old together).

☐ 3:1–66 *Third Lament: Despair, Hope, and Imprecation*

In this central poem, the author makes Jerusalem's despair his own and vice versa (vv. 1–18, already alluded to in 2:11). What seems to be at issue here is that the fall of Jerusalem meant the suffering of many who were faithful to Yahweh and innocent of her corporate crimes, but who yet felt relentlessly pursued by Yahweh. In the end, his only hope lies in the covenant faithfulness of Yahweh, whose love and faithfulness (echoing the words of Exod 34:6) are new every morning (vv. 19–24). These then are followed by a kind of personal dialogue about the meaning of suffering and its relationship to Yahweh, concluding with a call to repentance (vv. 25–42). Note that at the end the lament is then renewed (vv. 43–51), focusing finally on his enemies who are responsible for his suffering (vv. 52–62) and concluding with an imprecation against them (vv. 63–66).

☐ 4:1–22 *Fourth Lament: Groping in the Streets*

With this lament the author turns his attention to the present horrible conditions in Jerusalem, comparing them with the years of the siege and offering his belief that the dead are the lucky ones (vv. 1–11). He then focuses on the plight—and guilt—of the prophets and priests (vv. 12–16). Note that verse 17 begins the lament of the people themselves, in this case looking back to the last bitter days of the siege (including the flight and capture of the king, Jer 52:7–11), while the author himself concludes with an imprecation against Edom (Lam 4:21–22).

☐ 5:1–22 *Fifth Lament: The Remnant of Zion Weeps*

In this final poem, only the people speak, calling out to Yahweh to look on their present affliction, reflecting especially that occupied Judah is an unhappy and dangerous place in which to live (vv. 1–18). The poem and book then conclude with a prayer for restoration, which begins with an affirmation of Yahweh's eternal reign but is concerned, in characteristic lament fashion, with whether or not they have been forgotten (vv. 19–22).

The book of Lamentations reflects a significant turning point in the biblical story—the fall of Jerusalem—thus reminding us that God is true to his word about standing in judgment against unfaithfulness, while still holding out hope for the future based on his character.

The Prophets of Israel in the Biblical Story

The next part of the biblical story comes in the form of sixteen books that we call the Prophets. In Jewish tradition they are known as the Latter Prophets and were usually counted as four books, in this order: Isaiah, Jeremiah, Ezekiel, and the Book of the Twelve (the so-called Minor Prophets; Lamentations and Daniel were included among the Writings). The prophetic tradition had a long history in Israel, going back as far as Moses and including Samuel. But those whose words were eventually written down in scrolls bearing their names flourished from the middle of the eighth century B.C. (ca. 760) until the middle of the fifth century B.C. (ca. 460).

The prophets have an especially crucial role to play in the "story of Israel" part of the grand story. Indeed, they cannot be properly understood apart from their function in relation to the Law and the Former Prophets (Joshua through 2 Kings). As God's appointed spokesmen, they call Yahweh's people back to their covenant roots, announcing both the curses and blessings for covenant disloyalty or loyalty (see esp. Deut 27–30). The exilic prophets also helped the people through their twofold loss—of the divine presence and of the promised land—thus playing the role of Moses and Joshua in reverse.

Thus the prophets constantly call God's people back to divine realities: They belong to God, God does not belong to them; God has called them into being for his purposes of redeeming what was lost in the Fall and of blessing the nations. At the heart of the prophets' message, therefore, is deep concern that Israel reflect God's character by walking in his ways and keeping covenant with him. At the same time, they are constantly reminded that Yahweh is not a local Israelite deity, but is the sovereign God of the universe—Creator and Sustainer of all things and therefore also sovereign over all the other nations.

The nations, accordingly, play a very important role in the prophets' part of the grand story. On the one hand, the nations are included in the Abrahamic promise (Gen 12:2–3), so Israel is often reminded of her failure to be God's "blessing" for them. This dimension of the promise is thus regularly seen as part of God's final fulfillment of his promises (see Isaiah in particular), a part of the tradition that becomes central to the New Testament. On the other hand, since the Abrahamic promise included God's "cursing" those who "curse you," the prophets also regularly pronounce God's judgment on the nations. Thus Israel is not alone in coming under God's righteous judgments—indeed, Obadiah and Nahum are exclusively oracles against the nations (Edom and Assyria, respectively).

Much of what is said as you are guided through these books presupposes chapter 10 in *How to 1* as to the nature and function of the prophetic oracles (lawsuit, woe, promise, etc.). But three matters raised there are especially crucial and need to be repeated here in order to help you make sense of these (sometimes difficult) books as you read them.

1. In much the same way as the New Testament Letters, these writings were addressing ad hoc situations; therefore some awareness of the social-religious-political situation into which they were speaking is essential in order for you to read well. So in the section on "Specific Advice," the nature of the specific situation for each prophet will be pointed out.

For now, recall the three important matters that apply across the board for this time in Israel's history: that it was a time of (1) significant political, military, economic, and social upheaval, (2) a very high level of unfaithfulness and disregard for the Mosaic covenant, and (3) enormous shifts in the balance(s) of power on the international scene.

It is especially important to note that all of these prophets spoke at a time when Israel had been permanently divided into north (Israel/Ephraim) and south (Judah). Most of them address Judah, some of them speak into the situation of the exile, and several of them speak after the exile when a small remnant had returned to their historic land. Because it will be useful for you to relate these books to the sections of 1–2 Kings and 1–2 Chronicles to which they correspond, the relevant passages will regularly be called to your attention.

2. As you read, you will want to be aware of the frequent tension that exists in the prophets between the near future and the ultimate future, since the final consummation of the biblical story often serves as the backdrop for what is said about the near future. Thus Haggai, for example, is speaking directly to the situation of the rebuilding of the temple after the return from exile. Yet in encouraging the people to return to this work, he speaks both of the greater future of the temple and of the near future of Zerubbabel as the Davidic heir. And so it is with most of these books in their final form.

3. It is important also for you to be reminded that most prophetic speech takes the form of poetry. Here it would benefit you greatly to read pages 197–99 in *How to 1,* as well as perhaps an entry on Hebrew poetry in a recent Bible dictionary, so that you can appreciate the kinds of parallelism involved. Also, because these books are poetry, you will want to pause at times to notice the powerful and evocative images and metaphors that the prophets regularly use to capture the people's attention.

Here is God speaking in ways that are loud and clear (the latter more so than some are apt to think!). As you read, be aware not only of what God was saying to the people of the prophets' times but also of how much it is equally relevant to our own times and history. (Had Amos, you may find yourself asking, been reading the *New York Times*?)

Isaiah

ORIENTING DATA FOR ISAIAH

- **Content:** Yahweh's sovereign majesty and redemptive love, revealed in his dealings with his chosen people the Israelites, who are destined for both judgment and salvation, in which the nations will also be included
- **Prophet:** Isaiah of Jerusalem
- **Date of prophetic activity:** from about 740 to 687 B.C. (see 1:1)
- **Emphases:** the holiness, majesty, and righteousness of Yahweh; the compassion and saving mercy of Yahweh; the central role of Israel in Yahweh's plans for the nations and the world; the central role of Zion in these plans; the redemptive role of God's suffering servant; the glorious final future God has in store for those who are his

OVERVIEW OF ISAIAH

The book of Isaiah in many ways is the centerpiece of the story of Israel in the biblical story. Standing at the beginning of the Latter Prophets, even though not first chronologically, it serves to guide your reading of the rest of this tradition. But beyond that, its theological scope is all-embracing, constantly reminding Israel that Yahweh is the living God, the Creator and majestic Sovereign—and Judge—of all that is, as well as the compassionate Redeemer of Israel. Thus Isaiah looks forward to Israel's judgment, to her redemption from exile through a second exodus, and, through her coming Servant King, to the fulfillment of the Abrahamic covenant that includes the nations in Yahweh's salvation. And in the end it pictures the final redemption of Israel and the nations in a new heaven and new earth, when Zion, the place where Yahweh and people meet, is restored to its ultimate glory. Isaiah, therefore, had enormous influence on the New Testament writers, being cited or alluded to more often than any other Old Testament book except the Psalter.

The book itself presents this glorious panorama as a carefully crafted whole, which comes in two basic parts: Chapters 1–39 deal primarily with Jerusalem during the period of the Assyrian threat, but at the end Isaiah prophesies the future threat of exile in Babylon. Chapters 40–66 focus on the future of Israel and Jerusalem toward the end of the Babylonian captivity and beyond, climaxing with the hope of a new heaven and new earth and a final eschatological Zion.

Each of these parts has its own structures and rhythms. Chapters 1–5 introduce the major concerns of part 1—that Judah and Zion have failed in their calling to be Yahweh's people for him and the nations, so they must be judged (while 2:1–5 looks forward to the fulfillment of that calling). The failure is threefold: (1) lack of trust in Yahweh, which is expressed in (2) their constant flirtation with idols and (3) their lack of social justice. Isaiah's call (ch. 6) introduces the rest of part 1. His vision of the "Holy One of Israel" leads to his own cleansing and his commission to announce God's judgment on a people who are exactly like their idols—they have ears that do not hear and eyes that do not see. The rest of part 1 is framed by two sets of narratives (chs. 7–9; 36–39), one at the beginning (with Ahaz) and one at the end (with Hezekiah) of Isaiah's long career—both are during outside threats and both mention the same piece of geography (7:3; 36:2). In both cases at issue is trust in Yahweh: Ahaz does not, Hezekiah does. But Hezekiah then shows lack of trust with regard to envoys from Babylon, which leads to the second part of the book. Much of the inner frame of part 1 is a series of oracles against the nations, including nations on whom Israel has leaned for support rather than trusting Yahweh.

Part 2 is basically in two parts, each of which is also in two parts. Chapters 40–55 move the story ahead to a time toward the end of the Babylonian exile; chapters 40–48 are both consolation and confrontation—the latter to a people who are settled in Babylon and of no mind to take part in the new exodus—while chapters 49–55 reflect that the (now postponed) new exodus will finally be brought about by Yahweh's servant, who will thereby also gather the nations. Chapters 56–66 reflect the continuing failure of Israel (chs. 56–59), but then speak to the grand future that God has for his people and for the nations (chs. 60–66).

SPECIFIC ADVICE FOR READING ISAIAH

To read Isaiah well, you need to have some sense of the history it reflects, as well as of the theological concerns that energize the book from beginning to end.

The *history* reflected in chapters 1–39 is dominated by the role of Assyria on the international scene. Isaiah's call comes in the last year of Uzziah's long reign in Jerusalem (792–740 B.C.; see 2 Kgs 15:1–7), which had been a time of Assyrian decline and thus of relative peace in Judah and Israel. But by the time of Uzziah's death, Assyria had reasserted her power in the Near Eastern world through a new series of kings (Tiglath-Pileser III [744–727], Shalmaneser V [726–722], Sargon II [721–705], and Sennacherib [704–681]). Much of the political intrigue in Samaria and Jerusalem had to do with Israelite and Judean kings paying or withholding tribute to Assyria. It is these intrigues that lie behind the two sets of narratives in Isaiah 7–9 and 36–39. In each case Isaiah announces the deliverance of Zion, but he also foretells the exile to Babylon (39:5–7).

The siege and fall of Jerusalem and the twofold exile to Babylon is the story of Jeremiah and Ezekiel. The historical setting envisioned in Isaiah 40–55 is the later part of this exile, that is, the time after the message of Jeremiah and Ezekiel has been heeded and the exiles have settled into a new life in Babylon. The whole of this section of Isaiah is dominated by the expectation of a new exodus—from exile, across the desert with promises of water and safe passage back to Zion, the place where Yahweh will reestablish his dwelling. But the exiles will not receive this message of consolation—they cannot believe that Yahweh will use the Persian Cyrus to accomplish his purposes—and so the second exodus becomes part of a more distant future.

The *theological passions* of Isaiah find their focus at four points: (1) Yahweh as the "Holy One of Israel" (a term found thirty times in Isaiah and only six times in the rest of the OT); (2) Israel as Yahweh's "Holy People" (62:12); (3) Zion (Jerusalem) as God's "holy city" (48:2) and "holy mountain" (11:9; 27:13); and (4) the inclusion of the nations (Gentiles) in his people (2:2; 52:15).

Yahweh as the "Holy One of Israel" lies at the heart of everything—Isaiah's vision (ch. 6), Yahweh's justice and judgments (5:19–25), and Yahweh's mercy and compassion as Israel's Redeemer (41:14; 43:3–15; 62:12). Thus in Isaiah the term *holy* carries both of its essential characteristics: (1) Yahweh's absolute "otherness"—the Creator and Sustainer of all things and all nations, the one who has no rivals, since no other gods exist. You will not be able to miss this theme as you read, especially when it takes the form of scathing rebuke on the "lifeless" nature of such idols, who have eyes that cannot see and ears that cannot hear (see esp. 44:6–20). (2) Yahweh's absolute holiness in the moral/ethical sense. As a holy God, he requires holiness of his people—they are to bear his likeness (compassion, love, goodness, faithfulness) rather than that of their idols. After all, idolatry inevitably leads to injustice: The lifeless gods are unjust; their worshipers become like them.

At the center of Isaiah's story is Israel, redeemed but wayward, stubborn but loved, and it is Yahweh's relationship with them, told over and over again by pointing back to the exodus and the Davidic covenant, that reveals his mercy and compassion. Judge them he must, but give them up he will not—and it is here that the theme of Yahweh's saving a "remnant" belongs to the story. The story of this redemption thus climaxes with a servant Messiah who will redeem both Israel and the nations by dying for them—a story that finds its fulfillment in Jesus Christ and the cross.

The essential symbol of the relationship between Yahweh and his people is his presence with them in Jerusalem on Mount Zion. Here is where Israel has desecrated the relationship (1:10–25), yet here also is where Yahweh plans to restore the relationship (1:26–31) so that the nations will join them in worship on Zion (2:1–5). Thus the book begins with a desecrated Zion that is promised to be restored, and it ends (chs. 65–66) with the promised final expression of the Holy City and its Holy People, which includes the Gentiles.

There is much else that makes up this marvelous telling of the biblical story, but watching for these several themes, as well as being sensitive to the powerful imagery and cadences of the poetry, should help you catch something of the book's splendor, as well as its important place in the biblical story.

A WALK THROUGH ISAIAH

Yahweh's Complaint with Judah, and Isaiah's Call (chs. 1–6)

☐ 1:1–2:5 *Introduction: The Corruption and Future of the Holy People and Holy Place*

This section introduces both chapters 1–5 and the whole book; be watching for the pervading themes. Here Yahweh's complaint takes the form of a lawsuit against Jerusalem's ongoing *rebellion* against *the Holy*

One of Israel that has brought on his *judgment* (vv. 2–9, 24–25); their *religion* is useless (vv. 10–15d) because of their sins—*social injustice* (vv. 15e–17; cf. Amos) and *idolatry* (v.29)—but there is also the offer of *mercy* (vv. 18–20) and a bright *future* (vv. 26–28). In 2:1–4 Yahweh makes plain his commitment to redeem his creation, with Mount Zion functioning as the new Mount Sinai to which all *the nations* come (thus fulfilling Israel's true purposes in keeping with his covenant with Abraham). Note how the section ends with an invitation to Israel to thus walk in the light of Yahweh.

☐ **2:6–5:30** ***The Coming Day of the Lord***

In the first oracle (2:6–22) the key issues are arrogant trust in idols and lack of trust in Yahweh; also watch for some repeated themes that give power to the poetry. The coming disaster prophesied in 3:1–4:1 is directed especially at the leaders, and again the issue is *social justice*—the wealthy abusing the poor and the land (including the graphic portrayal in 3:16–4:1). But after disaster there is *hope* (4:2–6), the first expression of "second exodus" themes in Isaiah. Likewise, the song of the vineyard (5:1–7; picked up in Jer 12:10; Ezek 19:10–14; and by Jesus [Mark 12:1–12; John 15:1–8]) focuses on social injustice (Isa 5:7), as do the six woes that follow (vv. 8–25); hence, instead of the nations now coming to worship on Zion (2:2–4), they are summoned to destroy it (5:26–30).

☐ **6:1–13** ***Isaiah's Vision and Commission***

Uzziah has died (symbolic of what is happening to the Davidic dynasty). In the temple, the place of Yahweh's presence, Isaiah sees a vision of Israel's true King, the Holy One of Israel. Crushed because of his own and his people's uncleanness, Isaiah is pardoned and then commissioned to pronounce God's judgments on a people who have become like the idols they worship, that is, neither seeing nor hearing.

A Crisis of Trust: Ahaz and the Syro-Ephraimite Coalition (chs. 7–12)

At issue in chapters 7–39 is whether or not Jerusalem, represented by her king, will trust in Yahweh or in entangling alliances (a form of idolatry). Note that the narratives about Ahaz's (7:1–8:10) and Hezekiah's (ch. 39) failures to trust Yahweh bookend this larger section. And this is why there must be a future faithful king for Judah and the nations (9:1–7; 12:1–6; and throughout the oracles against the nations).

☐ 7:1–8:22 *Failed Kingship in Judah*

Watch how this opening narrative reveals Ahaz's wavering before a Syro-Ephraimite coalition. The names of Isaiah's two sons reflect Yahweh's response to Ahaz—the threat of Israel's being *plundered* (Maher-Shalal-Hash-Baz) and the mere *remnant* that will remain of the northern alliance after Yahweh judges them (Shear-Jashub)—while Immanuel, Yahweh's "sign" to Ahaz, reminds him of Yahweh's own presence in Zion (in this case, probably as a threat). Yahweh's word to Isaiah and Isaiah's response (8:11–22) indicate the issue at hand—trust in Yahweh.

☐ 9:1–12:6 *Future Kingship in Judah*

Central here is kingship in Israel. So note how Ahaz's failure to trust Yahweh is responded to by the announcement of a coming great Davidic king (9:1–7; 11:1–16). Together these oracles bookend (1) the announced fall of Samaria (9:8–10:4, who sided with Damascus against Judah), (2) the punishment of her destroyer, Assyria (10:5–19), and (3) the preservation of Judah (10:20–34). After the second announcement of the coming king (11:1–16), the section concludes with Yahweh on Zion as Judah's true king (ch. 12).

Yahweh's Complaint with the Nations (chs. 13–27)

☐ 13:1–14:27 *Against Babylon and Assyria*

Note that both oracles against these two historic enemies of Judah are distinguished at their heart by words of hope for Judah (14:1–3, 25). Babylon probably stands first in the series because eventually she would turn out to be *the* world power, whose collapse would be of monumental significance. Two things are noteworthy about this oracle: (1) It contains the imagery of the holy war, as Yahweh himself musters the army that will destroy Babylon (13:4–22), and (2) the king in particular is singled out because of his arrogance against Yahweh (14:12–21).

☐ 14:28–17:14 *Against Judah's Neighbors: Philistia, Moab, Damascus*

These oracles each put emphasis on the coming disaster, not on these nations' sins as such; in each case, as with the preceding two, look for the word of hope about the future of Zion and her people (14:32; 16:5; 17:6–7).

☐ 18:1–20:6 *Against Cush and Egypt*

Note how the two more general oracles (chs. 18–19) are concluded with a historically specific oracle against both Egyptian realms (ch. 20). In the two oracles, note that, as before, emphasis lies more on the announcement of judgment than on the reasons for it, and again it will result in the exaltation of Yahweh as king (18:7; 19:19–21). The length of the oracle against Egypt is probably related to the way it concludes: Judah's having sought help from Egypt.

☐ 21:1–23:18 *Against Babylon and Her Allies*

The oracle against Jerusalem (ch. 22) fits within these final oracles against Babylon and her allies (ch. 21), because Jerusalem's ruin will come at the hands of Babylon. Note the repeated motifs—emphasis on the doom, not the sins as such; turning from Yahweh on the part of Jerusalem, but with a future for the house of David (22:20–24); Yahweh's judgment of the arrogant (23:9).

☐ 24:1–27:13 *The Distress of the Nations, and Feasting on Yahweh's Holy Mountain*

The preceding oracles seem to imply that Yahweh is merely reacting to what the nations are doing; however, this next series makes it clear that he is the Sovereign Lord of the nations. In the first oracle, the coming destruction of Jerusalem (24:10–13) is appropriately placed in a context of the ultimate devastation of the earth. The nations respond by joining his people in a great eschatological feast on Mount Zion (ch. 25), while Judah's response (ch. 26) is to renew commitment to her trust in Yahweh and to enjoy his peace after discipline—to which Yahweh, having atoned for her guilt, responds by a renewed song of the vineyard, as Jacob takes root once more (ch. 27).

A Crisis of Trust: Hezekiah and the Babylonian Threat (chs. 28–39)

☐ 28:1–33:24 *Woe to Ephraim and Judah, Who Trust in Egypt*

Back to present reality in Judah once more; note how these oracles pick up themes from chapters 6–12. Again it is a crisis of trust regarding Yahweh. Watch for the sins that call forth this series of woes, first against Samaria (28:1–6) and then against Judah and her leaders (28:7–31:9)—especially the sins of injustice (the rich lying around getting drunk off the labor of the poor), mockery of God's prophet, and idolatry, all of which reflect Judah's arrogance, both in worship and foreign policy, with its accompanying failure to trust Yahweh, for which exhibit A is their going to Egypt for help (ch. 31). But note also how these threats are interlaced with words of hope that focus on the future of Zion and God's righteous king. Future hope then becomes the primary theme of chapters 32–33, interlaced with threats of judgment. Note especially that when Yahweh's righteous king reigns, the blind finally will see and the deaf hear (32:3–4; cf. 6:9–10).

Also be on the lookout for the many wordplays that mark these oracles (Samaria as a fading "flower" to be replaced by Yahweh as their "wreath" [28:1–5]; Judah's mockery is turned into God's mockery of them [28:9–13; cf. v.22]; the deaf will soon hear from the scroll [29:11–12, 18]; etc.).

☐ 34:1–35:10 *Once More: Judgment on the Nations, and the Future of Zion*

The final two oracles of this part of Isaiah conclude with Yahweh's love for Zion, first by announcing the Divine Warrior's judgment against the nations, especially Edom (ch. 34; cf. the similar phenomenon in Ezek 35–36), and second by announcing the coming new exodus (Isa 35:1–10); note how the judgment of 6:9–10 against the blind and the deaf, who have become like their idols, is finally reversed forever (35:5) and the ransomed of the Lord enter Zion with joy (v. 10). This final oracle also paves the way for chapters 40–55.

☐ 36:1–39:8 *Trusting Yahweh regarding Assyria, and Failure regarding Babylon*

Most of this narrative is repeated in 2 Kings 18:13, 17–20:19. In contrast to Ahaz earlier, Hezekiah listens to Isaiah and puts his trust in Yahweh, who miraculously delivers Judah from Assyria. Note again the emphasis on Zion and the remnant of Yahweh. But then Hezekiah fails to trust Yahweh by dallying with Babylon, not recognizing, as Isaiah does prophetically, that Zion's real threat lies in that quarter. So this narrative also serves as a transition to the oracles that come next.

Consolation and Confrontation (chs. 40–48)

☐ 40:1–11 *Introduction*

Watch how the theme of Israel's second, even greater exodus, which lies at the heart of the oracles contained in this section, is introduced here. Jerusalem's "hard service" in exile is coming to an end (vv. 1–2), as the desert is to be prepared like a highway, and Yahweh's glory will be revealed once more (vv. 3–5). All of this is the result of God's unbreakable word (vv. 6–8). Thus the prophet announces "good tidings to Zion"—that Yahweh will once more come with power and "shepherd" his people, bringing them safely home (vv. 9–11; note how v. 9 responds to 35:4).

☐ 40:12–41:29 *The Consolation of Israel*

But is exiled Jerusalem ready for this? Note how the oracles begin with Yahweh's contending with his people that he is the Sovereign Lord who can be trusted absolutely. His wisdom is unsearchable (40:12–14); no nation or idol can compare with him (vv. 15–26), so he will strengthen them for the journey (vv. 27–31; cf. v. 31 and Exod 19:4). Then Yahweh contends with the nations and their idols (41:1–7 [which have to be created in order to join the dispute!], vv. 21–29) to point out that he alone has raised up "one from the east" (v. 2, Cyrus), who comes on Babylon from the north (vv. 21–29). These oracles are obviously for Israel's consolation, since they bookend Yahweh's encouragement to Israel his "servant" that he is with them (as in the former exodus) and will provide for them through the desert (vv. 8–20).

☐ 42:1–44:23 *Israel As God's Reluctant Servant to the Nations*

As you read this series of stirring oracles, watch for the following repeated themes—that God's gracious redemption of Israel is so that she might become his servant for the nations; that Israel, still deaf and blind (cf. 6:9–10), is reluctant to receive this redemption; that Yahweh thus contends with them that he alone is God and that there is no other; that he will bring about a second exodus that will cause them to forget the first; and that all of this is for his own glory, he who is the gracious Redeemer of Israel.

☐ 44:24–45:25 *Yahweh's Chosen Deliverer, Cyrus*

Note the renewed emphasis on Yahweh's unbreakable word that accomplishes what he intends, including the raising up of Cyrus his servant for the sake of Israel his servant; especially note the repeated emphasis on "I am the LORD [Yahweh], and there is no other" (45:5, 6, 18; cf. 43:11; 45:14, 21, 22). Tucked into all this is also the note of

Israel's reluctance (45:9–10). Nonetheless Yahweh intends to use Israel's redemption as an appeal to the nations (vv. 14–25).

☐ 46:1–48:22 *Yahweh's Disputation with Stubborn Israel*

In this series of oracles Yahweh at last announces the actual fall of Babylon (46:1–2; 47:1–15). But his contention is with citizens of stubborn Israel, who are resistant to what Yahweh has planned for them (46:3–13; 48:1–19); he concludes with a final plea to flee Babylon (48:20–22).

Yahweh's Coming Servant Who Will Bring Salvation (chs. 49–55)

☐ 49:1–50:11 *Yahweh's Servant and the Salvation of Israel*

Note in these oracles how Yahweh's "servant, Israel," narrows down to one servant who will stand in for Israel and redeem both Israel and the nations. Note also that the new exodus is more clearly located in the relatively distant future. The first oracle paves the way: Yahweh's servant, Israel, becomes the one who brings Israel—and the nations—back to Yahweh (49:1–7). This is followed by the renewed announcement of the new exodus (49:8–13), along with Israel's continued reluctance (49:14, 24) and Yahweh's responses (49:15–23, 25–26), climaxing with the servant's own response to his commission (50:1–9) and the prophet's invitation for Israel to obey Yahweh (50:10–11).

☐ 51:1–52:12 *The Glorious Future of Zion*

After Yahweh appeals to the faithful in Israel who will inherit the promises (51:1–8), the prophet calls for Yahweh to lead the new exodus (51:9–11). Yahweh responds with words of consolation to Israel (51:12–16), so the prophet calls for Israel to respond (51:17–21), since their cup of wrath is to be passed on to Babylon (vv. 22–23). Zion must therefore prepare herself for the great exodus to come (52:1–6), which climaxes with Yahweh's return to Zion (vv. 7–10) and a final appeal to flee Babylon as they did Egypt, but not in haste this time (vv. 11–12).

☐ 52:13–53:12 *The Servant Atones for Israel's Sins*

How will this new exodus be achieved? Through the redeeming work of Yahweh's suffering servant, whose effective ministry is presented in 52:13–15, its means in 53:1–9, and its divine origins and assessment in 53:10–12. No wonder the New Testament sees the fulfillment of this passage in Jesus Christ (Mark 10:45; Acts 8:30–35; 1 Pet 2:21–25).

☐ 54:1–17 *The Glorious Future of Zion*

The climax of the servant's work is now expressed by means of echoes of three former covenants—Abraham (54:1–3), Sinai (vv. 4–8), and Noah (vv. 9–10)—as Zion's future glory is expressed with lavish imagery (vv. 11–17). Note especially that the exiles in chapter 52 are still in Babylon, but here they appear on Zion (v. 11). How did they get there? Through the suffering servant of 52:13–53:12!

☐ 55:1–13 *Yahweh's Invitation to Israel and the Nations*

Yahweh's final word in this section is one of invitation—to Israel and to the nations—to receive freely of God's gracious provision (55:1–7). Appealing once more to his sovereignty and unbreakable word (vv. 8–11), Yahweh announces the great reversal of fortunes for those who respond (vv. 12–13).

Present Failure, and Zion's Glorious Future (chs. 56–66)

☐ 56:1–59:21 *True Sabbath Keeping and True Fasting*

This final section of Isaiah begins with a kind of reprise—a return to the themes with which the book began. An opening oracle (56:1–8) sets the tone, with its concerns for Yahweh's soon-coming salvation, Israel's keeping covenant, Sabbath keeping in a context of justice, and the gathering of the nations on the holy mountain.

The series of oracles that follows picks up these themes, plus condemnation of Israel's leaders (56:9–57:4) and idolatry (57:5–13). But inserted between this condemnation of idolatry and of religion without justice (58:1–14) is an oracle of salvation for the humble (57:14–21). Note how all these themes echo 1:2–2:5.

The section concludes with an announcement of the sins that have kept Yahweh at a distance (59:1–8), a prayer of repentance by the people (vv. 9–15) and Yahweh's response of coming salvation (vv. 16–21), which echoes 1:18–20. Note especially how it ends by announcing the coming Redeemer and the Spirit (59:20–21).

☐ 60:1–63:6 *The Future Glory of Zion, and Yahweh's Anointed One*

This collection of oracles is the centerpiece of the final section of Isaiah. It starts with a marvelous picture of the future glory of Zion (ch. 60), which, as throughout Isaiah, includes the nations (vv. 10–14). Then comes the announcement of the coming Redeemer (ch. 61), who has remarkable resemblances to the servant of chapters 42–53—a passage that Jesus announces as fulfilled in himself and his ministry (Luke 4:16–21). Note also that the redeemed are the humble poor of the preceding oracles. This is followed by yet another oracle about Zion's glorious future (Isa 62), concluding with the Redeemer's eschatological judgment of the nations (63:1–6), a passage picked up by John (Rev 14:17–20).

☐ 63:7–64:12 *Yahweh's People Pray*

This prayer brings us back to present realities, as God's people await their great future. Note how it begins by recalling the first exodus—that Yahweh was present by his Spirit and in mercy redeemed them despite their rebellion (63:7–14)—which leads to the prayer for God to act again on their behalf (63:15–64:12), constituting one of the more poignant moments in Isaiah.

☐ 65:1–16 *Judgment and Salvation*

Yahweh's response to their prayer is to remind them of their waywardness (vv. 1–7), but also of his consistently promised redemption (vv. 8–16).

☐ 65:17–66:24 *Future Zion in a New Heaven and New Earth*

Isaiah now concludes with one more look at the future glory of Zion—what Yahweh has always been after—placed in an eschatological setting of a new heaven and a new earth, with a reminder of final judgment to come. Note how the end echoes 2:2–4: God's salvation encompasses a renewed Zion that will include the nations (66:18–21).

The book of Isaiah stands in the middle of the Old Testament as a reminder that Yahweh is the living God who will both judge the world in righteousness and will in mercy save his people and the nations through his "suffering servant" Messiah. It thus gathers up the whole of the Old Testament story and prepares the way for the New.

Jeremiah

ORIENTING DATA FOR JEREMIAH

- **Content:** oracles of judgment against Judah and the nations, along with oracles of future hope, interwoven with narratives of Jeremiah's role in the concluding days of Judah
- **Prophet:** Jeremiah, of priestly lineage from the village of Anathoth, about three miles south of Jerusalem
- **Date of prophetic activity:** from 627 to 585 B.C. (see 1:2–3)
- **Emphases:** Judah's unfaithfulness to Yahweh will end in its destruction; in keeping with the promises of Deuteronomy, God has a bright future for his people—a time of restoration and a new covenant; Yahweh's own heart for his people revealed through the heart of Jeremiah

OVERVIEW OF JEREMIAH

The book of Jeremiah is a collection of his many oracles—mostly in poetry and mostly against Judah and Jerusalem—plus a large number of narratives in which he is the leading player. The collection itself, perhaps "published" by Baruch (Jer 36:32; 45:1–5), comes in four major parts. Chapters 1–25 contain oracles and interpreted symbolic actions that announce the coming doom of Judah and Jerusalem. A large part of this material appears in the form of conversation/dialogue between the prophet and Yahweh. In chapters 26–36 two collections of (nonchronological) narratives enclose the highly important message of hope in chapters 30–33. Chapters 37–45 contain a series of narratives in chronological order, having to do with events that fulfill prophecies in part 1. Chapters 46–51 contain oracles against the nations, while chapter 52 is a historical epilogue, vindicating Jeremiah as a prophet. Thus:

A Prophecies of Judgment against Jerusalem (chs. 1–25)
  B Narratives Holding Out Hope for the Future (chs. 26–36)
  B* Narratives regarding the Fall of Jerusalem (chs. 37–45)
A* Prophecies of Judgment against the Nations (chs. 46–51)
Epilogue (ch. 52)

It is important to note that the narratives in chapters 26–36 have many correspondences with the preceding oracles. For example, the *content* of the famous temple sermon appears in 7:1–29, while the *reaction* to it appears as the first narrative (ch. 26); the policy to yield to Babylon and go into exile in 21:8–10 becomes the major focus of the narratives in chapters 27–29; and the reasons for judgments against Judah's kings and prophets given in chapters 22–23 find narrative expression in chapters 26–29 and 34–36. This suggests that the reason for the (nonchronological) first collection of narratives is topical—and intentional.

SPECIFIC ADVICE FOR READING JEREMIAH

To read Jeremiah well, you need to have some inkling about the man and his times, as well as the nature of the materials that make up the book.

First, a few comments about the times in which Jeremiah lived. Although Jeremiah received his call during the thirteenth year (of thirty-one years) of the reign of Josiah, only one of his oracles is dated to that period (3:6–10). Most of them come from the tumultuous years in Jerusalem after Josiah's death, during the reigns of two sons (Jehoiakim, 609–598 B.C., and Zedekiah, 597–586). Josiah himself had reigned during a lull on the international scene, as Assyria was in serious decline and both Egypt and Babylon were vying for supremacy in the coastal area that included Judah. Josiah had died in battle against the Egyptian pharaoh Neco (609), but Neco in turn was defeated by Nebuchadnezzar of Babylon in 605. The rest of Judah's final years are related to the political events that followed.

Josiah's sons (and one grandson, Jehoiachin) spent their few ruling years as political footballs between Egypt and Babylon, always under Babylonian control but repeatedly turning to Egypt for help to throw off the Babylonian yoke and gain a measure of independence. These policies eventually resulted in a siege by Nebuchadnezzar in 598 that brought Jehoiachin's brief reign of three months to an end, as he and most of the leading people of Jerusalem were sent into exile to Babylon (2 Kgs 24:8–17; Jer 29:2; see Ezekiel). Nonetheless, the final king of Judah, Zedekiah, returned to these hopeless policies, which eventually led to a second siege and the total destruction of Jerusalem (586). A still further rebellion by a remnant of those who remained in Judah finally resulted in a flight to Egypt in which both Jeremiah and Baruch were taken along.

It is not possible to make sense of Jeremiah apart from this history, since he played a major role in speaking into these political affairs over the twenty-two years of Jehoiakim's and Zedekiah's reigns. The narratives reveal a great deal about political intrigue, as both hawks and doves are represented, along with pro-Egyptian and pro-Babylonian voices. And because Jeremiah's oracles and narratives (until the events of the end, chs. 37–45) are not in their chronological order, you will do well to keep these names, dates, and political policies near at hand as you read.

Second, Jeremiah was given a most unenviable task, namely, to stand in opposition to the royal house of David and to the prophets, priests, and people by announcing the coming destruction of Jerusalem and urging them to accept exile in Babylon if they wished to live and have any future at all. At issue is Jeremiah's pro-Babylonian policy (following the first exile under Jehoiachin in 598), a view that had two things militating against it in the royal court: Many believed (1) that Jerusalem was secure because of the Davidic covenant and the presence of Yahweh's temple (see 7:4–11) and (2) that the present exile of Jehoiachin would be short-lived (see 28:1–4). Jeremiah's message is clear: Yield to Babylon and you will live—even if the return is a lifetime away(!); resist and you will die. Lying behind this resistance is a conviction, stemming from Yahweh's rescue of Jerusalem from the Assyrians (see Isa 36–37), that Zion was inviolable—because of its temple, Yahweh's resting/dwelling place.

Third, a few comments about Jeremiah's book. You need to note that chapters 1–25 form the heart of Jeremiah's prophetic word and probably represent much of the scroll that was burned by Jehoiakim and rewritten with the help of Baruch (ch. 36). The beginning oracles announce the coming judgment and the reasons for it (primarily unfaithfulness to Yahweh in the form of idolatry), while at the same time they are full of appeals to Judah, urging that if her people repent, Yahweh will relent. But the appeals go unheeded and eventually give way to the certainty of coming judgment. Included in this collection are the many intriguing moments of Jeremiah's own interactions with Yahweh (by argument, dialogue, lament, and complaint) over the coming disaster or over his own ill-treatment. You may find the going a bit easier when reading this collection if you mark carefully the changes of speakers. Also included are several interpreted symbolic actions, which serve to illustrate what Yahweh has to say to Judah.

Of the several influences on Jeremiah himself, the most obvious are Hosea and Deuteronomy. Jeremiah makes considerable use of the former's vivid imagery of Israel as a faithless bride-turned-prostitute, dearly loved by Yahweh, but whose unfaithfulness will cause him to give her over to her "lovers." This in turn reflects several Deuteronomic influences, especially the appeal to the stipulations of the covenant, including the curses for unfaithfulness at the key point of whether they will serve Yahweh alone (Jer 11:1–13; cf. 17:5–8). Related is the imagery of the un/circumcised heart (4:4; 9:25; cf. Deut 10:16; 30:6) and the promised restoration after exile with a new covenant (Jer 30–33). As in Deuteronomy, the issue is not merely idolatry, but syncretism—worshiping and serving Baal alongside Yahweh. But Yahweh is God alone and therefore a jealous God who cannot abide their idolatry, yet he is also compassionate and loving toward his people. It is this mixture of realities that finds poignant expression in Jeremiah.

A WALK THROUGH JEREMIAH

Oracles of Judgment against Judah and Jerusalem (chs. 1–25)

□ 1:1–19 *Introduction*

Watch for several important clues to the rest of the book as you read this introduction. The *heading* (vv. 1–3) places Jeremiah socially (from a priestly family in a village) and historically. The *call* itself (vv. 4–10) initiates the pattern of dialogue, as Jeremiah, in proper prophetic humility, resists his calling. The *first vision* (vv. 11–12) assures him of the certain fulfillment of God's word through him. The *second vision* (vv. 13–16) indicates the source of God's coming judgment (Babylon, from the north). The *final summons* (vv. 17–19) anticipates both his role and reception in these events.

☐ 2:1–6:30 *Oracles against Judah's Idolatry*

This first series sets up the rest of the book. Yahweh's charge against Judah/Jerusalem is given in 2:1–3:5. Watch for the following: the basic imagery of a formerly loving bride (2:2) who has turned to prostitution (2:20–25, 32–33; 3:1–5), mainly in the form of idolatry (but see also 2:34); the role of the leaders (kings, officials, priests, prophets; 2:8, 26; cf. chs. 21–23); and Yahweh's astonishment over such craziness (2:10–19).

In the next collection (3:6–4:4), watch for the many appeals to the faithless bride not to be like Samaria (who must also repent, 3:12–14), but to return to her husband, with the threat of sure doom if she fails to take heed. Next comes the announcement of disaster from the north (4:5–31, picking up from 1:14–16); note how this section alternates between direct words from Yahweh (4:5–6, 9, 11–12, 15–18, 22, 27–28) and Jeremiah's own words (vv. 7–8, 10, 13–14, 19–21, 23–26, 29–31).

Chapter 5 is a collection of short oracles, with two interventions by Jeremiah (vv. 3–6, 12–13) that alternately announce coming judgment (vv. 9–10, 15–17) and the reasons for it: Social injustice (vv. 26–28) again joins idolatry (vv. 7–8, 19). Note the thought echoed from Isaiah that the people have become like their idols (v. 21, eyes and ears that cannot see or hear).

Chapter 6 concludes this first collection by announcing the siege of Jerusalem. Note especially Jeremiah's own futile pleas with his people to take heed (vv. 10–11a, 24–26).

☐ 7:1–10:25 *More Oracles against Idolatry*

The first two sets of prose oracles (7:1–29; 7:30–8:3) spell out in stark detail Judah's syncretistic ways, all the while believing that the people's "devotion" to Yahweh and his presence will make them secure. You may wish to read chapter 26 in conjunction with the temple sermon (7:1–29), which narrates the response to it. The rest is a series of poetic oracles that picks up most of the themes from the first cycle (idolatry, forsaking the law, and judgment), but now heavily loaded with interventions by Jeremiah, mostly in the form of anguish over Jerusalem's coming destruction or in praise of the God whom Judah has spurned (note also the intervention by the people, 8:14–16). Note how it ends with a prayer (10:23–25) that echoes a common prophetic theme: Even though Judah deserves what it gets, so do the other nations, thus anticipating the oracles in chapters 46–51.

☐ 11:1–13:27 *The Broken Covenant*

Note how the first oracle (11:1–17) echoes what has gone before, but now in terms of the bride's breaking covenant with Yahweh. Look for Jeremiah's deep involvement in the rest of this section—a plot against him by his own people will result in their judgment (11:18–23); his renewed complaint about God's justice (12:1–4) is answered in terms of what Jeremiah's own people have done to him (12:5–13), yet justice will come to the nations as well (vv. 14–17); a symbolic action is then interpreted in terms of Judah's uselessness and coming destruction (13:1–14); and his own appeal to Judah (13:15–23) is answered again in terms of the unfaithful wife (vv. 24–27), thus returning to the theme of the broken covenant.

☐ 14:1–17:27 *Yahweh's Rejection of His People*

Note that this series continues the format of dialogue between Yahweh and Jeremiah: Yahweh announces judgment (14:1–6); Jeremiah prays for his people (vv. 7–9), but because their judgment is now set, he is told not to pray (vv. 10–16) but to weep over them (vv. 17–18). Jeremiah responds by reminding Yahweh of his covenant (vv. 19–22), to which Yahweh counters that even Moses and Samuel couldn't help them now (15:1–4, 5–9; cf. 15:12–14). Jeremiah responds with a lament (vv. 10, 15–18), and Yahweh with a call to repent and to stay with his calling, assuring him of deliverance (vv. 11, 19–21). After a series of personal prohibitions that are tied to judgments against the people (16:1–9), Jeremiah is commissioned to proclaim both judgment and hope (vv. 10–18), while another oracle of judgment (16:21–17:8) is followed by another dialogue (17:9–10) and personal lament (vv. 11–18). The concluding oracle announces judgment for breaking the Sabbath (vv. 19–27; cf. Exod 23:10–12; 31:12–17; 35:1–3).

☐ 18:1–20:18 *Symbols and Laments*

Two interpreted symbolic actions (18:1–17; 19:1–15) frame another personal lament (18:18–23), the second resulting in Jeremiah's being beaten (20:1–3), which in turn serves as another announcement of judgment (vv. 4–6), followed by a final personal lament (vv. 7–18). Note that the terror from the north is finally identified: It is Babylon (v. 4).

☐ 21:1–24:10 *Judgment against Kings and Prophets*

Oracles against Zedekiah bookend this section, which picks up from 2:8 and 2:26. A request from Zedekiah (ch. 21) that took place at the beginning of the siege (588 B.C.) thus heads a series of oracles against Judah's kings (ch. 22, note Jehoiakim [v. 18] and Jehoiachin [v. 24]), who will someday be replaced with a true Branch from David's line (23:1–8). These are followed by oracles against false prophets and priests (23:33–40) and a final oracle against Zedekiah and his officials (ch. 24). Note especially the messianic oracle in 23:5–6, which echoes Isaiah 11:1, 10. It is repeated in 33:15–16 and picked up in Revelation 5:5.

□ 25:1–38 *Summary of Part 1 and Anticipation of Part 4*

Note how the announcement of a seventy-year exile (vv. 1–14) is full of reasons for it that recall the preceding chapters. This is followed by an announcement of judgments against the nations (vv. 15–33), which will be spelled out in full in chapters 46–51, and a concluding word against the shepherds (vv. 34–38), bringing closure to chapters 21–24 as well. You will find the words against Babylon in 25:10 echoed in the final doom of John's "Babylon" in Revelation 18:21–23.

God's Word Offers Hope but Is Rejected (chs. 26–36)

□ 26:1–24 *Reaction to Jeremiah's Temple Sermon*

The brief summary in verses 1–6 introduces the narrative about Jerusalem's reaction to Jeremiah's temple sermon in 7:1–29. After the initial reaction (26:7–9), there is a hastily convened trial (vv. 10–19) in which Jeremiah is saved by a split between priests/prophets and officials and by a comparison with Micah. The final account compares Jeremiah with a prophet who did not fare as well (vv. 20–23) and another one who did (v. 24).

□ 27:1–29:32 *Jeremiah and the False Prophets*

This section is dominated by the conflict between Jeremiah and two false prophets (Hananiah and Shemaiah) over Jeremiah's pro-Babylonian policy. In contrast to Jeremiah himself (ch. 26) and over against his message of hope through exile, both of these men die. Note especially how the message of hope through exile prepares the way for the next section.

□ 30:1–33:26 *Promised Restoration and a New Covenant*

Here you will find the basic reason for Jeremiah's pro-Babylon stance: In it lies the only hope for the future. Thus, chapters 30–31 are a collection of short oracles that prophesy the return from exile and the restoration of Zion (see Deut 30:1–10); they are, however, interlaced with moments of judgment (Jer 30:5–7, 12–15, 23–24) in order to remind the people of what led to the exile. Note the various players in the restoration story—the people (of both Israel and Judah), the land, the city, the king, the priests, and especially the new covenant.

Jeremiah then buys a field in Anathoth (32:1–25) as down payment on this future that will come after his time! This is followed by another announcement of judgment at the time of the siege (32:26–35), followed by prose oracles of future restoration (32:36–33:26). Note how 33:15–16 picks up the promise of the Messiah from 23:5–6.

☐ 34:1–36:32 *Zedekiah, Jehoiakim, and Jeremiah's Scroll*

In response to chapters 30–33 these narratives illustrate covenant disloyalty (ch. 34) and then covenant loyalty (ch. 35), with the rejection of Jeremiah's words by Jehoiakim (ch. 36) concluding the section. True hope for Judah has been offered, but rejected.

The Fall of Jerusalem and Its Aftermath (chs. 37–45)

☐ 37:1–38:28 *Jeremiah and Court Politics*

The narratives in this final cycle are in chronological order, spelling out various episodes that marked the end of Jerusalem. The first (ch. 37) reflects the placing of false hope in Egypt by Zedekiah, resulting in Jeremiah's arrest; the second reflects Zedekiah's continuing anti-Babylonian policy (38:1–13), which results in Jeremiah's being thrown into a cistern; note that in the final episode (vv. 14–28), Jeremiah repeats the advice to yield to Babylon so as to live.

☐ 39:1–41:15 *Jeremiah and the Fall of Jerusalem*

This group of narratives tells the story of Jerusalem's fall, plus the sordid events that follow, including the assassination of Gedaliah.

☐ 41:16–45:5 *Jeremiah and the Flight to Egypt*

These final narratives contain Jeremiah's last oracles to the exiles in Egypt, who still resist Yahweh, plus a final word to Baruch.

Oracles against the Nations (chs. 46–51)

In keeping with the prophetic tradition, Jeremiah had over many years spoken oracles of Yahweh's judgment of the nations. These are placed at the end of his book—so that God's message of doom for Babylon would be the final word.

☐ 46:1–28 *The Doom of Egypt*

The promised oracles against the nations (see 1:10) now conclude the book. They begin with Judah's false hope, namely, Egypt. The defeat of Egypt's army (46:2–12) will be followed by the ruin of their land (vv. 13–24), with an appended note about Israel's hope (vv. 27–28).

☐ 47:1–49:39 *The Doom of Judah's Neighbors*

This series of oracles condemns Judah's closest neighbors, who are also historic enemies, judged primarily for pride and for their treatment of Israel. Starting in the south (Philistia), the focus moves to the east (Moab, Ammon, Edom), and then to the northeast (Damascus, Hazor, Elam). They are judged primarily for pride and for their treatment of Israel.

☐ 50:1–51:64 *The Doom of Babylon*

Although Jeremiah was pro-Babylon with regard to Israel's future, he also recognized that the destroyer must likewise be destroyed. Here especially you'll find the motif of Yahweh the Divine Warrior engaged in holy war against his enemies. Note in this collection of oracles announcing Babylon's doom how much is related to Israel's future, beginning with 50:2–7. Babylon's desolation will be even more complete than Jerusalem's, brought about by her cruelty to God's people, her arrogance, and her own idolatries. Several of these oracles will serve as the basis for John's announcement of doom on a later "Babylon"—the city of Rome (Rev 18).

An Epilogue (ch. 52)

Notice how this final historical epilogue serves to vindicate Jeremiah as a prophet. The king who rejected his words dies in ignominy (52:6–11); the king who accepted them, though imprisoned, lives on and dies in honor (vv. 31–34).

The book of Jeremiah is a constant reminder of God's faithfulness to his word in Deuteronomy that his elect will be cursed by exile for their unfaithfulness to Yahweh but will be restored at a later time with the hope of a new covenant—which was fulfilled through Jesus Christ, David's "righteous Branch" (Jer 23:5).

Ezekiel

ORIENTING DATA FOR EZEKIEL

- **Content:** a series of prophecies announcing the fall of Jerusalem, including the departure of Yahweh, followed by Israel's eventual restoration with the return of Yahweh
- **Prophet:** Ezekiel, an Israelite priest and prophet who was taken to Babylon among the first wave of captives from Judah in 598 B.C., and a younger contemporary of Jeremiah
- **Date of prophetic activity:** from 593 (Ezek 1:2) until 571 B.C. (29:17)
- **Emphases:** the inevitability of the fall of Jerusalem because of her sins, especially idolatry; the transcendent sovereignty of God as Lord of all the nations and all history; the loss and restoration of the land and of Yahweh's presence among the people of God; the promise of the life-giving Spirit as the key to covenant faithfulness

OVERVIEW OF EZEKIEL

The book of Ezekiel contains a variety of prophetic visions and oracles, which Ezekiel presented to the exiles in Babylon over a twenty-two-year period (593–571 B.C.), the most turbulent years in the history of Jerusalem. Except for the oracle and lament over Egypt (29:17–30:26), the oracles appear in chronological order.

The book is in three clear parts. Chapters 1–24 contain oracles from the five-year period preceding the siege of Jerusalem (588). These are primarily announcements to overconfident Judeans of God's certain judgment against the city and her temple. Next is a series of oracles against surrounding nations (chs. 25–32)—Babylon itself being notably excepted. The final oracles (chs. 33–48), which cover a sixteen-year period after the fall of Jerusalem, focus on hope for the future.

The structure of the book reflects Ezekiel's theology: Yahweh's *holy wrath* against his people's idolatries would cause Jerusalem to be destroyed, including her temple (the place of his presence)—despite disbelief and protest to the contrary (chs. 1–24). Yahweh is also *the sovereign God* over all the nations, so they, too, will experience judgment because of their idolatries and sins (chs. 25–32). But Yahweh is a God of *great mercy and compassion,* who intends to restore his people and be present with them once more (chs. 33–48).

SPECIFIC ADVICE FOR READING EZEKIEL

In order to read Ezekiel well, you need a measure of appreciation for the history of his times, some of which can be found in 2 Kings 22–25. Ezekiel was born into a priestly family in Jerusalem just before the reforms of Josiah (622 B.C.) and was presumably preparing for priestly duties to begin at age thirty (593). But in 598, disaster struck in the form of Nebuchadnezzar of Babylon. Over the span of Ezekiel's life, Judah's kings had made some bad political choices in the struggle between Egypt and Babylon over supremacy in the area. So Nebuchadnezzar eventually laid siege to Jerusalem; King Jehoiachin surrendered, and he and most of Jerusalem's prominent people, including Ezekiel's family, were taken into exile (see Jer 29:2) and placed in a refugee settlement south of Babylon near the Kebar River. Apparently many believed this exile was only a temporary blip on the screen of their glorious history as God's people (see Jer 28). But Jeremiah had already informed the exiles in writing (Jer 29:1–23) that they were going to be there for the long haul. Five years later Yahweh called Ezekiel to be a prophet who would announce God's judgment against Jerusalem, addressing his words to "the house of Israel"—primarily to the exiles in Babylon (Ezek 3:1, 11).

Lying at the heart of things was a theology to which both Ezekiel and the people were committed, although they had radically different views as to what it meant—the people of Israel as Yahweh's people, created and redeemed by him and ultimately defined by their *place* (the land, and especially Jerusalem) and by Yahweh's *presence* (symbolized by the temple in Jerusalem). Most people understood this theology to mean that Jerusalem was inviolable, a view reinforced by the miraculous salvation of Jerusalem after the fall of Samaria some 125 years earlier (see 2 Kgs 17–19). This theology had been continually fed to the people by the false court prophets (e.g., Hananiah, Jer 28), although opposed by Zephaniah and Jeremiah.

Ezekiel also understood that Israel was defined by place and presence (he was, after all, to become a priest in Jerusalem). But he also recognized that Judah had failed to keep covenant with Yahweh (see the arresting imagery of chs. 16; 23), thus they would forfeit the land and God's presence. Through a variety of visions, prophetic actions, and oracles, he announced over and over again that Jerusalem would soon be destroyed and that Yahweh would depart from his temple (ch. 10). This was both as unbelievable to the exiles in Babylon as it was excruciating for Ezekiel. But he also saw clearly that all of the best of the past was to be renewed in the future: king, land, people, covenant, and presence—which was eventually realized in Christ and his new-covenant people.

About the oracles themselves. You will observe that, in contrast to the prophets who preceded him, Ezekiel spoke his oracles primarily in prose rather than poetry. Indeed, reading Ezekiel is like entering into a verbal picture book, as one prophetic word after another comes either in the form of a symbolic action on his part or as a vision or allegorical picture, some of which are also interpreted. These latter cover a broad range, from the apocalyptic imagery in chapters 1 (cf. 10:1–22) and 37, to the interpreted symbolic visions of chapters 15 and 17, to the parable of chapter 16, which is so straightforward that it needs no separate interpretation.

You will want to be looking for other features that are also unique to Ezekiel, including his interest in the temple and things priestly. For example, watch for the frequency with which oracles are introduced by Yahweh's asking questions, and how often they conclude with the words "so you/they will know that I am the LORD [Yahweh]" (58*x*) or with "I the LORD [Yahweh] have spoken" (18*x*). His tendency to be repetitive may at times be burdensome to the modern reader, but for Ezekiel it was a way of reinforcing what he saw and reported. The repeated address to him as "son of man" is a Hebraism emphasizing his humanity in the presence of the eternal God.

Finally, you will meet many of Ezekiel's words and ideas when you come to the New Testament, especially in Paul's letters and John's Revelation. Many of John's own images are retakes of Ezekiel's as he joins them to some from Daniel and Isaiah to form a whole new set of images intended to express anew the unspeakable greatness of God and his ways.

A WALK THROUGH EZEKIEL

Oracles of Judgment against Israel (chs. 1–24)

☐ 1:1–3:27 *Ezekiel's Call and Commissioning*

Verses 1–2 place Ezekiel among the exiles and date the time of his call to his thirtieth year and to the fifth year of the exile (July 593 B.C.). His call begins with high drama (ch. 1), as Yahweh appears to him seated on a magnificent chariot throne borne by four cherubim (see 10:20), to which Ezekiel responds appropriately by falling facedown (cf. Dan 10:9; Rev 1:17). He is then commissioned and equipped (by the Spirit) for his exceedingly difficult assignment (Ezek 2:1–3:27). Note especially that his commission as a "watchman" (3:16–21) also stands at the beginning of the final series of visions/oracles (33:1–20).

☐ 4:1–7:27 *The Coming Siege and Doom of Jerusalem*

As you read this section, note that it is still part of the same sequence dated in 1:2. Thus, five years in advance, Ezekiel is to engage in three symbolic actions (4:1–3, 4–17; 5:1–4) by which Yahweh announces the coming siege and destruction of Jerusalem (5:5–17). These are followed by two straightforward oracles announcing the devastation of Jerusalem and the countryside alike (chs. 6–7); note that the first is addressed to "the mountains of Israel," a designation for the land (cf. 36:1–15), and that both conclude with "Then they will know that I am the LORD [Yahweh]." The singular reason for this devastation is idolatry, so the Israelites' dead bodies will be sacrifices to their idols (6:5).

☐ 8:1–12:20 *Israel's Idolatry and Yahweh's Departure from Jerusalem*

Over a year later (September 592), Ezekiel is taken by the Spirit to "see" Jerusalem's idolatry in the temple itself (ch. 8). This is one of the most poignant moments in the Bible. Can you feel Yahweh's utter dismay as the women weep over the god Tammuz and the men—with their backs toward Yahweh!—worship the sun in the place of the eternal God's very presence? Thus the people are symbolically marked for destruction (ch. 9) as Jerusalem is assigned to burning (10:2–8) and the glory of Yahweh leaves the temple (10:9–22) and eventually the city

(11:23). The judgment is especially against the present leaders in Jerusalem for their bad politics (11:1–15). But in anticipation of chapters 33–48, hope lies in the future (11:16–25) in keeping with Ezekiel's plea for a remnant to be spared (11:13). The final event prophesied in this sequence is the second deportation of exiles, announced by another symbolic action (12:1–20).

□ 12:21–14:23 *False Prophets and Misguided Elders*

Like Jeremiah, Ezekiel is plagued by false prophets, who in this case say that either Ezekiel's prophecies will not come to pass (12:21–25) or they will be long delayed (vv. 26–28); so Ezekiel is told by Yahweh to prophesy against those who cover flimsy walls with whitewash and those who make and use charms for divination in Yahweh's name (ch. 13). When the elders come to see him, their idolatrous hearts and their false prophets are exposed (14:1–11); Ezekiel concludes with a true prophecy—the inevitability of the coming disaster in Jerusalem (vv. 12–23). Despite her "prophets," Zion is simply *not* inviolable.

□ 15:1–19:14 *The Doom of Jerusalem and Her Kings*

These loosely related oracles—four allegories and a response to a proverb—variously reflect the situations of both the exiles in Babylon and current affairs in Jerusalem. The first two (chs. 15–16) focus again on Jerusalem's coming destruction, the first echoing Isaiah's song of the vineyard (Isa 5:1–7); note that it is the first of several oracles in the book that begin with Yahweh's asking questions. Ezekiel 16 graphically portrays the history of Israel's unfaithfulness to Yahweh (a prostitute who pays men to have her!)—by both her political intrigues and an insatiable appetite for idolatry. The allegories of eagles (ch. 17) and lions (ch. 19), the latter ironically taking the form of a lament, are directed especially at Zedekiah, present king in Jerusalem (17:15–21; 19:5–9; see 2 Kgs 25:6–7). These allegories enclose a complaint against God's injustice (the children pay for their parents' sins) brought to Ezekiel by the exiles (Ezek 18). Their proverb is rejected altogether and replaced with an offer to forgive if they repent. Note especially that their sins are expanded considerably beyond idolatry (cf. ch. 22).

☐ 20:1–24:27 *Countdown to Catastrophe*

This series, which begins August 591 (20:1), concludes (24:1) with the beginning of the siege of Jerusalem (January 588). The first oracle (20:1–44), picking up from chapter 16, puts Israel's history of unfaithfulness in plain terms, but concludes on a note of hope (anticipating chs. 36–37). In the brief oracle that follows (vv. 45–49), note that "south" is the direction to Judah from Babylon. God's "sword" for executing his judgment will be Babylon (ch. 21), again because of Judah's sins that demand judgment (ch. 22). The allegory of two sisters (ch. 23), also picking up from chapter 16, now sets Jerusalem's sins in light of fallen Samaria's, while the beginning of the siege is pictured in two ways as a cooking pot (24:3–8, 9–14). The siege coincides with the sudden death of Ezekiel's wife (24:15–27), and he is struck dumb by the enormity of his grief—a symbol for how the exiles will respond to the fall of Jerusalem.

Oracles of Judgment against the Nations (chs. 25–32)

Before the actual fall, at which point Ezekiel turns toward Yahweh's future for his people, he receives a series of oracles against the nations who were Judah's political allies, indicating that the same fate awaits them.

☐ 25:1–17 *Against Surrounding Nations*

This first set of oracles are against Judah's historic enemies, who became political allies only by the pressure of events, but who turned against her at the time of the siege.

☐ 26:1–28:26 *Against Tyre and Sidon*

Although not a political enemy, Tyre represents the economically exploitative powers; she lives in arrogance because of her position in the world's economic systems. The first oracle (ch. 26) is against the city herself, while the second (ch. 27) mockingly laments her coming demise. Here especially you get insight into the Phoenicians' role as merchants to the world, a passage from which John borrows heavily in his woe against Babylon (Rome) in Revelation 18. The third oracle (Ezek 28) focuses on the sheer arrogance of her king. But Yahweh alone is King of the nations, so Tyre must also fall.

☐ 29:1–32:32 *Against Egypt*

Here you find Ezekiel finally turning to the primary cause of so much of Judah's grief, namely, Egypt, from whom Judah's kings constantly sought help against Babylon. As with Tyre, there is an oracle of judgment (ch. 29) followed by a lament (ch. 30) and by an oracle against her king (ch. 31), but in this case concluding with a lament for this king as well (ch. 32).

Oracles of Hope and Consolation (chs. 33–48)

Watch for the clear sense of development you find in this final series of oracles. After positioning Ezekiel in the role of a watchman, Yahweh promises to restore, in turn, the Davidic kingship, the land, Yahweh's honor (by way of the new covenant), his people, his sovereignty over the nations, and finally his presence among the people in the land.

☐ 33:1–33 *Ezekiel's Role*

The word of hope begins by Ezekiel's returning to his role as watchman (33:1–20; cf. 3:16–21 to catch the new emphasis here). The news of Jerusalem's fall causes Ezekiel's mouth to open (33:22; cf. 24:25–27), and the first word is in keeping with Jeremiah's—that the *land* will be desolate for a long time (33:23–33).

☐ 34:1–31 *Restoring Yahweh's Role as Shepherd of Israel*

Note how the first word of hope focuses on *kingship,* since that has now failed in Israel. Using the imagery of shepherd (echoing David's kingship), Yahweh announces the failure of her past shepherds (vv. 1–10) and then his gathering of the scattered sheep whom "David" will once more shepherd in a future messianic age (vv. 11–31; cf. 11:16–17). Note especially the role of this passage in John 10, where Jesus announces himself as the fulfillment of this prophecy.

☐ 35:1–36:15 *Restoring Yahweh's Land*

You should not be surprised that the next focus for the future is on the *land.* This section begins with an oracle against Edom (ch. 35), who seized Judean lands after Jerusalem fell (cf. Obad 11–13). This is followed by an oracle to "the mountains of Israel" (Ezek 36:1–15; cf. 6:1–14)—that they shall produce abundantly in God's future for his people.

☐ 36:16–38 *Restoring Yahweh's Honor in Israel*

The next focus is on Yahweh's *honor*. Israel's past dishonor of his name will be reversed as the people are cleansed, and they will be given a new covenant and Yahweh's Spirit so that they can live by it (now written on their hearts; cf. Jer 31:31–33). Watch for Paul's development of this theme in 2 Corinthians 3:1–6. Finally, evidence of Yahweh's honor will be the productivity of the formerly desolate land to which he will bring them.

☐ 37:1–28 *Restoring Yahweh's People and His Covenant*

In order for all of this to happen, there must be a "resurrection" of the *people*, brought to life by Yahweh's word and Spirit (vv. 1–14), so that Israel again is *one nation* in the *land*, under their Davidic *king* and in the renewal of Yahweh's own *presence* among them (vv. 15–28).

☐ 38:1–39:29 *Restoring Yahweh's Supremacy*

Israel's restoration will be complete when Yahweh exercises his sovereignty over all her enemies, here symbolically represented by his defeat of Gog of Magog, from a distant land in the north (38:15). The point is that Yahweh will secure Israel's future restoration against all future enemies. Note how this section ends with Yahweh's victory banquet (39:17–20) and two summarizing promises of restoration (vv. 21–29) that prepare the way for the finale in chapters 40–48.

☐ 40:1–48:35 *Restoring Yahweh's Presence among His People and in the Land*

In April 573, fourteen years after the fall of Jerusalem, Ezekiel is given his final set of visions, which focus first on the restored temple and priesthood. What he sees is so grand that he includes its extraordinary measurements, thus symbolizing its grandeur and glory. All of the detail is a way of emphasizing the importance of the worship of Yahweh by the restored community of the future. And even if you do not share Ezekiel's own vested interest in the details, do not lose the central point, which Ezekiel himself makes by giving it center place in the vision—the return of Yahweh's presence among his people (43:1–9)! Also important for this great future for God's people is the redistribution of the transformed land (45:1–12), which is what the final two chapters (47–48) are all about. Note especially that the life-giving river is seen as flowing from the temple (47:1–12), the place of God's presence and of the people's worship, imagery that John picks up in his vision of the final city of God in Revelation 22:1–5. So the book ends with a new name for the city: "THE LORD IS THERE" (Ezek 48:35)!

The book of Ezekiel is a significant part of God's story as it tells of the final failure of the people of God as constituted by the first covenants, but looks forward to their being reconstituted by a new covenant that includes the true Shepherd and the gift of the Holy Spirit.

Daniel

ORIENTING DATA FOR DANIEL

- **Content:** a series of stories about how God brings honor to himself through Daniel and his three friends in Babylon, followed by four apocalyptic visions about future kingdoms and God's final kingdom
- **Prophet:** Daniel, one of the early exiles to Babylon, who was selected to serve as a provincial administrator in the Babylonian—and finally Persian—court
- **Date of composition:** unknown; presumably toward the end of the sixth century B.C. (ca. 520), although many have suggested it dates from the early second century B.C. (ca. 165)
- **Emphases:** God's sovereignty over all the nations and their rulers; God's care for the Jews in exile, with promises of final restoration; God's present overruling of and final victory over human evil

OVERVIEW OF DANIEL

The book of Daniel comes in two clear parts (chs. 1–6 and 7–12). The first half contains court stories, mostly about Daniel and three friends who remain absolutely loyal to Yahweh even while rising to positions of importance within the Babylonian Empire. The emphases are four: (1) on the four Hebrews' loyalty to God, (2) on God's miraculous deliverances of them, (3) on Gentile kings' acknowledging the greatness of Israel's God, and (4) on Daniel as the God-gifted interpreter of dreams—all of which emphasize God's sovereignty over all things, including the king who conquered and destroyed Jerusalem.

Part 2 is a series of apocalyptic visions about the rise and fall of succeeding empires, in each case involving a coming tyrannical ruler (7:8, 24–25; 8:23–25; 11:36–45)—most often understood to be Antiochus

IV (Epiphanes) of the Seleucid rulers of Palestine (175–164 B.C.), who because of his desolation of Jerusalem and sacrilege of the temple was to become the first in a series of antichrist figures in Jewish and Christian literature. But in each case the final focus is on God's judgment of the enemy and the glorious future kingdom awaiting his people.

SPECIFIC ADVICE FOR READING DANIEL

At the outset it is important to note that in the Hebrew Bible, Daniel is included among the Writings rather than the Prophets. In part this was due to its genre—stories about a "prophet" and apocalyptic visions, rather than prophetic oracles. Indeed, there is nothing else quite like Daniel in Jewish and Christian literature, with its combination of court stories and apocalyptic visions. Furthermore, its intent is to inspire and encourage God's people living under foreign domination, not to call them to repent in light of coming judgments. Daniel is thus never called a prophet, but one to whom God reveals mysteries.

It may be helpful, therefore, for you to review the brief description of apocalyptic in *How to 1* (pp. 251–52), since the dreams and visions in chapters 2 and 7–11 have most of the features of apocalyptic—the book was born in a time of oppression; it is a literary work altogether; it comes by means of visions and dreams that are given by angels; the images are those of fantasy symbolizing reality; and Daniel is told to seal up the visions for the last days (8:26; 9:24; 12:4).

Interestingly, chapters 1 and 8–12 are in Hebrew, while chapters 2–7 are in Aramaic, the lingua franca of the Near East from the sixth century onward through the time of Christ. Two things about this are important. First, the Aramaic portion consists of the stories, plus the first vision, suggesting that these are open reading for all, but the introduction and the interpreted visions are in Hebrew, implying perhaps that they are for God's people only. Second, the Aramaic portion is arranged in a chiastic pattern:

- Chapters 2 and 7 contain similar visions of future kingdoms, ending with God's final, eternal kingdom.
- Chapters 3 and 6 are stories of miraculous deliverance, where opposition has been directed against God.
- Chapters 4 and 5 are stories about the demise of two Babylonian kings, who both acknowledge the greatness of Israel's God.

Thus these stories tell us that God is in ultimate control of all human history (chs. 2; 7), illustrated both by the stories of miraculous deliverance (chs. 3; 6) and of the "overthrow" of the two Babylonian kings (chs. 4; 5). In each case they are marvelously narrated; to get their full benefit, you might try reading them aloud, as they were originally intended to be.

Also important for reading Daniel is to be aware of two historical contexts: (1) Daniel's own and (2) that predicted in his visions. Thus chapters 1–6 describe affairs within the Babylonian court from Nebuchadnezzar to the first of the Persian rulers of Babylon (ca. 605–530 B.C.)—from the time before the fall of Jerusalem, when the first captives from Judah were brought to Babylon, to that just beyond the demise of the Babylonian Empire in 539.

The visions (chs. 7–12) pick up at that point. Babylon was followed by the long-lived Persian Empire (539 to ca. 330). Then came the short-lived Greek Empire of Alexander (333–323), which at his death was divided among four generals (see 8:19–22). Of special interest for understanding intertestamental Jewish history is the long contest for Palestine between the Seleucids (of Antioch [the North]) and the Ptolemies (of Egypt [the South]), which is alluded to in the vision of Daniel 11 (see, e.g., the study notes in the NIV Study Bible). Crucial for Daniel is the rise of Antiochus IV, described in 11:21–32, who in fact set out to crush Jewishness in Jerusalem by forcing them to adopt his policy of Hellenizing his lands. Thus he forbade the keeping of the law and showed special favors to those who Hellenized (see 11:28). Eventually thwarted by Rome from seizing Egypt, he returned home by way of Jerusalem and poured out his fury on the Jews who resisted him, finally desecrating the Holy Place by erecting a statue of Zeus there in 167 (11:30–31). This event, which eventually led to the Maccabean revolt recorded in the Apocrypha's 1 and 2 Maccabees, is envisioned in Daniel 7–11. You can well imagine what it might have been like to read Daniel during this period—both the stories in chapters 1–6 (God honors loyalty and will humble arrogant kings!) and the visions themselves (God has foretold all this).

Finally, it is important to note that the coming of the messianic kingdom is pictured as taking place following the overthrow of Antiochus, which in fact it did a century and a half later—the only kingdom worth mentioning after Antiochus being not the Roman one, but that of Christ.

In keeping with the whole Hebrew prophetic tradition, these coming historical events were seen against the backdrop of God's great final eschatological future (see the introduction to the Prophets, p. 173).

A WALK THROUGH DANIEL

☐ 1:1–21 *Introductory Narrative: Daniel and Friends in Nebuchadnezzar's Court*

Watch for the ways this opening narrative introduces you not only to the stories that follow, but to a good reading of the whole book. Verses 1–2 give the historical setting, but also anticipate 5:1–2. Daniel and his fellows outshine all other provincials pressed into the king's service—and do so precisely because they maintain covenant loyalty with regard to the food laws (1:6–20), but note also the little insertion in v. 17, which anticipates the next story. And finally see that God is seen as directing these affairs (vv. 9, 17).

☐ 2:1–49 *Nebuchadnezzar's Dream Interpreted by Daniel*

This narrative serves three purposes: to exalt God over Nebuchadnezzar (vv. 27–28, 36–38, 44–45, 47), including God's exalting Daniel in the king's eyes (vv. 46, 48–49); to present Daniel as God's agent in interpreting dreams (vv. 14–45); and to anticipate the later visions (vv. 31–45). Note how the latter two items are highlighted in Daniel's prayer (vv. 20–23); note further that even though the dream is interpreted, there is no further interest in it at this point, merely intriguing you to read the coming visions. Note finally how verse 49 anticipates the next story, in which Daniel does not appear.

☐ 3:1–30 *Saved from Nebuchadnezzar's Fiery Furnace*

Now the "head of gold" (2:38) makes a monstrous image of gold and commands all provincials to worship it. But just as God watched over them in chapter 1, the three Hebrews are (now miraculously) delivered because of their absolute rejection of idolatry (3:16–18). Part of the power of the narrative lies in its fulsome repetitions. But its greater power lies in its point: The greatest king on earth is no match for the eternal God; not only does God deliver the three Hebrews in grand style from Nebuchadnezzar's arrogance and rage, but the king also promotes them (v. 30) and himself acknowledges the greatness of their God (vv. 28–29), which in turn anticipates the next story.

☐ 4:1–37 *Nebuchadnezzar's Madness*

This ultimate expression of God's sovereignty over earthly kings is magnificently told, highlighted in part by the fact that the whole narrative is a report from the king to the nations (v. 1). It begins with the king's acknowledgment that only God's kingdom is forever (vv. 2–3; cf. 2:44), again anticipating later visions (7:14, 18, 27), and it ends on the same note (4:34–35)—after the arrogant king is humbled by God to the role of an animal. Note that Daniel also reenters as the interpreter of dreams (vv. 8–27).

☐ 5:1–31 *Belshazzar's Feast and the Demise of Babylon*

Picture the drama as you read; also be watching, however, for the ways the story functions—to remind you that the Babylonian Empire came to an end because her king did not honor the true God (v. 23) and to relate this in a context where the king is defying God by using the sacred utensils from the Jerusalem temple (v. 2; cf. 1:2) for idolatrous purposes. Again, Daniel is the central figure, now interpreting the handwriting on the wall.

☐ 6:1–28 *Daniel in the Lions' Den*

This third attack on Jewish faith (see chs. 1; 3) again features Daniel, but now with Babylon under Persian rule. Note how much it corresponds to chapter 3: Daniel knows the decree, as well as its purpose and consequences—being thrown to immediate death—but he refuses to stop praying to his God, he is divinely delivered, and the king does homage to the "living God" (v. 26). And note how Darius echoes Nebuchadnezzar's acknowledgment of God's eternal kingship (vv. 26–27; cf. 4:34–35).

☐ 7:1–28 *The Vision of the Beasts from the Sea*

The four visions of these chapters are all dated—when Daniel is a relatively old man. This first one both echoes items from 2:36–45 and sets up those that follow. Note that in this case the interest centers on the little horn and the coming messianic kingdom. These are highlighted (1) by the way the narrative is set up (the little horn is introduced [v. 8], followed in turn by the divine court scene [vv. 9–10] and then by his ultimate demise [v. 11] and the eternal kingdom of the Most High and his "saints" [v. 18]), (2) by the lack of present interest in the other kingdoms (see ch. 8), and (3) by Daniel's singular interest in the fourth beast and the little horn (vv. 19–20). Note also that the last part of the vision itself, the little horn's oppression of the saints, has been left until verses 21–22 so that the interpretation can focus on this feature, on his ultimate defeat, and on God's everlasting kingdom (vv. 25–27).

☐ 8:1–27 *The Vision of the Ram and Goat*

The second and third kingdoms of chapter 7 are now envisioned as a ram and goat and are interpreted as the Medes and Persians, followed by Greece. Pictured are Alexander the Great's victory over Persia (vv. 6–8, 21) and the subsequent fourfold division of his empire among his four generals (vv. 8b, 22), from whom eventually would come the little horn (vv. 9–13, 23–25). Note again the focus of the vision—that he attacks the saints and their worship, and that he himself will be destroyed, but not with human power.

☐ 9:1–27 *The Interpretation of Jeremiah's Prophecy*

Daniel's prayer (vv. 4–19) is the theological centerpiece of the book, reflecting Israel's deserved exile for covenant unfaithfulness, but expressing hope in Yahweh's forgiveness and mercy (the only place in Daniel where the name Yahweh appears). This is enclosed by the need for a new application of Jeremiah's seventy years (vv. 1–3, in light of the devastation to be caused by the little horn). The answer (vv. 20–27) is a typical apocalyptic use of numbers, where the original number is multiplied by seven (= at the end of the devastation by the little horn), which, again typically, is portrayed against the backdrop of the final end.

☐ 10:1–12:4 *The Angel's Revelation of the Future*

All of the visions have been pointing to this final one. Note the elaborate preparations for it in Daniel's encounter with the angel in 10:1–21. What follows, after an introduction (11:2–4) that picks up from the vision in 8:19–22, is a forecast of the struggle between the Seleucids and Ptolemies over "the Beautiful Land" (11:5–20; cf. Jer 3:19). But, as before, everything leads to the rise and fall of Antiochus IV (Dan 11:21–45), concentrating especially on his devastation of Jerusalem but also again predicting his end. And, as before, his demise is set against the backdrop of the end (12:1–4), which will have the resurrection of the dead and eternal reward of the righteous as its centerpiece.

□ 12:5–13 *Conclusion*

Note that Daniel's concluding questions "How long will it be before these astonishing things are fulfilled?" and "What will the outcome of all this be?" are again given with cryptic number schemes, while Daniel himself will rest until the resurrection.

The book of Daniel, though focusing primarily on one period in Israel's history, looks forward to the great eternal reign of God inaugurated by Jesus Christ; as such it had great influence on the imagery of John's Revelation.

Hosea

ORIENTING DATA FOR HOSEA

- **Content:** Yahweh's compassion for the northern kingdom (Israel), yet his condemnation of them for their unfaithfulness to him
- **Prophet:** Hosea, a northern prophet, probably from Samaria
- **Date of prophetic activity:** ca. 758–722 B.C.
- **Emphasis:** Yahweh's unfailing love for his people, even when he must punish them for unfaithfulness

OVERVIEW OF HOSEA

The structure of this first—and longest—of the Book of the Twelve is less easy to discern than that of most of the prophetic books, due in part to the general lack of introductory or concluding formulas (e.g., "thus says the LORD [Yahweh]"). Two major divisions are clear (chs. 1–3 and 4–14). Part 1 seems intentionally introductory, and its own alternating pattern of judgment (1:2–9; 2:2–13; 3:4) followed by future restoration (1:10–2:1; 2:14–23; 3:5) may serve as a pattern for part 2 as well. The judgments are predicated on Israel's "adultery" (= idolatry, 2:8, 13, 17), and the restoration on Yahweh's unfailing love for his people (2:1, 14, 23; 3:1). Indeed, the tension in the book, as in Micah later, is between Yahweh's love for his people and his justice in carrying out the curses for covenantal unfaithfulness.

So images from Hosea's marriage both mirror Yahweh's long relationship with Israel (marriage, unfaithfulness, "divorce," restoration) and serve as a pattern for the book in its present form. A first cycle of oracles (4:1–10:15) tells the sordid story of Israel's unfaithfulness, both religiously and politically, along with Yahweh's (necessary) coming judgments; while 11:1–11 promises future restoration based on Yahweh's love and compassion. The story of unfaithfulness and judgment is repeated with even greater intensity in a second cycle (11:12–13:16), while 14:1–8 concludes the book with Yahweh's final love song for his people.

SPECIFIC ADVICE FOR READING HOSEA

Along with the close relationship between Hosea's own symbolic marriage actions and Yahweh's relationship with Israel/Ephraim, three other matters are crucial for a discerning reading of Hosea.

First, the *historical context* (see 2 Kgs 14:23–18:16) is influenced in large part by the downs and ups of Assyria. According to 1:1, Hosea began his prophetic calling toward the end of the relatively tranquil and prosperous days of Jeroboam II (see "Specific Advice for Reading Amos," pp. 223–24), but the list of Judean kings, as well as Hosea's own oracles, suggest that most of them were delivered during the years of rapid decline following the death of Jeroboam II (753). Six kings ruled in Samaria in rapid succession—through intrigue, caprice, and assassination (see 8:4)—until the northern kingdom was overthrown by Assyria in 722/1. Part of the intrigue was related to a king's willingness or unwillingness to pay tribute to Assyria, which in turn was related to looking elsewhere (7:8–11) for alliances to protect them against Assyria. In the end, Yahweh will use Assyria as his rod of punishment (10:6–7).

Second, and more important still, is the *religious/theological context*. Although Hosea regularly throws side-glances to Judah (see below), his passion and pathos are for Israel. Picking up where the reforming prophets Elijah and Elisha had left off a century earlier, he is both astounded and incensed at Israel's propensity to abandon Yahweh in favor of Baal—or to mix the two in syncretistic fashion (2:11, 13; see "Specific Advice for Reading Deuteronomy," pp. 57–58). Just as marriage is simultaneously both absolutely exclusive and deeply personal, so is Yahweh's covenant with Israel. Thus Hosea repeatedly reminds his hearers/readers of their beginnings (2:15; 9:10; 11:1–4; 13:4), while he also recalls Israel's history of unfaithfulness (9:10, 15; 10:9). The people's present unfaithfulness, reflected primarily in their idolatry, also finds expression in breaking most of the Ten Commandments, as the preamble in 4:1–3 spells out so forcibly.

At stake in all of this is Yahweh's own character. In turning to Canaanite fertility gods (the Baals and Asherahs), Israel has attributed fruitfulness of both crops and people to them (2:5, 12) and thus has abandoned

Yahweh, the Creator of all, who alone provides the crops and opens the womb (2:8, 18, 21–22; 9:11, 14). At the same time the Israelites have become like the gods they worship—full of lies, deceit, and caprice. Thus the bottom line for Hosea—and the reason for the coming judgment—is that although it should be otherwise, the people simply do not *know* Yahweh (4:1, 6, 14; 8:2–3); they have come to think of Yahweh, not in terms of their own story of redemption, but in terms of Canaanite religion—and the result is deadly.

Third, if at times you find Hosea a difficult read, that, at least in part, may be because he so clearly wears his heart on his sleeve. Here is *passion and pathos* let loose on Israel in oracle after oracle, irony upon irony—and such passion is not always easy to track in terms of where things are going (indeed, hardly any two commentaries agree on the details). At the same time, the oracles themselves do not always fit the ordinary formal patterns, since announcements of judgment and the reasons for it are not neatly packaged, and in many instances they simply blend in the same sentences. Furthermore, his Hebrew text has suffered much in transmission, so there are moments that are very difficult to figure out (observe the many footnotes in the NIV).

But at the same time this very passion is what makes Hosea such a great read. Striking metaphors are his specialty. Watch how Yahweh is lion, leopard, bear, eagle (vulture), trapper (5:14; 11:10; 13:7–8; 8:1; 7:12), as well as husband, lover, parent, green pine tree (2:14–23; 14:3–7; 11:8–9; 14:8). And Israel in her sins is even more vividly described: adulterous wife, stubborn heifer, snare and net, heated oven, half-baked bread, senseless dove, faulty bow, headless stalk, a baby refusing birth (2:2; 4:16; 5:1; 7:4, 8, 11, 16; 8:7; 13:13); she will disappear like mist, dew, chaff, and smoke (13:3); she will float away like a twig on water (10:7); she has sown the wind and will reap the whirlwind (8:7). It is hard not to get the picture. So enjoy, even as you weep with Yahweh and his prophet.

A final word about the book itself, as a book to be read. Although the prophecies are primarily directed toward the northern kingdom (Israel), it is very likely that the book itself was preserved in Judah. Evidence for this is in the heading, which takes the ministry of Hosea down to the reign of Hezekiah in Judah (715, six years after the fall of Samaria). This suggests that, even though Hosea seems to pay only passing attention to Judah in his oracles (see 1:7, 11; 4:15; 5:5, 10, 12–14;

6:4, 11; 8:14; 10:11; 11:12; 12:2), he will not expect his later Judean readers to do the same regarding Judah—nor should we who now read it from the hindsight of the fall of both kingdoms!

A WALK THROUGH HOSEA

☐ 1:1 *Heading*

Note that Hosea's book is "the word of the LORD" that came to Hosea over the time span of several Judean kings.

☐ 1:2–2:1 *Hosea, Gomer, and Children*

Here Hosea acts symbolically in marrying an "adulterous wife" (lit., "woman of prostitution," perhaps a metaphor for Gomer's disloyalty to Yahweh). His children are given names that speak of God's judgments against his own "faithless wife" (Israel), names they bear to symbolize the stigma of God's judgment and eventual rejection of Israel. But note also that the word of hope (1:10–2:1) reverses the meaning of their names! Note further the different destinies of Israel and Judah in 1:6–7, but their being reunited in God's promised future (v. 11).

☐ 2:2–23 *Israel Punished and Restored*

In a poetic oracle, the children of the adulteress are now called on to rebuke their mother (Israel), urging her to give up her idolatry or else Yahweh will show no love for her children (vv. 2–6). Israel feigns return to Yahweh (vv. 7–8), but will pay for her wantonness (vv. 9–13); observe how thoroughgoing her idolatry is. In the word of restoration (vv. 14–23), watch for the various reversals, including promised restoration to the land.

☐ 3:1–5 *Judgment and Restoration*

Note how this narrative, symbolizing the coming exile, corresponds to 2:14–23—just as 2:2–13 corresponds to 1:2–8; thus the two narratives (chs. 1 and 3) bookend the oracle in chapter 2. As you read the rest of the book, be looking for the ways the themes of these chapters are picked up.

☐ 4:1–5:7 *Yahweh's Charge against Israel for Unfaithfulness*

Much of this material takes the form of a lawsuit against Israel. It begins with an opening charge (4:1–3), where all the major themes of the book are laid out: no faithfulness to the covenant, no knowledge of Yahweh (NIV "acknowledgment"), the land mourns. Then picking up themes from chapters 1–3, charges are leveled against priest, prophet, and people (especially lack of knowledge [4:6–7, 14] that takes the form of idolatry [vv. 10–14, 15, 17–19]). Since they have now gone too far (5:1–4), they will be judged (vv. 5–7). Note that Judah is always in view as well (4:15; 5:5).

☐ 5:8–7:16 *Israel's Unfaithfulness through Entangling Alliances*

Yahweh now calls for the watchman (possibly Hosea himself, see 8:1) to sound the trumpet of warning (5:8). Judgment is sure (vv. 9–12, 14–15), and dallying with Assyria is no cure (v. 13), nor is false repentance (6:1–3), since it is like "morning mist" (vv. 4–10); even when Yahweh would restore them (v. 11), their sins continue to be exposed (7:1–7), especially as they continue to trust in other nations for help rather than Yahweh (vv. 8–16). And again watch for the references to Judah (5:10, 12, 13, 14; 6:4, 11).

☐ 8:1–9:9 *Once More: Judgment Because of Unfaithfulness*

Another call for the trumpet (8:1) announces again Yahweh's certain judgments, this time in the form of overthrow by the very nations she sold herself to (8:3b, 8–10, 14). Note again the charge of breaking covenant (8:1–3), but added now is the internal decay in the monarchy (8:4), while idolatry continues to be the main issue (8:4–7). The cycle then concludes with yet another announcement of coming judgment and the reasons for it (9:1–9).

☐ 9:10–10:15 *Israel Condemned for Not Living Up to Her Calling*

In 9:9 Yahweh reminded them of Gibeah (Judg 19–20); now he picks up a series of such reminders of past covenant disloyalty, which serve as examples for present judgments (Hos 9:10–14, Baal Peor [Num 25:1–9]; Hos 9:15–17, Gilgal [1 Sam 13; 15]; Hos 10:9–10, Gibeah again). Note the role of various kings in the oracles in Hosea 10 (vv. 3, 6–7, 15): Because Israel has rejected Yahweh as King, Israel's own king will be destroyed and her idols taken to the king of Assyria. And note also the invitation in 10:12, which anticipates the word of anguish and compassion that comes next.

☐ 11:1–11 *God's Undying Love for Israel*

In many ways this is the heart of Hosea's message. Yahweh's love for his "son," Israel (vv. 1, 3–4; see Exod 4:22); Israel's unfaithfulness (Hos 11:2, 7); Yahweh's judgment (vv. 5–6); and his promise of restoration (vv. 8–11)—all because he alone is the Holy One, totally other than his human creatures (v. 9). This paves the way for the coming of Jesus Christ.

☐ 11:12–13:16 *One More Time: Israel's Sins and Coming Judgment*

Note how the first of these oracles (11:12–12:14) picks up many of the themes from before—both Israel's (and Judah's) sins (lies, deceit, idolatry [bulls in Gilgal, v. 11]) and God's judgments (12:2, 14) and appeal (v. 6); here alone (vv. 7–8) Hosea explicitly reflects the social injustice found in Amos, Isaiah, and Micah. Observe also, however, that most of the oracle picks up (from 11:1–4) the reminders of their history, especially the roles of Jacob (the good and the bad!) and Moses (12:13).

The second oracle (13:1–16) again repeats the motif of the people's unfaithfulness to Yahweh, especially their ingratitude in turning to idolatry (vv. 1–2, 6, 9–12, 16) after Yahweh has done so much for them (vv. 4–6); therefore, they will come under judgment (vv. 3, 7–8, 15–16). Even so, the word of hope persists (v. 14).

☐ 14:1–9 *Invitation and Restoration*

Note how the book concludes with one more invitation to repent (vv. 1–3) and the promise of restoration and a glorious future (vv. 4–8); could Hosea have done it otherwise? So the book signs off with a word in Wisdom style, calling for discernment (v. 9)—a word that has similarities to Psalm 1.

The book of Hosea, which burns with the fire of God's love for his people, reminds us that the God of the biblical story judges unfaithfulness, even as he lays out hope beyond judgment.

Joel

ORIENTING DATA FOR JOEL

- **Content:** a devastating locust plague sets the stage for a twofold summons to repentance, to which God responds with a promise of mercy and an outpouring of his Spirit, with a day of judgment on the nations
- **Prophet:** Joel, who is otherwise unknown; his concern for Judah and Jerusalem (2:23, 32; 3:1) suggests that he was from the southern kingdom
- **Date of prophetic activity:** uncertain; perhaps ca. 590 B.C., but possibly after 500 B.C.
- **Emphases:** the impending day of Yahweh—a day of judgment and salvation; Yahweh chastens those he loves, and his chastening calls his people to repentance; Israel's God keeps covenant by showing mercy to his people; Yahweh is sovereign over all the nations and will judge those who have shown no mercy to his people

OVERVIEW OF JOEL

Joel centers much of his message in the concept of "the day of the LORD." Four scenes depict this decisive day, each scene having two parts. Chapter 1 describes the immediate disaster—a devastating locust plague (1:2–12)—which leads to a call for national repentance and prayer because of the severity of the plague (vv. 13–20).

In the second scene (2:1–17), all of this is repeated, but now the plague is likened to—or perhaps implicitly identified as—an army with Yahweh at their head, accompanied by cosmic signs (vv. 10–11), and the summons to repentance is based on Yahweh's character (vv. 12–17). This extended metaphor takes the picture in scene 1 a dimension further and probably refers to God's impending future judgments on Israel and the nations. It may be in fact that "locusts" serves as a kind of code word for the Babylonian armies that invaded Judah in 598 B.C.

The third scene (2:18–32) offers God's response—first to the immediate issue of the locust plague, by restoring "the years the locusts have eaten" (v. 25) through the return of agricultural bounty (vv. 18–27); and second with a special promise of the new age of the Spirit, thus pointing to a glorious future for God's people (vv. 28–32).

The final scene (ch. 3) depicts God's second response by bringing judgment against the nations (vv. 1–16) in the form of a great battle (in the Valley of Jehoshaphat, whose name means "Yahweh judges/has judged"). This scene ends with a picture of God's extraordinary blessings on his forgiven, purified people (vv. 17–21).

SPECIFIC ADVICE FOR READING JOEL

Joel offers us neither date nor specific, identifiable historical markers. This makes the reading of Joel a bit more difficult than in other cases, since understanding a prophet's times is so helpful in understanding his message (see the introduction to the Prophets, pp. 172–73). The "northern army" (2:20, lit., "the northerner") probably refers to the locusts in its first instance, but then metaphorically to the well-known dread of invading armies from the north (Jer 4:6 [referring to Babylon]; cf. Ezek 38:15; 39:2), but nothing more is made of it. Even more striking is the fact that, in a book where calls to repentance hold such a central place (Joel 1:13–14; 2:13–17), there is scarcely a mention of the sins that are responsible for the immediate or coming disasters. To be sure, the nations will be judged for their dividing up Yahweh's land and dealing treacherously with his people (3:2–3, 6), but the sins of Judah and Jerusalem seem primarily to be sins of complacency, and the summons takes the form of a wake-up call to the "drinkers of wine" (1:2, 5). The prophet seems to assume that the people know well where they have broken covenant with their God, but we later readers can only guess.

At the heart of Joel's message is "the day of the LORD," a concept that had been used by the prophets for some time before Joel came on the scene (see Amos 5:18–20; Isa 2:12–18; 3:7, 18; 11:10–11; Jer 30:7–8; Zeph 1:7–2:2). Its earliest mention in Amos indicates that Israel had a sanguine view of this day—that it was a day in their future when God would come to their aid because they were his. But Amos turned that understanding on its head, because Israel's covenant disloyalty has placed them at enmity with Yahweh, and Amos is followed in this by all the other prophets, including especially Zephaniah. Isaiah and Jeremiah further explain it as cutting both ways—a day of judgment on those whose sins deserve such, but followed by a day of salvation for God's gathered remnant. As you read Joel, you will see that he fits into this pattern of describing it. For him, the locust plague has set God's day in motion as judgment on Judah and Jerusalem, but its consummation clearly lies in a great future eschatological event of judgment on the nations and ultimately the restoration of God's people.

You should also note as you read that, even though Joel does not mention it as such, he presupposes Yahweh's covenant relationship with his people at every turn. Locusts and drought are part of the curses for disobedience to the covenant (Deut 28:22, 38–42), as is Israel's being scattered among the nations (Joel 3:2; see Deut 28:64); the call for repentance as the pathway to future restoration is deeply covenantal, as is the idea of God's chastening the people he loves (Deut 30:1–10; cf. Joel's "rend your heart and not your garments" [2:13] with Deut 30:2, 6). Note also that the appeal to God's character in Joel 2:13 is a replay of the language of Exod 34:6, a covenant-renewal moment; God's engagement in the holy war (Joel 2:10–11; 3:9–11) is also part of this motif.

A WALK THROUGH JOEL

☐ 1:1 *Heading*

In contrast to Hosea, Joel's heading is succinct, providing no knowledge of who he is or when he lived.

☐ 1:2–12 *Scene 1A: The Locust Plague*

Note how Joel's words "Hear this" (v. 2) are the beginning of his wake-up call (v. 5) for lamentation and repentance to a nation paying no more attention to her ways than drunkards would (v. 5). It is often pointed out that the description of the plague in verses 6–12 is painfully precise. Watch how the promised blessings in 2:18–27 respond directly to this scene.

☐ 1:13–20 *Scene 1B: A Summons to Repentance*

Not only would such a plague wipe out a people economically for years, but the sacrificial system comes to a grinding halt when there is nothing left to sacrifice; hence the focus on the first call to repentance is on the priests (vv. 13–14). The rest of the summons repeats the cause for mourning (vv. 15–18), followed by Joel's own prayer in the same vein (vv. 19–20).

□ 2:1–11 *Scene 2A: God's Invading Army*

Note how this second description of the plague pictures the locusts as something now in the future; it will come against God's people as a vast army led by God himself (the holy war turns against Israel!). There is perhaps a bit of irony here, as Israel expects God to come in their behalf accompanied by winged cherubim (Ps 18:10; Ezek 10:1–20), but instead he comes with winged creatures of destruction.

□ 2:12–17 *Scene 2B: The Summons to Repentance*

The second summons to repentance is one of the more memorable moments in the Old Testament. Note especially the echoes of Deuteronomy 30:1–6—that fasting and sackcloth and ashes mean nothing if there is no rending of heart. Here also (Joel 2:13) you find the covenant basis for such repentance: God is gracious and compassionate.

□ 2:18–27 *Scene 3A: God's Response—the Promise of Plenty*

Note how much this scene corresponds to the plague as described in 1:2–12 and responds to the assumed repentance in 2:12–17. The "locust" army is pushed into the two seas (v. 20), and abundance is restored. But the ultimate goal is the praise of Yahweh and the removal of the people's shame (vv. 26–27).

□ 2:28–32 *Scene 3B: God's Response—the Promise of the Spirit*

A part of the future restoration will be the fulfillment of Moses' yearning that all of God's people will be prophets (Num 11:29). Note how the list of those who will prophesy covers the whole gamut of the social order, including daughters and the lowest on the social ladder—female servants. Note also that this belongs to the eschatological future, accompanied by cosmic signs before the final expression of God's "day," when salvation is for all who call on Yahweh's name.

□ 3:1–16a *Scene 4A: God's Response—Final Judgment of the Nations*

As scene 3A corresponds to 1A, so this scene (4A) corresponds to 2A. Here you find a more typical "woe oracle" (see *How to 1*, p. 195) in which both the nature of God's judgment and the reasons for it are spelled out. Note especially how this fulfills the pledge of the holy war that God will drive out all their enemies.

☐ 3:16b–21 *Scene 4B: God's Response—Future Blessing of God's People*

As with 2:28–32, this final picture is overlaid with images of eschatological abundance: the lavish renewal of the land (v. 18a); a fountain flowing out of Jerusalem (v. 18b; cf. Ezek 47:1–12; Rev 22:1–5); Israel's traditional enemies finished forever (v. 19); an eternal habitation of Judah and Jerusalem (v. 20); and total removal of sin (v. 21). The ultimate basis for this is the return of God's presence to Zion (vv. 17, 21).

Besides prophesying of the great outpouring of God's Spirit, the book of Joel is especially concerned with the great themes of the biblical story: God's judgment on human sin, the need for repentance, and the merciful grace of God, so that all who call on his name will be saved.

Amos

ORIENTING DATA FOR AMOS

- **Content:** in a period of rare economic prosperity and political strength for Israel, Yahweh announces their doom because she has failed to keep covenant with him
- **Prophet:** Amos, a shepherd/farmer from Tekoa, south of Bethlehem in Judah
- **Date of prophetic activity:** ca. 760 B.C., for an apparently brief period (at the peak of the reigns of Jeroboam II in Samaria [793–753] and Uzziah in Jerusalem [792–740])
- **Emphases:** Yahweh is God over all the nations and the whole universe; Yahweh will bring utter ruin to Israel for her covenant disloyalty; syncretistic religion is anathema to Yahweh; Yahweh requires justice for the innocent and mercy for the poor; religious observances are no substitute for doing good and showing mercy

OVERVIEW OF AMOS

This third in the Book of the Twelve is the earliest of the prophetic books. Its basic message is that Yahweh has utterly rejected Israel's present religious and socioeconomic practices, so much so that he is going to bring the northern kingdom to an end and send the people into exile (5:5, 27; 6:7; 7:11, 17). At issue is covenant infidelity in the form of religious syncretism (see "Specific Advice for Reading Deuteronomy," pp. 57–58) and social injustice, carried on especially by the leaders and their indolent wives (4:1; 6:1–6). Indeed, they were glutted on religion, but didn't have a clue about Yahweh and his character (4:5; 5:21–23). So the Lion roars from Zion (1:2), and Amos gives him voice (3:8).

The oracles themselves were probably delivered at the sanctuary—the king's sanctuary—in Bethel (3:14; 7:10–17; cf. 1 Kgs 12:32) and within a brief period of time (Amos 1:1). They come to us carefully arranged.

The first series (1:3–2:16) proceeds from judgment on the surrounding nations for various forms of treachery (1:3–2:3), to Judah for infidelity (2:4–5), to an opening summary judgment against Israel (2:6–16). Then comes a series of three announcement oracles (3:1–5:17; cf. "Hear this word," 3:1; 4:1; 5:1) that spell out both Yahweh's coming judgment and the reasons for it. Next are two woe oracles, which reflect Israel's complacency, based on false security—religion (5:18–27) and material prosperity (6:1–14). Finally, Amos reports five visions, the first two (7:1–6) indicating that the coming judgment will not be like former ones but will involve total destruction, including the king and his sanctuary (7:7–9). This leads to an encounter with the king's priest at Bethel (7:10–17), followed by the final two visions of utter destruction (8:1–9:10).

In all of this there is scarcely a word of comfort and only a few words suggesting that Yahweh might relent (5:5–6, 14–15). But the book itself concludes with an oracle of salvation (9:11–15) that looks beyond the fall of Israel to the fall of Judah as well, promising that "David's fallen tent" (Jerusalem) will be restored in a future age of abundance.

SPECIFIC ADVICE FOR READING AMOS

Amos is the first of our four canonical eighth-century prophets (a contemporary of Hosea, and a bit older than Isaiah and Micah). The historical-political background to Amos can be found in 2 Kings 14:23–15:7 (cf. 2 Chr 26). Jeroboam II (in Israel) and Uzziah (in Judah) came to reign at about the same time, and both had long and prosperous reigns, which included territorial expansion of a kind that together nearly equaled that of David and Solomon. This was made possible mostly because their reigns coincided with a very low period in Assyrian fortunes (782–745), until the rise of Tiglath-Pileser III. And, of course, the royal house and the wealthy considered this period of growth and expansion as evidence of Yahweh's blessing, with a still brighter day of Yahweh awaiting them (Amos 5:18). But instead it turned out to be a brief halcyon period that lasted barely one generation. Thus, even though not mentioned by name in Amos, Assyria is still the ominous power on the political landscape, whose shadow lurks behind several passages (2:13–16; 3:11; 5:3, 27; 6:7, 8–14; 7:9, 17; 9:4). And within less than a generation after the death of Jeroboam the kingdom of Israel ceased to exist altogether (722/1), and Yahweh's voice was no longer heard there (8:11–12)—God having used Assyria as his rod of judgment against his wayward people (see 2 Kgs 17:7–41).

What Amos saw and spoke most clearly at the peak of this period (Amos 1:1) was that everything was in fact the opposite of what it seemed. Their "blessing" had nothing to do with Yahweh, but everything to do with their own corrupt practices; nor did their religion have much to do with Yahweh, even though it was undoubtedly still being carried on in his name. Thus only two broad categories of sin need be denounced: syncretistic religion (2:7–8; 4:4–5; 5:21–23, 25–26; 8:10, 14) and social injustice (2:6–8; 3:9–10; 4:1; 5:7, 10–13, 15, 24; 6:12; 8:4–6), which are clearly spelled out in the opening oracle, where they blend (2:6–8), as they do again in 5:21–24 and 8:4–6. It is this combination of oppression of the poor in a context of distorted religious enthusiasm that leads to Yahweh's judgment in the form of exile.

Crucial to this judgment is Amos's own loyalty to Yahweh and his covenant. At the heart of the covenant, as Jesus himself pointed out, is love for God and love for neighbor (Mark 12:30–31). Thus the Old Testament covenant, along with regulations for proper worship as a way of maintaining love for God, was full of laws that provided a form of equity for all, based primarily on land distribution (and thus creating a mostly rural rather than urban society). And those who were without land (widows, orphans, Levites, foreigners) were to be properly cared for by the others. The reason for this, as the Israelites were constantly reminded in the law (see e.g., Exod 22:21–27; Deut 16:18–20; 24:17–22), was that Yahweh himself had compassion for the poor (including a slave people called Israel, whom he had rescued and made his own).

But during this halcyon period enormous changes had taken place in both Judah and Israel, especially in the latter. An urban mentality developed, with luxurious dwellings and ornate appointments (3:12, 15; 5:11; 6:4–6), which was helped along by a collusion among royalty, priests, prophets, and judges, which became a wealthy aristocracy at the expense of the poor. Yahweh had had enough, so he chose a man of the land from the south, a Yahwist with powerful abilities of speech, to speak his word of judgment on the whole scene. Thus Amos renewed Moses' kind of prophetism among God's people—addressed to leaders and people alike, not just to individuals—announcing that the ultimate curse for not maintaining covenant loyalty, namely, desolation of the land and exile (Lev 26:27–45; Deut 28:25–68), was about to be carried out. And he became the forerunner of many others who were to come, most of whom brought the same message to the southern kingdom.

A WALK THROUGH AMOS

☐ 1:1–2 *Heading*

Note several important features of this heading: (1) Amos is a man of the land from Judah (Tekoa), who carefully dates his "words"; (2) note also that verse 2 is Amos's own words about Yahweh's speech through him, imagery that will be picked up again in 3:8; and (3) don't miss the geography: Yahweh roars in Zion; Carmel withers (NNW of Jerusalem on the Mediterranean, a straight line that would cross Bethel and Samaria!).

☐ 1:3–2:16 *Judgment on the Nations—and Israel*

Watch for three things that give this series its rhetorical power: (1) The patterns repeat ("for three sins . . . , even for four"); (2) they are directed against Israel's closest neighbors (beginning with a chiastic NE/SW–NW/SE pattern before going due east and south); (3) all of the sins are forms of treachery until you come to Judah (2:4–5), who has also broken covenant with Yahweh. You can imagine his Israelite hearers cheering Yahweh on—until the shoe drops, on Israel itself (2:6–16). Though patterned after the rest, this final oracle is considerably elaborated, since the main points of Amos's message lie here: first the reasons for judgment (vv. 6–8), then a brief replay of the Israelites' spurning of covenant history (vv. 9–12), concluding with the pronouncement of coming doom (vv. 13–16).

☐ 3:1–15 *First Announcement Oracle: Failure to Keep Covenant*

Watch for the various ways this first "Hear Yahweh's word" oracle sets up the rest of the book. It begins with Israel's covenantal privilege (vv. 1–2), followed by Amos's justification for prophesying (vv. 3–8)—to a people who have commanded him not to (2:12; 7:12–13). Then the Philistines and Egyptians are called on to witness Israel's coming destruction (3:9–10), followed by three announcements of doom (vv. 11, 12, 13–15).

☐ 4:1–13 *Second Announcement Oracle: Rejection of Divine Warnings*

This second "Hear" oracle announces judgment on the indolent wives of the wealthy (vv. 1–3), concluding with an ironic invitation to increase their beloved religious practices (vv. 4–5). This is followed by a series of reminders of past judgments Israel has failed to heed (vv. 6–11), with a call to prepare to "meet your God" in judgment (v. 12); it concludes with a fragment of a hymn (v. 13; cf. 5:8–9; 9:5–6) that describes their God as Creator and Revealer (cf., e.g., Ps 104:2–5).

☐ 5:1–17 *Third Announcement Oracle: False Religion and Injustice*

This third "Hear" oracle in many ways forms the heart of the book. Note its striking chiastic structure. It begins and ends with a lament over Israel's fall (vv. 2–3, 16–17), followed by an invitation to "seek [Yahweh] and live" (vv. 4–6, 14–15), while the inner circle spells out the recipients of this mixture of doom and invitation, namely, those who pervert justice (vv. 7, 10–12). The centerpiece is one more fragment of the hymn, reminding the people that the Creator is also the Judge (vv. 8–9).

☐ 5:18–27 *False Security in Religion*

This first "woe" oracle speaks directly to Israel's false security in multiplied religious exercises (more religion = more favor with God), but the day of the Lord they are looking for will in fact turn out to be a nightmare (vv. 18–20). Indeed, Yahweh hates Israel's religious practices (vv. 21–23), because the people themselves are full of injustice (v. 24). Note especially how the conclusion (vv. 25–26) makes clear the syncretistic nature of their present worship, ending with a final announcement of doom (v. 27).

☐ 6:1–14 *False Security in Material Goods and Military Success*

This second woe is directed at Israel's leaders (v. 1), who will be among the first to go into exile (v. 7). Their security lies in their great wealth and luxury (vv. 3–6 [v. 2 is much debated]) and in some minor military conquests (vv. 12–13; note esp. the pun on the name "Lo Debar" [= "nothing"]); note how both false securities are concluded with announcements of judgment (vv. 8–11, 14).

☐ 7:1–9 *Three Vision Reports: Locusts, Fire, Plumb Line*

With these three visions the final series of judgments begins its move toward Yahweh's determined end. Note how the first two indicate that what is to come will not be like former plagues (locusts/drought; cf. 4:6–9); Israel's future will be full of (lit.) "groaning" (NIV, "plumb line") because their destruction is now inevitable. Note especially that the king is finally specifically named in 7:9, which is what raises the ire of the king's priest, Amaziah.

☐ 7:10–17 *The Encounter with Amaziah*

This little report is full of interest. In turn you learn that (1) Amos is at Bethel, and Amaziah, the king's priest, reports him to the king (vv. 10–11); (2) when Amos is forbidden to prophesy (vv. 12–13), he indicates he is not a prophet by choice, nor does he belong to the prophetic guild (vv. 14–15); and (3) he then uses this encounter to pronounce Yahweh's judgment against Amaziah and his household (vv. 16–17). Thus both the king and the priest are singled out for individual pronouncements of doom.

☐ 8:1–9:10 *Two Vision Reports: The Certainty of Israel's Coming Destruction*

These two visions spell out the final doom of Israel. The first (overripe fruit, 8:1–14) especially recapitulates the issues of the Israelites' false religion mingled with injustice (vv. 4–6), in which their temple songs are turned into wailing (v. 3) and their treatment of the poor turned into the ultimate "famine"—the total loss of Yahweh's word in Israel.

The second (9:1–10) is climactic: Yahweh stands by the altar at Bethel, which crumbles on the heads of the people (vv. 1–4; note the reversal in v. 4 of their failing to seek good and hate evil [5:14–15]); after one more hymnic insertion (9:5–6), it concludes with the announcement of Israel's total annihilation (vv. 8–10). Israel is no better than her pagan neighbors (v. 7).

☐ 9:11–15 *Hope for the Future*

After all that has gone before, this word of hope is welcome relief. It comes in two parts, (1) the promised restoration of Jerusalem (vv. 11–12) and (2) the coming of the great messianic age (vv. 13–15), which have found their beginning fulfillment in Jesus Christ.

The book of Amos declares an important dimension of the biblical story in bold relief: True religion and social justice must go hand in hand, or one is breaking covenant with God.

Obadiah

ORIENTING DATA FOR OBADIAH

- **Content:** a doom oracle against Edom for taking advantage of (probably) the Babylonian conquest of Jerusalem in 588–86 B.C.
- **Prophet:** Obadiah, a prophet from Judah
- **Date of prophetic activity:** probably just after the fall of Jerusalem (586 B.C.?)
- **Emphases:** God's judgment on Edom for her sins against God's people; the defeat of those who think themselves unconquerable; Israel's deliverance and restoration on the day of the Lord

OVERVIEW OF OBADIAH

This fourth of the Book of the Twelve, which is also the shortest book in the Old Testament, is a single, unified prophecy against Edom that was probably spoken to various groups of Judeans to encourage them in the aftermath of their national tragedy. All the parts of a doom oracle are present: the announcement of doom—a prediction of Edom's coming defeat (vv. 1–9); the reasons for doom—a review of Edom's crimes against his "brother" while Judah was helpless (vv. 10–14); and the promised future (for Jacob, not Esau!)—on the day of the Lord Israel's sovereignty will be restored (vv. 15–21).

SPECIFIC ADVICE FOR READING OBADIAH

Edom was Israel's most tenacious foe throughout the history of the two "brother" nations (v. 10; cf. Gen 25:24–34), so it should come as no surprise that Edom is the subject of more foreign-nation oracles than any other people (Isa 21:11–12; 34:5–15; Jer 49:7–22; Ezek 25:12–14; 35:1–15; Amos 1:11–12; cf. Joel 3:19; Mal 1:2–5).

The principles for reading any foreign-nation oracle apply here. Yahweh is God not only of Israel but also of all the nations of the world; it reflects the "curse" side of the Abrahamic covenant ("I will curse those who curse you"); it is the prophet's engagement in the holy war, as a messenger of the Divine Warrior. If Israel's sins are great and deserve punishment, the treachery of Edom will also be punished, since it stands so completely over against God's own character of generosity and kindness. Moreover, if God is to deliver his people completely and permanently, he cannot leave their enemies free to strike again. Here again you find the typical final eschatological backdrop against which temporal judgments are to be understood (see *How to 1*, p. 201).

You may want to read Psalm 137 alongside this oracle to capture the sense of how deeply Israel felt about Edom's treachery. You may also want to read Obadiah 1–6 alongside Jeremiah 49:14–16 (for vv. 1–4) and 49:9–10 (for vv. 5–6); very likely Obadiah is restating and recasting Jeremiah's oracle as his starting point, an oracle that is probably well known to his hearers.

A WALK THROUGH OBADIAH

☐ Verse 1 *Title and Introduction*

Before Yahweh actually speaks (vv. 2–21), Obadiah presents himself as a messenger from the heavenly court who announces God's judgment on Edom in terms of the holy war.

☐ Verse 2–9 *Edom's Doom Announced*

At God's command, Edom will be conquered by a coalition of other nations (v. 1), and this in spite of its rocky, mountainous terrain in which it had rested secure for centuries (vv. 2–4); their plunder will far exceed the usual level (vv. 5–6). Note that, treachery for treachery, even Edom's old allies will turn against them and lead to their downfall (v. 7). Finally (vv. 8–9), Yahweh declares the ineffectiveness of two groups in which it took great pride—its famed wise men (Job and his counselors were from a part of Edom) and its warriors.

☐ Verse 10–14 *The Reasons for Edom's Doom*

The crime is treachery. When the Babylonians invaded Judah (2 Kgs 25), Edom quickly made a separate peace and then took advantage of Judah instead of helping its brother nation (Obad 11–12), seizing Judean towns and farmlands (v. 13) and capturing Judeans fleeing from the Babylonians (v. 14; handing them over probably to be sold as slaves).

□ **Verse 15–21** ***The Coming Day of the Lord***

You will note that Edom's judgment is part of the coming day of Yahweh in which all nations will experience his wrath (v. 15). The judgment takes the form of the *lex talionis* ("eye for an eye"), when Esau's and Jacob's fortunes are reversed (vv. 15b–18), as the returning exiles repossess the promised land (vv. 19–21; cf. Deut 30:1–10).

Obadiah reminds us of God's justice in punishing human sinfulness and of God's ultimate victory over earthly powers.

Jonah

ORIENTING DATA FOR JONAH

- **Content:** through a very reluctant prophet, God shows compassion for one of Israel's hated enemies
- **Prophet:** Jonah son of Amittai, who prophesied during the reign of Jeroboam II (see 2 Kgs 14:25)
- **Emphases:** Yahweh as Creator, Sustainer, and Redeemer of all; Yahweh's compassionate concern for the Gentiles (represented by Nineveh); Israel's reluctance (represented by Jonah) to acknowledge Yahweh's compassion for the nations

OVERVIEW OF JONAH

The book of Jonah is unique among the Latter Prophets. Rather than a collection of prophetic oracles, it is instead a narrative about God's compassion for some hated Gentiles by way of a Hebrew prophet who wants nothing to do with it.

The story is in four easily discernible parts (corresponding to our present chapter divisions): (1) Jonah is called to preach judgment against Nineveh — in Nineveh! — to which he responds by fleeing as far in the other direction as he can go. Yahweh sends a storm, and Jonah is thrown overboard and is rescued by God's miraculous provision of a large fish. (2) Jonah responds in prayer, a psalm of thanksgiving for deliverance. (3) Jonah accepts his mission to Nineveh, with these results: Nineveh repents and God relents (in keeping with Jer 18:7–8). (4) Jonah erupts in anger, to which God responds with an object lesson and a final question to Jonah (Jonah 4:9–10) — the point of everything.

SPECIFIC ADVICE FOR READING JONAH

In order to read Jonah well, you need to be watching for two things — the narrator's skill in telling his story and the theological concerns that he brings to it.

First, in order to appreciate the power of this narrative, you might try to put yourself in the sandals of its intended Israelite hearers. The story functions in much the same way as the parables of Jesus (see *How to 1*, pp. 151– 56), as the narrator draws his hearers/readers into the story and then catches them off guard with the final question.

The narrator's literary skills are reflected in several ways. For example, the basic story is framed by Jonah's flight from God (1:3) and his reason for it (4:2). Note also how the sailors' response to God's rescue of them anticipates God's compassion on Nineveh. Irony is used throughout to secure theological points: The pagan sailors end up sacrificing to Yahweh, after Yahweh's defiant prophet is thrown into the sea. At the end of his psalm Jonah exclaims (of his own deliverance): "Salvation comes from the LORD"—which is then played out by Nineveh's repentance and God's withholding of judgment. Jonah in his anger with Yahweh nonetheless speaks the truth about Yahweh's character (4:2), which turns out to be the very reason for his anger. And Jonah, rescued from death by Yahweh, in the ends wishes to die rather than to live—because the Ninevites get to live rather than die.

Second, this story is primarily about Yahweh and only secondarily about Jonah. Yahweh is the protagonist throughout: He calls Jonah; he sends a storm when Jonah disobeys—and intensifies it to keep the sailors from rescuing him; he provides a great fish to rescue Jonah; he is the object of praise and thanksgiving in Jonah's psalm; he sends Jonah a second time and then stays his hand when Jonah's preaching is successful; and in the end he provides both the plant and the worm and the scorching east wind to instruct Jonah in Yahweh's ways. Jonah, on the other hand, serves as the foil so that Yahweh's story can be told with power and punch.

At issue in all of this is the Abrahamic covenant (Gen 12:3)—that Yahweh is full of compassion and mercy for all that he has made (Ps 145:8–9, 13, 17) and that he intended all along to bless the nations through his election of Israel. But God's election, always an act of mercy, sometimes becomes the basis for pride and prejudice. And in this case remember that Assyria was the most cruel empire in ancient history (see the book of Nahum), yet God was giving such people a chance to repent—not conversion to Yahweh, but nonetheless a response sufficient for Yahweh to withhold his punishments. It is this "injustice" of God's mercy that is so offensive to Jonah.

A WALK THROUGH JONAH

☐ 1:1–17 *Jonah Runs from the Lord*

This opening narrative sets you up for the rest. Besides the basic story about Jonah, don't miss the two main elements: (1) Yahweh is in control of everything (note especially his role as Lord of land and sea, which the sailors come to recognize and Jonah does not understand), and (2) the deliberate contrasts between Yahweh's close-minded prophet and the increasingly open-minded pagan sailors.

☐ 2:1–10 *Jonah's Prayer of Thanksgiving*

Note that this "prayer" takes the form of an individual psalm of thanksgiving (see *How to 1*, pp. 218–19) and is thus expressed in terms of Yahweh's deliverance even while Jonah is still engulfed by the sea. The psalm is in three parts (vv. 2–4, 5–7, 8–9), the first two of which are parallel, as they interweave distress, rescue, and testimony, and conclude on a similar note—that of looking toward the temple. The final, testimonial, stanza (vv. 8–9) then anticipates the rest of the narrative, expressing Jonah's trust in Yahweh—from whom salvation comes—but doing so in contrast to those who "cling to worthless idols" (e.g., the Ninevites).

☐ 3:1–10 *Jonah's Preaching and Nineveh's Repentance*

Jonah is given a second chance, to which he responds with obedience (vv. 1–3). Note that the repentance of the city focuses on the king, who both sets the example (v. 6) and issues a decree that calls not only for fasting and sackcloth—even by the animals!—but a turning away from their evil ways and violence (vv. 7–8), hoping that such a display of repentance may cause God to relent (v. 9), which in fact he does (v. 10).

☐ 4:1–11 *Jonah's Anger at Yahweh's Compassion*

Here you come to the point of it all. Jonah does not want God to relent and is angry with Yahweh for being true to himself (see Exod 34:4–6)! The rest is dominated by Yahweh's twice-asked question, "Have you any right to be angry?/Do you have a right to be angry?" and Jonah's conviction that he does (vv. 4, 9). Using language from 1:17, the narrator three times points out that Yahweh "provides"—first the vine to give shade, then the worm, and finally the scorching wind. And then the second shoe drops. Jonah's selfish "compassion" over the *plant* more than justifies God's compassion for Nineveh's *people*—and *animals*. And we the readers are implicitly invited to answer Yahweh's question for ourselves—with regard to *our* enemies.

The book of Jonah continues the biblical story of the Creator and Redeemer God who shows compassion not only for his own but also for all whom he has created; the God of Scripture loves his enemies—and ours.

Micah

ORIENTING DATA FOR MICAH

- **Content:** alternating oracles of doom on Israel and Judah for their idolatry and social injustices and of future hope because of Yahweh's mercies
- **Prophet:** Micah, a Judean prophet from Moresheth, a town about twenty-five miles southwest of Jerusalem
- **Date of prophetic activity:** some length of time between the accession of Jotham (740 B.C.) and the death of Hezekiah (686)
- **Emphases:** the threat of divine judgment for breaking covenant with Yahweh; Yahweh as a God of justice and mercy who pleads the cause of the poor and requires his people to do the same; after judgment Yahweh will restore Jerusalem through the promised Davidic king; Yahweh as God of all the nations

OVERVIEW OF MICAH

The book of Micah, sixth in the Book of the Twelve, is a careful—and unique—collection and arrangement of oracles delivered by Micah over an apparently long period (1:6–7 was given well before the fall of Samaria in 722 B.C., while 1:10–16 traces the march of Sennacherib, which took place in 701; see 2 Kgs 18:13–19:37; Isa 36–37). Its uniqueness lies in its (not necessarily chronological) arrangement, which alternates between oracles of judgment and of future hope (basically Mic 1–2; 3–5; 6–7, which are marked off by the call to "hear/listen" 1:2; 3:1; 6:1).

The oracles in 1:2–2:11 are primarily pronouncements of divine judgment on Samaria and (especially) Jerusalem (the capitals representing the two kingdoms); they conclude with a brief promise of future restoration (2:12–13). The second set is introduced by a brief collection of three doom oracles (3:1–4, 5–8, 9–12); it concludes with a longer collection of oracles of hope (4:1–5:15) that focus on the promised (messianic) Davidic king. The third set is more evenly divided between threat (6:1–16) and hope (7:8–20), which are held together by Micah's lament over Israel's decadence (7:1–7).

SPECIFIC ADVICE FOR READING MICAH

Four matters are crucial for a good reading of Micah. First, the arrangement itself not only offers you a handle for reading the text but at the same time says something about Micah's own theology, which mirrors Deuteronomy 28–30. At the heart of things, as in Hosea, is the dynamic tension between the necessity of divine judgment (curses) because of Israel's breaking covenant with Yahweh and Yahweh's own longing to bless his people because they are his and because of his own character (compassion, mercy, forgiveness; see Mic 7:18–20). Micah himself is, as it were, both torn apart and held together by this twofold reality; the final composition of his book presents this tension in bold relief but concludes on the bright note of future hope.

Second, as is true for most of the prophets of Israel, the political history of the period plays an especially important role in understanding the oracles themselves. Micah is the fourth of the eighth-century prophets, a generation after Hosea and Amos, and a younger contemporary of Isaiah. Gone now are the halcyon days that characterized the reigns of Jeroboam II and Uzziah, and all of the seeds of decay and eventual destruction are settling in as the idolatry and social injustice condemned by Hosea, Amos, and Isaiah continued apace. At the same time Assyria is a constant threat on the international scene as she begins reasserting her power in the Near Eastern world (see "Specific Advice for Reading Isaiah," p. 176). Thus Assyria looms large in Micah, but her role is ambivalent: Although she is God's agent of judgment on Samaria (1:6–7, 10–16), she will fail against Judah (5:5–6) and will eventually experience God's judgment (5:15; 7:10). At the same time, as with Isaiah, the anticipation of Babylonian power is also prophesied (4:10).

Third, note especially the reasons for judgment on Judah. As it is with Isaiah and Amos, the issues are two: idolatry (1:7; 5:12–14) and social injustice (2:1–2, 8–11; 3:1–3, 8–11; 6:10–12; 7:2–3). Especially important for Micah is the role of the promised land as inheritance, which here goes in two directions—(1) exile from the land as part of the curse for unfaithfulness to Yahweh (1:16; 2:10; 4:9–10; cf. Deut 28:25–42) and (2) the unfaithfulness itself as the leaders and land barons deprive the rural poor of their traditional inheritance (Mic 2:2, 9; 3:2–3, 9–11; 6:10–12, 16; 7:2).

Fourth, Micah takes Israel's promised role in blessing the nations (Gen 12:3) with full seriousness (Mic 4:1–4; 7:11–13). This is the oath made to Abraham (7:20; the final word in the book), and this is the ultimate role of the messianic king, who will be God's agent for the peace of the nations (5:5). Note, therefore, that chapters 4–5, which express future hope in messianic terms, lie at the very center of the present arrangement. Thus, both the first and second oracles of hope center specifically on the coming messianic king (2:13; 5:1–6), and Micah 5:2 is cited in Matthew 2:6, in a Gospel that is particularly concerned about the Messiah's role in behalf of the nations (Matt 28:19–20).

Finally, you should also note that one hundred years later the oracle in Micah 3:12 is cited by some elders against King Jehoiakim, who wanted to take Jeremiah's life (Jer 26:17–19), a passage which also implies that Micah's preaching was in part responsible for Hezekiah's reforms (2 Kgs 18:1–8).

A WALK THROUGH MICAH

☐ 1:1 *Heading*

Note here (1) the emphasis on this being Yahweh's word, through the agency of Micah (from rural Moresheth, not Jerusalem), (2) its time, and (3) its subject matter.

☐ 1:2–16 *First Series of Threats (against Samaria and Jerusalem)*

Note how the first word (v. 2) sets the pace for the whole, by calling the whole earth to listen to Yahweh. This is followed by an oracle that begins with Yahweh as the Divine Warrior (vv. 3–4)—but now against his own people, whose sins center in the capital cities of Samaria and Jerusalem (v. 5). The threat of doom in this case is especially directed against Samaria for her idolatry (vv. 6–7).

The second threat (vv. 10–16), which begins with Micah's own response to it (vv. 8–9), is against Jerusalem, expressed in marvelous wordplays (see the NIV text notes) on the cities that Sennacherib had destroyed in his coming "even to the gate of Jerusalem" (v. 12). Although not as the result of Sennacherib's invasion, nonetheless the final word of threat is exile (v. 16).

☐ 2:1–11 *The Reasons for Judgment*

Watch carefully for the change of speakers: Micah (vv. 1–2), Yahweh (vv. 3–4), Micah (v. 5), false prophets (v. 6), Micah (v. 7a), Yahweh (vv. 7b–13). Note how the word of doom and its reasons (social injustice on the part of the land barons) come first (vv. 1–2), followed by Yahweh's threat, expressed in terms of the land being taken from them (vv. 3–5). The next oracle is God's judgment against the false theology of the prophets who have sided with the land barons (vv. 6–11).

☐ 2:12–13 *The First Word of Hope*

In direct response to verses 3–5 this first word of hope for the future is expressed in terms of regathering the people, with the messianic king in the lead.

☐ 3:1–12 *Second Series of Threats and Reasons*

With this collection of three oracles (vv. 1–4, 5–7, 9–12), Micah now focuses on the role of the leaders and prophets, who promote social injustice by their policies and prophecies. Note that Micah's own prophetic role is Spirit-inspired (v. 8; cf. 2:7) and that the final word (3:12) is judgment against Zion (Jerusalem and its temple).

☐ 4:1–5:15 *The Second Word of Hope: God's Messianic Kingdom and King*

As the centerpiece of the book, and now in direct response to 3:12, this series of oracles begins with the promised messianic restoration of Zion, where God's word will go forth and the nations gather to hear it (4:1–5; cf. Isa 2:1–4). This is followed in turn by (1) a long oracle promising return after exile, with the crushing of nations who oppose them (Mic 4:6–13), (2) the central role of the messianic king in the restoration (5:1–6), (3) the rest of the exiles triumphing over their enemies by bringing life and death (vv. 7–9), and (4) a final oracle in which Yahweh purges Judah (vv. 10–14) and punishes her enemies (v. 15).

☐ 6:1–16 *God's Case against Jerusalem (the Third Word of Threat)*

Here Yahweh takes Israel to court. He is the plaintiff—but also the judge! The mountains serve as jury (vv. 1–3). The plaintiff's case is made by rehearsing the essential moments in Israel's redemption—all

Yahweh's doing (vv. 4–5). Using the language of temple liturgy (Pss 15:1; 24:3), the defense responds with promises of increasingly more religion (Mic 6:6–7, note the gradual intensification of their offer), to which Yahweh responds by reminding them of what they already know about his character that they are to follow (v. 8). The judgment itself (v. 16) is based on Israel's failure precisely at this point (vv. 9–15).

□ 7:1–7 *Micah's Lament*

Once again (cf. 1:8) Micah himself laments over Jerusalem's inevitable fall, but his final word is one of hope (v. 7) and serves as a transition to the conclusion of the book.

□ 7:8–20 *The Third Word of Hope*

Hope for the future is Micah's last word; it begins with an expression of Israel's returning from exile and now fulfilling her role for the nations (vv. 8–13) and concludes with Micah's prayer (v. 14) and Yahweh's response (vv. 15–20). Note especially how the conclusion (vv. 18–20) is expressed in terms of Yahweh's character and prior promises to Abraham and Jacob: There is no God like Yahweh, who pardons sin and forgives transgression.

The book of Micah is a marvelous prophetic representation of the essentials of the biblical story, both in its Old Testament expression and in its anticipation of the New, with the promised Messiah and the restoration of his people.

Nahum

ORIENTING DATA FOR NAHUM

- **Content:** a prophecy of God's judgment against Nineveh (Assyria) for her oppression, cruelty, and idolatry, concluding with the announced destruction of the city
- **Prophet:** Nahum, from Judah, otherwise unknown (even his hometown is uncertain)
- **Date of prophetic activity:** sometime before the fall of Nineveh in 612 B.C., during the period of Judah's being a vassal to Assyria
- **Emphases:** Yahweh's sovereignty over all the nations; Yahweh's execution of justice against cruelty; Yahweh's overthrow of the arrogant who think of themselves as eternal

OVERVIEW OF NAHUM

This seventh in the Book of the Twelve is an unrelenting denunciation of, and pronouncement of God's judgment against, Assyria for her own unrelenting cruelty as master of the nations. As such, Nahum stands in contrast to the book of Jonah, which depicts at an earlier point in time Yahweh's concern for even his bitterest enemies (Assyria). But now Assyria's sin has "reached its full measure" (Gen 15:16), and Yahweh's famous patience is necessarily at an end. The key to Nahum's message is 1:7–8, which simultaneously expresses comfort to Judah and destruction for Nineveh.

The overall progression of the prophecy can be fairly easily seen. It begins with a Divine Warrior victory hymn (1:2–8), the last lines of which (vv. 7–8) serve also to introduce the first major oracle (1:9–2:2). This is followed by a vision of Nineveh's ruin (2:3–10), plus a taunt (vv. 11–13). Next come a series of oracles and taunts that declare the absolute certainty of Nineveh's demise (3:1–17), concluding with a satirical dirge over the fallen empire (vv. 18–19).

SPECIFIC ADVICE FOR READING NAHUM

The book of Nahum is a carefully crafted, brilliantly executed piece of poetry in which a whole variety of prophetic forms—hymn, salvation, doom, taunt, dirge—are carefully interwoven so as to effect what is basically a "woe oracle" over Nineveh (Assyria), along with a salvation oracle to Judah. Part of Nahum's mastery is his immediate introduction of Yahweh (1:2–6), followed by the interweaving of oracles against Nineveh and to Judah, without mentioning Judah until 1:15 and Nineveh until 2:8 (the NIV supplies the names earlier to help the reader through the alternating pattern in the first oracle; see "A Walk through Nahum"). All of this is expressed in wonderful poetic style with a whole variety of parallelisms (see *How to 1*, p. 198–99) and evocative imagery. An alertness to these various structural and metaphorical matters will enhance your reading of this book.

For the biblical/historical background to Nahum you may want to read 2 Kings 17–23 and 2 Chronicles 33–34. Three things about this background are essential for understanding Nahum: First, he is prophesying while Assyria is still at the height of her powers (Nah 1:12), having earlier established her presence in Egypt by conquering Thebes (3:8; ca. 663 B.C.). Second, Assyria was well known among the ancients—indeed, the records of her own kings verify it—as the most cruel of conquerors; her treacheries were legendary and barbaric, including the total destruction of peoples that were conquered (as with Israel, for example, who all but lost her identity when the people were resettled in Assyria and the land itself was resettled with pagans; see 2 Kgs 17:3–6, 24–41). Third, during the whole period in which Nahum could have prophesied, the kings of Judah (Manasseh and Josiah) were vassals of Assyria. All of this means that Nahum's prophesying was politically incorrect in every way—except from Yahweh's point of view.

Another important matter: Nahum (like Obadiah) is primarily directed against a foreign nation. As it always is in the Hebrew prophets, the theology that lies behind this is Yahweh's sovereignty over the entire universe, including all the nations as well as Judah, plus his covenant with Abraham in which he promised that "whoever curses you I will curse" (Gen 12:3). Judah's servitude to Assyria—plus her present political insignificance (except for Assyria's need for access to Egypt)—is to be understood in the light of God's omnipotence and justice. Be alert also for the reasons for Yahweh's judgments against Assyria: Besides her idolatries (Nah 1:14), her most pronounced sin is cruelty and injustice; she has enslaved nations (3:4), her cruelty is endless (3:19), and her merchants have stripped the lands clean (3:16). Against these evils, God's own goodness and compassion (1:7) stand as polar opposites.

A WALK THROUGH NAHUM

☐ 1:1–8 *Triumph of the Divine Warrior*

Note how the opening psalm is not case-specific, but introduces Yahweh as triumphant in the holy war, who as the all-powerful Ruler of the cosmos (vv. 4–5) takes vengeance on his enemies (vv. 2, 6, 8)—while at the same time he is the God who is slow to anger, good, and compassionate (vv. 3, 7; echoing Exod 34:4–6).

☐ 1:9–2:2 *Nineveh's Ruin and Judah's Salvation*

The NIV helps you see the alternation between comfort to Judah (1:12–13, 15; 2:2) and judgment of Nineveh (1:9–11, 14; 2:1) by adding their names at the appropriate places. After reading them in their canonical order, you might also try reading each set together to get the sense of crescendo in each case. Observe that the last in the series (2:1–2) also serves to set in motion the vision that follows.

☐ 2:3–13 *Vision and Taunt over Nineveh's Fall*

Note how Nahum now picks up "the attacker" from 2:1, describing in striking images the nature of Assyria's overthrow at the hands of Babylon (vv. 3–4, 9–10), while Nineveh's own mustering of troops will be of no avail (vv. 5–8). In light of that vision, Nahum then taunts Assyria as a lion (Assyria's national symbol) without a den (vv. 11–12), concluding with a word from Yahweh that summarizes both the vision and the taunt (v. 13).

☐ 3:1–7 *A Pronouncement of Woe and Taunt over Nineveh*

Listen to the powerful imagery in the short lines of the pronouncement of doom (vv. 1–3), again with Babylonian troops in view, while the reason for doom (v. 4) uses the imagery of an alluring harlot as the means of enslaving the nations. Note also how this taunt (vv. 5–7) begins the way 2:11–13 ends: " 'I am against you,' declares the LORD Almighty."

☐ 3:8–19 *Concluding Taunts and Dirge over Assyria's Fall*

After a satirical taunt over Nineveh (vv. 8–11; in light of her destruction of Thebes in Egypt), Nahum presents a series of insults (vv. 12–17) and concludes with a satirical dirge (vv. 18–19) that ends with a question. The only other prophetic book to end this way is Jonah, also regarding Nineveh, whose question stands in instructive contrast to this one.

Nahum reminds us of the essential character of the God whose story is told in the Bible, a God of goodness and salvation as well as of justice and judgment standing side by side in a way that is finally exhibited in the same way in the death of Jesus Christ on a cross.

Habakkuk

ORIENTING DATA FOR HABAKKUK

- **Content:** Habakkuk enters into dialogue with God over the question of injustice (How do people get away with evil and God seems to do nothing?) and receives grounds for trust
- **Prophet:** Habakkuk, a prophet of Judah, is unknown apart from this book
- **Date of prophetic activity:** sometime between 612 and 599 B.C., when Babylon had begun to dominate the international scene, but before she had attacked Jerusalem
- **Emphases:** prophetic indignation over God's apparent toleration of injustice; prophetic confidence in the justice and power of God; the stance of the righteous is faithfulness and trust in God; God's assurance that the wicked will be punished

OVERVIEW OF HABAKKUK

You may find this eighth in the Book of the Twelve to be among the easier of the prophetic books to read, because the structure is clear and the train of thought easy to follow. The first two chapters take the form of a dialogue between the prophet and Yahweh over injustice. Chapter 3 is the prophet's final response to God in the form of prayer in which he longs for the new exodus, yet affirms his trust in God no matter what.

In his complaint Habakkuk wrestles with what he knows to be true about God's character alongside God's apparent tolerance of the violence and injustice that abound in Judah (1:2–4). God's response—that he is raising up the Babylonians to handle this matter (1:5–11)—is small comfort to the prophet (1:12–17), since the Babylonians are more violent yet! So he takes his stand like the watchman of the night to see what answer will come in the morning (2:1). God's second response is twofold: (1) The prophet must wait and continue to trust in God (2:2–4), and (2) the arrogant will surely meet their doom in kind (plunder for plunder, 2:4–20). Habakkuk's prayer is a dramatic metaphorical remembrance of the exodus from Egypt, which inspires hope, trust, and rejoicing in God in the face of all difficulties.

SPECIFIC ADVICE FOR READING HABAKKUK

In many ways reading Habakkuk is like reading an extended lament such as one finds, for example, in Psalm 10 or 13. Everything is predicated on God's character—and the prophet's/psalmist's confidence that God will indeed eventually judge the actions of the wicked. In each case it is precisely because of who God is that the prophet or psalmist cries out, "How long?" at what seems to be divine tolerance of evil.

It is this relationship to the laments in the Psalter that best explains the most unusual feature of Habakkuk, namely, that there is no oracle directed toward God's people as such. Rather the prophet has himself taken on the role of the people in his dialogue with God over present injustice. And the liturgical notations at the beginning and the end of chapter 3 make it clear that Habakkuk intended his prayer/psalm to be sung in the community of the righteous.

For the biblical background to Habakkuk you will want to read 2 Kings 22–23 and 2 Chronicles 34:1–36:4. The way he mentions the raising up of Babylon in Habakkuk 1:6 suggests that she had not yet achieved full international ascendancy (after 605 B.C.), which also means that Habakkuk was a contemporary of Zephaniah, Nahum, and Jeremiah. The descriptions of Judah's sins in these four books confirm the Kings–Chronicles testimony that Josiah's reform was only short-lived and skin-deep, and that Judah was a society of continuing injustice, violence, and rejection of the law. Yet, like his contemporaries, Habakkuk saw the future with clarity—that God's justice would prevail.

You will recognize that the oracles against Babylon are quite in keeping with the whole prophetic tradition, which clearly understood Yahweh to be the sovereign God of all the nations. God is the one who raised up Babylon to execute judgment against Judah.

A WALK THROUGH HABAKKUK

☐ 1:1–4 *Habakkuk's First Complaint*

Note how much the complaint (vv. 2–4) is like the lament psalms—a cry for God to act in light of the present situation, plus a catalogue of reasons for the lament.

☐ 1:5–11 *Yahweh's Answer*

Yahweh's response is scarcely what the prophet is looking for! God is raising up Babylon to mete out his judgment against Judah. You might want to compare the relentless, unstoppable nature of the coming Babylonian attack with either Nahum's vision (Nah 2:3–4, 9–10; 3:1–3) or with Joel's (Joel 2:1–11).

☐ 1:12–2:1 *Habakkuk's Second Complaint*

Try to put yourself in Habakkuk's sandals in order to see how thoroughly unsatisfactory God's answer is. How can this be justice, when the God whose eyes are too pure to look on evil summons the treacherous to "swallow up those more righteous than themselves" (1:13)? So Habakkuk takes the place of the watchman to see how God will respond this time (2:1).

☐ 2:2–5 *Yahweh's Answer*

The answer is threefold: (1) Habakkuk must wait, for the answer ("the revelation") will come at its appointed time, (2) the Babylonians' present stance of arrogance is doomed, and (3) the righteous will live by their faithful trust in Yahweh (v. 4, the passage that became crucial in Paul's theology).

☐ 2:6–20 *Woe Oracles against the Oppressor*

Here watch for the *lex talionis* ("eye for eye") nature of God's justice as his judgment is meted out on Babylon. Picking up a different image in each oracle, God strikes his gavel five times: The plunderer is plundered (vv. 6–8), the haughty conqueror is shamed (vv. 9–11), the builder's building becomes fuel for the fire (vv. 12–14), the one who forces the other to get drunk will drink shame from the cup of God's wrath (vv. 15–17), and the silent idol is silenced before Yahweh, who is present in his holy temple (vv. 18–20).

□ 3:1 – 19 *Habakkuk's Prayer and Confession*

This marvelous psalm comes in three basic parts: verse 2, a prayer that God would renew his deeds of old; verses 3 – 15, a celebration of God's past victories as the Divine Warrior; and verses 16 – 19, Habakkuk's twofold commitment to "wait patiently for the day of calamity" and to put his trust and hope in God under any circumstances (cf. 2:2 – 4).

As with many readers, you may find the central section to be hard going. What is crucial to note here is that in three stanzas (3:3 – 7, 8 – 10, and 11 – 15) Habakkuk weaves together (1) God's dominion over the chaotic waters in creation, (2) his causing the sun to stand still for Joshua, (3) the theophany at Sinai, and (4) poetic descriptions of the exodus (cf. Exod 15:6 – 8; Ps 114) into a brilliant, breathtaking reminder of God's triumph over Pharaoh in delivering his people — a picture that makes Habakkuk's hair stand on end, as it were (Hab 3:16). All of this serves to assure God's people that he will act once more on their behalf.

Habakkuk carries on the biblical story in grand fashion — that the Creator, Redeemer God *will* do something about human iniquity, while his people live in hope and with faithful trust in him.

Zephaniah

ORIENTING DATA FOR ZEPHANIAH

- **Content:** oracles of coming catastrophic judgments against Jerusalem (thus Judah) and surrounding nations, plus an oracle of restoration for a remnant of Judah
- **Prophet:** Zephaniah of Jerusalem, possibly of the royal lineage of Hezekiah
- **Date of prophetic activity:** sometime during the reign of Josiah of Judah (640–609 B.C.)
- **Emphases:** the coming day of Yahweh; judgment against Judah for her sins; Yahweh as God of all the nations; judgments against the nations; eventual salvation of a remnant of Judah

OVERVIEW OF ZEPHANIAH

During the reign of Josiah (Judah's last good king), Zephaniah, who was possibly a member of the royal court, received a word from Yahweh, announcing that "the day of the LORD [Yahweh] is near" (1:7, 14, 18; 2:3). The burden of his prophecy is God's judgment on Judah for her idolatry and complacent wickedness (1:3b–18a; 3:1–5). But also included are a call to repentance (2:1–3), judgments against other nations (2:4–15), and the promise of restoration for a faithful remnant (3:9–20). Thus, as you will quickly recognize, Zephaniah—the ninth of the book of the Twelve—carries through with all of the significant concerns found in the Israelite prophetic tradition.

SPECIFIC ADVICE FOR READING ZEPHANIAH

The historical context of Zephaniah is in some ways similar to that of Habakkuk (2 Kgs 22–23; 2 Chr 34–35). In this case, however, since his prophecies are directed primarily against Jerusalem, you may also wish to read the relevant sections about syncretism in the "Specific Advice" for reading Deuteronomy and Kings. Although it is not possible to determine exactly when this marvelous set of oracles was proclaimed—though they would seem to precede rather than follow Josiah's reforms—you will not be able to miss seeing that God's judgment is being pronounced primarily because Jerusalem continues to be a city of religion, but not of pure Yahwism, while at the same time—also over against pure Yahwism—there is little concern for social justice.

Since most people do not find Zephaniah easy reading, it may help you in this regard to see his careful literary structure, which takes the form of a series of concentric patterns (chiasms). First there is the larger frame itself:

A God's Judgment of Judah, with Consequent Wailing (1:2–18)
  B God's Judgment of the Nations (2:1–3:8)
A* God's Redemption of the Remnant, with Consequent Rejoicing (3:9–21)

Within each of these, and sometimes interlocking between them, there are further concentric patterns. Note, for example, how 1:2–18 is framed by announcements of judgment against the whole earth (1:2–3//18b–c echoing the Flood [b–c = poetic lines in the verse]); in the same manner 1:2–3 and 3:8d frame the entire set of judgment oracles. Thus:

1:2–18 3:9–21
  1:2–3 3:8d
  1:2–3 1:18b–c

Similarly, the oracles against the nations are framed by a call to repentance on the part of Judah (2:1–3) and judgment because of her refusal to do so (3:6–8; see "A Walk through Zephaniah").

Second, all of this is expressed in brilliant and powerful images. Note, for example, his deliberate placing of God's judgment on Judah and Jerusalem in images and language that echo the Flood account in Genesis 6. This is related to Zephaniah's frequent use of hyperbole (purposeful exaggeration for effect). Thus, for example, he predicts at several points that God will destroy the whole earth and all its inhabitants (1:2–3, 18b–c; 3:8), yet also predicts a great future both for the peoples (3:9) and for Israel (3:10–19). Such overstatement is not to be taken literally (cf. a sports fan's understanding of the headline "Vancouver buries Boston" to indicate a lopsided victory, not the death and burial of a city);

its effectiveness lies in the people's taking seriously the extent of the tragedy that awaits them.

On the matter of the day of Yahewh, refer to "Specific Advice for Reading Joel," pp. 218–19. In Zephaniah "the day" (used 17*x* between 1:7 and 2:3!) refers to a time of decisive change on behalf of the righteous and against the wicked—and Judah is among the wicked.

A WALK THROUGH ZEPHANIAH

☐ 1:1 *The Prophet's Identity*

It is important not to go too fast here; note how the prophet is placed both in his lineage (possibly a descendant of the previous reforming king, Hezekiah) and in his own time (advancing the cause of the king who became the greatest reformer, Josiah).

☐ 1:2–18 *The Day of Yahweh Is Coming (against Judah)*

Don't forget as you read that this is a prophetic oracle, not a narrative, and thus written as poetry intended for oral presentation. Notice the outer frame (1:2–3b, 18b–c), where the judgment against Judah is set against the backdrop of a coming floodlike catastrophe. You will see that the judgment against Judah is in three parts: (1) Verses 3c–9 voice God's coming judgment expressly against Judah and Jerusalem because of their idolatries (note that the judgment is pictured in terms of God's preparing a sacrifice); (2) verses 10–13 describe the response to the day of Yahweh when it comes: the city wailing over its economic ruin and the laying waste of homes and estates; and (3) verses 14–18a describe the inevitable and inescapable nature of the day when it comes.

☐ 2:1–3:8 *Judgment on the Nations Detailed*

Observe the careful structuring of this section down to the smallest detail. It begins with a summons to Judah to repent and become like the humble righteous (2:1–3) and ends on the sad note of Jerusalem's refusal to do so (3:6–8). In between are five oracles, four against five other nations and one against Jerusalem herself, which are expressed in a perfectly balanced construction:

2:1–3	Summons to repent
2:4–7	Philistia (nine lines)—a neighbor's land will belong to Judah's remnant

2:8–11	Moab/Ammon (nine lines)—same as with Philistia
2:12	Cush (one line)
2:13–15	Assyria (nine lines)—a dreaded enemy will be destroyed
3:1–5	Jerusalem (nine lines)—Judah will be like her dreaded enemy
3:6–8	Refusal to repent

There are several other important matters to note as you read—that the reasons for judgment are barely given in the actual series against the other nations (Moab/Ammon for insulting God's people; Assyria for arrogance) but that reasons are amply given for Jerusalem's downfall (treachery by political and religious leaders); that 2:7 and 9 anticipate the remnant in the final oracle of the book (3:9–20); that the express reason for these oracles is to call Jerusalem to repentance (see esp. 3:6–7), although these kinds of oracles always exist in the prophets as reminders that Yahweh is also God over all the nations.

☐ 3:9–20 *Restoration of the Remnant*

As with the opening oracle of judgment, you will observe that this concluding oracle of hope is also in three parts: (1) Verses 9–13 express in Deuteronomic terms the purifying of the gathered remnant, who will rest secure in Jerusalem and live humbly and righteously; (2) verses 14–17, in contrast to the wailing in the opening oracle, describe the rejoicing (both the people's and Yahweh's) that now rings throughout the restored city; and (3) verses 18–20, again in Deuteronomic terms, describe the gathering of the people and their receiving praise and honor in exchange for shame.

The small book of Zephaniah speaks in powerful ways of both God's judgment on sin and his gracious act of salvation for the humble and undeserving, thus anticipating the gospel as expressed in the New Testament.

Haggai

ORIENTING DATA FOR HAGGAI

- **Content:** four oracles encouraging God's people to rebuild the temple in Jerusalem
- **Prophet:** Haggai, a postexilic prophet in Jerusalem and contemporary of Zechariah (see Ezra 5:1; 6:14)
- **Date of prophetic activity:** a four-month period during the second year of the reign of Darius of Persia (520 B.C.)
- **Emphases:** God's people need to rebuild the temple as the place of God's presence and of their worship; current hardships stem from failure in this matter; a glorious future awaits the people of God and Zerubbabel (thus David's kingly line)

OVERVIEW OF HAGGAI

Haggai, the tenth of the Book of the Twelve, consists of reports of four "words" addressed to Zerubbabel the governor, Joshua the priest, and the people in Jerusalem. His main concern is to encourage the people to get on with rebuilding the temple in Jerusalem.

Haggai's first "word" (1:1–11) announces that recent droughts and poor harvests (part of the curses for covenant disobedience; see Deut 28:20–48) are connected to the returned exiles' failure to build God's house (though they had already built their own houses), to which the people respond favorably (Hag 1:12–15). A month and a half later, the second "word" encourages them to continue the work, promising that the glory of the new temple would surpass that of the first (2:1–9). Priestly rulings on defilement serve as the basis for the third "word" (vv. 10–19), where God promises to bless them "from this day on." The final "word" (vv. 20–23) is addressed to Zerubbabel, assuring him that God will be with him.

SPECIFIC ADVICE FOR READING HAGGAI

It will help you in reading Haggai to also read Ezra 1–6, which serves as background for the words of Haggai recorded here. After a large group of exiles returned in 539 B.C. under the edict of Cyrus, they immediately rebuilt the altar and laid the foundations of the temple (Ezra 3). Then the work stopped as the people built their homes and worked their farms. Now, some nineteen years later, the work on the temple has gone no further; meanwhile they have regularly experienced drought and poor harvests. Through Haggai, Yahweh calls attention to the connection between these two realities and encourages them to return to the task of rebuilding the temple.

As you read, watch for several features that distinguish Haggai: (1) His oracles are not given in poetic form, but a kind of rhythmic prose; (2) they are most often carried on by way of questions (cf. Malachi), which lead to God's word to the people (Hag 1:4, 9; 2:3, 12–13, 19); (3) he also makes effective use of repetitions—"Give careful thought" occurs twice in the first and third oracles (1:5, 7; 2:15, 18); "I am with you" occurs in the first and second (1:13; 2:4); that God will "shake the heavens and the earth" occurs in the second and fourth (2:6, 21); and in language echoing Joshua 1:6–7, 9, 19, leaders and people are three times exhorted to "be strong" (2:4). Note also that while there is obvious progression in the four "words," there is also a clear correspondence between the first and third (the covenant curse is now to be overturned by covenant blessing) and between the second and fourth (encouraging Zerubbabel as leader).

Since the central issue of Haggai is the rebuilding of the temple, you will do well to recall the significant role the temple played in the life of Israel, which served as both the place of God's special presence (marking off Israel from all other peoples) and the place of proper worship. See "Specific Advice for Reading Exodus" (pp. 35–37) and the notes on Exod 25–40 (pp. 40–42), and recall that God's Spirit is the way God is present among them (hence Hag 2:5).

The specific days and dates given for these oracles are worth noting. The first (29 August 520) is given on the first day of the (lunar) month, thus in the setting of a New Moon festival (Num 10:10; 28:11) and at the time of the full maturing of the grain; the second (17 October 520) comes at the end of the Feast of Tabernacles (Israel's harvest festival);

and the third and fourth (18 December 520) during the growing season for spring harvest. All these were periods when people had no excuse that they were too busy to pay attention to the temple.

Here you also feel the frequent tension found in the prophetic tradition between present realities and the glorious future of God. As usual, the one (present hope) is spoken in light of the other (future glory). Note how this occurs regarding both the temple (2:1–5, 6–9) and Zerubbabel (2:20–22, 23), both being marked by God's eschatological shaking of the heavens and the earth.

A WALK THROUGH HAGGAI

☐ 1:1–15 *The Call to Rebuild the Temple*

Trace the unfolding of this "word." It begins with the setting (v. 1), God's complaint with his people (v. 2), and the primary question (v. 3)—failure to build God's house, even though the returned exiles have built their own. At the peak of the growing season, God calls them to start building his house! This is followed by two "Give careful thought to your ways" oracles about the present drought and the reasons for it (vv. 5–6, 7–11; drought is one of the curses for breaking covenant, Deut 28:38–40). Note how unlike the earlier prophets the third part is (Hag 1:12–15); the people's response is actually recorded—and it is positive!

☐ 2:1–9 *The Glory of the Second Temple*

You might try to imagine how someone seventy years old or older might have felt when they saw that the partly built temple was obviously not going to be like Solomon's—and far short of Ezekiel's grand vision (Ezek 40–43). Thus the people are encouraged to "be strong," because in time the second temple will exceed the glory of the first (fulfilled finally when Jesus assumes the role of the temple while standing in the courts of this temple; John 2:13–22).

☐ 2:10–19 *A Defiled People Purified and Blessed*

Note that two questions about defilement/undefilement (vv. 10–13) are used by way of analogy (vv. 14–19b) to repeat the essence of 1:8–11 (their land is "defiled" because the people are "defiled"), while verse 2:19c reverses the curse—from this day on God will bless them.

□ 2:20–23 *A Message to Zerubbabel*

Zerubbabel, heir of David's throne but a vassal governor of Judea under Persian rule, is promised a future overthrow of the worldly powers and that he will become God's "signet ring" ("official seal"; cf. Jer 22:24–25, where the last king of Judah was a "signet ring" to be discarded!)—a word also pointing forward to the time of David's greater Son.

Haggai reminds us that God's people are to be identified as a people of God's presence (the role of the temple), finally fulfilled in the coming of Jesus Christ and the Spirit.

Zechariah

ORIENTING DATA FOR ZECHARIAH

- **Content:** visions aimed at encouraging the postexilic community, especially the leadership, to rebuild the temple, plus oracles about the future coming King who would be slain and eventually triumph
- **Prophet:** Zechariah of Jerusalem, a contemporary of Haggai, but with a longer known ministry (cf. Zech 1:1 and 7:1 with Hag 1:1; see also Ezra 5:1; 6:14)
- **Date of prophetic activity:** 520 B.C. until sometime in the early 400s
- **Emphases:** God is with the remnant community of people who have returned from exile; God will prosper her leaders; the future of Jerusalem and Judah is bright and full of peace and glory; Israel's King will come back to Jerusalem in triumph, yet he will be slain for the sins of the people; God will punish his people's enemies, yet many of the nations will come to know the Lord

OVERVIEW OF ZECHARIAH

This eleventh of the Book of the Twelve has two such distinct parts (chs. 1–8; 9–14) that many scholars believe chapters 9–14 to be from someone else. But the Bible presents both parts together, with the second to be understood in light of the first. Here is a case where the near future and the great future of God exist in tension by the very structure of the book.

Both sections have recognizable parts. After an introductory call to repentance (1:2–6), you encounter a series of eight night visions (1:7–6:15), which are interpreted by an "angel who was talking with [Zechariah]" (1:9). These center in visions 4–5, which focus on the leadership of Joshua and Zerubbabel and the building of the temple. The rest of this section (chs. 7–8) uses a question posed about certain fasts to preach about the true nature of fasting and to announce God's future blessing of Jerusalem.

Chapters 9–14 contain two "oracles" (chs. 9–11 and 12–14) having to do with God's glorious future for his people and judgment on his/their enemies. The first contains a judgment against the nations (9:1–8) set in the context of the coming and subsequent rejection of God's kingly Messiah (9:9–17; 11:4–17) and the great regathering of his scattered people (10:1–11:3). The second oracle picks up all of these themes but sets them into an even more obviously eschatological context, as they focus on "that day," climaxing in chapter 14 with the final defeat of God's enemies and the establishment of his universal kingdom, when all the nations come to worship him.

SPECIFIC ADVICE FOR READING ZECHARIAH

Most people find Zechariah an especially difficult read, even for a prophetic book. This is undoubtedly due to the highly symbolic nature of the night visions plus the normally complex character of prophetic eschatological oracles—and these are what make up most of Zechariah. But with a bit of help you should be able to negotiate your way through the book and appreciate some of its grandeur.

For the history of the period and the basic concerns of the prophet, see "Specific Advice for Reading Haggai," p. 253. What is important to note here is that all of the primary concerns of Israel's prophetic tradition occur in Zechariah—judgments of God's people for their own sins; judgments against surrounding nations because of their sins against God's people and because Yahweh is sovereign over all the nations; a glorious future for the redeemed and purified people of God—and all of this set in tension between soon-to-be temporal realities and the final glorious future of God. What is also a pronounced feature of Zechariah is his expectation of God's future messianic king, which is why he is quoted so often by the New Testament writers (especially with regard to Christ and the final expression of the kingdom of God).

A couple of observations may help your reading of the night visions. First, they are arranged in a concentric (chiastic) pattern. Note that visions 1 and 8 (1:7–17; 6:1–8) both envision four groups of colored horses, whose purpose is to go throughout the whole earth, as the backdrop for the building of the temple. Visions 2 and 3 (1:18–21; 2:1–13) and 6 and 7 (5:1–4; 5:5–11) have to do with obstacles facing the restoration community and its building of the temple (in 2 and 3 the obstacles come from without and in 6 and 7 from within). Visions 4 and 5 (3:1–10; 4:1–14) are the centerpiece, dealing especially with Joshua's and Zerubbabel's leadership, both for the building of the temple and for leading the community.

Second, you will note a similar pattern to most of these visions: Zechariah describes what he sees, he asks about its meaning, and an interpreting angel gives the explanation. Four of the visions ([1] 1:14–17; [3] 2:6–13; [5] 4:6–10a; [8] 6:9–15) also contain one or more oracles, which make specific the message of the visions. The heart of all of this is a word of encouragement, declaring to the people that the time is ripe—the conditions are now in place for them to rebuild—while at the same time it is, as with Haggai, a word of encouragement to those in leadership.

The two oracles in chapters 9–14 are especially difficult to follow, but in the main they follow a pattern as well. Both have to do with the triumphal intervention of the Lord in the affairs of Judah and the nations. The first looks toward the more immediate future, the second toward the final coming of God's universal rule. Common to both is the central place of God's kingly Messiah, and the fact that he is rejected by the people.

One final note. Later prophets sometimes make use of the language and images of earlier ones. This is especially true of Zechariah, who not only mentions the "earlier prophets" (1:4, 6; 7:7, 12), but deliberately echoes their language in a number of places (e.g., cf. 1:4 with Jer 35:15). This may be the best explanation for the intriguing piercing and suffering of God's kingly Messiah in Zechariah 11–13, which sounds like further reflection on Isaiah's suffering servant (Isa 52:13–53:12). This also helps to explain why the New Testament writers refer to these two passages so often as the way to explain the Messiah's crucifixion.

A WALK THROUGH ZECHARIAH

□ 1:1–6 *Introduction*

Both the heading, which dates about two months after Haggai's initial word, and the words that follow serve as a validation of the prophet: This is what God has told Zechariah to tell the people, which affirms that the covenant is still in effect and calls for their obedience (in contrast to the way their ancestors behaved).

☐ 1:7–17 *Vision 1: The Horsemen: God's Return to Jerusalem*

Note the parts as you read: (1) the vision itself (v. 8); (2) Zechariah's question about meaning (vv. 9–10); (3) the interpreting angel's response: They are the patrol who has gone throughout the whole earth and find it at rest; (4) the oracle(s)—Yahweh is returning to Jerusalem, so the people must not rest but must rebuild the temple.

☐ 1:18–21 *Vision 2: Four Horns Destroyed*

Note how this vision is in two parts with explanations. The days of the nations responsible for the exile (of both Judah and Israel) are over.

☐ 2:1–13 *Vision 3: Jerusalem Cannot Be Measured—The Return of Prosperity*

Note how the explanation (vv. 4–13) takes the form of a series of oracles—the coming greatness of Jerusalem with Yahweh as her protector (vv. 4–5); a call to the exiles in Babylon to return (vv. 6–9; thus picking up from vision 2); Yahweh's dwelling in Zion as universal sovereign (vv. 10–13; thus filling out the present vision). Note also how verse 13 echoes Habakkuk 2:20.

☐ 3:1–10 *Vision 4: The Reinstatement of the High Priest*

Remember that this is the first of the two central visions. Since at stake is the rebuilding of the temple, the place of God's presence, this vision has to do with cleansing the high priest, who is to function in the temple once it is rebuilt. Note the progression from clean garments and turban (vv. 3–5) to recommissioning (vv. 6–7) to the promised Branch (v. 8, referring ultimately to the coming Davidic king; cf. Isa 11:1; 53:2; Jer 23:5); the vision concludes by anticipating the oracle in Zechariah 8:1–8.

☐ 4:1–14 *Vision 5: The Lampstand and the Olive Trees—God's Renewing Spirit/Presence*

Note the slightly different structure: the vision (vv. 1–3), now with two sets of questions (vv. 4–5, 11–13) and explanations (vv. 6–10, 14)—to encourage Zerubbabel that God's Spirit will bring about what human power cannot—plus an affirmation of his and Joshua's leadership.

☐ 5:1–4 *Vision 6: The Flying Scroll—Banishment of Evil from Judah*

Now you are back to a brief vision and explanation: The evil that persists in Judah will be banished from the land.

☐ 5:5–11 *Vision 7: The Woman in a Basket—Wickedness Exiled to Babylon*

Watch for the irony in this vision, as well as its relationship to previous visions: The people will return from exile (vision 3), Babylon has been overthrown (vision 2), the temple will be rebuilt (visions 4–5); so what happens to wickedness? It will be exiled to Babylon!

☐ 6:1–15 *Vision 8: The Four Chariots—God at Rest and a Crown for Joshua*

Note how this vision wraps up the series. This new patrol of four horsemen again goes throughout the earth and finds it at rest (especially Babylon, the "north country," v. 6)—all of this to say that the time for rebuilding is now.

The "word" that came to Zechariah that concludes the visions (vv. 9–15) both supplements and reinforces the concerns that have preceded (Joshua, the Branch, the rebuilding of the temple).

☐ 7:1–8:23 *In Response to a Question about Fasting*

A question related to special fasts in connection with the fall of Jerusalem becomes the catalyst for a series of oracles that take a concentric (chiastic) pattern similar to the visions.

- 7:1–3 The question: Do we continue to mourn and fast over Jerusalem's fall?
    - 7:4–14 A judgment against fasting without obedience to the covenant
        - 8:1–8 A picture of restored Jerusalem, which serves to inspire
        - 8:9–13 An encouragement to rebuild the temple
    - 8:14–17 True fasting expresses itself in showing mercy and justice (cf. Isa 58)
- 8:18–19 The question answered: Let the fasts be turned into joyful celebrations

Note how the two appended oracles (8:20–23) anticipate the fulfillment of the Abrahamic covenant that includes the Gentiles (Gen 12:3). And finally note how the two sections of the book end on this same note (Zech 8:20–23; 14:16–19).

☐ 9:1–11:17 *Zion's King and the Glorious Future for God's People*

This first oracle resorts to the poetic pattern of the earlier prophets. Look for the following progression: What begins with a judgment on the surrounding nations (9:1–8) turns into the promised restoration of the Davidic king (vv. 9–17) and of a united Israel (10:1, 3b–12). Note that the latter is enclosed by a denunciation of false shepherds (10:2–3a; 11:1–6, 14–17) and that the last of these encloses a picture of God's true shepherd who will be rejected by the people (11:7–13), which in turn anticipates the central section of the next oracle (12:10–13:9).

☐ 12:1–14:21 *The Smiting and Final Triumph of God's King*

Note how this second oracle picks up themes from the first one, especially the rejection of the true shepherd, while setting the whole in a more totally eschatological setting regarding the day of Yahweh ("that day"). This in turn is placed in the setting of the final eschatological expression of the holy war, where the enemy surrounds and ransacks Jerusalem (12:1–3a; 14:1–2) and the King is killed (12:10–13:7)—but in the end God's glorious final kingdom emerges (12:3b–9; 14:3–21).

The book of Zechariah advances the biblical story by reminding us that God's presence by his Spirit is at the heart of a restored Israel, while at the same time anticipating the sacrificial death of the Messiah who is to come.

Malachi

ORIENTING DATA FOR MALACHI

- **Content:** in six disputes with his people, Yahweh warns them of future judgments and promises redemption to the faithful
- **Prophet:** Malachi ("my messenger"), otherwise unknown
- **Date of prophetic activity:** unknown; perhaps ca. 460 B.C., just before the reforms of Ezra and Nehemiah
- **Emphases:** Yahweh is a covenant-keeping God and requires the same of his people; God's people show disdain for God by their apathy and moral and religious decline; God will judge his people in justice for their halfhearted obedience

OVERVIEW OF MALACHI

Malachi's oracle comes by way of six disputes between Yahweh and his people, all having the same root cause: In a time of spiritual disillusionment, Israel has grown weary of Yahweh and of keeping his covenant. The disputes come in two sets of three. The first set takes up the basic issue—their complaint that Yahweh does not love them (1:2–5), and Yahweh's "complaint" that they have shown contempt for him (1:6–2:9; 2:10–16). In the second set, Yahweh twice takes up their complaint that he has done nothing about evil and injustice (2:17–3:5; 3:13–4:3); these two bracket Yahweh's exposing their own form of injustice (3:6–12). At the same time they affirm that the great day of Yahweh will come indeed (3:1–4; 3:17–4:3). The book concludes (4:4–6) with words about the law (Moses) and the prophets (Elijah).

SPECIFIC ADVICE FOR READING MALACHI

Although one cannot be sure when Malachi prophesied, if it was just before the time of Ezra and Nehemiah, as seems likely, you would do well to review briefly what is said about these times in the "Specific Advice" for reading 1 and 2 Chronicles and Ezra-Nehemiah. Malachi's book is a graphic indicator of the moral and spiritual apathy of the time, which expressed itself in various forms of contempt for Yahweh and the covenant. In fact, most of the sins mentioned in Malachi are also mentioned in Ezra and Nehemiah—mixed marriages (Mal 2:11–15/ Ezra 9–10/Neh 13:23–27); failure to tithe (Mal 3:8–10/Neh 13:10–14); corrupt priests (Mal 1:6–2:9/Neh 13:1–9); and social injustice (Mal 3:5/Neh 5:1–13).

This general malaise and contempt for the covenant probably account in part for the unique form and structure of Malachi. You will see that each of the disputes tends to follow the same pattern:

- Declaration: the issue announced by Yahweh
- The people's question: basically taking the form of "How so?"
- Yahweh's response: reminding them of his past or coming actions, or revealing their actions that show contempt

These disputes function as a wake-up call in a time of disillusionment (see 3:14) when the returnees from Babylon felt generally abandoned by Yahweh. So rather than a court setting (as in Hosea and Micah, for example), Yahweh challenges them by means of declaration, question, and explanation.

There is a kind of progression to the disputes. They begin with Israel's questioning Yahweh's love (= compassion for and loyalty to them). To this, Yahweh responds that not only does he indeed love them (look what I did to Edom) but that there is plenty of evidence that they do not love Yahweh, in the form of contempt for the covenant by priests and people alike (offering blemished animals in sacrifice, and divorce and intermarriage with pagans). The final three disputes start the cycle again. Feeling abandoned by Yahweh, the people speak cynically about the prosperity of those who practice injustice. But, Yahweh responds, they themselves practice injustice by withholding tithes, the means of livelihood for the Levites and of provision for the poor (Num 18:21–32; Deut 14:28–29). In the final set, there are also assurances of God's coming justice—both judgment of the wicked and salvation of the (new) righteous remnant.

Thus, at the end of the Christian Old Testament (by way of the Septuagint) are prophetic words that Jesus and the New Testament writers see as speaking about his coming. Not only will God send "[his] messenger, who will prepare the way before [him]" so that "the Lord you are seeking will come to his temple" (Mal 3:1), but the final two words speak of Moses and Elijah, who make their appearance with Jesus on the Mount of Transfiguration.

A WALK THROUGH MALACHI

☐ 1:1 *Heading*

As with Joel, Malachi's heading does not help us identify either the prophet or his times.

☐ 1:2–5 *First Dispute: On Yahweh's Love*

Note how this first dispute sets both the tone and the structure for the rest. Yahweh does love them. How so? By his hating (= rejecting; allying himself against) their "brother"—but ancient foe—Edom, thus fulfilling Obadiah's prophecy.

☐ 1:6–2:9 *Second Dispute: On Offering Unacceptable Sacrifices*

Now it's Yahweh's turn. The basic issue is set forth in 1:6—the priests do not love (= they show contempt for) Yahweh. How so? By offering Yahweh blemished animals (see Lev 22:17–25) that they would not dare offer even to a governor. Better to close down the temple altogether than to show such disloyalty (1:10–14), which also dishonors Yahweh's name among the nations. Thus this dispute concludes with strong admonitions for the priests to change their ways (2:1–9).

☐ 2:10–16 *Third Dispute: On Intermarriage and Divorce*

Note that the form changes slightly here: Malachi now speaks for God (v. 10) as the dispute turns to the people themselves—over intermarriage with pagans (vv. 11–12), thus breaking covenant with Yahweh (= capitulation to idolatry). The issue of divorce (vv. 13–16) is related (= breaking covenant with a Jewish wife to marry a local woman).

☐ 2:17–3:5 *Fourth Dispute: On Wearying Yahweh with Words*

Back to the people's complaint. In their present malaise, they (cynically) call evil people good and ask about justice. Yahweh's answer is twofold: (1) The Lord whom they seek will come suddenly to his temple—as a refining fire (3:1–3a), and (2) his coming will result in both acceptable sacrifices at the temple (thus back to 1:6–2:9) and judgment against all forms of injustice (3:3b–5).

☐ 3:6–12 *Fifth Dispute: On Returning to Yahweh*

Notice how this dispute follows closely on what is said at the end of the previous one by putting the ball back in their court: They themselves must return to Yahweh (vv. 6–7). To their "How so?" the answer is to stop their own form of injustice—withholding the tithe (food, which is used for the Levites and the poor). Only then can the curse for covenant disloyalty be removed, so that the nations will see again God's blessing on his people (cf. Gen 12:3).

☐ 3:13–4:3 *Sixth Dispute: On Speaking Harshly about Yahweh*

This final dispute both wraps up the second set of three and brings the whole series full circle. It indicates why the first dispute was necessary: The people have been saying harsh things about Yahweh—that it is futile to serve him, and that in any case the arrogant prosper, while those who consider themselves as righteous do not (3:13–15; cf. dispute 4). Thus the final answer indicates that God will indeed divide the house—the arrogant will be judged (4:1)—and the "sun of righteousness will rise" for the righteous (4:2–3).

☐ 4:4–6 *Two Appended Words: the Law and the Prophets (Moses and Elijah)*

Malachi concludes by bringing Moses (the Law) and Elijah (the Prophets) into the picture. The people are urged to keep the covenant of law; they can anticipate the coming of a second Elijah who will precede the coming great day of Yahweh.

Malachi reminds God's people that they must take their covenant relationship with him seriously and that a great new day will dawn for them with the coming of Elijah (John the Baptist) to precede the Lord (Jesus Christ).

The Gospels and Acts in the Biblical Story

Jesus of Nazareth is the unmistakable centerpiece of the biblical story. The Gospels make it clear that his significance lies not simply in his death, but also especially in his person, life, and teaching. Nonetheless, each evangelist (Gospel writer) in his own way demonstrates by way of narrative that the death and resurrection of Jesus are the high points of his story (fully one-fourth to one-third of each Gospel is given over to the events of the final week).

Our interest in each of the Gospels is in their narrative about Jesus. Even though the first three are "synoptic" (seeing Jesus through common eyes), and Matthew and Luke use Mark in their telling of the story, they strike out on their own individual paths—all telling the same story, but each with his own concerns and emphases for the sake of his implied readers. Luke's Gospel is unique in yet another way, because he narrates the story of Jesus in two aspects: First, his Gospel, as do the others, tells about what Jesus "began to do and to teach" (Acts 1:1); second, in the book of Acts, he tells how the story of Jesus continues, now through the power of the Spirit, in the ministry of the early church.

The evangelists make it especially clear that you cannot understand Jesus without seeing how he fits into the Old Testament story that has preceded him—as the climax and fulfillment of the hopes expressed almost from the beginning of the story. On the one hand, they all see

Jesus as clearly fitting into the prophetic tradition—by his mighty words, mighty deeds, and symbolic actions (e.g., cleansing the temple; cursing the fig tree)—and so he is perceived by the crowds (Matt 21:46; Luke 7:16; 13:13). At the same time, all of them are writing from this side of the resurrection and know that he is none other than the expected "Son of David" (Mark 10:47–48), God's "Son" (Ps 2:7; Matt 3:17; 17:5; and parallels), who comes to his people as their King.

One key to this aspect of their narratives lies with the Old Testament understanding of the role of the king in Israel, who is often seen both to represent God to the people and to embody the people of Israel in his own person. This can be seen especially in the book of Psalms and in the suffering servant songs in Isaiah 42–53. It will be helpful for you as you read the Gospels to note how the evangelists tell the story of Jesus from this perspective. Take, for example, his baptism and the testing in the desert, where Jesus succeeds at the very places where Israel failed, as his own citations from Deuteronomy 6–8 make plain. Or take the discourse in John 15:1–8, where Jesus, picking up an image of Israel from the Old Testament (Ps 80:8–19; Isa 5:1–7; Jer 2:21), speaks of *himself* as the true vine and his disciples as the branches. And his death is clearly seen in light of Isaiah's suffering servant (Isa 52:13–53:12), as the one who bears the sins of the people, thus both representing the people and drawing them into the story themselves.

For each Gospel (and the book of Acts, too), therefore, we will also try to help you to see how the evangelist ties the story of Jesus to the story of Israel as the "fulfillment" of Jewish messianic hopes and expectations. Related to this, we also need to point out that each Gospel was written at a time when Gentile inclusion in the grand story (see comments on Gen 11:27–25:11, p. 30) was in full swing; we will therefore point out how each deals with this issue, especially in light of the rejection of Jesus by many of the Jews.

On other matters related to their composition and relationships to one another, as well as their essential message about the coming of the kingdom (as "already" and "not yet"), we point you to chapter 7 in *How to 1.*

The Gospel according to Matthew

ORIENTING DATA FOR MATTHEW

- **Content:** the story of Jesus, including large blocks of teaching, from the announcement of his birth to the commissioning of the disciples to make disciples of the Gentiles
- **Author:** anonymous; Papias (ca. A.D. 125) attributes "the first Gospel" to the apostle Matthew; scholarship is divided
- **Date:** unknown (since he used Mark, very likely written in the 70s or 80s)
- **Recipients:** unknown; but almost certainly Jewish Christians with a commitment to the Gentile mission, most commonly thought to have lived in and around Antioch of Syria
- **Emphases:** Jesus is the Son of God, the (messianic) King of the Jews; Jesus is God present with us in miraculous power; Jesus is the church's Lord; the teaching of Jesus has continuing importance for God's people; the gospel of the kingdom is for all peoples—Jew and Gentile alike

OVERVIEW OF MATTHEW

It is fitting that Matthew comes first in the New Testament, for two reasons: first, from the opening sentence it has deliberate and direct ties to the Old Testament; second, because of its orderly arrangement of Jesus' teaching, it was the most often used Gospel in the early church (cited by the early church fathers more than twice as often as the other Gospels).

The genius of Matthew's Gospel lies in its structure, which presents a marvelous tapestry of narrative interwoven with carefully crafted blocks of teaching. So well is this done that the most prominent feature of Matthew's story—the five blocks of teaching—is sometimes not even noticed because one is more aware of the flow of the narrative (which follows Mark very closely). The five blocks of teaching (5:1–7:29; 10:11–42; 13:1–52; 18:1–35; [23:1] 24:1–25:46) are presented on a topical basis. Each is marked off by a similar concluding formula ("When Jesus had finished [saying these things]"), which Matthew uses to transition back to the narrative.

The story itself begins with a twofold introduction about Jesus' origins (chs. 1–2) and about his preparations for public ministry (3:1–4:11). After that, each combined block of "narrative with discourse" forms a progressive aspect to the story, all having to do with Jesus, the messianic King, inaugurating the time of God's kingly rule—4:12–7:29, proclamation of and life in the kingdom; 8:1–10:42, the power and mission of the kingdom; 11:1–13:52, questioning and opposition to the kingdom and its mixed reception in the world; 13:53–18:35, growing opposition, confession by the disciples, and special instructions to the community of the King; 19:1–25:46, mixed responses to the Prophet who now presents himself as the King, and the judgment of those who reject him. The story concludes (chs. 26–28) with the trial, crucifixion, and resurrection of Jesus, and the commissioning of the disciples to take the story to the nations.

SPECIFIC ADVICE FOR READING MATTHEW

You cannot easily miss Matthew's way of tying the story of Jesus to that of Israel, since it is so direct and up-front. Jesus belongs to the genealogy of Israel's royal line, and he fulfills all kinds of prophetic messianic expectations. Note how often (eleven times in all) Matthew editorializes, "This was to fulfill what was said [spoken] through the prophet(s)." Moreover, Jesus' ministry and teaching presuppose the authoritative nature of the Old Testament law (5:17–48), and during his earthly ministry, Jesus focuses on the "lost sheep of Israel" (10:6).

But at the death of Jesus, the temple curtain is torn in two (27:51), indicating that its time is over and that the time of Jesus and his followers has begun. You will see as you go along how Matthew presents Jesus as being in unrelieved opposition to the Pharisees and the teachers of the law (e.g., 5:20; 12:38; 21:15; 22:15; 23:2–36), so much so that he speaks of "their [your] synagogue(s)" as over against his disciples (e.g., 10:17; 13:54; 23:34). And an alternative story explaining away Jesus' resurrection still circulated among some Jews at the time Matthew is writing (28:11–15).

At the same time, look for the ways that Matthew also exhibits clear concern for the mission to the Gentiles. For example, four women—primarily, if not all, Gentiles—are included in the genealogy (Tamar, Rahab, Ruth, and Uriah's wife [Bathsheba]). The story proper begins in Galilee (Matt 4:12–16), which Matthew sees as fulfilling Isaiah 9:1–2—that the people living in darkness, in Galilee of the Gentiles, have seen a great light—and it ends (Matt 28:16–20) with a commissioning of the apostles to make disciples of all the nations (= Gentiles).

This interweaving of themes suggests that the Gospel was written at a time when church and synagogue were now separated and were in conflict over who is in the true succession of the Old Testament promises. Matthew's way of answering this issue is by telling the story of Jesus, who "fulfills" every kind of Jewish messianic hope and expectation: After his birth as "king of the Jews" (2:2), he is honored (worshiped) by Eastern royal figures; at his birth, baptism, and transfiguration he is signaled as God's Son; his virgin birth fulfills Isaiah 7:14 that "God is with us" (cf. 12:6, 41, 42; 28:20); he dies as "THE KING OF THE JEWS," 27:37; and is acknowledged as "Son of God" by the Roman centurion (27:54). At the same time Matthew also recognizes Jesus as Isaiah's suffering servant (20:28) and extends this recognition to include his whole ministry, including his healings (8:17) and the opposition (12:17–21).

Equally important for Matthew, Jesus is presented as the true interpreter of the law (5:17–48; 7:24–27), especially over against the Pharisees and the teachers of the law. The latter have turned the law into a heavy yoke (11:28) and bind heavy burdens on people's backs (23:4); Jesus, who as Son knows and reveals the Father (11:25–27), offers an easy yoke and light burden (11:28–30). His "law" is mercy and grace (9:13; 12:7; 20:30, 34; 23:23). Those who experience such mercy are thus expected to be merciful in return (18:21–35; cf. 5:7). Jesus did not come to abolish the Law and Prophets but to fulfill them (5:17; 7:12), to bring the new righteousness of God's kingdom that goes infinitely beyond the teachings of the Pharisees (5:20). At the same time, Matthew shows concern about some within the believing community who prophesy but do not live obediently (7:15–23). In his Gospel, therefore, the twelve disciples play the role of learners who are to model life in the kingdom. You will want to look for these features as you read.

Thus, for Matthew, Jesus is the center of everything, and those who follow him not only proclaim the coming of the kingdom—the coming of God's mercy to sinners—but they are also expected to live like him (7:15–23). And when they have success in their own proclamation of the kingdom, especially among Gentiles, they are to make disciples of them by teaching them to observe the way of Jesus (28:19–20), both in their individual lives (chs. 5–7) and in their church communities (ch. 18). Matthew almost certainly intends his Gospel to serve as the manual for such instruction!

A WALK THROUGH MATTHEW

☐ 1:1–2:23 *Prologue: Jesus' Divine and Human Origins*

Here you find the well-known features of Matthew's narrative of Jesus' origins (the annunciation to Joseph; the visit of the Magi; the slaughter of the innocents; the flight to Egypt). As you read, note how many of Matthew's concerns and themes surface here. His genealogy explicitly places Jesus in the royal lineage (son of David) and anticipates the Gentile mission (son of Abraham). His birth from a virgin both fulfills prophecy and emphasizes his divine origins (by the Holy Spirit, as "God with us"). Note especially how the narrative of chapter 2 places worship of Jesus by Gentile royal court figures in the context of an attempted execution by Jewish royalty.

☐ 3:1–4:11 *Introduction to Jesus: His Baptism and the Testing*

Jesus is introduced to Israel by way of a new prophet, John the Baptist; John consents to baptize him (how could the Messiah accept a baptism for repentance?). Jesus is immediately led by the Spirit into the desert to be tested as to who he is (Son of God) and why he is here (his royal/suffering servant mission). Note how in his baptism and forty-day testing Jesus steps into the role of Israel (= through the Red Sea followed by forty years in the desert) and foils Satan with passages from Deuteronomy 6 and 8, precisely at points where Israel failed the test; thus the (now humble) Divine Warrior wins the first round against the enemy.

☐ 4:12–7:29 *The Proclamation of the Kingdom*

The *narrative* portion of part 1 is very brief: Starting in Galilee of the Gentiles, Jesus gathers disciples, proclaims the good news of the kingdom, and heals the sick (note the summary nature of 4:23–25; the first actual "miracle stories" appear in the next section).

The *discourse* in this case is by far the best known. Set in the context of a mountain (as Moses on Sinai), the new Torah (teaching from the law) is the carefully structured Sermon on the Mount, much of which you will recognize even if you have never read Matthew before. The collection emphasizes first the "gospel" setting of the discourse (5:3–16, nine beatitudes, plus affirmations of God's people being salt and light).

The rest instructs the disciples on the new righteousness (the way of living in the kingdom), setting it in the context of "fulfilling" the Law and Prophets (5:17) and going beyond that of the Pharisees and the teachers of the law (traditionally "scribes") in every way—especially ethical life over against the scribes (5:21–48) and the three religious duties of the Pharisees, namely, almsgiving, prayer, and fasting (6:1–18).

These are followed by admonitions to single-hearted trust in God, which renders life in the kingdom as without anxiety (6:19–34), to just treatment of others (7:1–12), and to obedience (7:13–27). Note the conclusion in 7:28–29, "When Jesus had finished saying these things."

☐ 8:1–10:42 *The Power and Mission of the Kingdom*

The *narrative* portion of part 2 is dominated by eight miracle stories (that contain nine actual miracles). Notice how these stories emphasize the power of the kingdom, beginning with mercy for an outcast (8:1–4) and a Gentile (8:5–13), and they include triumph over the raging sea and over demons. And so the humble Divine Warrior wins round two against Satan. Included also are three short narratives that in turn illustrate the cost of discipleship (8:18–22) and the beginning of opposition (9:9–17); note especially the citation from Hosea 6:6, "I desire mercy, not sacrifice" (Matt 9:13), in the context of opposition. A nearly identical summary (9:35–38) to what you read in 4:23–25 sets the stage for the second discourse.

The *discourse* in this section is set in the context of Jesus' sending out of the Twelve (10:1–14)—the workers sent out "into his harvest field" (9:37–38). But as the collection of sayings proceeds (beginning with 10:17), you will see that they speak primarily to the church's later mission in the world, especially anticipating the rough reception those who carry on the mission of Jesus are going to experience in days to come. Note how the summarizing statement begins the next section (11:1a).

☐ 11:1–13:52 *Questioning of and Opposition to Jesus and the Kingdom*

In the *narrative* part of this section, be looking for the rough reception that Jesus himself experienced as he is both questioned and opposed by "this generation" (11:1–19; 12:1–14). Note how these two narratives bracket Jesus' judgment on unrepentant Israel (11:20–24) and his invitation to the humble, the "little children" who are oppressed by the burden of Pharisaism (11:25–30). And note how Matthew includes a second time the citation of Hosea 6:6, "I desire mercy, not sacrifice" (Matt 12:7), again in the context of opposition.

The opposition is seen as "fulfillment" regarding Jesus as Isaiah's suffering servant (12:15–21; citing Isa 42:1–4, the first of the servant songs). This is followed by two more narratives of opposition (Matt 12:22–45, God's stronger man has come and bound the strong man and is plundering his house [the Divine Warrior theme again], and one affirming the humble poor who follow Jesus and do God's will [12:46–50]).

You will recognize the *discourse* to be made up of seven parables (13:1–52). Note their generally common thread—instructing the disciples on the mixed reception of the kingdom in the world, which will be made evident at the end, while two of them (13:44–46) emphasize the surpassing worth of the kingdom. Again, watch how the opening sentence of the next section serves to summarize this discourse.

☐ 13:53–18:35 *Opposition to and Confession of Jesus*

As you read the *narrative* portion of part 4 (13:53–17:27), watch for the ways it further illustrates preceding themes (varied responses to Jesus from ch. 13) while at the same time gains momentum toward the final week in Jerusalem.

It begins with the rejection of God's prophets (Jesus in his hometown, 13:53–58; John the Baptist by Herod, 14:1–12), followed by two mighty deeds (14:13–36). Matthew then sets controversy with the Pharisees (15:1–20) in contrast with the faith of a Gentile woman (15:21–28).

Note how a second feeding miracle (15:29–39) leads to Jesus' being tested by the Pharisees and Saducees (16:1–4), which in turn leads Jesus to warn his disciples against their teaching (vv. 5–12), all of which leads to the climactic moment in verses 13–20, when the disciples confess Jesus as the Messiah. This leads in turn to their being let in on what is to come—Jesus' death in Jerusalem (vv. 21–23)—which in turn leads to special instruction on discipleship (vv. 24–28), while three of them see his resurrection glory in advance (17:1–13).

Another triumph over demons provides for teaching on faith (17:14–21), followed by a second prediction of Jesus' death (vv. 22–23) and his announcement that his followers are exempt from temple regulations (vv. 24–27).

Note how the *discourse* in this section (ch. 18) picks up the discipleship theme from the preceding narrative, being singularly concerned with relationships within the believing community. After establishing the nature of discipleship (God's "little ones," the humble poor), Matthew includes instructions—not causing the little ones to stumble (vv. 6–9), seeking the wandering ones (vv. 10–14), dealing with sin against one another (vv. 15–20), and forgiveness (vv. 21–35). Again note how the first sentence in the next section concludes this discourse.

□ 19:1–25:46 *Jerusalem Receives and Rejects Her King*

Be watching here as the *narrative* portion of this final section (19:1–22:46) puts Jesus first in "the region of Judea" (19:1) and then in Jerusalem itself (21:1), which Jesus enters for the events of the final week. You will observe that the narratives in the first half (chs. 19–20) continue the themes of opposition and discipleship. After opposing the Pharisees' easy view of divorce (19:1–12), the childlike nature of discipleship is reinforced over against the rich, who find it difficult to enter the kingdom (vv. 13–15, 16–26).

This leads to further instruction on discipleship—the "last" will be "first" in the kingdom (19:27–30); they are the undeserving who receive mercy, to the consternation of those who consider themselves worthy (20:1–16). Yet the disciples are still not fully on board, as a third passion prediction (vv. 17–19) is followed by a desire for positions of authority in the kingdom (vv. 20–24). Jesus responds by assuming the role of the suffering servant (vv. 25–28), which they are to model.

On the way to Jerusalem Jesus heals two blind men (20:29–34; the eyes of the blind are opened, while those who see will be shown to be blind). Then Jesus presents himself to Israel as its long-awaited King (21:1–11, fulfilling Zech 9:9 and Ps 118:25–26) and marks off the temple as his own (Matt 21:12–17; cf. Mal 3:1–4). You will see that most of the rest of this narrative (Matt 21:23–22:46) is a series of "conflict stories" interspersed with parables, which together illustrate the clash over Jesus' authority that will lead to his execution. Note especially the role that Psalms 118 and 110 play in these events.

The *discourse* that follows is prophetic, first announcing judgment on the teachers of the law and the Pharisees (23:1–39), after which Jesus leaves the temple ("your house is left to you desolate," 23:38) and pronounces judgment against Jerusalem (24:1–28) in light of the end itself (vv. 29–35), calling for watchfulness and service on the part of his followers (24:36–25:46).

☐ 26:1–28:20 *The King Is Tried, Crucified, and Raised*

Here you come to the climax of the Gospel—the final rejection of Jesus in Jerusalem (26:1–27:66), including the trial, denial, crucifixion, death, and burial of Jesus. Note Matthew's interest in two events at Jesus' death that mark the end of the old and the beginning of the new: (1) The temple curtain was torn in two, and (2) some holy people from the former era were raised to life (27:51–53).

But the conclusion offers hope for the future: "He is not here; he has risen, just as he said" (28:1–10). After noting an alternative report that was circulating among the Jews who opposed Matthew's church (vv. 11–15), he concludes with the commissioning of the disciples and the affirmation that all authority belongs to the risen Lord, who is still present with us to the end of the age as we continue to carry out their commission from him (vv. 16–20).

What a wonderful way to begin the New Testament part of God's story—of his saving a people for his Name through the death and resurrection of Jesus, and sending them into the world to be the bearers of his Good News and to make disciples from all the nations, thus fulfilling the Abrahamic covenant!

The Gospel according to Mark

ORIENTING DATA FOR MARK

- **Content:** the story of Jesus from his baptism to his resurrection, about two-thirds of which tells of his ministry in Galilee, while the last third narrates his final week in Jerusalem
- **Author:** anonymous; attributed (by Papias, ca. A.D. 125) to John Mark, a sometime companion of Paul (Col 4:10) and later of Peter (1 Pet 5:13)
- **Date:** ca. A.D. 65 (according to Papias, soon after the deaths of Paul and Peter in Rome)
- **Recipients:** the church in Rome (according to Papias), which accounts for its preservation along with the longer Matthew and Luke
- **Emphases:** the time of God's rule (the kingdom of God) has come with Jesus; Jesus has brought about the new exodus promised in Isaiah; the kingly Messiah came in weakness, his identity a secret except to those to whom it is revealed; the way of the new exodus leads to Jesus' death in Jerusalem; the way of discipleship is to take up a cross and follow him

OVERVIEW OF MARK

Although Mark is the earliest of the four Gospels (see *How to 1*, pp. 135–39), because it is shorter and has much less teaching than the others, it has often tended to suffer neglect. At one level his story is straightforward. After a prologue, which introduces us to the good news about Jesus Christ (1:1–15), the story unfolds in four parts. In part 1 (1:16–3:6), Jesus goes public with the announcement of the kingdom. With rapid-fire action he calls disciples, drives out demons, heals the sick, and announces that all of this has to do with the coming of God's rule; in the process he draws amazement from the crowds and opposition from the religious and political establishment, who early on plot his death.

Part 2 (3:7–8:21) develops the role of the three significant groups. Jesus' miracles and teaching are sources of constant amazement to the *crowds;* the *disciples* receive private instruction (4:13, 34) and join in the proclamation (6:7–13), but are slow to understand (8:14–21; cf. 6:52); the *opposition* continues to mount (7:1–23; 8:11–13).

In part 3 (8:22–10:45), Jesus directs his attention primarily to the disciples. Three times he explains the nature of his kingship—and hence of discipleship (8:34–38)—as going the way of the cross (as Isaiah's suffering servant; Mark 10:45), and three times the disciples completely miss it.

Part 4 (10:46–15:47) brings the story to its climax. The king enters Jerusalem and the crowds go wild with excitement, but in the end the opposition has its day. Jesus is put on trial, found guilty, and turned over to the Romans for execution on a cross—as "the king of the Jews" (15:2).

A brief epilogue (16:1–8) reminds Mark's readers that "[Jesus] has risen!"

SPECIFIC ADVICE FOR READING MARK

It was a killing time in Rome. The church was experiencing the Neronian holocaust, in which many believers had been burned alive at Nero's garden parties and two of the church's more important figures (Peter and Paul) had been executed. Soon after, there appeared among them a small book (Mark's Gospel), written to remind them of the nature of Jesus' own messiahship (as God's suffering servant) and to encourage cross-bearing discipleship.

Mark has been described as one who cannot tell a story badly. In part this is due to his vivid style, which is what also gives his Gospel the sense of being rapid-fire. Almost every sentence begins with "and" (cf. KJV); forty-one times he begins with "and immediately" (which does not always refer to time but to the urgency of the telling), and twenty-five times with "and again." But he also includes little details, including the Aramaic words of Jesus on six occasions. All of this reflects both a written form of oral recounting and the memory of an eyewitness.

The prominent place of Peter in the Gospel and the fact that early on so much happens in and around Peter's house in Capernaum suggest that the tradition has it right—that the Gospel in part reflects Peter's own telling of the story. But Peter's role in the Gospel is anything but that of a hero. He who urged others to "clothe yourselves in humility" (1 Pet 5:5) does not forget his own weaknesses while following Jesus; you will want to look for these features as you read. But at the end, after he vehemently denied knowing his Lord (Mark 14:66–72), he also remembers that the angel told the women at the tomb, "Go, tell his disciples *and Peter*" (16:7, emphasis added).

But brief and breathtaking as Mark's Gospel is, it is not at all simple. Indeed, Mark tells the story with profound theological insight. Absolutely crucial to your reading with understanding is to note how he presents Jesus as Messiah. Three things emerge at the beginning that carry all the way through to the end: (1) Jesus is the kingly Messiah, (2) Jesus is God's suffering servant, and (3) Jesus keeps his identity secret.

Mark's telling of the story thus emphasizes the "messianic secret," the "mystery of the kingdom of God," namely, that the expected coming King knew he was destined to suffer for the sake of the people. The demons, who recognize him, are silenced (1:25, 34; 3:11–12); the crowds to whom the King comes with compassion are told not to tell anyone about his miracles (1:44; 5:43; 7:36; 8:26); when finally confessed as Messiah by the disciples, he tells them to tell no one (8:30). What no one expects is for God's King to be impaled on a cross! But Jesus knows—and he silences all messianic fervor, lest it thwart the divine plan that leads to the cross. When the disciples are clued in to the "mystery," even they fail to get it (8:27–33); they are like the blind man who has to be touched twice (8:22–26; in their case, by Jesus' resurrection).

But in reminding his readers of the nature of Jesus' messiahship, Mark also reminds us that this is the way of discipleship as well. Indeed, the first instruction on discipleship (8:34), which calls for cross bearing, appears only after the first disclosure to the disciples of Jesus' own impending death (v. 31).

Mark also uses the theme of God's kingly suffering Messiah to show Jesus' connection to the story of Israel, especially Isaiah's (now long-delayed) new exodus. The key moments in the first exodus are deliverance, the journey through the desert, and arrival at the place where the Lord dwells. Isaiah (chs. 35; 40–55) announces the return from Babylonian exile as a new exodus. Notice how Mark puts us in touch with this theme in his very first sentence: "The beginning of the gospel about Jesus the Messiah, as it is written in Isaiah the prophet." Jesus then steps into the role of Israel (through the water and testing in the desert). The theme carries all the way through. Mark *cites* Isaiah at key points (the opposition's hardness of heart, "those on the outside" [Mark 4:10–12; 7:6; 9:48]; the inclusion of Gentiles [11:17]). He echoes Isaiah in all kinds of ways: Jesus' ministry is expressed in the language of Isaiah 53 (Mark 10:45); the parable of the tenants (12:1–12) recasts Isaiah's "song of the vineyard" (Isa 5:1–7); the motif of eyes that see but don't perceive and ears that hear but don't understand (Isa 6:9–10). The long-awaited Deliverer has now come, but contrary to common expectations, he has come to suffer for the people in order to lead them from exile into the final promised land (Mark 13).

A significant part of the new exodus included the gathering of the Gentile nations. Since Mark's Gospel is intended for people who are already a part of that mission, his way of placing them in the story of Jesus is by relating a series of non-Galilean (Gentile) narratives in 6:53–9:29. In this context he places the matter of ceremonial washing, for example, and he comments that Jesus in effect abolished the food laws (7:19b). Moreover, the Gentile mission delays the dropping of the final curtain on history (13:10), and in repossessing the temple as Israel's "king" (11:17), Jesus cites Isaiah 56:7 ("my house will be called a house of prayer for all nations" [= Gentiles]).

By looking for these various features as you read, you may find yourself among those who know Mark's Gospel as one of the rich treasures in the Bible.

A WALK THROUGH MARK

The Prologue—Introduction to Jesus and the Kingdom (1:1–15)

As you read Mark's very brief introduction, notice how all of his major concerns appear here. The "good news about Jesus" begins with the announcement that Isaiah's new exodus has begun: "Prepare the way for the Lord" (1:3), proclaims John the Baptist—the new Elijah (Mal 4:5–6)—who thus presents Jesus to Israel. Jesus then assumes the role of Israel in the new exodus. At his baptism the voice from heaven defines Jesus' messianic destiny in words from Psalm 2:7 (the Davidic king), Genesis 22:2 (God's beloved Son), and Isaiah 42:1 (God's suffering servant). After his testing in the desert, he comes into Galilee announcing the "good news of God": "the time has come" for God's kingdom to appear, which calls for faith and repentance.

Part 1: The Kingdom Goes Public — Disciples, Crowds, Opposition (1:16–3:6)

☐ 1:16–45 *The Disciples and the Crowds*

Note how Mark starts the story with the call of disciples to "come, follow [Jesus]" (1:16–20), a key to much of the Gospel. Even so, the disciples are in the background for most of this section, as Mark focuses first on the crowds (vv. 21–45). They are the "amazed" on whom Jesus has compassion and with whom he has immense popularity (vv. 22, 27–28, 32–33, 37–38, 45)—so much so that at the end of the short narrative, Jesus can "no longer enter a town openly." Note that Mark accomplishes all this with just three short narratives!

☐ 2:1–3:6 *The Opposition*

Now comes the opposition (2:1–3:6), presented in a series of five narratives. Look for the question "why?" in each of the first four, whereby Mark shows the *reasons* for opposition: 2:7 (blasphemy = making himself equal with God); 2:16 (eating with sinners); 2:18 (failure to keep the rules); 2:24 (breaking the Sabbath). Note at the end (3:6) the solidifying of the opposition both religious and political—with the first hint of Jesus' coming death.

Part 2: The Mystery of the Kingdom — Faith, Misunderstanding, Hard Hearts (3:7–8:21)

☐ 3:7–4:34 *Presenting the Mystery of the Kingdom*

The plot thickens. Notice how the three groups are immediately brought back into the picture (crowds, 3:7–12; disciples, vv. 13–19; opposition, vv. 20–30; even his family is bewildered, vv. 31–34). The disciples are now "appointed" as the Twelve (representing the remnant of Israel), and their role is stepped up considerably.

In 4:1–34 Mark uses Jesus' teaching in parables to introduce the mystery of the kingdom, which will be revealed to them (those on the inside). The opposition (those "on the outside"), in their failure to hear with their ears (4:9), fulfill Isaiah's prophecy (Isa 6:9–10; cf. his scathing rebuke of people becoming like their idols that cannot hear [Isa 42:18, 20]), but as the story proceeds, the disciples fare little better.

☐ 4:35–6:6a *The Kingdom Present in Power: The Blindness of the World*

Next you encounter a series of mighty deeds (4:35–5:43). In turn Jesus displays his power over the sea, demons, death, and uncleanness (an "untouchable" [cf. Lev 15:25–27] touches Jesus and is made whole, thus restored to life in the community). Note the emphasis on *faith:* those to whom the mystery is being revealed lack faith (Mark 4:40); the people across the lake want Jesus to leave (5:17); the woman's faith makes her whole (5:34); the synagogue leader is encouraged to have faith (5:36); Jesus' hometown lacks faith (6:6a). Wonder and awe come easy; true faith does not.

☐ 6:6b–8:21 *The Kingdom Extends to Gentiles: The Blindness of the Disciples*

Watch for two things in this section: (1) the role of the disciples and (2) Jesus' ministry among Gentiles. It begins with the Twelve joining Jesus in ministry—with such success that Herod gets wind of it (6:6b–30). But note how the two "feeding" stories (6:31–44; 8:1–10) are both followed by the "hardness of heart" motif (6:45–52; 8:11–21).

In between (6:53–7:37), Jesus ministers among the Gentiles, who show both faith (7:24–30) and amazement (vv. 31–37). Significantly, Mark brings the Pharisees into this scene as well, as Jesus eliminates the food laws by pronouncing all things clean (7:1–23).

The "hardness of heart" narrative at the end (8:11–21) is especially important to Mark's narrative. The Pharisees "test" Jesus about "a sign from heaven"; they are looking for a Messiah of worldly power. When his disciples fail to understand his warning about the Pharisees, note how his questions reflect Isaiah 6:9–10 (cf. Mark 4:9–12): "Do you have eyes but fail to see, and ears but fail to hear?" (8:18).

Part 3: The Mystery Unveiled—The Cross and the Way of Discipleship (8:22–10:45)

You can scarcely miss the central feature of this section, which frames the whole, namely, the three passion predictions and the disciples' hardness of heart. Thus the crowds and opposition recede into the background, while Jesus, on the way to Jerusalem, devotes himself primarily to instructing the disciples.

☐ 8:22–9:29 *The First Passion Prediction and Its Aftermath*

Note how the narrative of the twice-touched blind man (8:22–26) serves to bridge the disciples' "blindness" (vv. 17–21) and their "first touch" at Caesarea Philippi (vv. 27–30). But they clearly need a second touch. Peter gives the right answer: Jesus is the Messiah. But when told that the Messiah must die, he is infused with "the yeast of the Pharisees" and vehemently rejects such a wild idea (vv. 31–33).

Watch for two things in the crucial teaching on discipleship that follows (8:34–9:1): (1) This is the first instruction on discipleship in the Gospel (coming only after the nature of Jesus' messiahship is disclosed), and (2) here the crowds are (significantly) included.

The Transfiguration (9:2–13), with its affirmation of the Son as the one to hear, is the divine response to Jesus' suffering before it happens; note how both the Law (Moses) and the Prophets (Elijah) are witnesses. But it is also set in contrast to the continuing hardness of heart on the part of the disciples (Peter on the mountain, and the rest with the demon-possessed boy, 9:14–29).

☐ 9:30–10:31 *The Second Passion Prediction and Its Aftermath*

Watch how the second foretelling of Jesus' death is now followed by squabbling among the disciples over who is the greatest (9:33–34). Jesus responds by pointing out the nature of discipleship—servanthood and childlikeness (vv. 35–37). Note how this theme is immediately picked up in the instructions that follow—on welcoming Jesus' little ones and not causing them to sin (vv. 38–50). When Mark returns to it in 10:13–16, he sets it in contrast to the rich (10:17–31), for whom it is hard "to enter the kingdom of God"—an obvious shock to the disciples, who assume the rich have God's blessing.

☐ 10:32–45 *The Third Passion Prediction and Its Aftermath*

One more time, but briefly in this case, Mark points to the disciples' hardness of heart. Note that this time it is set in the context of "on their way up to Jerusalem." So while Jesus is heading toward his death as God's suffering servant (v. 45), the disciples covet positions of authority!

Part 4: The King Comes to Jerusalem to Die (10:46–15:47)

In this section you will see the religious opposition coming to the fore, while the disciples and crowds play only supportive roles.

☐ 10:46–13:27 *The King Comes to Jerusalem: The House Is Divided*

Note how the Bartimaeus story (10:46–52) serves as the bridge to this section—a blind man, who "sees" Jesus as "the Son of David," is given sight, while the seeing, who don't recognize David's son (12:35–40), remain blind. You might want to check out how this narrative and the next two (triumphal entry and cleansing/judgment of the temple) echo God's coming to Israel in Isaiah 35.

Thus with three prophetic symbolic actions—the triumphal entry, the cursing of the fig tree, and the cleansing of the temple—Jesus presents himself to Israel as their long-awaited King. The Lord whom they seek comes suddenly to his temple—but in judgment (see Mal 3:1). This is followed by a series of six conflict stories between Jesus and the religious authorities (Mark 11:27–12:40), to which the widow with her two small coins stands in bold relief (12:41–44).

The disciples reappear in chapter 13 to hear the announcement of God's eventual judgment on Jerusalem (vv. 14–23) in the context of final judgment and salvation (vv. 24–27), with emphasis on the disciples' being watchful.

☐ 14:1–15:47 *The King Is Crucified*

Finally the story reaches its dreadful/marvelous climax. The King is anointed for burial (14:1–11) and has a final meal with his disciples, who are assured they will eat and drink anew with him in the coming kingdom (vv. 12–26)—and this in the context of their present disowning of him (vv. 27–31, 66–72). He is then led away to be humiliated by the religious opposition, as they spit on the Messiah (vv. 32–65) before turning him over to Rome to be executed by crucifixion (15:1–41), as "the king of the Jews." What Pilate intended as warning—this is what happens to messianic pretenders—Mark sees as the ultimate truth about Jesus as kingly Messiah. Jesus is then buried under the watchful eye of some women who will be the first to hear the good news of his resurrection.

Epilogue: The Story Is Not Over (16:1–8)

The epilogue remains a mystery. Jesus has been raised (but no recorded appearances); the story obviously goes on, but the final word is fear. Did Mark write more that was lost (see the two later endings in the New Revised Standard Version)? Or did he intend his readers to change "fear" into "awe," and follow Jesus along the way that leads to the cross and the resurrection? We may never know, but the latter is certainly what he intends his Gospel as a whole to do.

This superb telling of the story of Jesus as the fulfillment of the story of Israel is crucial to our understanding the emphases of much of the rest of the New Testament, especially the letters of Paul and the books of Hebrews and 1 Peter. As Paul put it in 1 Corinthians 1:18–25, in the weakness and folly of a crucified Messiah, God has shown his power and wisdom at work in the world for salvation.

The Gospel according to Luke

ORIENTING DATA FOR LUKE

- **Content:** the story of Jesus as part 1 of Luke-Acts, which is the story of the salvation of "Israel," which Christ and the Spirit have brought about; part 1 begins with the announcement of Jesus' birth by the Spirit and carries through to his ascension
- **Author:** according to very early tradition, Luke the physician and sometime companion of the apostle Paul (see Col 4:14), the only Gentile author in the Bible
- **Date:** uncertain; scholars are divided between a date before the death of Paul (ca. A.D. 64; see Acts 28:30–31) and one after the fall of Jerusalem (A.D. 70, because of his use of Mark)
- **Recipient(s):** Theophilus is otherwise unknown; in keeping with such prefaces in Greco-Roman literature, he was probably the patron of Luke-Acts, thus underwriting its publication; the implied readers are Gentile Christians, whose place in God's story is ensured through the work of Jesus Christ and the Spirit
- **Emphases:** God's Messiah has come to his people, Israel, with the promised inclusion of Gentiles; Jesus came to save the lost, including every kind of marginalized person whom traditional religion would put outside the boundaries; Jesus' ministry is carried out under the power of the Holy Spirit; the necessity of Jesus' death and resurrection (which fulfilled Old Testament promises) for the forgiveness of sins

OVERVIEW OF LUKE

If Mark is one of those who cannot tell a story badly, Luke is the one who can tell it to perfection. His vision is all-embracing: The story of Jesus, now placed in the context of world history (Luke 2:1; 3:1–2), includes the Spirit's ongoing ministry in the church as well. So you need to read part 1 in connection with part 2, as Luke himself intended, and not just in the context of the other three Gospels (thus we will guide you through Acts in the next chapter, out of canonical order). Luke's story is thus in two major parts: (1) how the good news of God's salvation for all people began, through the power of the Spirit, with Jesus in Galilee and in Jerusalem (Luke's Gospel), and (2) how the good news of God's salvation through Jesus was, by the power of the Spirit, carried by the apostles from Jerusalem to Rome (Acts).

Chapters 1 and 2 of Luke both introduce the story and anticipate all its major themes and concerns—the links with Old Testament promises; the Davidic kingly role of Jesus; the restoration of Israel; the inclusion of Gentiles; God's concern for the poor; the role of the Holy Spirit; the anticipated opposition; the joy caused by the good news about Jesus.

In 3:1–4:13 the ministries of John and Jesus are linked, as anticipated in chapter 1. Jesus is presented to Israel through his baptism and testing; he is also linked to the Gentile mission by a genealogy that takes him back through Abraham to Adam.

The rest of the Gospel is in three parts, set off by geographical notations. In 4:14–9:50 Jesus teaches and heals in Galilee. The introductory narrative of a Sabbath in Nazareth (4:16–30) serves as a prototype for the rest of the story—fulfillment of Old Testament promises; the Spirit descending on the Messiah; good news to the poor; inclusion of Gentiles; rejection by some of Israel.

In 9:51 Jesus "resolutely set out for Jerusalem"; he does not arrive there until 19:45. Although regularly portrayed in this long section as on the way to Jerusalem (10:38; 13:22; 17:11; 18:31), Jesus still gathers disciples around him, challenges all with his teachings, rejects a pharisaic understanding of God, and in turn is finally rejected by the religious and political authorities.

Finally in Jerusalem (19:45–24:53), Jesus is rejected by the Jewish leaders and is crucified. But the crucifixion and resurrection were of divine necessity—evidence of God's faithfulness to his people. So part

1 ends with the ascension and on a note of joy, as the disciples stay at the temple, awaiting part 2.

SPECIFIC ADVICE FOR READING LUKE

Luke's primary concern (in both parts) is with the story of salvation—God's salvation of "Israel," with its promised inclusion of the Gentiles. Salvation for Luke means God's acceptance and forgiveness of sinners, which, picking up an Old Testament theme, is especially expressed as "good news to the poor" (4:18; 7:22; cf. 1:51–53)—all those who have been marginalized by society at large and especially by the religious power brokers. They are the "lost" (19:10) and include wealthy tax collectors (19:1–9), "the [economically] poor, the crippled, the lame, the blind" (14:13; cf. 16:19–31), a Samaritan (17:11–19; cf. 10:25–37), and women (7:36–50; 8:2–3; 10:38–42; cf. the three women in chs. 1–2). Be looking for these as you read. It also includes the Gentiles, but that dimension of the story is reserved for Acts. Thus in part 1 the universalizing of salvation is vertical, covering every strata of society within Israel; in part 2 it is horizontal, focusing especially on the Gentiles and the march of the gospel from Jerusalem to Rome.

Thus in Luke's Gospel Jesus comes both as Israel's kingly Messiah (the announcement to Mary [1:32–33] is full of the language of the Davidic covenant from 2 Sam 7:14, 16) and as the one who has come to help God's "servant Israel, remembering to be merciful to Abraham and his descendants forever, just as he promised our ancestors" (Luke 1:54–55; cf. 1:68–75; 2:30–32). Luke begins part 2 with the disciples' question, "Lord, are you at this time going to restore the kingdom to Israel?" (Acts 1:6).

It is in this context that the temple (Zion) plays a significant role in Luke-Acts. Not only is the Messiah presented—and recognized—in the temple (Luke 2:21–38), but the only narrative of Jesus' childhood in the Gospels (2:41–52) places him in the temple courts having discussions with the teachers. This anticipates his return to the temple to teach in 20:1–21:38, after he had "cleansed" it (19:45–48). Fittingly, the outpouring of the Holy Spirit and the first proclaiming of the gospel happen at the temple in Acts 2–6. But the God who has thus returned to his earthly temple has also announced its coming destruction (Luke 21:20–24); in this new era of salvation God no longer dwells in a temple made by hands (Acts 7:48–50). And that leads to the other side of the story—that many in Israel, especially the "religious" and their leaders, reject Jesus, thus fulfilling

Simeon's prophecy (Luke 2:34)—"This child is destined to cause the falling and rising of many in Israel, and to be a sign that will be spoken against." This begins in the programmatic narrative in 4:16–30 and continues throughout the Gospel, climaxing at the end with the rejection of Jesus by the Jewish leaders in Jerusalem. It becomes a major theme in Acts.

In this regard, watch especially for the significant role the books of Isaiah and the Psalms play in Luke's presentation. Isaiah's concern for the nations in the context of Jewish rejection frames the whole of Luke-Acts, beginning with Simeon's echo of Isaiah 49:6 (Luke 2:32), followed by Luke's own citation of Isaiah 40:3–5 regarding John the Baptist (Luke 3:4–6, "and all people will see God's salvation"), and finally with Jesus' citation of Isaiah 61:1–2 as he begins his public ministry (Luke 4:18–19). At the very end (Acts 28:26–27), Diaspora Jewish rejection of Jesus in Rome is seen to fulfill Isaiah 6:9–10 (cf. the citation of Isa 49:6 in the significant speech by Paul in Acts 13:47). At the same time Isaiah's suffering servant is the key to understanding Jesus' earthly ministry (Luke 22:37; Acts 8:32–33; cf. Mark), while Jesus' coming to the temple as Israel's rightful King and his present exaltation as Lord are seen in light of Psalms 2, 118, and 110 (see Luke 20:17, 42–43; Acts 2:34–35; 4:11, 25–26; cf. 7:56; cf. Hebrews).

Although salvation comes through Jesus, Luke especially emphasizes the role the Holy Spirit plays in God's salvation. You will notice how the Spirit predominates in the events in chapters 1–2 of Luke's Gospel, as well as in the ministry of Jesus himself. Everything Jesus does by way of preparation (3:1–4:11) is guided by the Spirit. His ministry begins with the citation of Isaiah 61:1, "the Spirit of the Lord is on me because he has anointed me" (4:18). That Luke intends his readers mentally to insert "by the Spirit" throughout this narrative about his earthly ministry is made clear by Peter in Acts 10:38—"how God anointed Jesus of Nazareth with the Holy Spirit and power, and how he went around doing good and healing all who were under the power of the devil, because God was with him." This theme is thoroughgoing in Acts.

You should also note the emphasis throughout the Gospel on prayer and joy. Jesus himself prays at every major point in the story, and Luke includes more *teaching* on prayer than all the other Gospels. And salvation as "good news for the poor" causes people regularly to glorify God with great joy. Here is one Gentile who is deeply grateful to be included in God's salvation of his people Israel.

A WALK THROUGH LUKE

The Story Begins (1:1–4:13)

☐ 1:1–4 *The Prologue*

Luke's preface follows a well-known literary convention, where an author sets forth the *reason* for his narrative, usually in light of what others have done and almost always addressing his patron as someone to be honored. Luke himself learned of the events about Jesus from some who were eyewitnesses (including Mary? see 2:51); he also knew of earlier such narratives (Mark was one of these, which he used in writing his own account).

☐ 1:5–2:52 *The Announcement and Birth of Jesus, the Messiah*

Four things are important to watch for here: (1) Luke deliberately ties the story of Jesus to Israel; for example, the story of Elizabeth and John echoes that of Hannah (1 Sam 1–2), the mother of Samuel—the prophet who anointed David; the Messiah's birth is announced to Mary in the language of the Davidic covenant (2 Sam 7:14, 16); Mary bursts into a song that echoes the Psalter, as does John's father, Zechariah, at John's birth. God is at last "remembering to be merciful to Abraham and his descendants" (Luke 1:54–55), to raise up "a horn of salvation for us in the house of David" (1:69). The narrative concludes (2:52) in words that echo the growth of young Samuel (1 Sam 2:26).

(2) All the people involved are among the poor of Israel. Thus (in chapter 2), Jesus is born in a manger because there was no guest room; his birth is announced to lowly shepherds; at Jesus' and Mary's "purification," his parents offer the sacrifice of the poorest of the poor; a widow prophesies about Jesus. (3) Simeon's blessing and prophecy are especially programmatic: Jesus will be the glory of Israel, he will bring salvation to the nations, and he will "cause the falling and rising of many in Israel." (4) Luke especially emphasizes Jesus' humanity (see 2:52); the miraculous element is regularly attributed to the work of the Spirit. The whole story develops in this mode.

☐ 3:1–4:13 *Jesus' Preparation for Ministry*

Already linked to Jesus in chapter 1, John the Baptist comes on the scene announcing the new exodus. But John is not the Messiah; rather, he points people to the coming of the Messiah (and his baptism with the Holy Spirit and fire). Jesus is baptized and is himself anointed by the Spirit. After a genealogy (tracing Jesus back to Adam), the Spirit leads him into the desert to be tested (as was Israel following its "baptism" through the Red Sea). And so Jesus is prepared for his public ministry.

The Ministry of Jesus in Galilee (4:14–9:50)

In this first major section of his Gospel, Luke weaves together a series of short narratives that illustrate Jesus' powerful ministry on behalf of the poor and the captives; also included are several illustrations of his teachings, with emphasis on hearing God's word and putting it into practice (8:21). You will see how Luke holds the narrative together by use of repeated short summaries that help to keep you focused on the greatness of Jesus and on his bringing the kingdom (4:14–15, 44; 5:15; 7:17; 8:1–3). Also woven through the narrative, but not in a prominent role, is the beginning of opposition (5:17–21, 30; 6:7; 7:31–35, 44–49).

□ 4:14–44 *Good News for Nazareth and Capernaum*

After an introductory summary (vv. 14–15), Luke uses Jesus' visit to the synagogue in his hometown of Nazareth to introduce the whole of his ministry (vv. 16–30)—fulfilling Old Testament promises; Spirit-empowered; with good news for the poor, including release of captives; justified by two Old Testament stories of the inclusion of Gentiles, resulting in opposition. Note especially that the opposition is the result of Jesus' reminding some Jews of God's prior inclusion of Gentiles (thus anticipating the story in Acts).

This is followed by two short narratives illustrating Jesus' powerful ministry on behalf of the poor and captives. Thus in his driving out demons and healing the sick (4:31–44), Jesus, the (humble) Divine Warrior, engages Satan in the holy war on Satan's own supposed turf (see 4:6; cf. 10:18).

□ 5:1–6:11 *Mission and Controversy*

After calling his first disciples (5:1–11), Jesus' healing of a man with leprosy causes Jesus' fame to spread (vv. 12–16). It also sets up a series of conflict stories—on Jesus' right to forgive sins (vv. 17–26), his eating with sinners (vv. 27–32), his disciples' not fasting (vv. 33–39), and his breaking traditional Sabbath rules (6:1–11).

☐ 6:12–49 *Jesus Instructs His Disciples and Others*

Jesus now appoints the Twelve (Israel again!), whom he instructs (v. 20) in the presence of others (vv. 17–19) on the nature of discipleship. Note the emphases—on the humble poor, who are persecuted for Jesus' sake; on loving and not judging; and finally on obedience.

☐ 7:1–50 *Good News to the Poor*

Again Jesus shows compassion on the poor, in this case a Gentile (vv. 1–10), a widow (vv. 11–17), and a town prostitute (vv. 36–50). Note that the second story concludes with the exclamation that "a great prophet has appeared among us" (v. 16), which then leads to the narrative about Jesus and John the Baptist (vv. 18–35). Note further how the Pharisees' rejection of John (v. 30) leads to the final story in this section, where a view of the Pharisees emerges that will become thoroughgoing in the next section.

☐ 8:1–56 *Authentic Hearing, Fear, and Faith*

Luke now presents Jesus as a teacher of parables, so as to emphasize authentic hearing (the kind that leads to obedience, vv. 1–21). This is followed by three miracle stories (with four miracles), demonstrating Jesus' power over creation, demons, death, and uncleanness (see comments on Lev 11:1–16:34, p. 47). Note also how the first and last of these stories pick up the themes of *fear* and *faith.*

☐ 9:1–50 *The Identity of Jesus and Authentic Discipleship*

Watch for the significant role the Twelve play in this final series of narratives, beginning with Jesus' sending them out for ministry (vv. 1–9). The larger section then concludes with the confession of Peter and the first two predictions of Jesus' death (9:18–27; 9:43b–50), plus the transfiguration (vv. 28–36), where Jesus talks with Moses and Elijah about the "exodus" (vv. 30–31; see TNIV note) he is about to accomplish in Jerusalem.

On the Way to Jerusalem (9:51–19:44)

As you read this long travel narrative, you will find that even though the entire narrative is set "on the way to Jerusalem," that thread is often let go (among other things, the mission of the seventy-two and the events of two different Sabbaths are included). Luke probably intends us to read this section in light of the events already predicted, which are soon to transpire in Jerusalem. Also watch for several previous themes woven throughout: (1) the coming of God's salvation to all people, especially the poor and the lost; (2) regular, and sometimes harsh, confrontation between Jesus and the Jewish leaders; (3) the closely related theme that Jesus is going to Jerusalem to suffer and be killed; and (4) the formation of the disciples, especially preparing them for the time after his departure.

☐ 9:51–11:13 *Discipleship: Hearing and Doing the Word*

Notice how much of this material is aimed at instructing the disciples. Their attitude toward Samaritan opposition (9:51–55) is eventually challenged by Jesus' parable in 10:25–37, whose point is to demolish the question "Who is my neighbor?" Between these stand "the cost of discipleship" (9:57–62) and the mission of the seventy-two (10:1–24). Then comes the story of how one truly welcomes Jesus (vv. 38–42, by "listening to what [Jesus] said") as well as instruction on prayer (11:1–13).

☐ 11:14–54 *Opposition to Jesus*

In the next narratives, Jesus' authority is called into question first by some in the crowds over his driving out demons and then through their demanding a sign (vv. 15–16), to which Jesus responds in verses 17–32, and second by the Pharisees (vv. 37–38), to which Jesus responds with a series of woes on the Pharisees and their teachers (vv. 39–54).

☐ 12:1–13:9 *Discipleship and Preparedness*

Note the two emphases in this series of materials: (1) not pursuing wealth, but being content with what one has and being generous to the poor, and (2) vigilance in light of the coming eschatological crisis.

☐ 13:10–17:10 *Jesus in Opposition to Pharisaism*

You will see that this next series begins with a controversy between Jesus and the Pharisees over his showing compassion on the Sabbath (13:10–17). After two parables about the kingdom of God (vv. 18–21), he then responds to the question of who will be saved by implying that many will not (vv. 22–30), which in turn leads to his sorrow over Jerusalem (vv. 31–35). Following this, watch for two recurring themes in Jesus' conflict with the Pharisees—(1) their attitude toward the poor and the lost and (2) their attitude toward money (14:1–16:31). Note that the greatly loved parable of the prodigal son indicates that what is at stake between Jesus and the Pharisees is their opposing views of God (not a slaveholder [15:29], but a gracious, forgiving Father). The section then concludes with further instruction to the disciples on forgiveness and faithful servanthood (17:1–10).

☐ 17:11–19:27 *Responding to the Presence of the Kingdom*

Note how this final series begins with the reminder that Jesus is "on his way to Jerusalem." At issue is the proper response to the presence of the kingdom—thankfulness (17:11–19, involving a Samaritan again); faithfulness (17:20–18:8); humility (18:9–17); and the problem of wealth (18:18–30). After the third prediction of his coming death (18:31–34), Jesus heals a blind man and finds a lost man in Jericho (18:35–19:10). The final parable (19:11–27) is especially intended to prepare the disciples for his absence.

The Events of the End (and New Beginning) in Jerusalem (19:45–24:53)

☐ 19:45–21:38 *Jesus Teaches in the Temple*

As anticipated in chapters 1 and 2, Jesus now returns to the temple. After driving out the money changers, he takes his rightful place as teacher in the temple, an event which is set in the context of the religious leaders plotting to kill him (19:47). Note how this whole section thus portrays the conflict between Jesus and the opposition in the context of the temple, while "the people" (v. 48) play the role of learners who are on God's side. Note also how the parable of the tenants in the vineyard (20:9–19) makes it clear that the vineyard (cf. Isa 5:1–7) is about to be given over to others (Gentiles).

☐ 22:1–23:56 *The Trial and Death of Jesus*

Having shaped the narrative toward this point, Luke now recounts the events surrounding Jesus' death. Jesus is brought before three different tribunals (the Jewish Sanhedrin, Herod, and Pilate); note that before the political figures he is declared innocent of wrongdoing (23:4, 13–15). For the sake of his Gentile audience, who know that the Romans reserved crucifixion for slaves or noncitizen insurrectionists, Luke makes sure to note that Jesus himself "has done nothing to deserve death" (23:15). Even in his crucifixion, Jesus extends salvation to one of the "lost ones" (vv. 39–43)—who also affirms Jesus' innocence.

□ 24:1–53 *The Vindication and Exaltation of Jesus*

Luke has the longest resurrection narrative among the four Gospels. Recognized in the breaking of bread, Jesus himself repeatedly interprets his death in terms of its divine necessity and prophetic fulfillment: Christ *must* suffer and rise from the dead, "and repentance for the forgiveness of sins ... be preached in his name to all nations, beginning at Jerusalem" (24:47), thus pointing to part 2 (Acts). Note that Luke concludes in the temple with rejoicing and waiting.

Luke's Gospel is one of the great treasures of the biblical story, emphasizing God's fulfillment of his promises to Israel—that "the year of the Lord's favor" (Luke 4:19) had come with Jesus' compassionate ministry of deliverance for and acceptance of the poor and helpless.

Acts

ORIENTING DATA FOR ACTS

- **Content:** part 2 of Luke's account of the good news about Jesus; how by the power of the Spirit the good news spread from Jerusalem to Rome
- **Author:** see the Gospel according to Luke
- **Date:** see Luke
- **Recipients:** see Luke
- **Emphases:** the good news of God's salvation through Jesus is for Jew and Gentile alike, thus fulfilling Old Testament expectations; the Holy Spirit guides the church in spreading the good news; the church has the good sense to side with God regarding his salvation and the inclusion of the Gentiles; salvation for all is God's thing and nothing can hinder it; the good news is accepted in joy by some and rejected in anger by others

OVERVIEW OF ACTS

In writing his larger account of the good news about Jesus, Luke has shaped the two parts to correspond in some significant ways. In Acts, for example, the geography is now reversed; it starts in Jerusalem and then branches out to other parts of Judea (chs. 1–12); its large central section is another travel narrative, as Paul takes the gospel from Antioch to Europe (chs. 13–20); the final third (chs. 21–28) portrays Paul's trials before the same three tribunals as Jesus (the Jewish Sanhedrin [Luke 22:66–71/Acts 22:30–23:10]; the Roman procurator [Luke 23:1–5, 13–25/Acts 24:1–27]; and one of the Herods [Luke 23:6–12/Acts 25:23–26:32])—which in Paul's case results in his getting the gospel to the heart of the empire (Rome).

The key to your reading of Acts is to recognize the "movement" of the gospel from Jerusalem to Rome, narrated in six parts (panels) and signaled by Luke's little summary statements in 6:7; 9:31; 12:24; 16:5; and 19:20. In each case the narrative seems to pause for a moment before it takes off in a new direction—sometimes geographically, sometimes ethnically, and sometimes both. The good news that is being spread, of course, is God's salvation (the forgiveness of sins) offered to all people (Jew and Gentile alike) through the death and resurrection of Jesus and by the power of the Holy Spirit. Here at last the promise to Abraham (Gen 12:2–3; see Acts 3:25), expressed repeatedly by the prophets as part of their hope for the future—that Gentiles would join Israel as the people of God (e.g., Isa 2:1–5; Mic 4:1–5; Zech 14:16–18)—had found its fulfillment.

The first panel (1:1–6:7) tells the story of the spread of the good news about Jesus in Jerusalem by the apostles. The second (6:8–9:31) marks the first geographical expansion to neighboring Judea and Samaria (see 1:8), where Stephen and the Hellenists play the major role. The third (9:32–12:24) narrates the first expansion to the Gentiles (Cornelius) and the conversion of the key figure (Paul) in what is to be its still greater expansion. With Paul now the central figure, the fourth panel (12:25–16:5) narrates the expansion to Gentiles in Asia, and how the early leaders dealt with the "problem" of Gentile inclusion "law-free." The fifth (16:6–19:20) marks the jump of the gospel from Asia to Europe; the church is also now steadily more Gentile than Jewish. The sixth (19:21–28:31) tells how Paul (the apostle to the Gentiles) finally got to Rome (the capital of the Gentile world) with the good news—but he did so, Luke reminds us, by way of Jerusalem through a series of trials very much like those of Jesus.

SPECIFIC ADVICE FOR READING ACTS

The story in part 2 is still about Jesus, as the brief prologue (1:1–2) reminds us. The first part was about what "Jesus *began* to do and to teach until the day he was taken up to heaven" (emphasis added). With some carefully chosen connections to part 1, Acts begins by picking up the prophecy from Luke 3:16 by John the Baptist about the coming Holy Spirit (Acts 1:5). The disciples are promised the "power" of the Holy Spirit (cf. Luke 24:49, "clothed with power from on high") so as to bear witness to Jesus. Luke then narrates the ascension (cf. Luke 24:51) in the context of Jesus' promised return; the clear implication is that through the Spirit they are to carry on the story until he comes (cf. the parable in Luke 19:11–27).

How Luke does this is the genius of Acts. First, note the large number of speeches that Luke records throughout the narrative (e.g., Peter in 2:14–39; 3:11–26; 10:27–43; Stephen in 7:1–53; Paul in 13:16–47; 17:22–31; 20:17–35). These tend to appear at key points and illustrate how the gospel is preached (or defended) in a variety of settings. In each case the speech either includes the essence of the story of Jesus or focuses on him at the end. Thus Jesus' story continues in Acts as the early believers bear witness to him.

Second, note (1) the connection between Jesus Christ and the Spirit and (2) that the Spirit is ultimately responsible for every major turning point in the narrative. How Luke connects Jesus and the Spirit is especially important. You will remember from reading Luke that the Spirit is the key to Jesus' earthly ministry (cf. Acts 10:38). Now "exalted to the right hand of God, he has *received* from the Father the promised Holy Spirit and *has poured out* what you now see and hear" (Acts 2:33, emphasis added). Christ, the great bearer of the Spirit, is also the great "baptizer" in the Spirit so that others will receive the Spirit and thus bear witness to Christ. It is therefore not surprising that at every turn, the Spirit is the driving force behind the forward movement of the gospel.

Third, because the gospel is God's thing, initiated by him and expressing his faithfulness to Israel through Christ, and carried out by the power of the Spirit, Luke also regularly reminds us that nothing can hinder it—not the Jewish leaders in Jerusalem (chs. 3–5; "you will not be able to stop these men; you will only find yourselves fighting against God," 5:39); not unbelieving Jews, like Saul of Tarsus, bent on destruction (8:1–3); not the church in Jerusalem (11:1–18; "who was I to think that I could stand in God's way?" Peter asks, v. 17); not secular leaders, like Herod (12:1–24, "Herod ... was eaten by worms and died. But the word of God continued to increase and spread"[!], vv. 23–24); not Judaizers within the church (15:1–35; "why do you try to test God?" v. 10); not religious or secular opposition from Greeks (16:16–40; 19:23–41); not shipwrecks or snakes (chs. 27–28). With the coming of Jesus and the Spirit, the time of God's favor has come. The gospel is God's activity in history; salvation is for all people, Jew and Gentile alike, and nothing can hinder it. And so the book concludes with Paul preaching in Rome with all boldness and without hindrance (28:31).

You will remember about Luke's Gospel that the universal nature of salvation was expressed in a *vertical* way to include the poor of every imaginable kind. In Acts Luke has concentrated *horizontally* on the Gentile mission—those ultimately marginalized by Israel. But throughout the narrative the restoration of Israel (Acts 1:6) is also always kept in view. The gospel begins as good news to Israel, "heirs of the prophets and of the covenant" (3:25), so that thousands turn to Christ from the start. As it moves outward, carried by Hellenistic Jews, it embraces fallen Jews (the Samaritans, 8:4–25) and a Jewish proselyte (8:26–40). The first Gentile convert is a "God-fearer" (10:2), and wherever Paul goes, he always begins in the synagogue, where some believe. And at the end, in Rome, he still pleads with Israel to believe in Jesus (28:17–28), but they refuse, so "God's salvation has been sent to the Gentiles, and they will listen!" (v. 28).

That leads us to remind you of the other side of Simeon's prophecy (Luke 2:34–35)—that Jesus will be a "sign that will be spoken against." You will want to note as the narrative progresses that the church becomes more and more composed of Gentiles, while Diaspora Jews and the Jewish leaders in Jerusalem lead the opposition. This obviously saddens Luke, but it also is part of the reminder to his implied (Gentile) readers that they belong to the Israel that God is reconstituting through Christ and the Spirit.

Finally, you will want to watch for the sudden insertion of "we" in the narrative at 16:10 (in Troas), which goes on until verse 17 (in Philippi), is picked up again at 20:5 (again in Troas), and continues through 21:19 (in Jerusalem) and again at 27:1 through 28:16 (from Caesarea to Rome). Two things are noteworthy about this phenomenon: (1) The author presents himself without fanfare as a sometime traveling companion of Paul, and (2) in these passages the details are far more abundant and vivid, suggesting that he may be using something like a diary.

A word about its placement in the canon. Luke understands his Gospel and Acts to be two parts of one story. It ended up in two books of about equal length (rather than one long book) because each would fit on one papyrus scroll. But in putting together the New Testament canon, the early church separated Luke from Acts (since both would have existed on separate scrolls, even when copied) through inspired insight. In the canon Luke now belongs to the fourfold Gospel, while Acts serves as a bridge between the Gospels and Paul. But in reading Acts, you need always to remember how it fits into Luke's inspired plan.

A WALK THROUGH ACTS

☐ 1:1–6:7 *The Good News Begins in Jerusalem*

After the prologue that picks up where the Gospel left off (1:1–11), Luke first narrates the *filling up* of the Twelve (1:12–26), since they serve as the representatives of/to Israel. The coming of the Spirit then marks a new beginning (2:1–13; the Gentile world is already present in microcosm), followed by Peter's explanation of the phenomenon of tongues and the results (2:14–41). This is followed by a series of sketches that illustrate the early life of the church in Jerusalem—its common life (2:42–47; 4:32–37); its preaching and healing ministry (3:1–26; 5:12–16); the opposition (4:1–22; 5:17–42); and judgment within the community for "testing the Spirit" (5:1–11). What you will discover as you read is a new community that believes in Jesus but continues to live within Judaism.

Be looking also for two things that carry over from the last chapter of Luke's Gospel: (1) The disciples' ministry is primarily in the temple courts—the same temple courts cleansed by Jesus and made the arena of his final days of teaching (see Luke 19:45–21:38)—and (2) everything in this section is seen as fulfillment of very cardinal moments from the Old Testament story: the end-time gift of the Spirit promised by Joel (Acts 2:16–21); the resurrection of Jesus, as David's true heir (2:24–32); the present exaltation of Jesus as the exalted Lord of Psalm 110:1 (2:33–35); that the Messiah would suffer (3:17–23); that the promise to Abraham that he would bless the nations is about to be fulfilled (3:25); that the rejected Jesus is the rejected cornerstone of Psalm 118:22 (4:11) and the Messiah against whom the nations rage (4:25–26). Be on the watch for this motif as you continue through the rest of Acts.

The section ends (6:1–7) by noting that two groups have emerged within the community: Greek-speaking (Hellenistic) Jewish Christians and Aramaic-speaking (Jerusalem-based) Jewish Christians. The former of these, who belong to the Hellenistic synagogue in Jerusalem, become the key to the next expansion. Note how verse 7 brings this panel to a conclusion.

☐ 6:8–9:31 *The Good News Spreads to Judea and Samaria*

Note that this section picks up where the last one left off. You will see that the gospel has made significant inroads into the Greek-speaking synagogue (6:8–15). The first two of the leaders mentioned in 6:5 (Stephen and Philip) are responsible for the next phase of the story. Stephen's speech (ch. 7), patterned after such passages as Nehemiah 9:6–37 and Psalms 105 and 106, takes up the two crucial issues—from their accusation (Acts 6:13)—where the new wine cannot be contained in the old wineskins (Luke 5:36–39): (1) the temple (God does not dwell in buildings made by hands, in fulfillment of Isa 66:1–2) and (2) the law (the true lawbreakers are those who crucified Jesus, not the believers). Especially watch for the role of Moses in this speech—that he who was "rejected" by Israel (Acts 7:23–29, 35, 39) also foretold that God would send them "a prophet like me from your own people" (v. 37), who was also rejected (vv. 51–52).

Next comes the expansion to Samaria and to a Gentile proselyte through Philip's ministry (ch. 8); note here that Jesus is understood to be Isaiah's suffering servant (vv. 32–35). The panel then concludes with the conversion of one of the chief leaders of the opposition in the Hellenistic synagogue—Saul of Tarsus, who will be responsible (for the most part) for the next two phases of the expansion (Asia, Europe). Note how Saul is first introduced (8:1, 3); you might also want to look ahead to the two instances where Paul himself repeats this story (22:1–21; 26:2–23), in both cases emphasizing his role in the Gentile mission. Again, watch how 9:31 sums up and thus concludes this section.

☐ 9:32–12:24 *The Good News Spreads to the Gentiles*

Note how Luke begins and ends this panel with Peter stories (9:32–43; 12:1–19). The first one is intended to set the stage for the Cornelius story and to remind you that the apostles continue to do mighty works. The conversion of Cornelius is so important that Luke narrates it twice (10:1–48; 11:1–18). The significance is that the first Gentile was brought to faith, not through the Hellenists (who might be suspect in Jerusalem), but through Peter, resistant though he is. The whole is orchestrated by the Holy Spirit. When criticized in Jerusalem, Peter tells the story all over again. Because of the work of the Spirit, Peter could not hinder God (11:17). Jerusalem is amazed: "even the Gentiles" (v. 18) get in on the good news. Also crucial to this panel is the founding of the church in Antioch by the Hellenists (vv. 19–30), since it will be the sending church for the mission to Asia and Europe. The Peter story with which the section ends (12:1–19) not only illustrates the "nothing can hinder it" motif but also sets the stage for the death of the opposition in this case (12:19–23). Note especially how the summary sentence of 12:24 sits in direct contrast to verse 23.

☐ 12:25–16:5 *The Good News Spreads to Asia*

Look for several pivotal matters as you read this phase of the story: (1) The church in Antioch is the new center (12:25–13:3; 14:26–28); (2) Paul becomes the predominant figure (13:4–12); (3) the sermon in Pisidian Antioch (13:16–41) illustrates preaching in the Diaspora synagogues; and (4) the spread of the gospel also leads to the first open breach with Judaism, specifically over the Gentile mission, supported by Isaiah 49:6 (Acts 13:47).

Note how the three accounts in Acts 14 reinforce these themes, especially the power of God that accounts for the inclusion of many Gentiles and the widening breach between Diaspora Jews and the early believers in Christ. The Jerusalem council (15:1–35), with the chief roles being played by Peter and James, affirms a "law-free" gospel to the Gentiles. Note how brief the summarizing sentence is in this instance (16:5).

☐ 16:6–19:20 *The Good News Spreads to Europe*

Here Luke records Paul's second and third missionary trips (16:6–18:22; 18:23–19:20); note how Paul always goes out from and returns to Antioch. The mission to Europe is especially orchestrated by the Spirit (16:6–10)—and here the author joins the story. In this panel Luke also records instances of conflict with pagan authorities (16:16–40; 17:5–9; 18:12–17), which tend to be instigated by Diaspora Jews (17:5, 13; 18:12). In each case the state either will not intervene or apologizes. Luke also includes here an example of preaching in a totally pagan environment (17:16–34). Again note how 19:20 functions to conclude the section.

☐ 19:21–28:30 *The Good News (and Paul) Reaches Rome*

You should find this final section an absorbing narrative. As you read, don't miss that most of it deals with how Paul gets to Rome—through a series of trials similar to those of Jesus. Again be watching for the entrance and exit of the author. At the beginning and at the end, Paul is still reaching out to his fellow Jews (21:17–26; 28:17–28). But they resolutely reject Christ, so the final word is one of judgment in the words of Isaiah 6:9–10 (cf. Luke 8:10) and acceptance by the Gentiles (Acts 28:26–28). Note especially that in Paul's two "defenses" (22:1–21; 26:2–23), he tells his story so as to highlight his role in the Gentile mission. Also crucial to the story is the constant reminder that just as with Jesus (who, even though he died as a state criminal, had three times been pronounced "not guilty"), so with Paul: He and the church are found "not guilty" of wrongdoing against Rome (22:29; 23:26–30; 26:32).

In his vivid narrative of shipwreck in 27:1–28:16, Luke also makes it clear to us that Paul's getting to Rome was ultimately God's doing. So when the apostle to the Gentiles arrives in the Gentile capital, still reaching out to the Jews but affirming the Gentiles, Luke's grand story comes to an end.

It is hard to imagine how impoverished the biblical story would be without part 2 of Luke-Acts. Here we not only have a lot of the gaps filled in, but we are constantly reminded that the gospel is *God's thing* in the world—salvation for all through Jesus Christ and the Spirit.

The Gospel according to John

ORIENTING DATA FOR JOHN

- **Content:** the story of Jesus, Messiah and Son of God, told from the perspective of postresurrection insights; in his incarnation Jesus made God known and made his life available to all through the cross
- **Author:** the beloved disciple who "wrote [these things] down" (21:24; cf. 13:23; 19:25–27; 20:2; 21:7) most likely refers to John the apostle, son of Zebedee (otherwise not named in this Gospel); the "we" of 21:24 suggests another person is responsible for the Gospel in its final form
- **Date:** unknown; probably ca. A.D. 90–95
- **Recipients:** see 1 John, to which this Gospel is closely related
- **Emphases:** Jesus is the Messiah, the Son of God; in his incarnation and the crucifixion, he both revealed God's love and redeemed humanity; discipleship means to "remain in the vine" (Jesus) and to bear fruit (to love as he loved); the Holy Spirit will be given to his people to continue his work

OVERVIEW OF JOHN

John's Gospel is one of the great treasures of the Christian faith. Intentionally telling the story from a perspective after Jesus' resurrection and the gift of the Spirit (see 2:22; 12:16; 14:26; 16:13–14), John writes to reassure believers of the truth of what they believe (in light of defections and rejection)—that through the Incarnation God is fully and finally known. Here is God's love in full and open display.

In so doing, John puts the story of Jesus into the broadest biblical framework: The Incarnate One is none other than the Word, present with God from the beginning and responsible for creation (1:1–4, 10). But the Incarnate One is also the Crucified One, who, as God's Lamb, "takes away the sin of the world" (1:29). John is also concerned to demonstrate that the incarnate Son of God is in fact the long-awaited Jewish Messiah; thus Jesus bursts onto the world's stage, fulfilling every imaginable Jewish hope, while at the same time becoming "the Savior of the world" (4:42). Since he is the Son of (the living) God, what he gives is *life* (= the life of God himself)—eternal life (= the life of the coming age available now).

John begins with a prologue that puts much of this in poetic form (1:1–18), weaving theology and history together as he sets the stage for his telling of the story. The story itself is in two major parts (1:19–12:50; 13:1–20:31); it concludes with a commissioning epilogue and explanation of the (not-expected) death of the "disciple whom Jesus loved" (21:1–25).

In part 1 Jesus first manifests himself as Son of God to his disciples (1:19–2:11), who thus see "his glory" (1:14) and "put their faith in him" (2:11). He is then revealed to "the world" (2:13–12:50) as both the Messiah and the Son of God. John brings this off by telling the story in the setting of the Jewish feasts, where Jesus acts and speaks in ways that fulfill the rich messianic expectations expressed (especially) through the ceremonies connected with these feasts (Passover, 2:13–4:54; Sabbath, 5:1–47; Passover, 6:1–71; Tabernacles, 7:1–10:21; Dedication, 10:22–42; [prelude to the final] Passover, 11:1–12:36). Also in this section one finds the seven "signs" (John's *sign-ificant* word for miracles) and the seven "I am" sayings (Jesus' self-identification). Part 1 ends with a double conclusion, narrating first Jesus' rejection by some of the Jews (12:37–43) and then the meaning of Jesus and his mission (12:44–50).

The two narratives connected with the Passover (2:13–4:54; 6:1–71) also anticipate the final Passover narrated in part 2. Here the interest focuses first on the disciples as those who will carry on Jesus' mission (chs. 13–17) and then on the crucifixion itself (chs. 18–19), where the Son of God cries (triumphantly) about his work, "It is finished" (19:30). The narrative proper concludes with the resurrection (ch. 20), focusing especially on the commissioning of the disciples (20:19–23) and using Thomas's need to see as a foil for those who believe without seeing (vv. 24–31).

SPECIFIC ADVICE FOR READING JOHN

The thing that should most strike you when coming to John's Gospel from having read the Synoptics is how different it is. Not only is the basic scene of Jesus' ministry different (Jerusalem instead of Galilee), but the whole ministry looks quite different. Here you find no messianic secret (Jesus is openly confessed as Messiah from the start); no parables (but rich use of symbolic language); no driving out of demons; no narratives of the testing in the desert, the Transfiguration, or the Lord's Supper. Rather than placing emphasis on the kingdom of God, the emphasis is on Jesus himself (the Life who gives eternal life); rather than short, pithy, memorable sayings, the teaching comes most often in long discourses. As one scholar put it, "John seems to belong to a different world."

The reason is that John deliberately sets out to tell Jesus' story from the perspective of what he had come to know about him after the light had dawned (brought about by Jesus' resurrection and the gift of the Spirit). Moreover, John's interest in Jesus at his point in history (ca. A.D. 90–95) is shaped in particular by the false prophets who are denying the Incarnation and the saving significance of Jesus' death and resurrection, and who are marked by a failure to love others (see "Specific Advice for Reading 1 John," pp. 412–13). So part of the reason for his postresurrection perspective may be traced to this historical setting. You should note how often John emphasizes that Jesus is rooted deeply in flesh-and-blood history (he grows weary, thirsts, weeps at death; blood and water flow from his side while on the cross). The point is that the one whom John and his readers know as the exalted Son of God lived a truly human life on planet Earth and did so within the context of historical Judaism.

John's special perspective accounts for two other phenomena peculiar to his telling of the story—(1) the nature of many of his narratives and (2) the use of double meanings of words, closely related to the rich symbolism. You need to be ready to hear some things at two levels. John often starts with a narrative, which then evolves into a discourse—and at times you cannot tell where Jesus stops talking and John himself is interpreting (this Gospel is especially problematic for red-letter Bible editions!). For example, in 3:1–21 he starts with a straightforward narrative of Jesus' encounter with Nicodemus, but at its heart are wordplays on the Greek word *anōthen* (which can mean either "again" or "from above," which Nicodemus hears as "again" while John clearly intends both) and *pneuma* (the same word means "wind" and "Spirit"). And at verse 11 the "I/you [singular]" shifts to "we/you [plural]" and then moves into straight discourse, which from verses 15 to 21 comes in the language and style of 1 John. This has all the earmarks of Christian preaching, and it recurs throughout John's Gospel.

John's passion in this "preached" retelling of the story is threefold, two parts of which occur in his statement of purpose in 20:30–31. First, he cares especially to demonstrate that Jesus is deeply rooted in history as the Jewish Messiah, which is explicitly confessed by the disciples (1:41, 45; cf. 11:27) and confirmed by Jesus (4:25–26; 5:46; 10:24). Thus some of the "I am" sayings are full of Old Testament allusions—shepherd (Ezek 34), vine (Isa 5:1–7), bread (Exod 16:4; Ps 78:24)—where Jesus steps into the role of Israel itself (vine), as well as Israel's kingly Messiah (shepherd). Most significantly, John sets the entire story in the context of Jesus' being the fulfillment of Jewish messianic hopes associated with various aspects of the festival celebrations, matters often hidden to us but well known to him and his readers.

For example, at the Feast of Tabernacles there was a special water-pouring rite in the temple (described in the Talmud). This rite was related first to the giving of water from the rock in the desert (Exod 17:1–7); it came to be interpreted in a messianic way as pointing to the giving of the Spirit by the Messiah. It is on the "greatest day" of this feast that Jesus cries out, "Let anyone who is thirsty come to me and drink," which John then interprets in light of the gift of the Spirit (John 7:37–39). You are not necessarily expected to catch all of this as you read (a good commentary will guide you as to the details), but it is important to point out that there is often more than meets the eye in the reading of this Gospel. We will call your attention to some of this as you read along.

Second, John is concerned to demonstrate that Jesus, the Jewish Messiah, is none other than the Son of God (the Jewish messianic title from Ps 2:7 now understood as the Second Person of the Trinity). In Jesus, God himself has become present by incarnation. John takes every opportunity he can to press this point over and over again (cf. 1 John).

These two matters lead to the third—the "pathos" of the Gospel, which is to be found in Jewish rejection of their Messiah, precisely because of his claims to divinity. This emerges first in the prologue (1:10–13) and becomes a subtheme throughout the whole Gospel, but especially in 2:13–12:50. This is not anti-Semitism, as is often claimed (any more than when Jewish prophets even more fiercely denounced their fellow Jews for failure to follow God); rather it is expressed out of a heart broken over the failure of the people to follow their Messiah. Those who were best positioned to understand Jesus rejected him because they were unwilling to risk letting go of their own safe categories. But whatever else, John clearly believes that Jesus died for the Jewish nation, as well as for the world (11:51–52).

A WALK THROUGH JOHN

Prologue (1:1–18)

This wonderful passage you will want to come back to again and again. Here John emphasizes both the prehistorical and historical aspects of Jesus as the Word, the Son of God. Beginning with the Word before creation (vv. 1–2), John then tells of the Word's role in creation (vv. 3–5) and of the twofold response to his coming into the world (vv. 9–13), concluding with a confession (note the shift to the first-person plural) about his incarnation (v. 14) and deity (v. 18). Here also the *new exodus* motif begins: Believers in Jesus are the true "children of God" (cf. Exod 4:22–23), while Jesus is presented as greater than Moses (vv. 16–17), who led the first exodus. Interspersed is a contrast with John the Baptist (vv. 6–8, 15), which anticipates the beginning of the story itself.

The Messiah/Son of God Is Manifested to His Disciples (1:19–2:12)

Picking up from 1:1, John tells the beginning of the *new creation* in a seven-day scheme (five actual days; the last deliberately specified as three days after the fourth [2:1]), which in turn anticipates the seven days of the final week (12:1). What starts with the ministry of John the Baptist—some of whose disciples follow Jesus—climaxes at the wedding of Cana, where his disciples "put their faith in him" (2:11).

☐ **1:19–42** ***Days 1 to 3: Not John, but Jesus, Is the Messiah***

Note how these first three days pick up the three things said about John the Baptist in the prologue (1:7–8): He was not the light (vv. 19–28); he came to bear witness to the light, in no less than four different messianic confessions (vv. 29–34); his witness was so that others—in this case, John the Baptist's own disciples—might believe in Jesus Christ (vv. 35–42). Note especially how this series ends with the confession by some of John's disciples, "We have found the Messiah."

□ 1:43–51 *Day 4: Jesus Is Recognized by a True Israelite*

Watch for the ways this fourth day anticipates the *fulfillment of Jewish hopes* motif that pervades the rest of the story: A genuine Israelite without guile (playing on the name of Jacob ["he deceives"], Gen 25:26) confesses Jesus in the most Jewish confession in the Gospel ("Son of God … King of Israel"; see Ps 2); he (and the others) will see the fulfillment of Jacob's ladder (Gen 28:10–22; "surely the LORD is in this place") come to pass in Jesus Christ.

□ 2:1–12 *Day 7: Jesus Is Recognized As the Fulfillment of Jewish Messianic Hopes*

And now for the climax on the seventh day of the new creation: The best wine ("saved … till now") is drawn out of six stone jars used for Jewish ceremonial washings! This outpouring of the best wine is seen by his disciples as fulfilling a significant aspect of Jewish messianic hopes (e.g., Isa 25:6; Jer 31:12; Amos 9:13–14). With this revelation of his "glory," the "first of his miraculous signs," his disciples "put their faith in him."

The Messiah/Son of God Is Manifested to the World (2:13–12:50)

In this section John places each of the narratives in the context of Jewish festivals; and in each case Jesus fulfills some aspect of messianic expectations associated with that feast.

□ 2:13–4:54 *The First Passover*

In the context of Passover, John first narrates the temple cleansing, the significance of which lies at two points: (1) Jesus' actions divide the world into those who believe and those who do not, and (2) Jesus himself replaces the temple as the locus of God's presence (cf. 1:51).

This is followed by a series of four narratives (Nicodemus, John the Baptist, the Samaritans, the official's son), which continue motifs already in place—the exaltation of Jesus as Son of God in the context of some who do and do not believe (3:1–36); Jesus, not Jerusalem or Mount Gerizim, as the place of God's presence; and the confession of Jesus as "Savior of the world" (4:1–54). Note how the two narratives of chapter 4 also point toward the gathering of the nations—Samaria (vv. 1–42) and the "royal official" (vv. 43–54)

☐ 5:1–47 *An Unnamed Feast*

The next feast is unnamed because John's interest is in the *weekly* feast day, the Sabbath (5:1–47). The whole narrative assumes a Jewish belief that God continued to work on the Sabbath in three areas of his special divine prerogatives, namely, birth, death, and rain—all of which could and did occur on Sabbath days, giving evidence of God's "working" on the Sabbath.

Watch how John uses the healing of the invalid on the Sabbath as the basis for a discourse (vv. 16–47) on Jesus' assuming the divine prerogative of "work" on the Sabbath (giving life and judging [taking life]), which results in a confrontation with the Jewish leaders.

☐ 6:1–71 *The Second Passover*

As you read this second Passover narrative, you find Jesus functioning as the expected "prophet like [Moses]" (Deut 18:18) as he feeds the multitude and then offers them the bread of life. Playing on the Exodus theme of *bread from heaven,* which Jews expected to be renewed in the messianic age, Jesus offers himself as that bread, by offering them his "flesh" and his "blood" (John 6:48–58), thus anticipating the final Passover (chs. 13–20). Note that this feast ends with a winnowing of disciples.

☐ 7:1–10:21 *The Feast of Tabernacles*

For the Feast of Tabernacles John selects narratives where Jesus deliberately fulfills the three great symbols from Exodus celebrated in various ways during this feast in Jerusalem: (1) the water from the rock (Exod 17:1–7), (2) the light (pillar of cloud/fire) that guided the Israelites (Num 9:15–23), and (3) the giving of the divine name (Exod 3:13–15)—for background see especially Zechariah 14:6–9, 16–19. The concluding narrative—giving sight to a blind man (John 9)—illustrates how Jesus is the Light of the World. The Jewish leaders now threaten to put out of the synagogue any who confess Jesus as the Christ (vv. 22, 34). As you read the whole narrative note how Jesus is regularly the cause of division in Israel.

This narrative climaxes with the formerly blind man and the Pharisees standing in marked contrast with regard to Jesus (9:35–41), to which Jesus responds (10:1–21) by telling the Pharisees that he himself is the great messianic shepherd foretold by the prophet (Ezek 34:11–16, 20–31). Note how it ends (John 10:19–21): Jesus as the cause of division.

☐ **10:22–42** ***The Feast of Dedication***

The Feast of Dedication celebrated the Maccabean restoration of worship in the second temple after it had been desecrated by Antiochus Epiphanes (see Dan 7–12); it was therefore a feast where Jewish patriotism and messianism ran high. Note how Jesus in this context presents himself—in the temple courts—as Messiah and Son of God, which again brings division in Israel: Some would now seize him (John 10:39); others believed in him (v. 42).

☐ **11:1–12:36** ***Prelude to the Final Passover***

This prelude to the final Passover (note 11:55–12:1) is full of events and sayings that anticipate chapters 13–20—the climactic sign by the one who offers eternal life is the raising of Lazarus, which (ironically) will lead to Jesus' death, where God's glory is fully revealed; as the Resurrection and the Life (11:25), he both gives life and will raise his own on the last day; the high priest "prophesies" that one man will die for the Jewish nation and the "scattered children of God" (= Gentiles; 11:51–52); Jesus is anointed for his burial (12:1–11); he enters Jerusalem as their long-expected King (vv. 12–19); and to Greeks who want to "see Jesus" he responds by pointing to his exaltation on the cross (vv. 20–36).

☐ **12:37–50** ***Conclusion: The House Is Divided***

Note that John now offers a double conclusion to Jesus' manifesting himself to the world (vv. 37–43, 44–50). You will not be surprised by now that the first one summarizes the mixed response to Jesus, as fulfillment of Isaianic prophecies. The second then summarizes what you have learned about Jesus in this section of the Gospel.

The Final Passover: The Messiah/Son of God Dies for the World (13:1–20:31)

Besides the narratives of Jesus' crucifixion (chs. 18–19) and resurrection (20:1–10), watch for John's special emphasis during this final Passover on the disciples, who will continue Jesus' ministry (13:1–17:26; 20:19–29).

☐ **13:1–17:26** ***Jesus at Table with His Disciples***

In this long table talk, you will find Jesus repeating three themes over and over: I am going; you are staying to continue my work; but you can't do it alone, so I am sending you the Spirit.

Note especially how chapter 13 sets up the whole—Jesus' servant action that symbolizes his whole ministry (coming from heaven [he strips off his outer garment], he takes the servant's place in their behalf and calls them to follow him). Watch how the two major players in the next two scenes (Judas, who will betray Jesus, and Peter, who will deny knowing Jesus) are already presented in the first scene (vv. 2, 6–11).

Now see how the three main themes are emphasized in chapter 14: Jesus is going back to the Father, whom he has now fully revealed (vv. 1–10); they are staying to continue his works (vv. 11–14); he will return to them in the person of the Spirit (vv. 15–31). This leads to Jesus' applying Isaiah's vineyard parable (Isa 5:1–7) to himself and them (John 15:1–8), which leads to further expounding of the main themes (15:9–16:33), which now includes the world's hatred of them as the world hated Jesus.

Finally, Jesus' prayer (17:1–26) not only echoes these same themes but also anticipates the success of the disciples' mission to the nations—for whom Jesus also prays.

□ 18:1–20:31 *Jesus: Slain and Raised Lamb*

Note how John's crucifixion narrative begins by narrating the fulfillment of the prophetic words from chapter 13—first Judas (13:18–30) in 18:1–14; second Peter (13:31–38) in 18:15–27. Thereafter John makes two special points: (1) Jesus is indeed the Jewish Messiah/King, but of a kingdom not of this world (18:28–40), and (2) Jesus dies at the same time as the Passover lambs (19:14), as he is "lifted up" on the cross (cf. 3:14–15; 12:32–33) to God's glory (cf. 11:4). His last utterance, "It is finished" (19:30), is a play on the word *fulfill* and thus has intentional double meaning: Jesus now dies; his death fulfills the work he came into the world to do.

The resurrection narrative then focuses especially on the disciples, leading to the commissioning. Note especially the significance of the Thomas narrative for the readers of John's Gospel: Thomas believed because he saw; blessed are those (John's readers, now including us) who believe on the basis of this Gospel, without otherwise seeing.

Epilogue (21:1–25)

After the beatitude and statement of purpose in 20:29–31, the epilogue focuses especially on Peter and the "disciple whom Jesus loved," with concern over the longevity of the life of the latter, but whose death has now either taken place or is imminent—before the coming of Christ. So the epilogue explains what Jesus really said in light of some apparent misunderstandings.

If the Synoptic Gospels care about Jesus' place in the history of Israel and beyond, John cares about Jesus' place in the whole scheme of things—from creation to redemption and beyond (final resurrection). That the Messiah is none other than the eternal Son of God is the ultimate good news of the Christian story.

The Epistles and Revelation in the Biblical Story

In our introductory chapter on the biblical story (see pp. 14–20), we noted the central role the people of God play in God's story (as the human "agonists"); we saw too that the "plot resolution" to the story is their redemption and reconciliation (with God and with one another).

The Epistles play a crucial rolc in thc grand story, both defining how the plot resolution works out and how God's newly redeemed and reconciled people are to live in the present age, as they hopefully and joyfully await the final chapter of the story. Collectively, the Epistles presuppose the story of Jesus as told in the Gospels; their main concerns lie in the instruction, encouragement, and exhortation of God's people. As such, the Epistles share several things in common.

First, since the writers of the Epistles are primarily concerned with the salvation of God's people, Christ's death and resurrection play the absolutely key role in everything the writers say and do. At the same time, they also understand the role of the Spirit to be vital—as the way God and Christ are now present with God's people.

Second, all the Epistles are written to first-generation converts—even if sometimes after many years of living in the faith—and do not set out to give a full summary of Christian doctrine or ethics. As noted in *How to 1* (pp. 56–59), they are all ad hoc, written to specific situations in the lives of believers, most often in direct response to some false teaching that is circulating among the churches. This means that they tend to highlight those aspects of the gospel that expose and counter the errors they are combating.

Third, each of the Epistle writers lives and breathes an understanding of present existence that is eschatological (see *How to 1*, pp. 145–48). That is, they believe that with Jesus and the Spirit the time of the end has already begun and that they live between the times of Jesus' inauguration of God's rule and of his coming again to bring God's rule to full consummation. Thus, both the writers and the people addressed understand their new life in Christ to be "already" a reality but "not yet" what it will be at the end (1 John 3:2). By indwelling the individual believer as well as the gathered church, the Spirit is both the evidence that the future has already dawned (the down payment, or "deposit," Paul calls him, 2 Cor 1:22) and the guarantor of the final glory that is to be.

Fourth, the ethical imperatives (the supposed do's and don'ts) that occur throughout are not a new form of the law. Rather they are understood as expressions of God's own likeness as revealed in Christ (2 Cor 3:18; 4:4–6), and therefore they reflect what life in the final kingdom is to be like. The emphasis of the Epistles is that this life of the future is to be lived out now in the believing community as we await the final end. And here again the Spirit of God, who is now also known as the Spirit of Christ (Rom 8:9; 1 Pet 1:11), plays the central role.

About the Revelation of John: Although it functions as an epistle, it is in fact a word of prophecy expressed in the form of apocalyptic. As we point out in our chapter on the Revelation (see pp. 426–29), although writing primarily to encourage God's people in light of their soon-coming conflict with the Roman Empire over emperor worship, John at the same time gathers up strands of the story from both the Old and New Testaments and weaves them into a glorious tapestry of the final chapter of the story—so that the New echoes the Old in every imaginable way. When God's people live in God's eternal presence (Rev 21–22), the biblical story will have turned the final page.

In the meantime, don't forget as you read that this part of the story is ours as well. Here is where God writes us into his story. So read and enjoy.

Romans

ORIENTING DATA FOR ROMANS

- **Content:** a letter of instruction and exhortation setting forth Paul's understanding of the gospel—that Jew and Gentile together form one people of God, based on God's righteousness received through faith in Jesus Christ and on the gift of the Spirit
- **Author:** the apostle Paul
- **Date:** ca. A.D. 57, from Corinth (cf. Rom 15:25–26 with 1 Cor 16:1–7)
- **Recipients:** the church in Rome, which was neither founded by Paul nor under his jurisdiction—although he greets at least twenty-six people known to him (16:3–16)
- **Occasion:** a combination of three factors: (1) Phoebe's proposed visit to Rome (16:1–2; which would begin in the house church of old friends Priscilla and Aquila, 16:3–5), (2) Paul's own anticipated visit to Rome and desire that they help him with his proposed mission to Spain (15:17–29), and (3) information (apparently brought by visitors) about tensions between Jewish and Gentile believers there
- **Emphases:** Jews and Gentiles together as the one people of God; the role of the Jews in God's salvation through Christ; salvation by grace alone, received through faith in Christ Jesus and effected by the Spirit; the failure of the law and success of the Spirit in producing true righteousness; the need to be transformed in mind (by the Spirit) so as to live in unity as God's people in the present

OVERVIEW OF ROMANS

This letter is arguably the most influential book in Christian history, perhaps in the history of Western civilization. But that doesn't necessarily make it easy to read! While theologically minded people love it, others steer away from it (except for a few favorite passages), thinking it is too deep for them. But the overall argument and the reasons for it can be uncovered with a little spadework.

At issue is tension between Jewish and Gentile Christians in Rome, who probably meet in separate house churches and who appear to be at odds regarding Gentile adherence to the Jewish law—especially over the three basic means of Jewish identity in the Diaspora: circumcision (2:25–3:1; 4:9–12), Sabbath observance, and food laws (14:1–23). What is at stake practically is whether Gentiles must observe the Jewish law on these points. What is at stake theologically is the gospel itself—whether "God's righteousness" (= his righteous salvation that issues in right standing with God) comes by way of "doing" the law or by faith in Christ Jesus and the gift of the Spirit.

What drives the argument from beginning (1:16) to end (15:13) is expressed in the conclusion—that God might give Jews and Gentiles "the same attitude of mind toward each other that Christ Jesus had," so that together "with one mind and one voice you may glorify the God and Father of our Lord Jesus Christ" (15:5–6). The focus of the argument is on what makes such unity possible: God's righteousness given to Jew and Gentile alike on the basis of faith in Christ Jesus and effected through the gift of the Spirit. This primary issue is surrounded by matters having to do with Paul's hoped-for relationship with this church at the strategic center of the empire (1:1–15; 15:14–33), followed by a commendation of Phoebe (16:1–2) and greetings to friends (16:3–16), concluding with a final exhortation, greetings, and doxology (16:17–27).

The argument itself is in four major parts (1:16–4:25; 5:12–8:30; 9:1–11:32; 12:1–15:12), each of which concludes on a confessional note that also serves as a transition to the next part (5:1–11; 8:31–39; 11:33–36; 15:13). In turn the parts take up (1) the issue of human sinfulness, showing first its universality (Gentile and Jew alike, with the law offering no advantage to the Jew) and then the effectiveness of Christ in dealing with sin, so that right standing with God is based on faith alone—for which Abraham, the "father of us all" (4:16), serves as exhibit A; (2) how faith in Christ and the gift of the Spirit effect the kind of righteousness that the law intended but could not pull off, since it lacked the power to deal with human sinfulness; (3) how God is faithful despite Jewish unbelief, having a place for both Gentiles and Jews in the new "olive tree" (11:24); (4) what the righteousness effected by Christ and by the Spirit (thus apart from the law) looks like in terms of relationships within the believing community and beyond.

SPECIFIC ADVICE FOR READING ROMANS

The key to a good reading of Romans is not to get bogged down over the many bits of detail that beg for an answer. Rather, use "A Walk through Romans" to get the big picture, and then perhaps come back and, with the help of a good commentary, try to discover answers to its many pieces.

Knowing two things may help you as you read. First, the argumentation Paul employs in this letter is patterned after a form of ancient rhetoric known as the diatribe, in which a teacher tried to persuade students of the truth of a given philosophy through imagined dialogue, usually in the form of questions and answers. Very often an imagined debate partner (interlocutor) would raise objections or false conclusions, which, after a vigorous "By no means!" the teacher would take pains to correct.

You will notice as you read how thoroughgoing the diatribe pattern is. The imaginary interlocutor appears at several key places (2:1–5, 17–24; 8:2; 9:19–21; 11:17–24; 14:4, 10). Paul debates first with a Jew (2:1–5, 17–24), with whom he dialogues in most of the argument that follows, as he raises and answers questions and responds to anticipated objections (2:26; 3:1–9, 27–31; 4:1–3; 6:1–3, 15–16; 7:1, 7, 13; 8:31–35; 9:19; etc.). A Gentile interlocutor is finally introduced in 11:13–24. In both cases Paul begins by attacking ethnic pride (2:17–20; 11:18). Notice further how all of this is suspended when he comes to the exhortations that begin part 4 (12:1–13:14), only to be picked up again when the issue of Jew-Gentile relationships over food and days is brought to the fore (14:4, 10). Sometimes this form of argumentation can be dizzying, especially when in the course of it Paul makes some sweeping statements that may look contradictory. But in the end, all individual statements have to be kept in the context of the whole argument.

Second, the nature of the argumentation is such that it follows a logical sequence of ideas, but you should not think that this also represents a sequence of Christian experience (justification [chs. 1–5] followed by sanctification [chs. 6–8], as is often suggested). For example, even though the role of the Spirit is not examined thoroughly until 7:4–6 and 8:1–30, his role is already anticipated in 2:28–29 and 5:5. Likewise the inadequacy of the law is first presented in chapter 2, but in the context of the life of the Spirit it is raised again in 7:7–8:4 and hinted at again in 13:8–10. And what is said about the Spirit in 8:1–30 makes clear that his presence is presupposed in the argument of 6:1–14. Likewise the ethical specifics in chapters 12–14 presuppose the argument of chapters 6 and 8. The point is that Paul does not present the whole gospel at every turn; as you move forward in the letter, you will need constantly to try to keep the whole argument in view.

A WALK THROUGH ROMANS

☐ 1:1–7 *Salutation*

In this, the longest by far of his salutations, note how Paul already focuses on the gospel (vv. 2–4, to be resumed in vv. 16–17) as including the Gentiles (vv. 5–7).

☐ 1:8–15 *Thanksgiving and Prayer*

Watch how Paul's standard thanksgiving and prayer evolve into a narrative about his longing to come to Rome, a narrative that will be resumed in 15:14. Note especially how he backs away from pressing his apostolic status.

☐ 1:16–17 *The Thesis Stated*

As you read the rest of the letter, you will see how many of its ideas and concerns are anticipated in this thesis sentence (together with vv. 2–4): the gospel is about God's Son; it is God's power bringing salvation to Jew and Gentile alike; it is the revelation of God's righteousness, available to all on the same basis, namely, faith in Christ Jesus.

☐ 1:18–5:11 *Part 1: On Sin, the Law, Christ, and Faith*

Paul begins by painting the dismal picture of the human condition, starting with Gentile sinfulness: Idolatry leads both to the worship of the creature and to injustice and hatred of every kind (1:18–32). But note that he quickly counters by arguing that having the law does not thereby advantage the Jews, allowing them to judge others (2:1–11): (some) Gentiles who do not have the law do what the law demands (2:12–16) and (some) Jews who have the law still break the law (2:17–27). The only hope lies with *heart circumcision* (see Deut 30:6) by the Spirit (Rom 2:28–29).

After a brief (diatribal) look at the issue of God's faithfulness in light of Jewish sinfulness (3:1–8), Paul concludes with the bad news—that Jew and Gentile alike are sinful and need help, which the law could not provide (3:9–20).

God's own response is the greatest good news ever: Through the death of Jesus Christ, God's righteousness is given apart from the law and is available to Jew and Gentile alike by faith (3:21–26). Note how Paul then raises the three questions (3:27–31) to be answered in the rest of the argument: (1) "Boasting" is excluded; (2) its exclusion is based on the "law" of faith, apart from the Mosaic Law; (3) faith is the only answer, since there is only one God—for Gentiles as well as Jews.

For all of this Abraham serves as exhibit A (4:1–25). Note the emphasis that Abraham not only believed God and thus was credited with righteousness but also that this happened while he was still uncircumcised (a Gentile), thus making him the father of all, both Jew and Gentile alike (that is, those who believe God as he did, vv. 23–25).

Paul's response to this good news is to burst into confessional rhapsody, urging all his readers to enter into "peace" and to boast/rejoice in their hope and in their sufferings, since "we" have experienced God's love in Jesus Christ (5:1–11).

☐ 5:12–8:39 *Part 2: On Sin, Christ, the Law, and the Spirit*

Note how part 2 begins as part 1 did, with the universal scope of human sinfulness. But now Paul goes back to Adam in order to point out the equally universal scope (= for Gentiles as well as Jews) of the righteousness made available in Christ (5:12–21).

Paul then takes up the issue of sins, given that sin itself is taken care of through the death and resurrection of Christ. Using three analogies—death/burial/resurrection pictured in Christian baptism (6:1–14), slavery and freedom (6:15–23), and death in marriage (7:1–3)—he concludes in 7:4–6 by urging that we die to the old (the flesh [sinful nature] and the law) and live in the new (Christ and the Spirit).

Since Paul has been so hard on the law to this point, he digresses momentarily to exonerate the law—it is God-given, after all—despite its role in our death (7:7–25). Lacking the Spirit, it stood helplessly by while "another law"—the sin that it aroused—took over and "killed" Paul (vv. 14–24).

God's response to this (8:1–30) is a *third law,* the Spirit (v. 2), who fulfills the law in us (v. 4) and stands against the sinful nature (vv. 5–13).

The Spirit also leads us in the present (vv. 14–17) and guarantees the future (vv. 18–25), while aiding us in prayer in the midst of suffering (vv. 26–27) and conforming us to Christ's likeness (vv. 28–30).

Paul's response to all of this is the ecstasy of 8:31–39. God is "for us," not against us, in Christ, from whose love we can never be separated and in whom we are more than conquerors in all situations. Thus believers (especially Gentiles) don't need to go the way of the law.

☐ 9:1–11:36 *Part 3: God's Faithfulness and Jewish Unfaithfulness*

Paul turns now to address the tension between God's faithfulness (in bringing Jew and Gentile together as one people) and Jewish unfaithfulness (in that the majority of Jews have not responded to the good news in Christ). The argument is in three phases, bookended by a lament over those of Israel who have rejected Christ (9:1–5) and a confessional conclusion, where Paul bows in praise and wonder before God's awesome sovereignty (11:33–36).

Note how the first phase (9:6–29) resumes the question of God's faithfulness from 3:3. Despite Jewish rejection, God's word has not failed; election needs to be understood along the new lines of a remnant and God's mercy on Gentiles.

Watch how the second phase (9:30–10:21), although still dealing with God's faithfulness, presents Israel's own responsibility for missing out on what God is now doing (with Gentiles now "in" and much of Israel "out").

The third phase (11:1–32) takes up the very tough question of whether God has rejected Israel altogether. Despite appearances, God has not cast off his ancient people; they have stumbled, but not totally fallen. Returning then to the concept of "remnant," Paul argues that God's new remnant people includes both Jew and Gentile; both have served, in different ways, to help bring the others in.

☐ 12:1–15:13 *Part 4: The Practical Outworking of God's Righteousness*

The (preceding) mercies of God call us to service of God, based on a renewed mind (by the Spirit) that can determine what pleases God (12:1–2). Note that verses 3–8 offer the basic theological grounding for the exhortations that follow: The believing community (of Jew and Gentile together as one body) is the arena in which all of this is to be worked out, first at the interpersonal level (vv. 9–21) and then in the world (13:1–7). Love is the linchpin (vv. 8–10), holding everything together (it fulfills the law and makes the rest of the argument work).

After pointing out to Gentile believers that the end of the law does not mean the end of righteousness (13:11–14), Paul concludes the whole argument on the very practical issue of Jew and Gentile respecting each other's attitudes toward food and days (14:1–15:13), urging each to accept the other (14:1; 15:1, 7). Notice how, in marvelous argumentation, he sides with the Gentiles theologically (14:17–18) but with the Jews practically (vv. 19–21). And note especially how the whole argument concludes in 15:5–8 with prayer and exhortation to "accept one another," followed by a series of Old Testament texts that include the Gentiles in God's story (vv. 9–12). The whole argument from 1:16 then concludes with the prayer of 15:13.

☐ 15:14–33 *Paul, the Gentile Mission, and Rome*

Picking up where the argument left off in 15:5–13, Paul points out his own role in bringing the gospel to Gentiles (vv. 14–22), which in turn leads him to lay out his plans to come to Rome—by way of Jerusalem (vv. 23–33).

☐ 16:1–27 *Concluding Matters*

The conclusion to the letter begins with a commendation of its bearer, Phoebe (16:1–2). This is followed in turn by greetings to friends in Rome (vv. 3–16), a final exhortation (vv. 17–20), final greetings (vv. 21–24), and a doxology (vv. 25–27). Note how at the very end Paul again stresses that it is in keeping with the prophets that "the Gentiles ... come to faith and obedience" (cf. 1:2–7).

Here God's story gets told in its primary theological expression. God's love for all, both Jew and Gentile alike, found expression in Christ's death and resurrection; the gift of the Spirit makes it all work out in everyday life.

1 Corinthians

ORIENTING DATA FOR 1 CORINTHIANS

- **Content:** a letter of correction, in which Paul stands over against the Corinthians on issue after issue, mostly behavioral, but which are nevertheless betrayals of the gospel of Christ and the life in the Spirit
- **Author:** the apostle Paul
- **Date:** ca. A.D. 53–54, from Ephesus (see 16:8)
- **Recipients:** the church in Corinth, composed mostly of Gentiles (12:2; 8:7)
- **Occasion:** Paul responds to a letter from the church (7:1) and to reports he has received (1:11; 5:1)
- **Emphases:** a crucified Messiah as the central message of the gospel; the cross as God's wisdom and power; Christian behavior that conforms to the gospel; the true nature of life in the Spirit; the future bodily resurrection of the Christian dead

OVERVIEW OF 1 CORINTHIANS

First Corinthians is the most difficult of the New Testament letters to summarize, because Paul deals in turn with no less than eleven different issues, sometimes in a length similar to some of his shorter letters (2 Thessalonians, Titus). Some items (on *divisions* and on *wisdom,* 1:10–4:21; on *incest,* 5:1–13; on *litigation,* 6:1–11; and on *going to prostitutes,* 6:12–20) are in direct response to reports from members of Chloe's household (1:11, probably an Ephesian Christian whose servants have been in Corinth on business). This may very well be true of the *head covering* of women in 11:2–16 as well and is almost certainly true of the *Lord's Table* correctives in 11:17–34.

The rest is in response to the Corinthians' letter to him mentioned in 7:1, where he starts by taking up the question of *sex and marriage* (7:1–24). At 7:25 the formula "Now about [virgins]" occurs, repeated in 8:1 ("Now about food sacrificed to idols"); 12:1 ("Now about spiritual gifts"); 16:1 ("Now about the collection"); and 16:12 ("Now about our brother Apollos"). Most of these are in direct response to behavior that is being embraced by some or most of the believers in Corinth; in each case Paul is *correcting* them, not informing them about things they do not yet know (notice how often he prods them with "Don't you know . . ." where the implication is that they do in fact know; see 3:16; 5:6; 6:2, 3, 9, 15, 16, 19; 9:13, 24). The only issue raised that is not behavioral is the bodily resurrection of believers in chapter 15, and here Paul specifically says that "some of you say that there is no resurrection of the dead" (v. 12).

There is a degree of logic to the overall arrangement. He begins with matters reported to him (1:10–6:20), starting with the basic issue of divisions—within the community itself, but primarily over against Paul—before picking up other forms of breakdown in community relationships (incest, litigation, prostitution). Beginning at 7:1, he takes up issues from their letter, very likely in the order they occur. But when he comes to a couple of matters dealing with worship (attending idol feasts and the abuse of tongues), he inserts two other matters of worship that he has information about (head coverings and abuse of the Lord's Table). He puts the issue of the resurrection at the end of his response to Spirit giftings, because it probably reflects the false theology (or spirituality) that is responsible for the Corinthians' attitudes on most of the other issues as well. He concludes with more practical matters in chapter 16.

SPECIFIC ADVICE FOR READING 1 CORINTHIANS

To read 1 Corinthians well, you need some understanding of the city where the Corinthian believers lived. After lying dormant for nearly a hundred years, Corinth was refounded by Julius Caesar in 44 B.C. as a Roman colony. Because of its strategic location for commerce both north-south and east-west, by the time of Paul (one hundred years later) it had become the largest city in Roman Greece. By ancient standards it was a relatively new city, but it had quickly become cosmopolitan (having attracted people from all over the empire) and full of the *nouveau riche*. It was also very religious (all of the immigrants brought their deities), while at the same time morally decadent. So those who had become believers were from among this diverse population, both slave and free, Gentile and Jew (12:13), who brought a lot of their prior baggage with them to the Christian faith.

It is important as you read 1 Corinthians to be aware that the opposition to Paul in this letter (e.g. 4:3–5, 18–21; 9:1–2) was not from the outside—as in Galatians, 2 Corinthians 10–13, and 1 Thessalonians—but from within the church itself. A careful reading suggests that he and they (at least many of them) are at odds on every issue. They have either misunderstood or deliberately misinterpreted an earlier letter from him that prohibited certain vices (1 Cor 5:9–10) and have written to tell him why they think they are right and he is wrong (e.g. chs. 8–10; 12–14). And the conduct of some of them, which they have *not* written about, is so grotesquely unchristian that Paul is horrified that a Christian community could have brought itself to believe as they do. At times you can even pick out where Paul is citing them, often in agreement with their statement itself, but disagreeing with how they understand it (see 6:12–13; 7:1–2; 8:1, 4).

The primary place where he and they are at odds is over the question of *being spiritual*—what it means to be a person of the Spirit. This surfaces most sharply in chapters 12–15, where they apparently believe that speaking in tongues is to speak the language of angels (13:1)—they have thus already arrived at the ultimate state of spirituality, so much so that some of them have no use for a bodily resurrection (6:13–14; 15:12). This has also led to a triumphalist view of life in the present. Full of "wisdom" by the Spirit, they see Paul's weaknesses as evidence of a lesser spirituality (4:6–21). In such a view there is no room for the life of the cross. Hence the ease whereby they reject Paul's view on so many issues. Very likely their spirituality also lends itself to their low view of bodily activities (meaning they can indulge or be ascetic at will) so that some are even arguing against sexual life in marriage (7:1–7), and the traditional head coverings are being cast aside "because of the angels" (11:3–16, esp. v. 10).

Paul's basic response to all of this is to remind them that the gospel has a crucified Messiah, risen from the dead, at its very heart, and thus he bookends the letter with these two basic theological realities (the cross, 1:17–2:16; the resurrection, 15:1–58). Everything else in the letter must be understood in light of these; indeed, the most crucial role of the Spirit is to reveal the cross as the key to God's wisdom (2:6–16).

Because Paul sees the gospel itself at stake (especially because of the Corinthians' rejecting the centrality of the cross in Christian life), you will find his moods to run a wide gamut of emotion—confrontation (4:18–21; 9:1–12; 14:36–38), appeal (4:15–16; 10:31–11:1), sarcasm (4:8; 6:5, the "wise" aren't wise enough to settle disputes!), irony (1:26–28, no one in the name of wisdom would have chosen them to be God's people!), eloquence (13:1–8), and rhapsody (15:51–57)—but there is very little joy or pleasure to be found currently in his relationship with this church (and 2 Corinthians tells us it gets worse before it gets better).

A WALK THROUGH 1 CORINTHIANS

☐ 1:1–9 *Salutation, Prayer, and Thanksgiving*

Note how, typically, these formal elements are elaborated in ways that anticipate the rest of the letter ("sanctified in Christ Jesus"; "enriched in every way" [with Spirit giftings]). Significantly, Paul still thanks God for them—all of them—because they are God's people, after all, not his.

As you read the rest of the letter, look for the various elements of and reasons for the specific problems Paul is dealing with, and note now he responds to each.

☐ 1:10–4:21 *Divisions over Leaders in the Name of Wisdom*

The problem: a combination of (1) their anti-Paul sentiment, which (2) has broken out as strife over their leaders, which (3) is being carried on in the name of wisdom.

Paul's response: Note how he takes on the problem of wisdom first (1:13–3:4), urging that everything about the Corinthians' existence in Christ gives the lie to their present wisdom—the gospel of a crucified Messiah (1:18–25); their own calling (1:26–31); Paul's preaching (2:1–5). Indeed, one role of the Spirit is to reveal the cross as God's wisdom (2:6–16).

Second (3:5–23), he corrects their inadequate understanding of (1) leaders, who are merely servants (vv. 5–15), and of (2) the church, which is the temple of the living God in Corinth (vv. 16–17); thus there should be no boasting in mere mortals (vv. 18–23).

Third (4:1–21), he responds to their criticism of him: Since he is God's servant, they have no right to judge him; their pride reeks, so he appeals to them and warns them.

☐ 5:1–13 *A Case of Incest*

The problem: A believer is living incestuously with his "father's wife" (another wife of his father, but not his biological mother; see Lev 18:8); note that this is an instance where they are directly at odds with his previous letter to them (5:9).

Paul's response: Since Paul has already judged the offender, they are to gather in the power of Christ and turn him over to Satan (= put him back out of the church into Satan's sphere; cf. 1 Tim 1:20)—for the sake of the church in the present and finally for the offender's own salvation.

☐ 6:1–11 *External Litigation of an Internal Squabble*

The problem: One brother has cheated another (v. 8), who has taken him to the pagan courts for judgment (v. 1), and the church has done nothing (vv. 2–5).

Paul's response: Horrors! By doing nothing, the church has betrayed its existence as God's end-time people (vv. 2–4); shame on the litigant (vv. 6–7); warning to the defendant (vv. 8–10). But note how Paul ends by affirming their redemption through Jesus Christ and the Spirit (v. 11).

☐ 6:12–20 *On Going to the Prostitutes*

The problem: In the name of their rights as believers (v. 12) and on the basis of a low view of the body (v. 13), some men are arguing for the right to visit the prostitutes (understandable in light of 7:1–16).

Paul's response: Against *their* view of rights, only what is "beneficial" counts, and to be mastered by anything is a form of bondage (v. 12). Against their wrong view of the body, he appeals to the Lord's resurrection as affirming the body (v. 14) and to the nature of sexual intercourse as uniting two people (v. 15); one cannot thus be united to the Lord by the Spirit and united to a prostitute by sex (vv. 16–17), since the body belongs to the Lord as his temple (vv. 18–20).

☐ 7:1–24 *To the Married and Once-Married*

The problem: On the basis of a slogan, "It is good for a man not to have sexual relations with a woman," some women apparently (see v. 10) are arguing for no sex within marriage (because they have already assumed their "heavenly" existence in which there is no marrying or giving in marriage?), and if not regarding no sex, then for the right to divorce.

Paul's response: To the *already married* (vv. 1–7), stop depriving each other on this matter; instead, maintain full conjugal relationships. To *widows* and (probably) *widowers* (vv. 8–9), stay as you are. To the *presently married* (to a believing spouse, vv. 10–11), no divorce (= stay as you are). To the "rest" (= *presently married to an unbeliever,* vv. 12–16), do not seek divorce (= stay as you are).

The "rule" (vv. 17–24), based on God's calling and Christ's redemption is this: Stay as you are, since God's call sanctifies your present situation, but if change comes, that too is acceptable.

□ 7:25–40 *To the Never-Before Married*

The problem: Based on the premise of 7:1, some are arguing that virgins (= betrothed young women) surely should not marry.

Paul's response: Note how Paul agrees with the conclusion but not the premise; hence he offers different reasons for staying single (the "present crisis"; unencumbered freedom to serve the Lord)—but whatever else, do not be anxious (v. 32), because marriage is also God's plan.

□ 8:1–11:1 *On Idol Feasts and Marketplace Idol Food*

The problem: Since idols have no reality because there is only one God (8:4), some have argued against Paul that they should have the right to continue attending temple feasts (8:10), where all family celebrations were held; related is the matter of Jewish scruples about buying food once offered to an idol (10:23–11:1). They have apparently called into question Paul's right to forbid temple attendance—denying his apostleship on the basis of his not accepting their patronage (9:1–18) and his being wishy-washy about marketplace food (eating it in Gentile homes, but remaining kosher in Jewish homes, 9:19–23).

Paul's response: Note that Paul does not begin with a prohibition (that will come later; 10:14–22), but with their acting on the basis of *knowledge* (spiritual elitism again) rather than love (8:1–6). For most former idolaters the "god" had subjective reality, and being encouraged to return to the temples would destroy them (8:7–13).

Paul then (9:1–18) defends his apostolic right to their support, even though he has given that right up, and maintains that his actions regarding marketplace food are strictly in the interest of evangelism (9:19–23). After urging the need for self-discipline, with himself as a positive example (9:24–27), he warns them on the basis of Israel's negative examples (10:1–13). Finally, he explicitly forbids eating in the temples, since to do so is to participate in the demonic (10:14–22).

Turning to marketplace food itself in 10:23–11:1, Paul argues that Scripture itself makes clear that God doesn't care one way or the other—so buy and eat unless it bothers a pagan's conscience (someone who understands Christianity as a Jewish sect).

☐ 11:2–16 *On Head Coverings in Worship*

The problem: Most likely some women were discarding a traditional loose-fitting shawl on the basis of being as the angels, which apparently brought tensions in marital relationships (the women were, in their husbands' view, being like men).

Paul's response: Although women do have authority over their own heads on this matter (v. 10), in the Lord women and men are interdependent (vv. 7–9, 11–12), so the women should maintain the customs (vv. 13–16) so as not to appear like men (otherwise, he argues, go the whole way in looking like a man and be "shaved," vv. 5–6).

☐ 11:17–34 *Divisions at the Lord's Table*

The problem: Note that their division here is along the lines of rich and poor (v. 22) and is related to the eating of a meal in connection with the Lord's Table (vv. 17–21), at which the poor were being excluded (the church met in the houses of the well-to-do).

Paul's response: He reminds them of the words of institution (vv. 23–25) and that they must "discern the body of Christ" when they eat (= the church; see 10:16–17); otherwise they eat for judgment instead of blessing (11:27–32). Eat private meals privately; at community meals "make everyone equally welcome" (vv. 33–34).

☐ 12:1–14:40 *The Abuse of Speaking in Tongues*

The problem: Their view of tongues as the language of angels (13:1) caused them to overemphasize this gift in worship (14:18–19, 23), with the result that their community worship was nonintelligible and thus could not build up the body.

Paul's response: First, the primary criterion for Spirit utterances is the confession of Jesus as Lord (12:1–3). On the basis of their Trinitarian experience of God (vv. 4–6), Paul then urges diversity of giftings in the unity of the Spirit (vv. 7–31); in any case, love should rule at every point in their worship (13:1–13).

Pursuing love means first that only what is intelligible should occur in the community for the sake of edification (14:1–25) and second that everything must have a measure of order (vv. 26–40), because one's worship reflects what one believes about God's character (v. 33).

□ 15:1–58 *The Bodily Resurrection of Believers*

The problem: Some are denying a bodily resurrection of believers (v. 12), apparently ridiculing the idea of a raised body (v. 35). Note that the placement of this issue in the letter suggests that it is closely related to chapters 12–14.

Paul's response: On the basis of Christ's resurrection, which they do believe (vv. 1–11), Paul argues for the certainty of our own resurrection (vv. 12–34), including (1) the folly of believing in the one and not the other (vv. 12–19); (2) both the inevitability (the firstfruits guarantees the final harvest) and necessity (death is God's final enemy to be overcome) of our resurrection (vv. 20–28); and (3) the senselessness of their actions, and of life itself, without such a hope (vv. 29–34).

As to "what kind of body," the answer is *the same, but not quite the same*—it will be spiritually refitted for heavenly existence (vv. 35–50). Notice how he concludes by taunting death in light of the certainty of our future (vv. 51–58)—here let your heart soar!

□ 16:1–11 *On the Collection for the Poor*

The problem: Paul intends to take a substantial contribution from his Gentile churches to relieve the poor in Jerusalem; apparently the Corinthian believers have asked him about it.

Paul's response: Set some money aside weekly—to which he adds information about future plans, both his and Timothy's.

□ 16:12–24 *Concluding Matters*

Note how he takes up their request for Apollos's return (v. 12) in a way that brings the letter to conclusion in typical style (staccato exhortations,

vv. 13–14; commendation of the letter's bearers, vv. 15–18; final greetings, vv. 19–24). But note also that here he adds a final curse and prayer (v. 22) and a word following the grace (v. 24, reassuring them of his love for them, given how strongly he has had to respond).

This letter holds an important place in the biblical story, reminding us constantly that (1) God calls a people to himself so that they might be conformed to his own likeness, reflected in the (apparent) weakness and folly of the cross, and that (2) in the end he will overcome our (and his) final enemy—death—by resurrection and/or transformation.

2 Corinthians

ORIENTING DATA FOR 2 CORINTHIANS

- **Content:** probably two letters (chs. 1–9; 10–13) combined into one, dealing primarily with Paul's tenuous relationship with the Corinthian church and in the process touching on several other matters as well (Paul's ministry, the collection for the poor in Jerusalem, and some Jewish Christian itinerants who have invaded the church)
- **Author:** the apostle Paul, joined by Timothy
- **Date:** ca. A.D. 54–55, from Macedonia (2:13; 7:5)—most likely Philippi
- **Recipients:** see 1 Corinthians
- **Occasion:** Titus's return from a recent visit (7:5–7) and Paul's anticipated third visit to the church (13:1) in light of (1) the church's need to have the collection ready before Paul gets there and (2) their readiness to embrace some "false apostles ... masquerading as apostles of Christ" (11:13)
- **Emphases:** Christian ministry as servanthood, reflecting that of Christ; the greater glory of the new covenant in contrast to the old; the glory of the gospel exhibited in the weakness of its ministers; the gospel as reconciliation; giving to the poor as an expression of generosity, not of obligation

OVERVIEW OF 2 CORINTHIANS

Reading 2 Corinthians is something like turning on the television in the middle of a very complicated play. People are talking and things are happening, but we're not at all sure who some of the characters are or what the plot is. In fact, in coming to this letter from 1 Corinthians, one has the sense of entering a new world. Few of the issues raised in the earlier letter appear here, except the concern over the collection (1 Cor 16:1–4/2 Cor 8–9) and perhaps a return to the matter of idol food in 2 Corinthians 6:14–7:1. But that is a surface view; what holds the two together is the overriding relational tension one senses between Paul and the Corinthians regarding true apostleship.

Four matters that play off against one another in the course of our letter(s) account for all of its parts: (1) Paul's change of plans regarding visits to Corinth, (2) the collection, (3) his apostleship and ministry, and (4) the presence of the Jewish Christian itinerants.

The first three matters carry over from 1 Corinthians and are dealt with in 2 Corinthians 1–9. A chronological explanation of his immediate past relations with them, apparently touched off by his change of mind about proposed and actual visits, is found in 1:12–2:13 and picked up again in 7:5–16. The long interruption of 2:14–7:4 is the crown jewel of the letter. Here Paul defends his apostleship-in-weakness (recall 1 Corinthians), a matter that has been aggravated by Paul's opponents (2:14–4:6). The need to have the collection ready before he comes is addressed in chapters 8–9. Chapters 10–13 contain a vigorous attack against his Jewish Christian opponents—comparable to that in Galatians (cf. Phil 3:2)—interspersed with indignation, biting sarcasm, and gentle appeals to the Corinthians to come to their senses.

SPECIFIC ADVICE FOR READING 2 CORINTHIANS

By any reckoning, you will find that 2 Corinthians is not easy to read, in the sense of seeing how it hangs together. Three things make it so. First, it is the most intensely personal of Paul's legacy of letters, made so because at issue throughout is Paul's ongoing, mostly painful, relationship with this church. The intensity of this personal dimension accounts for a number of things, including both the way Paul speaks and the difficulty we have at times in following the flow of thought (e.g., 2:14–7:4).

Second is the probability that 2 Corinthians is Paul's fourth and fifth letters to this church, joined as one in the transmissional process (a letter precedes our 1 Corinthians [see 1 Cor 5:9]; between 1 and 2 Corinthians there is the sorrowful letter mentioned in 2 Cor 2:3–4). There are two reasons for believing so: (1) Even though Paul speaks against the itinerants in 2:17–3:3 (those who "peddle the word of God for profit"), the rest of chapters 1–9 reflects a relatively stable situation, including appeals and terms of endearment (e.g., 1:7; 2:1–4; 6:11–13; 7:13–16), of a kind wholly lacking in 1 Corinthians. Almost everyone agrees that something has happened between his writing these words and what appears in chapters 10–13. (2) In 8:16–18 Paul commends Titus and another brother who will carry letter 4 (chs. 1–9) and pick up the collection; in 12:18 Paul refers to this sending as a past event.

Third is the question of how the four matters that make up the letter hang together. Our suggestion: Paul's relationship with this church, which was already tenuous when he wrote 1 Corinthians, had obviously soured. This is related in part to a change of plans regarding the itinerary outlined in 1 Corinthians 16:5–9. Instead of coming by way of Macedonia, he came directly from Ephesus, both to their great surprise and chagrin (the collection was not ready). A serious encounter with someone, alluded to in 2 Corinthians 2:1–2, 5–11, and 7:11–12 (perhaps one of the itinerants), caused Paul to leave just as abruptly as he had appeared.

In the meantime he changed plans yet again! Instead of returning to Corinth from Macedonia (1:15–16), he went on to Ephesus and sent Titus with his sorrowful letter (2:3–4), partly to make sure that the collection was under way (8:6). When he and Titus finally met in Macedonia (2:12–13; 7:5–7), Titus brought essentially good news. Even though Paul's letter had hurt them, as he knew it would, it had also led to repentance and (too much) discipline of the man who had attacked Paul (2:5–11). All of this is dealt with in chapters 1–7.

Paul's first reason for coming, however, is still in the forefront—to pick up the collection (chs. 8–9). Titus is thus being sent on ahead with letter 4 (chs. 1–9), which offers explanations for his actions and especially hopes to ensure that the collection will in fact be ready when Paul and some Macedonians come a bit later (9:1–5).

Meanwhile the itinerants were still plying their trade. By the time Titus arrived with letter 4, they appear to have gotten the upper hand, so Titus rushed back to Macedonia with the bad news, causing Paul to write again, this time confronting both the Corinthians and his opponents for their playing false with the gospel and with the true meaning of apostleship. This letter was preserved as chapters 10–13 of our 2 Corinthians.

In getting these matters into perspective for an easier reading of this letter, be sure not to lose sight of the grandeur of its theology, both of ministry and of the gospel. Here Paul picks up the theology of the cross as applied to ministry, which began in 1 Corinthians 4:9–13, and plays it out in full detail. God's glory—and the power of the gospel—is not minimized, but enhanced, through the weakness of the "jars of clay" (2 Cor 4:7; cf. 12:7–10) who proclaim it. Such ministry is in keeping with the Crucified One, after all. Hence Paul repeatedly glories in his weaknesses—not because he liked to suffer, but because it meant that attention was focused on the Savior, not on the messenger. And the passage dealing with the glory of the new covenant through Christ and the Spirit (3:1–18) is "worth the price of the book." So read, and enjoy!

A WALK THROUGH 2 CORINTHIANS

☐ 1:1–11 *Salutation and Praise to God*

Instead of the ordinary thanksgiving and prayer following a brief salutation (vv. 1–2), note in this case that Paul bursts into praise of God for comfort/encouragement in suffering (vv. 3–7), which serves as a way of bringing the Corinthians on board regarding his most recent escape from death (vv. 8–11).

☐ 1:12–2:13 *An Explanation of Paul's Change of Plans*

As you read this section, be alert to the fact that everything is in chronological order. So note that Paul feels compelled at the outset to give reasons for his most recent change of plans (1:12–17). This is because, at the end of the day, the gospel itself is at stake if its messengers are not themselves trustworthy (vv. 18–22). He then explains why he wrote the sorrowful letter instead of returning after the painful visit (1:23–2:4). After urging compassion on the man who caused Paul grief (2:5–11), resulting from his just-mentioned letter, he picks up with his itinerary from Ephesus to Troas to Macedonia, reflecting especially on his own anxiety over the sorrowful letter (2:12–13).

☐ 2:14–7:4 *Paul, Minister of the New Covenant*

Watch how Paul's anxiety with regard to receiving no news about Corinth in Troas results in this truly grand digression. Although the whole reads like a stream of consciousness, you can still trace how the stream flows. After an initial thanksgiving for victory despite present anxiety (2:14), he moves into wonder at his own God-given ministry

(vv. 15–16), which he then sets in contrast to the itinerants, now in terms of the new covenant brought about by Christ and the Spirit (2:17–3:6).

This launches a contrast between the new and the old (3:7–18, evidence of the Jewishness of his opponents). To make some sense of this passage you might want to read Exodus 34:29–35, since this is a perfect example of what is known as a Jewish midrash—a sermonic application of an Old Testament text to a new situation. Note how it climaxes with the past work of Christ and the present work of the Spirit (2 Cor 3:14–18).

Paul then applies what has been said up to this point to his and their situation (4:1–6), which in turn leads to reflection on the tensions of living "already but not yet," contrasting present bodily weakness and suffering with eternal glory and future resurrection (4:7–5:10).

Returning to his own role in proclaiming Christ, Paul urges that Christ's death and resurrection change our perspective on everything—including how the Corinthians should view him and his sufferings as an apostle (5:11–17)—but note that mention of the gospel typically means elaboration of its glory and purposes, now (notably) in terms of reconciliation (5:18–21)!

Finally he appeals to them to accept both him and his gospel (6:1–2, 11–13), again set in a rhetorically powerful affirmation of present existence as "already but not yet" (vv. 3–10).

The unusual digression in 6:14–7:1 is probably over the issue of eating in the idol temples (cf. 1 Cor 8:1–13; 10:14–22), touched off by his appeal to openness regarding affection (2 Cor 6:11–13), to which he returns in 7:2–4, which finally brings him back to where he left off in 2:13.

□ 7:5–16 *The Explanation Renewed*

Note how 7:5 picks up the chronological accounting of recent events from 2:13. Paul now explains how he has responded to Titus's return with the good news of their godly sorrow and generally open attitude toward Paul. He is especially pleased that Titus found them to be as Paul had boasted of them.

□ 8:1–9:15 *Have the Collection Ready When I Come*

But for all their readiness to repent (7:11), there still remains the business that Titus could only begin (8:6) but not bring to completion, namely, the collection for the poor in Jerusalem. You will see that what now concerns Paul is that he has boasted to the Macedonians of the Corinthians' readiness, and some representatives of these churches are about to accompany him to Corinth (9:1–5). So surrounding the commendation of Titus and the two who will accompany him (8:16–24, Titus is to make sure the collection is ready), Paul appeals in turn to (1) the example of Macedonia (8:1–5), (2) their own excelling in so many things, including beginning the collection (8:6–12), (3) the biblical principle that those who have plenty should share with the needy (8:13–15), and finally (4) generosity as a true expression of godliness (9:6–15).

□ 10:1–13:14 *Defense of Paul's Ministry against False Apostles*

Even though this issue is anticipated in 2:17–3:3, after the "sugar and honey" of 7:5–16 we are hardly prepared for the present barrage. You will see that the whole is a fierce defense of Paul's ministry, both personally and in terms of its character—all in light of the false apostles, whose slanders of Paul emerge throughout.

So Paul begins by taking one accusation of the opponents head-on—the alleged duplicity between his letters and his personal demeanor when with the Corinthians (10:1–11), pointing out in turn the opponents' duplicity of working his turf rather than evangelizing on their own (10:12–18).

This leads to a direct attack against them—they are deceitful purveyors of a false gospel (11:1–4)—followed by a scathing contrast between them (as servants of Satan, who take the Corinthians' money for their own gain) and himself (11:5–15). Personally ill at ease over what he feels he has been forced to do, he finally resorts to a "fool's" speech (11:16–33, the "fool" in the Greek theater enabled a playwright to speak boldly to his audience and get away with it). Since his opponents boast in their achievements (10:12–13; 11:18), Paul will "boast" in his *non*achievements, thus deliberately—and ironically—putting his ministry into a context of *conforming to the cross*. The ultimate irony is his escaping Damascus through a window in the wall (the highest honor in the Roman military was given to the first person to *scale* a wall in battle!).

He continues the boasting in weakness by refusing to give prominence to visions and revelations, as his opponents do, concluding on the ultimate theological note—that Christ's "power is made perfect in [Paul's] weakness" (12:1–10), reflecting again the theology of the cross articulated in 1 Corinthians 1–4. This is followed by a series of (mostly personal) appeals (2 Cor 12:11–21).

The final exhortations (13:1–10) then sum up the preceding arguments before the final greetings (vv. 11–13)—and the ultimate Trinitarian benediction (v. 14).

The significance of this letter for the biblical story must not be downplayed because of its strongly personal dimension. At stake is God's own character—his loving grace expressed most strikingly in the weakness of the cross, which Paul insists is the only true expression of discipleship as well. Hence Paul's readiness to boast in his weaknesses, since they serve to magnify the gospel of grace, God's true power at work in the world.

Galatians

ORIENTING DATA FOR GALATIANS

- **Content:** a heated argument with the (Gentile) Galatian believers against some Jewish Christian "missionaries" who insist that Gentiles be circumcised if they are to be included in the people of God
- **Author:** the apostle Paul, joined by "all the brothers and sisters" with him (1:2)
- **Date:** probably ca. A.D. 55 (although some think as early as 47–48), with no indication of place of origin
- **Recipients:** Gentile believers in Galatia, either ethnic Galatians (whose territory in central Asia Minor had been earlier settled by people from Gaul [modern France]) or those in the Roman province of Galatia, which also included peoples of Pisidia, Lycaonia, and Phrygia (Acts 13–14; 16)
- **Occasion:** the churches of Galatia have been invaded by some agitators (5:12) who have questioned Paul's gospel and his apostleship; apparently some Galatians are on the verge of capitulating to them, which sparks a vigorous defense by Paul of his gospel and his calling
- **Emphases:** Paul's apostleship and gospel come directly from God and Christ, not through human mediation; the death of Jesus has brought an end to ethnic religious observances; the Spirit produces the righteousness the law could not; the Spirit enables believers not to yield to sinful desires; one receives the Spirit through faith in Christ Jesus

OVERVIEW OF GALATIANS

Like 2 Corinthians 10–12, this letter is clearly three-sided—*Paul*, to the *Galatians*, against the *agitators*. Paul is obviously red-hot (just like God in the Old Testament when his love for Israel has been spurned). Full of the Holy Spirit and in keeping with the nature of rhetoric under such circumstances, Paul writes with passion and forcefulness. Here you will encounter caustic and biting jibes at the agitators as well as fervent, sometimes cajoling, pleas to the Galatians not to give in to them. What could have inflamed such intensity?

The answer: The gospel is at stake, especially as it includes the Gentiles, law-free, in the people of God—not to mention Paul's own calling as apostle to the Gentiles. If the Galatians cave in to circumcision, everything God has done in Jesus Christ and is doing by the Spirit to include Gentiles in the people of God will have come to nothing (2:21). God's story itself is on the line.

Thus Paul comes out with guns blazing. First, he takes on the agitators' slander of his apostleship. In a series of three narratives, he starts by distancing himself from Jerusalem (1:13–24; his apostleship and gospel do not have human origins in any form), then points out Jerusalem's concurrence with him (2:1–10), and finally notes that any failure to keep the accord came from Jerusalem itself (2:11–14).

He then uses his speech to Peter on the latter occasion to launch his argument with the Galatians (2:15–21). The rest of the letter fluctuates three times between argument, application, and appeal (3:1–4:7/4:8–11/4:12–20; 4:21–27/4:28–31/5:1–12; 5:13–24/5:25–6:10/6:11–17). His *argument* is that the cross of Christ and the gift of the Spirit have brought observance of the Jewish law to an end. Notice how his *appeals* run the gamut, sometimes reflecting on past relationships (4:12–20; 5:7–10), sometimes pointing out the consequences of their proposed actions (4:8–11; 5:2–6), and sometimes disparaging the agitators (5:7–12; 6:11–13).

SPECIFIC ADVICE FOR READING GALATIANS

You may find the argument sections of this letter a bit hard to follow; this will be because of its "in house" nature, where Paul is arguing with the agitators on their own grounds. But with a little background knowledge you should be able to unpack it well enough.

Here is an instance where special vocabulary tells much of the tale. Note how often these key words occur: law 32*x*; flesh (TNIV 7*x* "sinful nature") 16*x*; works 7*x* (6*x* "observing the law," lit. "works of law"; 1*x* "acts of sinful nature," lit. "works of flesh"); circumcision/circumcise 13*x*; Christ 38*x*; the Spirit 17*x*; faith/believe 22/4*x*; grace 8*x*; justified/justify 8*x*; Abraham 9*x*; promise 10*x*; son/seed 13/5*x*; freedom/free 4/6*x*; enslave/slave/slavery 11*x*; Gentiles 10*x*. While most of these words also occur in Paul's other letters, the number of times they appear in Galatians (and Romans as well) is out of proportion to their occurrences elsewhere.

At issue is the question, Who are the true *children/seed* of *Abraham* and thus true heirs of the *promises* made to Abraham? Paul's answer: Those, especially *Gentiles*, who have *faith* like Abraham's, who are thus *free*born *sons* and not *slaves*. They have become so by *faith in Christ* and the (promised) gift of *the Spirit;* on the other hand, those who would enforce Gentile believers to be *circumcised* are bringing them under the Jewish *law* and thus into *slavery. Justification* comes only by *grace;* to revert to *circumcision* is to seek advantage with God through *works of law,* which Paul sees as of the *flesh* (= ultimately putting trust in one's own achievements). All of this boils down to one basic matter: On what grounds are Gentile believers included in the people of God (= become part of Abraham's seed)? On their trusting Christ and their reception of the Spirit (their true identity marker), or by adding Jewish identity markers as well?

But why Abraham, you might well ask? Why not simply remind the Galatians of the story of Christ? The answer lies almost certainly with the arguments of the agitators, who have taken Genesis 17:1–22 as their primary text. There God established circumcision as "an everlasting covenant" in a context where Abraham was again promised to be the father of "many nations" (repeating the blessing of the Gentiles from Gen 12:3); in this context God promises that Sarah herself would bear a child, the legitimate heir—while Ishmael is already a young man. In all fairness, the agitators were not advocating a righteousness based on works; they had themselves put their faith in Christ. But, they would have argued, just as Abraham believed God (Gen 15:6) and then was given the covenant of circumcision, so the Gentiles who believe in Christ need to be circumcised in order to become the true children of Abraham, and thus heirs of the promise. At stake for them in the end is their own identity as the people of God, since the *marks of identity* for Jews in the Diaspora were especially circumcision, the food laws, and the sacred calendar, including Sabbath keeping.

Paul sees clearly where such an argument leads—to an equation that reads, "grace + works of law = favor with God." But adding a *plus factor* to grace in fact nullifies grace. Thus he argues that "grace + nothing = favor with God." Otherwise, believing Gentiles must in fact become Jews in order to be completed as Christians (3:3). Thus Paul appeals first to the Galatians' own experience of the Spirit (3:1–5) and then to Genesis 15:6 (which *precedes* 17:1–22 in the story), which says of Abraham that his *faith alone* was what God counted as righteousness (Gal 3:6–9). The rest of chapters 3 and 4 spell out various implications of these first two arguments. Paul shows first the preparatory and thus secondary nature of the law in relation to Christ and the Spirit (3:10–4:7), and then he shows that by rejecting Christ, the contemporary Jews have in effect made themselves the heirs of Ishmael rather than of Isaac (4:21–27). In any case their observance of the law is selective, and for Paul, to be under law means that one must observe the *whole* law (3:10; 5:3; cf. 6:13), not just parts of it.

The final argument (5:13–24) points out that the Spirit alone is sufficient for the kind of life in the present that reflects the likeness of Christ and stands over against the "desires" of the "sinful nature" (= flesh, referring to living in a self-centered way that is hostile to God)—which is precisely where the law failed. It could make people religious, but not truly re-formed so as to be shaped into God's own character (which is what the fruit of the Spirit reflects).

A WALK THROUGH GALATIANS

☐ 1:1–5 *Salutation*

Note how this unique salutation anticipates the argument by focusing on the heart of the gospel (vv. 4–5).

☐ 1:6–9 *A Curse on the Agitators*

You may find this paragraph abrupt, and for good reason, since this is Paul's only letter to a church that does not include a thanksgiving and prayer. Instead, he assumes the role of the prophet, pronouncing a double curse on those who are derailing the Gentile Galatians with a foreign gospel (and on any others who would do so).

□ 1:10–2:14 *In Defense of the Gospel—Part 1: Paul and Jerusalem*

It is significant to note that Paul begins the defense of his gospel by defending his apostleship (which was a direct commission to take the gospel to the Gentiles). Thus, after a transitional sentence (1:10) against those who imply that by not insisting on circumcision, Paul is merely trying to please people, Paul begins by asserting that his gospel is not of human origin but came to him by revelation (vv. 11–12). The defense of this assertion then proceeds by way of a three-part chronological narrative—(1) that his gospel and apostleship (in contrast to that of the agitators) are absolutely *independent* of Jerusalem (vv. 13–24), thus capitalizing positively on what his opponents see as a negative; (2) that his gospel is nonetheless *in agreement* with Jerusalem and has their blessing (2:1–10, only spheres of ministry differ); and (3) that *Jerusalem* (in the person of Peter), not he, *broke faith* with the agreement (vv. 11–14).

□ 2:15–21 *The Theological Propositions Set Forth*

Using his speech to Peter at Antioch as the point of reference, Paul makes the primary assertions about his gospel that the rest of the letter will argue—(1) that righteousness is "not by observing the law," (2) that righteousness is "by faith in Jesus Christ" (who brought law observance to an end), and (3) that the indwelling Christ (by his Spirit, of course) is the effective agent for living out the new righteousness (v. 20). Otherwise, Christ died for nothing (v. 21).

□ 3:1–4:7 *In Defense of the Gospel—Part 2: Christ and the Law*

As you move now to Paul's theological defense of his gospel, note especially that it begins and ends with an appeal to his readers' experience of the Spirit (3:1–5; 4:6–7). The rest of this first argument is based on Scripture. The heart of it shows Christ's role in support of the first two propositions of 2:15–21: Having brought the time of the law to an end, he has ushered in the time of faith. Thus, Paul argues (in sequence):

3:7–9—Abraham's true heirs are those who, like Abraham (and now including the Gentiles), have faith (in Christ Jesus).

3:10–14—The law is not based on faith but on *doing,* which means doing the *whole law* (not just selected portions), which is also a "curse" because it excludes people from living by faith; thus Christ died so as to remove the curse so that Gentiles might be included by faith and through the Spirit.

3:15–18—Here Paul argues that the law, which came much later than the covenant with Abraham, is quite unrelated to the "promise" (that Gentiles will be included in the people of God—through the promised Holy Spirit) given to Abraham's "seed" (personified eventually by Israel's king, and thus finally realized in Christ).

3:19–22—Why then the law? It was added to *confine* God's people (keep them fenced in, as it were) until the promise was to be realized. And in any case, it was not intended to bring life, nor could it bring life (only Christ and the Spirit can do that).

3:23–4:7—The merely supervisory role of the law is over. Using the analogy of a child coming of age, Paul concludes (twice: 3:23–29; 4:1–7) that only faith in Christ Jesus produces true children/heirs, thus setting them free from slavery, through the gift of the Spirit (the Spirit of the Son, the true heir!).

☐ 4:8–20 *Application and Appeal*

In verses 8–11 Paul applies the preceding argument to his readers' specific situation. Since God *knows* them as his children, why go back to slavery? Notice the more personal, relational nature of verses 12–20, where he appeals to the Galatians to return to their earlier loyalty to him and devotion to Christ.

☐ 4:21–5:12 *Once More: Argument, Application, Appeal*

In 4:21–27 Paul returns to the scriptural argument of 3:6–4:7. By taking up the themes of Abraham, slavery, and freedom, he demonstrates by an analogy from Genesis that "doing the law" would mean slavery, while Christ and the Spirit mean freedom.

Note how this is followed by a threefold application and appeal. The Galatians are like Isaac, the free son of the "free woman" by "the power of the Spirit," and like Isaac, they are being persecuted by the slave woman's son, Ishmael—the Jewish Christian agitators (4:28–31). Again, note the personal nature of the appeals—(1) with a fervent call that the Galatians face up to the consequences of capitulating to circumcision, including their need to keep the whole law (5:1–6), and (2) with a scathing denunciation of the agitators, who have themselves abandoned faith in Christ and are acting like a runner who cuts off others to keep them from winning (5:7–12).

☐ 5:13–6:10 *In Defense of the Gospel—Part 3: The Spirit and Righteousness*

Paul concludes by taking up the third proposition from 2:15–21—the indwelling Spirit has replaced law observance, because the Spirit can do what the law could not, namely, effect true righteousness (5:13–14, 22–23) and effectively combat the desires of "the sinful nature [flesh]" (vv. 16–21). Be sure to catch that this is set in the context of community disharmony (vv. 15, 26; note that eight of the fifteen "acts of the sinful nature" are sins of discord!). They are thus urged to live by the Spirit, who has brought them to life following Christ's death and resurrection (vv. 24–25). All of this is applied to very practical issues in 6:1–10.

☐ 6:11–18 *Conclusion: Circumcision No, the Cross Yes*

Paul concludes with another blistering attack on the agitators, who compel Gentiles to be circumcised but do not themselves keep the (whole) law (vv. 12–13), before turning the Galatians' attention once more to the cross (vv. 14–15). The final blessing (v. 16) is for all who live by the "rule" of verse 15 (circumcision is utterly irrelevant; only the new creation counts).

Because of the nature of the opposition, in this letter the basic lines of the truth of the gospel are most clearly drawn. Our understanding of the Christian faith would not be the same without this letter. Above all else, it serves as our own charter of freedom.

Ephesians

ORIENTING DATA FOR EPHESIANS

- **Content:** a letter of encouragement and exhortation, set against the backdrop of "the powers" (6:12), portraying Christ's bringing Jew and Gentile together into the one people of God as his ultimate triumph and glory
- **Author:** the apostle Paul (although many have doubts)
- **Date:** A.D. 61–62 (see "Orienting Data for Colossians," p. 359), probably from Rome
- **Recipients:** uncertain; perhaps a circular letter to many churches in the province of Asia, of which Ephesus is the capital (no city is given in the earliest manuscripts; Paul assumes the readers do not know him personally, 1:15; 3:2)
- **Occasion:** Tychicus, who is carrying this letter (6:21–22), is also carrying two letters to Colosse (Colossians and Philemon [Col 4:7–9]); perhaps after reflecting further on the Colossian situation and on the glory of Christ, and knowing the Asian fear of "the powers of this dark world," Paul writes a general pastoral letter for the churches of that area
- **Emphases:** the cosmic scope of the work of Christ; Christ's reconciliation of Jew and Gentile through the cross; Christ's supremacy over "the powers" for the sake of the church; Christian behavior that reflects the unity of the Spirit

OVERVIEW OF EPHESIANS

Writer and poet Eugene Peterson tells the story of his four-year-old grandson hopping up into his lap to hear a troll story. "Tell me a story, Grandpa," he begged, "and put me in it!" That is what Paul is doing in Ephesians, telling the ultimate story—God's story—and putting some Gentile believers—and us—in it (1:13–14; 2:13).

The churches of Asia Minor are in a period of difficulty. Some outside influences are putting pressure on Gentile believers to conform to Jewish identity markers (circumcision, food laws, religious calendar; see "Specific Advice for Reading Colossians," pp. 360–61). Others are discouraged, distressed by magic and the power of the demonic ("the spiritual forces of evil in the heavenly realms," Paul calls them, Eph 6:12), which had held them in their grip for so many years. As Paul is in prison thinking about these things and reflecting on the grandeur of Christ as expressed in his letter to the Colossians, his heart soars, and what he sees he writes down as encouragement for these churches.

You will hardly be able to miss the note of affirmation and encouragement in this letter. It begins with praise to God (in the form of a Jewish *berakah*: "Blessed be God") for the abundant blessings he has given in Christ (1:3–14); it carries on through the thanksgiving and prayer (vv. 15–23), into the narrative of Jew and Gentile reconciliation (2:1–22)—plus Paul's role in it (3:1–13)—and concludes with yet another prayer and doxology (3:14–21). The rest of the letter urges them to maintain the unity God has provided through Christ's death and resurrection and the Spirit's empowering (4:1–5:20), especially in Christian households (5:21–6:9), and concludes (6:10–20) by urging them to stand boldly in Christ and the Spirit and so to withstand the powers that are still arrayed against them (and us), while they (we) live in the present age.

SPECIFIC ADVICE FOR READING EPHESIANS

As you read you will want to be on constant alert for the three concerns that dominate the letter. The first is the passion of Paul's life—the *Gentile mission,* but not just the salvation of individual Gentiles. Rather, he asserts that by reconciling both Jew and Gentile to himself, God thereby *created out of the two a new humanity*—the ultimate expression of his redeeming work in Christ (2:14–16). This theme first emerges at the end of the opening blessing (1:11–14); it is developed in a thoroughgoing way in 2:11–22 and picked up again in 3:1–13. It is also this "unity of the Spirit" (between Jew and Gentile) that chapters 4–6 are all about by way of exhortation. Thus the whole letter is held together by this theme.

The second theme is *Christ's victory over "the powers"* for the sake of the church, with the Spirit playing the key role in our participation in that victory. You will see how Paul brings these first two concerns together early on in the letter—(1) in the "blessing" in 1:3–14, where Christ's redemptive, reconciling work embraces all things, both those in heaven (the "heavenly realms" are now his) and those on earth (Jew and Gentile as the one people of God), and (2) in telling them about his own role in the gospel (3:1–13), where the reality of Jew and Gentile together as the one people of God is on display before the powers so that they become aware of their present—and ultimate—defeat in Christ (vv. 10–12).

The first theme in turn lies behind the third concern as well, which makes up the second major part of the letter (chs. 4–6)—that they "walk" (4:1, 17; 5:2, 8, 15, usually translated "live" in the TNIV) so as to *maintain the "unity of the Spirit"* (4:1–16). This includes living out the life of Christ in their relationships (4:17–5:17), their worship (5:18–20), and in their Christian households (5:21–6:9)—those places where the worship would have taken place.

All three concerns are brought into final focus in 6:10–20, where, through the weapons and armor provided by Christ and the Spirit, Paul's readers are urged to stand as one people in their ongoing conflict with the powers.

As you read you will also want to note how Paul's Trinitarian experience of God lies behind everything. This comes out in the structure of the opening praise rendered to God: Father (1:3–6), Son (vv. 7–12), and Holy Spirit (vv. 13–14); note that each of these concludes with "to the praise of his glorious grace"; "for/to the praise of his glory." It is picked up again in the thanksgiving and prayer that follow (1:17), as well as in the narrative of reconciliation in 2:11–22, and serves as the basis for maintaining unity in chapters 4–6 (see 4:6–8; one Spirit, one Lord, one God and Father).

A WALK THROUGH EPHESIANS

□ 1:3–14 *Praise to the Triune God*

Note that where he usually begins with thanksgiving and prayer for the recipients, Paul here begins with an opening "blessing" of the God who has blessed them through Christ and the Spirit. Besides being aware of the Trinitarian structure (as noted above), you should observe how Paul here introduces two of the major themes: (1) The Spirit's (TNIV "spiritual") blessings, provided through Christ, are theirs in the heavenly realms, the place of the habitation of the powers to whom they were formerly in bondage (v. 3), and (2) these blessings, especially redemption in Christ (vv. 4–10), have come to Jew and Gentile alike so that both together inherit the final glory of God (vv. 11–14).

☐ 1:15–23 *Thanksgiving and Prayer*

Here you find Paul's typical thanksgiving (vv. 15–16) and prayer (vv. 17–19). Notice how the prayer (for the Spirit's enlightenment) functions primarily to set the stage for the affirmations of his readers' present position in Christ, who presently sits at God's right hand as head over the powers for the sake of the church (vv. 20–23); note especially how this echoes the messianic Psalm 110:1.

☐ 2:1–10 *Reconciliation to God through Christ*

Flowing directly out of 1:20–23, Paul reminds his readers first of their past enslavement to the powers (2:1–3) and then of their present position with Christ in the heavenly realms, where he sits enthroned above the powers (vv. 4–7). Paul concludes with a kind of creedal statement: Life in the present is based on grace—not by "works" but for "good works" (vv. 8–10)—thus setting the stage for verses 11–22. You might want to read this section through and then read it again to see how much you can identify with the original readers.

☐ 2:11–22 *Reconciliation of Jew and Gentile through Christ and the Spirit*

This section, on the other hand, should keep us from reading verses 1–10 in a purely individualistic way. At stake for Paul is Gentile and Jew (and all other expressions of ethnic hatred) being joined together as the one people of God; they are made so, first, through Christ, whose death on the cross tore down the barriers that divide people, and, second, through the Spirit, who makes us one family as well as God's temple, the place of his present habitation on earth.

☐ 3:1–13 *Paul's Role in the Reconciling Work of Christ*

Note how Paul starts a prayer—picked up again in verse 14—but interrupts himself to emphasize both his own role of proclaiming the "mystery" as well as the nature of the mystery itself, namely, that Gentiles are coheirs with Jews and therefore together with them form the one people of God, now especially as a reality on display before the powers—as evidence of their defeat!

☐ 3:14–21 *Prayer and Doxology*

Paul now prays that they—and we—might *experience* what he has just related, now in terms of knowing the *unknowable love of Christ* and thus to be filled, through the power of the Spirit, with all the fullness of God himself. Such prayer and its potential realization through the Spirit calls once more for praise to God (vv. 20–21).

☐ 4:1–16 *An Exhortation to Maintain the Unity (between Jew and Gentile)*

Note that narrative and prayer are now followed by imperative (words of exhortation). This is how Paul addresses his third major concern—that the Ephesian believers maintain "the unity of the Spirit" noted in 2:11–22. After giving the Trinitarian basis for it (vv. 4–6), he reflects on the gifts Christ has given to the church for its growing up into this unity.

☐ 4:17–6:9 *The Practical Outworking of Unity*

In this very important section you will find Paul now applying what he has urged in verses 1–16 to his readers' corporate and household existence as God's people in the world. They must give up their former way of life as Gentiles who lived in opposition to God (4:17–24). Notice that most of the sins mentioned next (vv. 25–31) are those that destroy harmony in human relationships; to continue in such sins is to give place to the devil (v. 27) and thus to grieve the Holy Spirit (4:30); rather they should walk in the way of Christ (5:1–2).

After a series of exhortations to abandon their former ways as Gentiles and become God's light in the darkness (5:3–17), Paul focuses on their corporate worship (which took place in the context of households). Thus the exhortation to "be filled with the Spirit" (5:18) for worship also serves as the hinge between relationships in general and within households in particular, where this worship would take place. After all, the Christian household was the basic expression of the Christian community.

Note especially that in the *household rules* (5:21–6:9), the householder himself (husband, father, master) is addressed in each case in relationship to the other three kinds of people in the household (wife, children, slaves). The key element in making the Christian household work is for the householder to "love [his wife], just as Christ loved the church and gave himself up for her" (5:25).

☐ 6:10–20 *Conclusion: Stand Strong against the Powers*

Paul concludes by urging his readers, in light of all that has been said to this point, to contend against the powers by means of the *armor* provided through redemption in Christ (vv. 13–17a) and the *weapons* of the Spirit (vv. 17b–20)—the word of God and prayer.

This letter is an essential part of the biblical story. It is clear that God takes the church far more seriously than some of his people in later times have done, precisely because it is the place where God has brought about reconciliation between diverse people, who were often bitter enemies, and made them his people who bear his likeness *in their life together*—and all of this as evidence that he has defeated "the powers."

Philippians

ORIENTING DATA FOR PHILIPPIANS

- **Content:** Paul's thanksgiving for, encouragement of, and exhortation to the suffering community of believers in Philippi, who are also experiencing some internal struggles
- **Author:** the apostle Paul, joined by his younger companion Timothy
- **Date:** probably A.D. 62, almost certainly from Rome
- **Recipients:** the church in Philippi (mostly Gentile), founded around A.D. 48–49 by Paul, Silas, and Timothy; Philippi is located at the eastern end of the vast plain of Macedonia on the very important Egnatian Way, which connected Rome with Byzantium (later Constantinople and Istanbul)
- **Occasion:** Epaphroditus, who had brought information about the church to Paul in prison and delivered their gift to him (2:30; 4:18), is about to return to Philippi, having now recovered from a nearly fatal illness (2:26–27)
- **Emphases:** Paul's and the Philippians' partnership in the gospel; Christ as the key to all of life, from beginning to end; knowing Christ, by becoming like him in his death (sacrificing oneself for others); rejoicing in Christ even in suffering; unity through humility and love; the certainty and pursuit of the final prize

OVERVIEW OF PHILIPPIANS

Philippians is the favorite letter of many Christians, full of wonderful and memorable passages. To his longtime friends at Philippi Paul bares his soul more than anywhere else in his letters (1:12–26; 3:4–14). Here you get a good look at what made Paul tick—Christ crucified and raised from the dead, whose story is recounted in 2:5–11. Paul has given up all his past religious "profits" and counts them as "loss," as "garbage," in comparison with knowing Christ, who is also the final prize he eagerly pursues (3:4–14).

But the community in Philippi is experiencing some inner tensions at the very time they are also undergoing suffering because of pagan opposition to their gospel, so Paul addresses this matter head-on (1:27–2:18). He also warns them against adopting Jewish marks of religious identity, especially circumcision (3:1–4), which would, in fact, make them enemies of Christ (3:18–19).

Thus even though Paul's and their "circumstances" make up the heart of this letter, everything finally focuses on Christ. Indeed, Paul urges the Philippians to follow his own example just as he follows Christ (3:15, 17; 4:9; cf. 2:5). Since the letter will be read aloud in church and since they are his friends no matter what, he saves his thanksgiving till the end (4:10–20)—acknowledging their gift with overflowing gratitude and reminding them that God himself accepted it as a sweet-smelling sacrifice (4:18), which leads to doxology (v. 20).

SPECIFIC ADVICE FOR READING PHILIPPIANS

Although Philippians is much loved, most people have a difficult time following its flow of thought, since it is not easy to see how everything fits together. Knowing three things should help you to see how the letter works and hopefully make it even more special to read—and obey!

First, friendship was a much more significant matter in the Greco-Roman world than it is in Western cultures, so much so that the highest level of friendship—between equals and based on mutual goodwill and trust—was the topic of several tracts among the philosophers, starting with Aristotle. Such friendship was entered into consciously, almost contractually. It was always accompanied by *social reciprocity* (that is, friends expected to "benefit" one another by their mutual goodwill and trust), which was most often expressed by way of metaphors from commerce, especially mutual *giving and receiving.* A striking feature of such friendship was the assumption that friends had mutual enemies, so that those who stood in opposition to one party in the friendship became the automatic enemies of the other (see John 19:12).

One type of ancient letter, the letter of friendship, arose out of this relationship; here the writer would share his or her own present thinking (often including reflection on one's circumstances) and inquire about the other's circumstances. Mutuality and goodwill always find expression in such letters, as do the obligations of benefits received and given.

That Paul had entered into such an arrangement with the Philippians (alone among all his churches) is explicitly stated in 4:14–16. All kinds of other features of friendship thus appear in Philippians—their mutual partnership in the gospel from the very beginning (1:3–5; 4:15); Paul's special affection for them (1:8; 4:1); Paul's enemies must also be theirs (3:1–4, 17–19). The whole letter fluctuates between his and their circumstances (the language referring to each other's circumstances, distinct to such letters, appears in 1:12, 27; 2:19, 23).

Second, another kind of letter was the letter of moral exhortation, usually written by the recipient's friend or moral superior. Such letters aimed to persuade or dissuade toward or away from certain kinds of attitudes or behavior. In such letters the author usually appealed to examples, including sometimes his own.

This is where the story of Christ in 2:5–11 fits into our letter, as well as Paul's own story in 3:4–14, whose point is that knowing Christ means to "become like him in his death." Those who do not follow Paul's example (3:17) are called "enemies of the cross" (3:18). These appeals are designed to curb the bickering that is going on in the community (2:1–4, 14; 4:2–3).

Third, the opposition to the church in Philippi is almost certainly related to the fact that Philippi was a Roman military colony. The town had been reconstituted by the first Roman emperor, Augustus (Octavian), and given to troops defeated and disbanded by him (at the battle of Philippi) during the Roman civil war. Because they had been thus favored by Octavian, the citizens of Philippi developed a fierce loyalty to the emperor as such. It is not surprising, therefore, that the cult of the emperor, with its devotion to the emperor as "lord and savior," flourished in Philippi. This loyalty brought its citizens into direct conflict with Christians and their devotion to Jesus Christ as the only Lord and Savior (cf. 3:20). Since Paul was also a prisoner of Rome because of the gospel (1:13), this meant that he and the Philippian believers were currently going through "the same struggle" (1:30).

This background makes it easy to think that part of the reason for the narrative of 1:12–26 is also to offer the Philippians an example of how to respond to such attempts to suppress the gospel, namely, to rejoice in the Lord and to determine, whatever the outcome, that "to live is Christ and to die is gain" (1:21).

As you read through the letter, see how often these things help you see how Paul is trying both to encourage and to exhort the Philippians to be like Christ, and like Paul his servant.

A WALK THROUGH PHILIPPIANS

☐ 1:1–11 *Salutation, Thanksgiving, and Prayer*

Because of his friendship with the addressees, in the (otherwise typical) salutation (vv. 1–2) Paul designates himself (and Timothy) as servants of Christ Jesus, rather than asserting his apostleship. Also, only in this letter does he mention "overseers and deacons" (v. 1, perhaps because two women leaders [4:2–3] were not seeing eye to eye on things?).

As usual, the prayer of thanksgiving (1:3–8) and petition (vv. 9–11) anticipates many of the concerns of the letter. You may wish to see how many of these you can spot as you read through the rest of the letter.

☐ 1:12–26 *Paul's Circumstances: Reflections on Imprisonment*

Paul begins by telling them how things are with himself (1:12–26): His own suffering at the hands of Rome has furthered the gospel through both friends and enemies, which is a cause for rejoicing in the Lord. The ground for such rejoicing is that Paul's life is not determined by circumstances ("life" or "death" in v. 20 means to be set free or executed), but by his relationship to Christ. Hence to "live" or "die" means Christ.

☐ 1:27–2:18 *The Philippians' Circumstances: Exhortation to Steadfastness and Unity*

The opening exhortation (1:27–30) sets out the two major concerns: (1) unity among the believers, in (2) a setting of opposition and suffering. The following appeal to unity and love (2:1–4) sets forth both the attitudes that destroy unity (selfish ambition and vain conceit) and that promote it (humility, putting others first), which is modeled by Christ.

Over against their attitudes and behavior he places Christ's self-emptying and his humility (by dying on the cross; 2:5–8). Before the ultimate Humble One, now exalted to the highest place, all human beings (including "lord" Nero), angels, and demons shall bow the knee and confess Christ's lordship (vv. 9–11). This is followed by further exhortations to "work out" their common salvation by not grumbling but rather by holding firmly to the word of life in Philippi (vv. 12–16). Note that the section concludes on a note similar to how it began—Paul's present suffering for their sake, with the invitation to joy (vv. 17–18).

☐ 2:19–30 *What's Next? Regarding Paul's and Their Circumstances*

Paul hopes to return to see his friends, but he is still in prison, so he will send Timothy as soon as there is news (vv. 19–24), and he is sending Epaphroditus now (vv. 25–30), who in God's mercy has recovered from his illness and is carrying Paul's letter to them.

☐ 3:1–4:3 *The Philippians' Circumstances Again: Warning and Appeal*

Since friendship also meant having *enemies* in common, Paul warns his friends one more time against those from "the circumcision," who would impose Jewish identity markers on Gentiles so as to "secure" them before God (3:1–3). This is simply "putting confidence in the flesh," Paul says, and that launches his own story (vv. 4–14). "Been there, done that," he says regarding such religious boasting; for him the heart and goal of everything is to know Christ now—by sharing in his sufferings—and to vigorously pursue the final prize of knowing him finally and completely.

All who truly follow Christ, Paul concludes, will see it this way, and as citizens of heaven they will finally be conformed to Christ's heavenly existence as well (3:15–21). Thus he returns one final time (4:1–3) to the earlier appeal to unity.

☐ 4:4–9 *Concluding Exhortations*

Although these are common to most of Paul's letters, note how the present exhortations are also shaped by the situation in Philippi (rejoicing in the Lord; being thankful; knowing God's peace, both in their hearts and in the community).

☐ 4:10–20 *Acknowledging Their Gift: Friendship and the Gospel*

In acknowledging their gift, Paul also returns to the theme of learning to live in the present with contentment, because he "can do all this [live in plenty or in want] through him who gives me strength" (vv. 11–13).

But he concludes by bringing all the matters of friendship to a glorious conclusion. With their ample supply toward his present needs, social reciprocity now lies on his side. But he is in prison and cannot presently *benefit* them, so he turns the matter over to "my God," who "will meet all your needs according to the riches of his glory in Christ Jesus" (vv. 14–19), which causes Paul then to burst into doxology (v. 20).

□ 4:21–23 *Closing Greetings*

These are especially brief in this letter, probably because Paul wants the words of verses 18–20 to be the final ones ringing in the Philippians' ears as the letter is read in church. But he does add a final encouragement by noting that among those sending greetings as followers of the Lord are members of "lord" Caesar's own household!

The whole of this wonderful letter is dominated by the story of Christ in 2:5–11, the Christ we are called both to serve and to be like. To "know Christ" means to live and act in the believing community as he did in his incarnation and crucifixion.

Colossians

ORIENTING DATA FOR COLOSSIANS

- **Content:** a letter encouraging relatively new believers to continue in the truth of Christ they have received, and warning them against outside religious influences
- **Author:** the apostle Paul, joined by his younger companion Timothy
- **Date:** probably A.D. 60–61 (if Paul is in Rome, as is most likely)
- **Recipient(s):** the (mostly Gentile) believers in Colosse (Colosse was the least significant of three towns noted for their medicinal spas [including Hierapolis and Laodicea] at a crucial crossroads in the Lycus River Valley, approximately 120 miles southwest of Ephesus); the letter is also to be read, as an exchange, in Laodicea (4:16)
- **Occasion:** Epaphras, a Pauline coworker who had founded the churches in the Lycus Valley, has recently come to Paul bringing news of the church, mostly good but some less so
- **Emphases:** the absolute supremacy and all-sufficiency of Christ, the Son of God; that Christ both forgives sin and removes one from the terror of "the powers"; religious rules and regulations count for nothing, but ethical life that bears God's own image counts for everything; Christlike living affects relationships of all kinds

OVERVIEW OF COLOSSIANS

Although Paul has never personally been to Colosse (2:1), he knows much about the believers there and considers them one of *his* churches—through his coworker Epaphras (1:7–8). His primary concern is that they stand firm in what they have been taught (1:23; 2:6–16; 3:1). After a glowing thanksgiving and encouraging prayer report (1:3–12), much of the first half of the letter reiterates the truth of the gospel they have received (1:13–22; 2:2–3, 6–7, 9–15). The rest of these two chapters exposes the follies of the errors to which some are being attracted (2:4, 8, 16–23). One may rightly guess, therefore, that the emphases in Paul's recounting the gospel are also there in response to the errors.

At the heart of the errors is a desire to regulate Christian life with rules about externals—"Do not handle! Do not taste! Do not touch!" (2:21, which sounds very much like certain forms of present-day Christianity). Most of chapters 3–4, therefore, take up the nature of genuinely Christian behavior. "Rules" and "regulations" have an appearance of wisdom, but no real value (2:23). Christian behavior results from having died and been raised with Christ (2:20; 3:1) and now being "hidden with Christ in God" (3:3), thus expressing itself "in the image of [the] Creator" (3:10). Note especially that the imperatives that flow out of these realities (3:12–4:6) are primarily directed toward community life, not toward individual one-on-one life with God.

SPECIFIC ADVICE FOR READING COLOSSIANS

As you read Colossians, you will want to be looking for four things. First, since so much that is said in Colossians is in direct (and indirect) response to some false teaching, be on the lookout for everything Paul says about these errors. Even though this matter does not emerge in a direct way until 2:4, by the time you are finished with chapter 2 you cannot help but see how important it is. Probably, therefore, much of what is said in 1:13–23 also was written with an eye toward what was falsely being taught.

Because of its importance for understanding this letter, a lot of scholarly energy has been devoted to the *false teaching,* trying to match it with what is otherwise known (or guessed at) in the Greco-Roman world. But at the end of the day all we know about it is what Paul says in this letter. We can't even be sure that there were "false teachers" as such; Paul's references are invariably to "anyone," "no one," etc. (2:4, 8, 16, 18). In any case, as you read, at least be looking for the various elements found in these errors.

The most obvious element is its Jewish flavor, which includes circumcision (2:11, 13), food laws, and the observance of the Jewish religious calendar (2:16); for Paul these are simply a written code standing over against us (2:14), merely "human commands and teachings" (2:22) that Christ has done away with. This element is apparently mixed with superstitions about angelic or spiritual powers (1:16; 2:8, 15, 18, 20), which seem also to have a powerful appeal both as divine "philosophy"—elite wisdom—(2:3, 8, 20) and divine "mystery" (1:26; 2:2). These teachings also seem to be in conflict with the physical side of Christ's earthly life and redemption (1:19, 22; 2:9).

Second, you will not be able to miss Paul's primary emphasis on the absolute *supremacy of Christ* over all things. This begins in 1:13, as the thanksgiving gives way to the exaltation of the Son, and carries through verse 22. It then recurs at every key point in the letter. Paul argues that Christ is the key to everything they need. All that God is ever going to do in and for the world has happened in and through him (1:19; 2:2–3, 9, 13–15, 20; 3:1). Paul also emphasizes the absolute supremacy of Christ over the powers, including Christ's role in creation and redemption. Christ is the whole package, so don't let go of him. He is the true "Head" trip (1:18; 2:10, 19).

Third, you will now want to think through the *situation in the church* one more time. Paul has never been there, but he has heard of their genuine faith in Christ. Notice the ways he tries to encourage them (1:3–12; 2:2; etc.), but note also the warnings (1:23; 2:4; etc.). At the same time think about how some things are said precisely because they do not know Paul personally but only through Epaphras. This is especially true of 1:24–2:5, where he sets his calling and ministry before them, especially in terms of the Gentile mission and what God has done through him by the power of the Spirit.

Fourth, at the end you may wish to read the whole letter again, this time with the knowledge that Onesimus (4:9) is being returned to Philemon for forgiveness, so Paul is preparing the church to *receive Onesimus* back as well (see Philemon). Read it at least once as you think Onesimus might have heard it; then perhaps try to put yourself in the shoes of a member of the church in Colosse.

A WALK THROUGH COLOSSIANS

☐ 1:1–2 *Salutation*

This is pretty standard, but note especially the emphasis on the Colossian believers already being holy and faithful.

☐ 1:3–14 *Thanksgiving and Prayer*

As usual, these anticipate much that is in the letter. The thanksgiving emphasizes the Colossians' already existing faith and love; the prayer asks for the Spirit's wisdom and understanding so that they might live lives worthy of Christ, made possible by God's power. Note how at the end the prayer gives way once more to thanksgiving (v. 12), which then trails off into a sentence that gives the reason for it—redemption through God's Son so as to share in his inheritance.

☐ 1:15–23 *The Supremacy of the Son of God*

This marvelous passage, which has a profoundly hymnic quality to it, actually continues the sentence that began in verse 12 (and continues through verse 16). Notice how what began with the Father's redemption through his Son, now proceeds to exalt the Son, who bears his image. In turn Paul proclaims first the Son's supremacy in relationship to the whole created order, including "the powers," as the creator of all things (vv. 15–17), and then in relationship to the church as its redeemer (vv. 18–22), concluding with a concern that the Colossians stay with Christ (v. 23).

☐ 1:24–2:5 *Paul's Role*

As you read this section, think about how it functions in a letter to a church that Paul has not founded or visited. His present imprisonment is to be understood as carrying on the sufferings of Christ for the sake of the (especially Gentile) church (1:24–27); his present role is to "strenuously contend" (an athletic metaphor) for members of churches like theirs and Laodicea, who have not known him personally, so that they might be encouraged and not fall prey to false teaching.

☐ 2:6–23 *Christ over against Religious Seductions of All Kinds*

Here you come to the heart of the letter. Christ in his incarnation and crucifixion both exposes and eliminates the "hollow philosophy" some are entertaining—a philosophy that first of all has to do with "the powers" (vv. 6–10). But note how in verses 11–19, this philosophy has been tied to an attempt to bring Gentile believers in Christ under the three primary identity markers of the Jewish Diaspora (see "Specific Advice for Reading Galatians," pp. 342–43), expecially food laws and the Jewish calendar (v. 16), and perhaps circumcision.

Note how Paul responds: They have received a new and truly effective circumcision—in the cross Christ has forgiven sin and triumphed over "the powers" (vv. 11–15); food laws and sacred days were a "shadow" of the reality, Christ himself, whose death and resurrection has forever eliminated the need to live by rules (vv. 16–23). Observe especially how Paul concludes: Rules "have an appearance of wisdom," but "lack any value in restraining sensual indulgence." Rules simply aim too low; believers are made for higher and better things.

☐ 3:1–11 *The New Basis for (Christian) Behavior*

Our participation in the death (2:20) and resurrection (3:1) of Christ eliminates the need to follow religious rules. Believers in Christ have died to those merely human things, having been raised to life by the one who is now exalted to the Father's right hand (see Ps 110:1). Paul then describes what we have died to (Col 3:5–9) and, by a shift of images (changing clothing), urges us to a life that reflects God's own image (v. 10). Verse 11 anticipates the imperatives that follow by reminding his readers that Christ has eliminated all cultural, religious, socioeconomic, and racial barriers.

☐ 3:12–4:6 *What Christian Life Looks Like*

Based on God's love and election (3:12), Paul proceeds to illustrate how God's image (in Christ) is to be lived out in their relationships with each other. Notice how everything flows out of the character traits of verse 12, two of which describe Christ in Matthew 11:29, and most of which are called "fruit of the Spirit" in Galatians 5:22–23. Remember as you read that these instructions in Christian behavior are *not* directed toward individual piety, but toward life in the Christian *community,* the basic expression of which is the Christian household.

☐ 4:7–18 *Final Greetings*

We learn much here, so don't read too hastily. Note especially the description of Onesimus (v. 9) as a "faithful and dear brother, who is one of you" (cf. Philemon). Note also how the greetings (Col 4:10–15) function to remind the Colossian believers that they belong to a much larger community of faith, including some mutual acquaintances.

What an important part of the biblical story this letter is, by its exaltation of Christ and by reminding us that behavior counts for something—but only as it is a reflection of Christ's own character and redemption.

1 Thessalonians

ORIENTING DATA FOR 1 THESSALONIANS

- **Content:** a letter of thanksgiving, encouragement, exhortation, and information for very recent Gentile believers in Christ
- **Author:** the apostle Paul, joined by his traveling companions Silas and Timothy
- **Date:** A.D. 50 or 51, while Paul is in Corinth, probably the earliest document in the New Testament
- **Recipients:** quite new converts to Christ in Thessalonica, mostly Gentile (1:9–10)—Thessalonica was a northern Aegean seaport that also sat astraddle the Egnatian Way (see "Orienting Data for Philippians," p. 353); in the time of Paul it was the chief city of Macedonia
- **Occasion:** the return of Timothy to Paul and Silas in Corinth; Timothy had been sent to Thessalonica to see how the new believers were doing (see 3:5–7)
- **Emphases:** Paul's loving concern for his friends in Thessalonica; suffering as part of Christian life; holiness regarding sexual matters; the need to do one's own work and not live off the largesse of others; the resurrection of the Christian dead; readiness for Christ's coming

OVERVIEW OF 1 THESSALONIANS

Put yourself in Paul's shoes. You have recently been to Macedonia's major city, where you had had good success in preaching the good news about Christ. But your success also aroused enormous opposition. Your host was arrested and charged with high treason, while friends ushered you out of the city by night so that you wouldn't be brought before the authorities. Thus your stay was much shorter than you had expected, and the new believers are now pretty much on their own, without a long period of seasoned instruction in the way of Christ. (See the account in Acts 17:1–9; the three Sabbath days mentioned in verse 2 does not mean that Paul was in the city for only that long. Rather that was how long he was able to work in the synagogue. Our letter indicates a church of much greater stability, Christian instruction, and renown than two or three weeks would have produced.)

So what would you have done? Try, as Paul did, to return, despite the danger (1 Thess 2:17–18)? And what if you could not return, because "Satan blocked [your] way"? And all the time you know nothing about what has happened in Thessalonica since you left (these were the days before postal service, not to mention telephone and e-mail service!). Very likely you would do what Paul did: Send a younger colleague, who could return without fear of being recognized or of suffering personal danger.

Now Timothy has returned to Paul and Silas in Corinth. A full half of our letter (chs. 1–3) is about Paul's past, present, and future relationship with these new converts, told in basically chronological fashion. Two clear things about Paul emerge in this section: (1) his deep, personal anxiety about the Thessalonians' situation and (2) his equally deep relief to learn that things are going basically very well (you can almost hear his sigh of relief in 3:6–8). Two things also emerge about the Thessalonian believers in these two chapters: (1) They continue to undergo suffering and persecution, but (2) they are basically hanging in there with regard to their faith in Christ—although there are also some things lacking.

The rest of the letter takes up matters that have been reported to him by Timothy. Most of them are reminders (see 4:1–2, 9; 5:1) of instructions they had been given when Paul and his companions were among them—about sexual immorality; mutual love, which includes working for one's own sustenance; and the return of Christ. One altogether new item is also included, namely, what happens to believers who have died before the coming of Christ (4:13–18).

SPECIFIC ADVICE FOR READING 1 THESSALONIANS

Keep in mind in reading this letter that it is most likely the earliest extant Christian document. To see how Paul deals with very new converts is part of the delight of reading. Notice especially how often Paul reminds them of things they already know (1:5; 2:1, 5, 9, 10, 11; 4:2, 9; 5:1). Given that Timothy's report about their faith was essentially positive and that on two matters Paul says there is no need to write (4:9; 5:1), the question is, Why then write at all? The answer lies in 3:9–10, where Paul thanks God that overall they are doing quite well, but that there are also some deficiencies. Since he cannot come now, he sends a letter as his way of being present and supplying "what is lacking in your faith."

On three matters (2:1–12; 4:1–8; 4:13–5:11) it is especially important to be aware of Greco-Roman culture in general and Thessalonian sociology in particular. First, every charge Paul defends himself against in 2:1–6 can be found in pagan philosophical writings—charges leveled against religious or philosophical charlatans. Almost certainly part of the suffering of the Thessalonian believers comes in the form of accusations against Paul (after all, he left town in the dead of night with political charges hanging in the air!). Second, the Greeks and Romans never considered immoral the kind of sexual behavior outside of marriage that both Jews and Christians saw as breaking the seventh commandment; what we would call sexual promiscuity—of all kinds—was simply an accepted way of life. Third, there is plenty of archaeological evidence indicating that the pagan Thessalonians were intensely interested in matters of life after death.

It is also of some interest to read 1 Thessalonians in conjunction with Philippians, since both are directed toward Macedonian (and therefore Greek) cities, yet their citizens are well known in antiquity for their loyalty to Caesar; in both cases Paul and the churches are undergoing persecution because of their loyalty to a "King" other than Caesar.

But there are differences as well. While 1 Thessalonians shows characteristics of a letter of friendship, that friendship was not of the more contractual kind Paul had with the Philippians. Note that in Philippi Paul had accepted financial support, whereas in Thessalonica, even though he stayed with Jason, he chose in this case to work with his own hands. This appears to mark a change in missionary strategy, which will serve Paul's theological interests in both Thessalonica and Corinth—here, because in 2 Thessalonians he will eventually appeal to his own example in order to reinforce the instruction given in 1 Thessalonians 4:9–12. See further the comments on 2 Thessalonians 3:6–15 on page 372.

A WALK THROUGH 1 THESSALONIANS

After the briefest of all of Paul's salutations (1:1), he begins with what turns out to be an extended "thanksgiving turned report" on their relationship (1:2–3:10), followed by a typical prayer report (3:11–13).

☐ 1:2–10 *Thanksgiving for Their Conversion*

Thanksgiving over the Thessalonian believers' faithfulness very soon gives way to a reminder of their conversion. Four things are stressed: (1) Paul's and the Holy Spirit's role in their conversion; (2) as with Paul—and in imitation of Christ—they experienced suffering in coming to faith, plus joy in the Holy Spirit; (3) news of their conversion had preceded Paul to Corinth (Achaia); (4) conversion included a turning from idolatry and a waiting for Christ's return.

☐ 2:1–12 *Recalling Paul's Ministry*

For their own sakes, Paul defends himself against charges of being a religious huckster. Notice that in verses 7–12 he uses three family images (infant, mother, father!) to refer to his relationship with them.

☐ 2:13–16 *The Thanksgiving—and Thessalonians' Suffering—Renewed*

Note how much this echoes 1:4–6. Here we also learn the source of their suffering ("your fellow Gentiles"), which reminds Paul of the source of his suffering (fellow Jews), whom he indicts for having crucified Christ and for trying to keep Gentiles from coming to faith (cf. Acts 17:1–8).

☐ 2:17–3:10 *Paul, the Thessalonians, and Timothy*

In successive paragraphs Paul picks up the narrative of his relationship with the Thessalonians since he (and Silas and Timothy) were "orphaned [!] ... from you for a short time." First (2:17–20), he reports on his own attempts to return and the reason for it; second (3:1–5), he reports on the sending of Timothy—to see how they were doing in light of their suffering; third (3:6–10), he expresses his great relief over Timothy's report "about your faith and love." All of this ends with a renewed thanksgiving.

☐ 3:11–13 *Prayer Report*

You should note that Paul prays for the very things he will now go on to speak about, namely, holiness, love, and the coming of Jesus Christ.

☐ 4:1–8 *On Sexual Purity*

Observe the clear shift here, as Paul moves on to pick up "what is lacking" in their faith (3:10). The first item is sexual immorality, reminding them that the God who called them and gave his Holy Spirit to them also calls them to a monogamous sexual life.

☐ 4:9–12 *On Love and Working with One's Own Hands*

Paul now moves on to the matter of mutual love—that some are not to be unnecessarily burdensome to others. On this matter, and the need to speak to it again, see 2 Thessalonians.

☐ 4:13–18 *On the Future of Christians Who have Died*

This paragraph reminds us of how brief Paul's time with them must have been. They had heard plenty about Christ's return (see 1:9–10; 5:1–11), but in the meantime, some of their company had died (because of the persecution?), and they simply didn't know what was to become of them. The answer: The dead will be resurrected; the living will be transported into the presence of Christ at his coming.

☐ 5:1–11 *On the Coming of Christ*

In light of the anxiety caused over the matter just addressed, Paul adds some encouraging words about the coming of Christ and his readers' participation in it. Although often read as warning, the passage is clearly intended to be an encouragement to a suffering community of believers (v. 11, "therefore encourage one another"). Since they are children of the day, they neither engage in nighttime activities nor should be caught by surprise at Christ's coming.

☐ 5:12–22 *Concluding Exhortations*

In turn Paul encourages respect/honor for leaders (vv. 12–13), urges healthy community relationships (vv. 14–15), exhorts basic piety (continual rejoicing, prayer, and thanksgiving; vv. 16–18), and prods them to encourage prophecy, but to test it and hold fast the good (vv. 19–22).

☐ 5:23–28 *Concluding Prayer and Greetings*

The prayer in particular recapitulates many of the items just addressed.

Here is a letter full of good things for the building up of relationships within the Christian community as we await the sure coming of our Lord, who will bring the present story to an end.

2 Thessalonians

ORIENTING DATA FOR 2 THESSALONIANS

- **Content:** a letter of further encouragement in the face of suffering, of warning against being misled regarding the coming of the Lord, and of exhortation for some to work with their own hands and not sponge off others
- **Author:** the apostle Paul, joined by his traveling companions Silas and Timothy
- **Date:** A.D. 51 (probably), very shortly after 1 Thessalonians (although some would reverse the order of our two letters)
- **Recipients:** see 1 Thessalonians
- **Occasion:** Paul has received word that some (probably by prophetic word) have spoken in Paul's name to the effect that the day of the Lord (= the coming of Christ) has already taken place, plus the fact that the disruptive loafers spoken to in 1 Thessalonians have not mended their ways
- **Emphases:** the sure salvation of the Thessalonian believers and the sure judgment of their persecutors; the day of the Lord is still ahead and will be preceded by "the rebellion"; those who are idle and disruptive should work for their food

OVERVIEW OF 2 THESSALONIANS

If you read this letter hard on the heels of 1 Thessalonians, you may notice that in general it lacks the warmth of feeling that you found in the first letter; and the material in 2 Thessalonians 2:1–12 is just obscure enough, especially in light of 1 Thessalonians 4:13–5:11, to cause you to wonder what gives. But what has caused the tone of this letter is easy to see. Both of the major items taken up (2 Thess 2:1–12; 3:6–15) give good reason for Paul to be upset—even more than he actually comes across as. In any case, the other sections of the letter (the thanksgiving and prayer in 1:3–12 and the prayer and request for prayer in 2:16–3:5) are full of the same kind of affection and concern Paul expresses in the earlier letter.

So what does give? First, Paul has learned from someone that the church is being thrown into confusion (2:2) by a declaration given in Paul's name that the day of the Lord has already happened. Both sides of this matter are enough to upset him—the falsehood itself and the fact that it is being put forward under Paul's authority. Since in 2:15 he tells them to hold fast to what he himself had taught them—by "word of mouth" (when he was present with them) and by "letter" (1 Thessalonians)—the problem in 2 Thessalonians 2:2 probably comes from an untested prophetic utterance (see 1 Thess 5:19–22) claiming to speak in Paul's name on this matter.

Second, he also has reason to be a bit miffed over those who are idle and disruptive, since he has already spoken to this issue in his first letter (1 Thess 4:9–12; 5:14).

Together these account both for the ambivalent tone and the specific content of the letter.

SPECIFIC ADVICE FOR READING 2 THESSALONIANS

For a brief letter, 2 Thessalonians has more than its share of difficult moments. First, although Paul expects certain events to take place before the coming of Christ (as you will see in 2:1–12), the specific nature of these events is less than certain. Most of our difficulty stems from the fact that at two crucial places (the identity of "the man of lawlessness" and "what is holding him back"), the Thessalonians had previously been informed, so Paul does not here repeat himself (2:5–6). Although these questions are obviously matters of interest for us as later readers, we will very likely have to be content to live with the main point of the passage, since we are outside the loop on these matters.

Second, there is also plenty of speculation—often given out as though it were plainly in the text—on the reason why the disruptive-idle continue not to work. The reason most commonly suggested is that they've quit working because they are expecting the soon coming of Jesus. But that hardly squares with what is actually being promoted in 2:2, that the day of the Lord has *already* come. More likely it is related to the general disdain of manual work on the part of Greek aristocracy.

But nothing can be known for certain about the why; Paul's concern is, and ours should be as well, altogether with the *what*—both the exhortation to the disruptive-idle to get to work and the instruction to the church on how to treat such people.

A WALK THROUGH 2 THESSALONIANS

☐ 1:1–12 *Salutation, Thanksgiving, and Prayer*

Note several things as you read: (1) how the thanksgiving (vv. 3–10) affirms the Thessalonians in areas that need reinforcing; (2) that, as with 1 Thessalonians, it soon turns into narrative (vv. 6–10)—about the sure coming judgment of those who are persecuting them, while ending on the note of their own sure salvation—and (3) that the coming has a "can't miss the action" dimension to it (v. 7b), over against the teaching of those who claim it has already happened.

Watch how the prayer (vv. 11–12) then picks up the twin matters of faith and love from verse 3 (now in terms of deeds prompted by goodness and faith).

☐ 2:1–12 *Correcting Erroneous Teaching about Christ's Coming*

Paul begins the body of the letter (vv. 1–2) by urging the Thessalonian believers not to be shaken by the erroneous teaching (even though he is not quite sure of its source). As you read Paul's response (vv. 3–12), note first that he reminds them (vv. 5–6) of his earlier instruction on this matter to the effect that certain events must precede the coming of the Lord. Second, note how "the man of lawlessness" mentioned in verse 3 is the central figure in the whole narrative. A great rebellion will accompany his appearance (v. 4), effected in part by satanic miracles that dupe those who refuse to embrace the truth (vv. 9–12), but in the end he will be destroyed by Christ himself at Christ's coming (v. 8).

☐ 2:13–17 *Application and Prayer*

Paul next encourages the Thessalonian believers (vv. 13–14) by immediately setting them—those who have believed the truth and received the Spirit—in contrast to those mentioned in verses 10–12. He then urges them to stand firm in their former instruction (v. 15), finally praying both for their encouragement and their continuing faithfulness to Christian life and teaching (vv. 16–17).

☐ 3:1–5 *Request for Prayer*

Friendship in antiquity requires reciprocity (see "Specific Advice for Reading Philippians," p. 354); thus, having prayed for them in their present circumstances, he now asks them to pray for him in his.

☐ 3:6–15 *About Those Who Are Idle and Disruptive*

Before reading this section, you may wish to reread 1 Thessalonians 4:9–12. In returning to this matter, Paul uses himself as an example as he urges the disruptive-idle to work with their own hands so as not to burden anyone (2 Thess 3:6–13). Next (vv. 14–15), he tells the church what they are to do, namely, dissociate from those who refuse to obey, but always to think of them as brothers and sisters, not as enemies.

☐ 3:16–18 *Concluding Matters*

After passing the peace (v. 16), Paul takes quill in hand to sign off and thus guarantee the authenticity of the letter (v. 17), before the final grace-benediction (v. 18).

This letter fits into the biblical narrative as part of God's reassuring his people that Christ alone holds the key to the future and that they can trust him to defeat the enemy once and for all in his own time; in the meantime, love for one another also means not to impose on others' kindness.

1 Timothy

ORIENTING DATA FOR 1 TIMOTHY

- **Content:** an indictment of some false teachers—their character and teachings—with instructions on various community matters these teachers have brought to crisis, interspersed with words of encouragement to Timothy
- **Author:** the apostle Paul (although doubted by many)
- **Date:** A.D. 62–63, from Macedonia (probably Philippi or Thessalonica), apparently after his (expected) release from the imprisonment noted in Philippians 1:13 and 2:23–24
- **Recipient(s):** Timothy, a longtime, younger companion of Paul; and (ultimately) the church in Ephesus (the grace-benediction in 6:21 is plural)
- **Occasion:** Paul has left Timothy in charge of a very difficult situation in the church in Ephesus, where false teachers (probably local elders) are leading some house churches astray; Paul writes to the whole church through Timothy in order to strengthen Timothy's hand in stopping these straying elders and some younger widows who have followed them
- **Emphases:** the truth of the gospel as God's mercy shown toward all people; character qualifications for church leadership; speculative teachings, asceticism, and love of controversy and money disqualify one from church leadership; Timothy, by holding fast to the gospel, should model genuine Christian character and leadership

OVERVIEW OF 1 TIMOTHY

The letters to Timothy and Titus have long been called the Pastoral Epistles, under the assumption that they are intended to give instructions to young pastors on church order. But that tends both to read later concerns back into these letters and to lump them together in a way that loses their individual (and quite different) character and life setting. This letter is the first of the three, written soon after Paul had left Timothy in Ephesus. Having disfellowshipped the ringleaders of the false teaching (1:19–20), he left Timothy there while he went on to Macedonia, charging him to stop "certain persons [from teaching] false doctrines any longer" (1:3).

The letter fluctuates between words to the *church* through Timothy and words to *Timothy* himself, although even these latter are intended to be overheard by the church. Much of the letter points out the follies of the false teachers/teaching (1:4–10, 19b–20; 4:1–3, 7; 6:3–10, 20–21). The words to Timothy (1:3, 18–19a; 4:6–16; 6:11–16, 20–21) charge him with regard to his duties and encourage him and strengthen his hand before the community to carry out these (sometimes unpleasant) duties. These two matters merge in the final charge to Timothy in 6:20–21. The rest of the letter deals with community matters, obviously deeply influenced by the false teaching—matters such as the believers' gathering for prayer and teaching (2:1–15); qualifications for, and replacement of, leaders (3:1–13; 5:17–25); caring for older widows, but urging younger ones to marry (5:3–16); attitudes of slaves toward masters (6:1–2).

Despite the many words directed personally to Timothy, this letter is all business, as is made clear by a lack of both the ordinary thanksgiving and prayer reports that begin Paul's letters (cf. 2 Timothy) and the greetings to and from friends that conclude them (again, cf. 2 Timothy).

SPECIFIC ADVICE FOR READING 1 TIMOTHY

As you read, note especially what Paul says about the false teachers and their teaching—since concern about them appears to lie behind every word in this letter. There are good reasons to assume that these teachers were local elders who had embraced some ideas that are quite incompatible with the gospel of grace (1:11–17): First, unlike the other letters of Paul that deal with false teachers (2 Corinthians, Galatians, Philippians), 1 Timothy gives no hint that these teachers might be outsiders. Second, Paul has already excommunicated two of them, clearly insiders (1 Tim 1:19–20), and the later evidence from 2 Timothy 2:17–18 indicates that one of them (Hymenaeus) refused to leave (note that he is named first both times, implying that he is the ringleader). Now, third, read Paul's address to the elders of this church in Acts 20:17–35, and note that, some five years or so earlier, Paul had predicted this very thing would happen (vv. 29–30, that from among their own number some would arise and distort the truth).

If you add one additional factor, that these elders have made use of some younger widows who have opened their homes to their novelties—as 2 Timothy 3:6–7 states—then the whole letter falls into place. Note how these factors together explain (1) why Paul writes to Timothy, and not to the church as in other such cases, since his letter would not get a hearing in the hands of these elders; at the same time Paul is authorizing Timothy before the church to see that these elders are replaced by people with proper qualifications; (2) why he gives careful instructions, not about the duties of elders, but about their qualifications; (3) why he gives such detailed instructions about caring for older widows, while urging the younger ones, some of whom have already gone astray after Satan (1 Tim 5:15), to marry—against his general advice in 1 Corinthians 7:40—and why he forbids them to teach in this setting (1 Tim 2:11–15); and (4) why, although his primary concern is for the gospel (1:11), Paul gives so little of its content in this letter—since Timothy does not need instruction here—and why on the other hand so much is said about the nature of the false teaching.

The false teaching seems to be a mixture of things Jewish and Greek. Errantly based on the law (1:7), it was full of Old Testament speculations ("myths and endless [wearisome] genealogies," 1:4); it was being presented as *gnōsis* ("knowledge," 6:20) and appeared to have an esoteric and exclusivistic appeal (1:4–7; note in 2:1–7 and 4:10 that God wants *all people* to be saved), which included a false asceticism that denied the goodness of creation (4:3–5; perhaps 5:23). Beyond their teaching, Paul indicts the teachers for their love of controversies, including battles over words (1:6; 6:4), and especially for their greed (6:5–10; cf. 3:3, "not a lover of money").

All in all, Paul has left Timothy with a very difficult assignment—which seems not to have been altogether successful in light of the evidence of 2 Timothy—making the words to Timothy all the more poignant. You might try to put yourself in Timothy's shoes as you read through the letter.

A WALK THROUGH 1 TIMOTHY

☐ 1:1–2 *Salutation*

Despite their long and close relationship, note how Paul emphasizes here his apostleship and Timothy's being his "true son" (= legitimate child). This is surely for the sake of the church, in light of what they must hear from this letter.

☐ 1:3–20 *First Charge to Timothy*

This first charge (v. 3, renewed in v. 18) reminds Timothy of his duty to stop the false teaching (v. 3), which is then described (vv. 4–11) in contrast to Paul's testimony (vv. 12–17). Notice how the latter both articulates the content of the gospel and authorizes Paul's apostleship. Verse 15 gives the first of three trustworthy sayings cited in this letter (see 3:1; 4:9) and emphasizes that Christ came to save sinners (not ascetics). The renewed charge (1:18–20) reminds the church that Hymenaeus and Alexander have been disfellowshipped.

☐ 2:1–15 *Instructions on Community Matters*

The first matter Paul brings up is community prayer, that it is to be for "everyone" (v. 1), because God wants "all people" to be saved (vv. 3–4), as Christ's sacrifice for "all people" is the sure evidence (vv. 5–6). This is followed by instruction about proper decorum at community prayer: When the men lift up their hands to pray, they are not to be soiled with the disputings of the false teachers (v. 8), and the women are not to dress seductively (for that culture), but to "wear" good deeds (vv. 9–10); because of the influence of the younger widows (2:15 and 5:14 should be read side by side), Paul forbids women to teach (using Eve's deception by Satan that led to transgression as the biblical analogy for their being deceived by Satan; cf. 4:1 and 5:15).

☐ 3:1–13 *Qualifications for Church Leaders*

With a second "trustworthy saying" (v. 1), Paul offers the character qualifications for three kinds of leaders (the verb "is to be" in v. 2 grammatically controls vv. 2, 8, and 12): overseers (vv. 1–7), deacons (vv. 8–10, 12), and women deacons ([v. 11], probably; certainly not "wives"). Note the singular lack of duties, except for "able to teach" in verse 2, and how many of these qualities stand in sharp contrast to what is said elsewhere of the false teachers.

☐ 3:14–4:5 *The Purpose for the Letter*

Paul writes so that God's people will know how to conduct themselves in God's household. They are to be God's temple (pillar and foundation) that preserves "the mystery from which true godliness springs," set forth in hymnic style in 3:16; this is set in direct contrast to the satanic teachings of the fallen elders (4:1–5). Note that the hymn emphasizes Christ's incarnation (line 1), apparently over against a false asceticism (4:3–5), and the universal nature of the gospel (lines 4–5), over against the (apparent) exclusivism of such asceticism.

☐ 4:6–16 *Renewed Charge to Timothy*

As in chapter 1, Timothy's charge is given over against the false teachers (vv. 6–8). The third trustworthy saying (v. 8) emphasizes that "training" in the godliness noted in 3:15–16 (versus ascetic "discipline") holds promise for life both in the present and the future, while the additional word about "labor" (= Paul's and Timothy's as ministers of the gospel) again emphasizes the universality of the gospel.

Notice how the rest of the charge (4:11–16), while clearly intended to bolster Timothy's courage, explicitly sets him before the congregation as a model to emulate—despite his youth—and reaffirms his ministry among them, before concluding with personal words.

☐ 5:1–6:2b *On Widows and Elders (and Slaves)*

Paul now specifies how to handle the two groups that have been causing the grief. After introductory words about all the people (5:1–2), he takes up in turn the younger widows (vv. 3–16) and the straying elders (vv. 17–25), concluding with instructions to slaves (6:1–2). Note how in both primary cases he first sets those who are going astray in contrast to those who are genuine. Thus the church is to care for "widows who are really in need" (5:3–9), but he counsels the younger ones to marry, bear children, and manage their households (vv. 11–16).

Likewise, the church must honor (and pay) faithful elders (5:17–18), but try (with impartiality), dismiss, and replace "those who sin" (vv. 19–22, 24–25). The parenthetical word to Timothy (v. 23) is probably for both his and the church's sake: "Keeping yourself pure" (v. 22) does not include (ascetic?) abstinence from wine, which Timothy needs for his health.

□ 6:2c–10 *Final Indictment of the False Teachers*

Here Paul once more impeaches the false teachers for their love of controversy, but finally he scores them for their love of money. Note how he borrows here from the Old Testament Wisdom tradition (Job 1:21; Eccl 5:15).

□ 6:11–20 *Final Charge to Timothy*

Note how, as in 4:1–16, Timothy is once again set in contrast to the false teachers, with emphasis now on his persevering to the end, "which God will bring about in his own time." Verses 17–19 qualify the indictment against greed in verses 6–10: Those who happen to be rich (in that culture, handed down as inheritance) are to be "rich in good deeds," especially in the form of generosity to the needy.

Note how the sign-off (vv. 20–21) summarizes Paul's urgencies; its abruptness highlights how urgent the matter is.

This letter's special contribution to the biblical story lies in its emphasizing the role of good leadership for the sake of the people of God, thus echoing the contrast between false and genuine prophets from the Old Testament.

2 Timothy

ORIENTING DATA FOR 2 TIMOTHY

- **Content:** an appeal to Timothy to remain loyal to Christ, to the gospel, and to Paul, including a final salvo at the false teachers (of 1 Timothy)
- **Author:** the apostle Paul (although doubted by many)
- **Date:** ca. A.D. 64, from a prison in Rome (the lion in 4:17 is an allusion to Nero or to the empire itself)
- **Recipient(s):** Timothy primarily; secondarily to the church (the first "you" in 4:22 is singular, the final one is plural)
- **Occasion:** Paul has been once more arrested and taken to Rome (most likely from Troas and at the instigation of Alexander, 4:13–15 [probably the same man who was disfellowshiped in 1 Tim 1:19–20]); the letter urges Timothy to come to Paul's side, but mostly offers him a kind of last will and testament
- **Emphases:** the saving work of Christ, "who has destroyed death and brought life ... through the gospel" (1:10); loyalty to Christ by perseverance in suffering and hardship; loyalty to Paul by recalling their longtime relationship; loyalty to the gospel by being faithful in proclaiming/teaching "the word" (= the gospel message); the deadly spread, but final demise, of the false teaching; the final salvation of those who are Christ's

OVERVIEW OF 2 TIMOTHY

This is Paul's final (preserved) letter. At the end, we learn that its primary purpose was to urge Timothy to join Paul in Rome posthaste (4:9, 21) and to bring Mark and some personal items along with him when he comes (4:11, 13). Timothy is to be replaced by Tychicus, the presumed bearer of the letter (4:12). The reason for haste is the onset of winter

(4:21) and the fact that Paul's preliminary court hearing has already taken place (4:16).

But the majority of the letter is very little concerned about this matter and very much an appeal to Timothy to remain loyal to Paul and his gospel by embracing suffering and hardship. And in this sense it also becomes a community document (hence the plural "you" in 4:22b), implicitly urging the believers to loyalty as well. This appeal is made in the context of the continuing influence of the false teachers (2:16–18; 3:13), the defection of many (1:15), and Paul's expected execution (4:6–8).

Everything in the letter reflects these matters, including the thanksgiving (1:3–5) and the concluding personal matters and instructions (4:9–18). The body of the letter is comprised of three major appeals to loyalty (1:6–2:13; 2:14–3:9; 3:10–4:8), each of which follows a similar ABA pattern, which together create the same pattern for the whole letter. In the first appeal it is loyalty-defection-loyalty (1:6–14/1:15–18/2:1–13); in the second it is opposition-loyalty-opposition (2:14–19/2:20–26/3:1–9); in the third it is Paul's loyalty-appeal-Paul's loyalty (3:10–12/3:14–4:2, 5/4:6–8), interspersed with notes about opposition and desertion (3:13; 4:3–4). In the larger picture, the first and third sections are mostly appeal, while the sandwiched section is mostly about the opposition.

SPECIFIC ADVICE FOR READING 2 TIMOTHY

This letter does not fit comfortably the category Pastoral Epistle (see "Overview of 1 Timothy, pp. 373–74), in the sense of offering instruction on church matters to a young pastor. But it is certainly pastoral in the sense of Paul's concern for Timothy personally, which is intertwined with his concern for Christ and the gospel. You may want to mark these instances as you read.

Second Timothy is not the first letter we have from Paul while he was "chained" (2:9). But in contrast to the earlier ones (Philippians, Colossians, Ephesians, Philemon), where he expects to be released (Phil 1:24; 2:23–24; Phlm 22), here he just as clearly expects to be executed (2 Tim 4:6–9, 16–18). Although this adds a dimension of poignancy to the whole (the desertions are obviously painful, 1:15; 4:9–12), there is no despair. To the contrary, hardship is simply part of the package (1:8; 2:3; 3:12; 4:5). You cannot miss the note of Christ's triumph over death and his bringing life, which rings out loud and clear (1:10; 2:8–10, 11–12a; 4:8, 18).

Even the long section condemning the false teachers (2:14–3:9) is interlaced with words of hope: "The Lord knows those who are his" (2:19, echoing Num 16:5). This section also helps to substantiate what you learned about the false teachers in 1 Timothy: They like to quarrel over words (2 Tim 2:14, 23); they have wandered away from the truth, arguing that the resurrection has already taken place (2:18); they have had noteworthy success among some "gullible women" (3:6–7); and their lifestyle does not conform to the gospel (3:1–5).

A WALK THROUGH 2 TIMOTHY

☐ 1:1–5 *Salutation and Thanksgiving*

Be on the lookout for the significance of the words in the salutation, "in keeping with the promise of life," for the rest of the letter. And note how, in contrast to 1 Timothy and Titus, which are more businesslike, this letter has a thanksgiving, which also (typically) anticipates much that is in the letter; note especially the emphasis on Paul's and Timothy's relationship, and on Timothy's loyalty to the faith of his forbears.

☐ 1:6–2:13 *First Appeal*

The first appeal sets the tone for the whole; it is basically twofold—for Timothy to (1) join Paul in suffering for the gospel (v. 8) and (2) guard what has been entrusted to him (v. 13–14). The basis of the appeal is the work of the Spirit (vv. 6–7, 14), Christ and the gospel (vv. 9–10), and Paul's example (vv. 11–12).

The appeal is then interrupted to set in contrast the many who were not loyal (v. 15) and one who was (Onesiphorus, vv. 16–18).

Note the new twist when the appeal is renewed (2:1–13): Timothy must entrust to others what has been entrusted to him (v. 2)—because he is being pulled out of Ephesus. After a series of analogies emphasizing loyalty, single-mindedness, and expectation of final reward (vv. 3–7), Paul reinforces the appeal once more by reminding Timothy of Christ and of Paul himself (vv. 8–10), concluding with a "trustworthy saying" (vv. 11–13) that emphasizes God's faithfulness, no matter what.

☐ 2:14–3:9 *Context for the Appeal: The False Teachers*

You will want to notice that, as in 1 Timothy, words to Timothy are set in the context of the false teachers. The first warning against the false teachers (2 Tim 2:14–18) emphasizes their "quarreling about words" and "godless chatter" and their corrosive influence. Yet God "knows those who are his," and these "must turn away from wickedness" (v. 19, which prepares the way for what follows).

The contrasting appeal to Timothy (2:20–26) starts with an analogy (he must cleanse himself and the church of articles used for refuse) before emphasizing the need for a gentle, not quarrelsome, spirit—even in dealing with the opponents.

Paul returns to the false teachers in 3:1–9, describing their gruesome self-centeredness (vv. 1–5) and their deceitful sway over some "gullible women" (vv. 6–7), comparing them to the Egyptian sorcerers (vv. 8–9).

□ 3:10–4:8 *Final Appeal*

The first appeal focused primarily on Christ and the gospel; this appeal focuses primarily on Timothy's long relationship to Paul, and Paul's own modeling of the gospel (3:10–13; 4:6–8). These two passages sandwich the appeal itself, first to Timothy's own past (3:14–17), and second to Timothy's ministry, given the many defections from the truth (4:1–5).

□ 4:9–18 *The First Reason for the Letter*

Paul concludes with his primary reason for writing in the first place—to urge Timothy to come quickly (before winter, v. 21) and bring some personal things with him (vv. 9, 13). This is said against the backdrop of deserters and some others having been sent out on ministry (vv. 10–12). Since Timothy will come through Troas, Paul warns him about Alexander (vv. 14–15). He concludes with information about his "first defense" (= a kind of grand-jury inquiry), which for him was a moment of triumph for the gospel. Rescued from the "lion's mouth" in this first instance, he nonetheless looks forward to the heavenly kingdom.

□ 4:19–22 *Final Greetings*

Unlike 1 Timothy, 2 Timothy is more truly a letter in its overall style; thus it concludes with greetings to and from friends, plus the grace-benediction.

With this letter Paul's role in the biblical story comes to an end. Since we are so much in his debt, we would do well to heed carefully the appeals to loyalty in this letter.

Titus

ORIENTING DATA FOR TITUS

- **Content:** instructions to Titus for setting in order the church(es) on Crete, including the appointment of qualified elders and the instruction of various social groups, set against the backdrop of some false teachers
- **Author:** the apostle Paul (although doubted by many)
- **Date:** ca. A.D. 62–63, apparently from Macedonia at about the same time as 1 Timothy (see 3:12; Nicopolis is on the Adriatic coast of Macedonia)
- **Recipient(s):** Titus, a Gentile and sometime traveling companion of Paul (see Gal 2:1–3; 2 Cor 7:6–16; 8:6, 16–24; 12:17–18); and the churches on Crete (Titus 3:15, "you all")
- **Occasion:** Paul had left Titus on Crete to finish setting the churches in order, while he and Timothy (apparently) went on to Ephesus, where they met a very distressing situation (see 1 Timothy). But Paul had to go on to Macedonia (1 Tim 1:3; cf. Phil 2:19–24); perhaps the Holy Spirit reminded him while writing 1 Timothy that some similar problems had emerged in Crete, so he addressed the churches through a letter to Titus
- **Emphases:** God's people must be and do good—this is especially true of church leaders; the gospel of grace stands over against false teachings based on the Jewish law

OVERVIEW OF TITUS

In some ways Titus appears to be a smaller version of 1 Timothy, where false teaching prompted instruction on qualifications for church leadership; at the same time Paul addresses other matters that the false teachers have triggered. Hence, both the qualifications for elders and the indictment of the false teachers have some striking similarities to what is said about them in 1 Timothy.

But there are also some significant differences. The most noteworthy is the fact that *Timothy* was left in a situation where the church had been in existence for nearly twelve years, and he had to deal with elders who were leading the church astray. *Titus* has been left in Crete to set new churches in order. Thus, in this case, Paul begins with the qualifications for church leaders (1:5–9), before taking on the false teachers (1:10–16). This is followed by general instructions on how to deal with older and younger men and women and with slaves, with emphasis on doing good (2:1–10), which looks like an expansion of 1 Timothy 5:1–2 and 6:1–2. The rest of the letter then emphasizes, in light of the grace of God, their "doing good" in the world (2:11–3:8), which is again set in contrast to the false teachers (3:9–11).

SPECIFIC ADVICE FOR READING TITUS

While problems with the false teachers lie behind much of what is said in Titus, they do not seem to be such a dominant factor as in 1 Timothy. They themselves are to be silenced (Titus 1:11), while people who would follow them must be rebuked (1:13). There are enough similarities with 1 Timothy to make one think that the same kind of teaching is in view: They are into Jewish myths (Titus 1:14) and genealogies (3:9), based on the law (3:9); they love controversies (1:10; 3:9); they are deceivers (1:10) and lovers of money (1:11); and they use the law (apparently) to promote ascetic practices (1:15). This final item gets more emphasis in Titus, which Paul responds to with a much greater emphasis both on grace and on doing good.

So as you read, look especially for Paul's emphasis on *doing good.* Although found also in 1 Timothy (1 Tim 2:10; 5:10), this theme permeates Titus (Titus 1:16; 2:7, 14; 3:1, 8, 14; cf. 1:8). For Paul there is no tension between grace and doing what is good. The latter is the proper issue of the former. What is at odds with grace is the "religious" use of the law, maintaining purity through observance of regulations, as a way of maintaining God's favor. But a genuine experience of grace results in a people who are eager to do good (2:14). Thus these two themes merge in two great theological passages (2:11–14; 3:4–7), the latter of which constitutes another of the five trustworthy sayings in these letters.

A WALK THROUGH TITUS

☐ 1:1–4 *Salutation*

As with 1 Timothy, and in contrast to 2 Timothy, this letter is more "business" than personal, thus it lacks a thanksgiving/prayer report. For whose sake (Titus's or the churches'), do you think, is the long elaboration on Paul's apostleship? After you've read through the whole letter, you might want to come back to this passage and list the ways it anticipates items in the letter.

☐ 1:5–9 *Appointing Elders*

This list is very similar to 1 Timothy 3:2–7. The fact that "appointment" is in view here (not "replacement") is expressly stated (Titus 1:5), which also accounts for the one major difference with 1 Timothy, namely, the *duties* mentioned in Titus 1:9. On their being "hospitable" (v. 8), see 3 John. And don't miss the next item in Titus 1:8: They are to "love what is good."

☐ 1:10–16 *Opposing False Teachers*

The false teachers must be silenced because they play right into the hands of a proverbial understanding of Cretans. Believers who would be tempted to follow them must be rebuked. Again note how the section ends: These people are "unfit for doing anything good."

☐ 2:1–10 *Godly Living for Various Social Groups*

Picking up the same four groups as in 1 Timothy 5:1–2, plus the slaves from 6:1–2, Paul gives instructions on "sound doctrine" (medical imagery for being healthy) for older men, older women, younger women, younger men, and slaves. Note how often the reasons given for godly living are for the sake of those on the outside (Titus 2:5, 8, 10). Again, note verse 7: Titus is to set an example "by doing what is good."

☐ 2:11–15 *The Basis for Godly Living*

Now Titus is given the theological bases for the preceding instructions—the grace of God, our future hope, and Christ's redemption, which has as its goal a people of his own, who are "eager to do what is good" (v. 14).

□ 3:1–8 *The People of God in the World*

As in 2:1–10, notice how "doing good" is pointed outward—how to live in a godly manner for the sake of an ungodly world (3:1–2), since we were once there ourselves (v. 3). The basis for such living is salvation wrought by the Triune God (vv. 4–7)—rebirth initiated by God's love and effected through Christ's justifying grace and the renewing work of the Holy Spirit, who is poured out on us generously through Christ. Verse 8 offers the motive.

□ 3:9–11 *Final Indictment of the False Teachers*

You might want to compare what is said here with 1:10–16. Thus the letter signs off the way it began.

□ 3:12–15 *Concluding Personal Notes and Greetings*

Note that after some personal words to Titus about his and others' comings and goings (vv. 12–13), Paul hits the main theme of "doing what is good" one final time (v. 14), before a concluding exchange of greetings and the grace-benediction.

The significance of this letter for the biblical story is Paul's insistence that grace and doing good belong together, as long as the latter is not confused with religious observances.

Philemon

ORIENTING DATA FOR PHILEMON

- **Content:** the sole purpose of this letter is to secure forgiveness for a (probably runaway) slave named Onesimus
- **Author:** the apostle Paul, joined by his younger companion Timothy
- **Date:** probably A.D. 60–61 (see "Orienting Data for Colossians," p. 359).
- **Recipient(s):** Philemon is a Gentile believer in Colosse (see Col 4:9), in whose house a church meets; the salutation and final greeting indicate that Paul expected Philemon to share the letter with the church
- **Occasion:** Onesimus has recently been converted and has been serving Paul, who is in prison; now Onesimus is being sent back to Philemon, accompanied by Tychicus, who is also carrying letters to the churches in Colosse (Colossians) and Asia (Ephesians)
- **Emphasis:** the gospel reconciles people to one another, not only Jew (Paul) and Gentile (Philemon), but also (runaway) slave and master, making them all brothers!

OVERVIEW OF PHILEMON

This, the shortest of Paul's letters, was an extremely delicate letter to write. Paul is explicitly asking forgiveness for a crime that deserved punishment (Onesimus's crime)—and implicitly for another crime that could have been brought before the proper authorities (Paul's harboring a runaway slave).

You will want to observe how carefully Paul puts all of this into gospel perspective, beginning with the prayer and thanksgiving (vv. 4–7), where he praises God for the way the gospel has already been at work in Philemon's life. Note especially that Paul refuses to lean on his apostolic authority (see vv. 1, 8–10, 17, 21); rather, he appeals on the basis of the gospel of love (vv. 8–11). He also reminds Philemon that he, too, is one of Paul's converts (v. 19), whom he regards now as a "partner" in the gospel (v. 17).

Verses 12–16 are the coup. Onesimus has really been in the service of Philemon without his knowing it, and his having been a runaway may finally serve the greater interests of all, especially the gospel. Even though Onesimus is returning as a repentant slave, the first relationship between slave and master, Paul reminds Philemon, is that of brother in Christ.

SPECIFIC ADVICE FOR READING PHILEMON

Slavery in the first-century Greco-Roman world was not based on capture and race, as in North American (and European) history, but, by Paul's time, on economics—and birth. But even household slaves, as Onesimus probably was, were at the bottom of the social ladder, having absolutely no rights under Roman law. Thus they could be treated as a master willed, and runaways were often crucified as a deterrent to other slaves.

So imagine yourself in Onesimus's shoes. Apparently he had stolen from Philemon (vv. 18–19) and run away as far as he could get (Rome). But he became repentant, fell in with Paul, who was in prison in Rome, and now, back home, stands in the midst of the Christian community, while Colossians and this letter are read to the congregation. How do you think you would feel?

But we may surmise that the letter had already been read by Philemon so that the reading of it in church was a public expression of Philemon's acceptance of both Paul's letter and his wishes. You might also want to go back and do a quick reread of Colossians, keeping in mind that the Colossian believers are hearing it read with Onesimus present and that they, too, must accept Onesimus back as "a dear brother" in Christ.

Did the letter work? Of course it did; it is hard to imagine either of these letters being preserved if it hadn't! Whether this Onesimus is the one who eventually became overseer of the church in Ephesus cannot be known for certain, but Christian tradition believed it so. We know about him from Ignatius, who, on his way to Rome to be martyred, wrote to the church in Ephesus: "In God's name, therefore, I received your large congregation in the person of Onesimus, your bishop in this world, a man whose love is beyond words. My prayer is that you should love him in the Spirit of Jesus Christ and all be like him. Blessed is he who let you have such a bishop. You deserved it." The gospel does things like that!

A WALK THROUGH PHILEMON

☐ 1–3 *Salutation*

Fortunately, the salutation proper gives us a lot of helpful information noted under "Orienting Data for Philemon." (Apphia is probably Philemon's wife; in light of Col 4:17, Archippus is likely a teacher in the church). In any case, be certain that Onesimus's return will affect the whole household, as well as the church.

☐ 4–7 *Thanksgiving and Prayer*

As in Paul's other thanksgiving and prayer reports, he thanks God and prays mostly for the effects of the gospel in Philemon's life. Note the emphasis on love and faith (v. 5), which are then elaborated in reverse order in verses 6 and 7; note also how the end of verse 7 anticipates what is coming.

☐ 8–21 *The Appeal*

Watch for the wordplay on Onesimus's name in verses 10–11. The formerly-useless-now-useful one is urged not only to be welcomed (v. 17), but taken back as a "brother in the Lord." It is not clear how Paul could have repaid Onesimus's debt (vv. 18–19)—after all, Paul is in prison and wholly dependent on outside help himself! He surely expects Philemon to wipe the slate clean, but just in case, he models the gospel by taking on the debt himself.

☐ 22–25 *Personal Word and Greetings*

Verse 22 indicates that Paul expects release from this imprisonment (cf. Phil 1:24; 2:23–24), a concern that in this case takes the place of "greet all the saints," which usually occurs. You may wish to compare the greetings in Philemon 23–24 with those in Colossians 4:10–15.

This semiprivate letter is in our Bibles because the truth of the gospel lies not only in its history and the theological interpretation of that history; it is also anecdotal. God's story has been told a million times over in stories like this one.

Hebrews

ORIENTING DATA FOR HEBREWS

- **Content:** a "word of exhortation" (13:22) sent in letter form, encouraging faithful perseverance in light of the superlative final word God has spoken in Christ
- **Author:** unknown; a second-generation believer (2:3), who was a skilled preacher and interpreter of Scripture, with an excellent command of Greek (it came into the canon among Paul's letters, but definitely not by him)
- **Date:** unknown; guesses range from A.D. 50 to 90; probably before 70 (since the author gives no hint that the Jewish temple has been destroyed)
- **Recipients:** an unknown but specific group of (predominantly) Jewish Christians; perhaps a house church in Rome (13:24) that is opting out of relationships with the larger Christian community (10:25; 13:7, 17)
- **Occasion:** the community is discouraged because of suffering (10:35–39) and perhaps from doubts about whether Jesus really took care of sin; the author writes to convince them to "not throw away your confidence" (10:35; cf. 2:1; 4:14)
- **Emphases:** God has spoken his absolutely final word in his Son; to abandon Christ is to abandon God altogether; Christ is superior to everything that went before—the old revelation, its angelic mediators, the first exodus (Moses and Joshua), and the whole priestly system; God's people can have full confidence in God's Son, the perfect high priest, who gives all people ready access to God

OVERVIEW OF HEBREWS

Hebrews is a long, sustained argument, in which the author moves back and forth between an argument (based on Scripture) and exhortation. What drives the argument from beginning to end is the absolute superiority of the Son of God to everything that has gone before; this is what his *exposition of Scripture* is all about. What concerns the author is the possibility that some believers under present distress will let go of Christ and thus lose out on the Son's saving work and high priestly intercession, and thus their own experience of God's presence; this is what the interspersed *exhortations* are all about.

The introduction (1:1–3) sets the pattern with a sevenfold description of the Son and his work that makes him God's last word. This is followed by a series of two major arguments (1:4–4:13; 4:14–10:18), each with several subsets, and a final major application and exhortation (10:19–13:21), in this case interlaced with some further biblical arguments.

Part 1 is all about the Son—his superiority to angels despite (and because of!) his humanity (1:4–2:18), to Moses (3:1–19), and to Joshua (4:1–13). Here the author also sets the stage for part 2: Christ's effective high priestly ministry is made possible through the preexistent and now exalted Son's having become incarnate. And the failure of the first exodus lay not with Moses and Joshua, but with the people's failure to faithfully persevere; the readers are urged not to follow in their footsteps.

Part 2 is all about the Son as the perfect high priest. After a transitional exhortation (4:14–16), the author then introduces Jesus as high priest (5:1–10), followed by a series of two warnings and an encouragement (5:11–6:3 [slacking off]; 6:4–8 [apostasy]; 6:9–20 [God's sure promises]). Then, drawing on the royal messianic Psalm 110, he uses Melchizedek as a pattern for a priesthood of a higher order (7:1–28). Based on a new, thus superior, covenant, the perfect priest offered the perfect (once-for-all) sacrifice in the perfect sanctuary (8:1–10:18).

Part 3 is all about faithful perseverance. It begins with an appeal—in light of all this, "let us ..." (10:19–25)—followed by warning (10:26–31), encouragement (10:32–39), example (11:1–12:3), instruction (12:4–13), and another warning (12:14–17). Finally, using marvelous imagery that contrasts Mount Sinai with the heavenly Mount Zion, the author affirms their future certainty (12:18–29), then concludes with very practical exhortations about life in the present (13:1–25).

You will want to watch how the author makes this work—by a series of seven expositions of key Old Testament texts, while making the transition between each by way of exhortation: (1) Psalm 8:4–6 in Hebrews 2:5–18; (2) Psalm 95:7–11 in 3:7–4:13; (3) Psalm 110:4 in 4:16–7:28; (4) Jeremiah 31:31–34 in 8:1–10:18; (5) Habakkuk 2:3–4 in 10:32–12:3; (6) Proverbs 3:11–12 in 12:4–13; and (7) the Sinai theophany (Exod 19) in 12:18–29.

SPECIFIC ADVICE FOR READING HEBREWS

Most contemporary Christians do not find Hebrews an easy read, for at least two reasons: (1) its structure (just noted) of a single, sustained argument, interlaced with application and exhortations, and (2) the author's thought-world (basic ways of perceiving reality), which is so foreign to ours. Thus there are two keys to a good reading.

First, keep in sight the two foci that concern the author throughout: (1) the overwhelming majesty of Jesus, the Son of God, who stands at the beginning and the end of all things and whose suffering in his incarnation made him a perfect high priest on their behalf (he both dealt with sin finally and perfectly and is also a merciful and empathetic intercessor), and (2) all of this is spoken into the present despondency of the people to whom he writes, who have had a long siege of hardship (10:32–39) and who are beginning to wonder whether Jesus really is God's final answer. Try to put yourself in their shoes: Jews who had long ago put their trust in Christ, believing that at long last the fulfillment of their messianic hopes had come—only to have suffering (and sin) continue long after they had first believed.

Second, since everything for him (and them) hinges on his exposition of Scripture as pointing to Christ, it is especially important for you to have a sense of how the writer of Hebrews uses Scripture and what Scriptures he actually uses.

Four things are important about his use of Scripture: (1) His and their only Bible was the Septuagint, the Greek translation of the Hebrew Bible. This means at times that his citations, which are very exact, do not always read as does your Old Testament, and sometimes his point is made from the wording in the Greek Bible. (2) He regularly uses a very common rabbinic way of arguing, namely, "from the lesser to the greater" (= if something is true of *a*, how much more so of *z*). (3) He reads the entire Old Testament through the lens of Christ, understanding well that the royal psalms point to David's greater son, the Messiah. (4) His form of scriptural argument is to cite his text and then show how other texts and the event of Christ support his reading of these texts.

It is especially important for you to be aware of what Scripture the author actually cites and then argues from. For example, even though he alludes to the sacrificial system in 9:1–10:18, he never cites from Leviticus. Rather, he focuses his argument almost altogether on Jesus as fulfilling a key royal psalm—Psalm 110. At the same time he presupposes that Jesus also fulfills the first royal psalm—Psalm 2. The latter declares that the Messiah is God's Son (Ps 2:7), which is the very *first* thing the author says in his introduction (Heb 1:2). He then elaborates in terms of the Son's being heir (as well as the Creator and Sustainer) of the universe, and of his being "the radiance of God's glory and the exact representation of his being." Psalm 2:7, joined with the Davidic covenant (2 Sam 7:14), is then the first citation (Heb 1:5) in the series of proof texts that follow. You will find it cited again—for the final time—in 5:5, where it is joined with a citation from Psalm 110:4.

Observe next how the *last* thing said in the introduction of the Son (Heb 1:1–3) is that he "provided purification for sins" and "sat down at the right hand of the Majesty in heaven." These allusions to Psalm 110 (vv. 4, 1) are then picked up as the final citation in the following series (Heb 1:13). Thus in this one messianic psalm, you find two crucial matters: (1) the Son, now called "Lord," is seated at the right hand of God (Ps 110:1), the place of his high priestly ministry (see Heb 8:1; 10:12; 12:2), and (2) God by oath promised that the exalted King/Son will also be a priest forever in the order of Melchizedek (Ps 110:4). So after the author joins Psalm 110:4 to Psalm 2:7 in 5:5–6, the rest of the argument from that point on will be about Christ's fulfilling this promise.

Now add to these points the following: (1) the failure of Israel to enter into rest (Heb 3–4, based on Ps 95); (2) the fact that God promised a new covenant (Jer 31:31–34, cited in full in Heb 8:8–12); (3) the fact that Christ's death effected both that new covenant and a perfect, once-for-all sacrifice for sins (9:1–10:18, thus bringing the old order to an end); (4) the long list (ch. 11) of those who faithfully persevered as they awaited the future promise; and (5) the concluding analogy in 12:18–29 of the superiority of heavenly Zion to Mount Sinai—and you should be able to see not only where the whole argument is going but also how persuasive it should have been for these early Jewish Christians. So read and enjoy!

A WALK THROUGH HEBREWS

☐ 1:1–3 *Introduction*

Watch how these verses offer a true introduction to the argument: The Son, who is superior to the prophets, is the heir of all things; he also stands at the beginning of all things. Moreover, he who is God's glory, being his exact representation, also presently sustains all things; and it is he who dealt with sin and now sits at the place of authority at God's right hand.

☐ 1:4–4:13 *The Supremacy of God's Son*

Here you enter at once into the author's way of arguing, as he begins with a series of Old Testament quotations (1:4–14) that do two things simultaneously—show the Son's superiority to angels and support the affirmations of verses 2–3.

After an initial warning (2:1–4), he expounds Psalm 8:4–6 to argue for the significance of the Incarnation: The Son was made "lower than the angels" for a brief time so that he could (1) fully identity with us, (2) through his sufferings effect salvation for us, and (3) thus also become a merciful high priest for us—and therefore be better than the angels.

Next you come to the author's contrast with Moses (Heb 3:1–6; note the form of argument, from the lesser to the greater). The mention of Christ's superiority to Moses leads to exhortation and warning, based on Psalm 95:7–11, that those who are Christ's must not follow in the unbelief (= lack of faithful obedience) of those who belonged to Moses (Heb 3:7–19). Watch how this in turn leads to a further exposition on the theme of entering God's rest (4:1–10; from Ps 95:11), which the first Joshua ("Jesus" in Greek) did not secure, and which now awaits those who persevere. The transitional exhortation (Heb 4:11–13) serves to remind the Jewish Christians of the certainty of God's word.

☐ 4:14–10:18 *The Supremacy of the Son's High Priesthood*

In this section you will encounter the author's long, sustained argument about Jesus as the ultimate high priest. The theme is introduced by way of a transitional exhortation (4:14–16), which picks up the theme from 2:17–3:1 and urges that Christ as high priest makes it possible for all people, not just priests, to "approach God's throne of grace with confidence, so that we may receive mercy"—because Christ also shared our humanity, with all of its suffering.

The sustained argument then begins in 5:1–10 with an exposition of Psalm 110:1 and 4, emphasizing first the humanity and duties of priests and their divine appointment, before citing the two royal psalms and showing how Jesus' humanity and suffering qualified him for priestly service—but now of a new and higher order, namely, that of Melchizedek.

Before the author elaborates this point, he feels constrained to remonstrate with them over their slowness to become mature (Heb 5:11–6:3), which leads to a warning against apostasy (6:4–8), but note that he concludes with encouragement (6:9–12). As he begins to move back to the exposition about Melchizedek, he argues that God's promise (Ps 110:4, about the Messiah's priesthood) is confirmed by his oath in the same verse, thus making his promise absolutely guaranteed (Heb 6:13–20).

The exposition about Melchizedek is in two parts: First (7:1–10), the author draws on the Genesis account (Gen 14:18–20) and glories in Melchizedek's lack of a genealogy (no predecessor or human successor) and in the fact that Levi (understood to be present in Abraham's loins) is already foreshadowed as inferior to the greater; second (Heb 7:11–28), the author shows that, by fitting the Melchizedek order, Christ's priesthood is both legitimate and superior to that of Aaron.

Not only so, but (8:1–6) Christ's priesthood takes place in a superior sanctuary (heaven itself; note the allusion to Ps 110:1 in Heb 8:1) and is based on the new (and thus superior) covenant promised in Jeremiah (Heb 8:7–13). Watch how the exposition that follows shows how Christ, the perfect "sacrificer," is also the superior (perfect) sacrifice (9:1–10:18). After describing the old (9:1–10), he shows how Christ's sacrifice of himself both obtained eternal redemption (9:11–14) and mediated the new covenant through his death (9:15–22). He then summarizes the argument and brings it to a conclusion (9:23–10:18) by emphasizing the eternal, "once for all time" nature of Christ's sacrifice (no condemnation for past or present sins!).

□ 10:19–12:29 *Final Exhortation to Perseverance*

Note how the author's concerns emerge in the five "let us" exhortations in 10:22–25, based on the sure work of Christ (vv. 19–21): Let us draw near to God (we now have access to the Most Holy Place!); let us hold fast to our hope; let us spur one another on toward love and good deeds; let us not forsake meeting together with others; and let us encourage one another. After a strong warning against deliberate sin (grace does not mean license; vv. 26–31), he urges perseverance (vv. 32–39), citing Habakkuk 2:3–4.

The exposition of the Habakkuk text that follows (Heb 11:1–12:3) is so well known that it is easy to miss what is going on. Note that the author's singular point is the faith (faithful perseverance) of many who did not "shrink back" (10:39)—despite adversity and not obtaining the promised future; at the same time he insists that we are in continuity with these believers and they with us, since the promise has now been realized as we all await the glorious future. He concludes by pointing his readers once more to Jesus as an example of endurance in suffering (12:1–3).

Besides, he goes on (with an exposition of Prov 3:11–12), there is an educative dimension to suffering. After a final exhortation to holy living in community (Heb 12:14–17), he concludes with the analogy of the two mountains (12:18–24), including both warning and encouragement (12:25–29).

☐ 13:1–25 *Concluding Practical Exhortations and Greetings*

Watch for the ways these exhortations emphasize his readers' need to love others in the community and to submit to their leaders, all the while still contrasting Christ with what has preceded him (thus, e.g., the sacrificial system is out, but a sacrifice of praise and of doing good to others is in [vv. 15–16]).

This is an especially important document in the biblical story in that it shows both the continuity of the new with the old (Christ has fulfilled the old, thus completing its purpose) and the nature of discontinuity (the people of God are now newly constituted through God's royal Son and the Spirit)—all of this by the one and only living God.

James

ORIENTING DATA FOR JAMES

- **Content:** a treatise composed of short moral essays, emphasizing endurance in hardship and responsible Christian living, with special concern that believers practice what they preach and live together in harmony
- **Author:** James, brother of our Lord (Gal 1:19), who led the church in Jerusalem for many years (Acts 15; Gal 2:1–13)—although questioned by many
- **Date:** unknown; dated anywhere from the mid–40s A.D. to the 90s, depending on authorship; probably earlier than later
- **Recipients:** believers in Christ among the Jewish Diaspora
- **Occasion:** unknown, but the treatise shows concern for real conditions in the churches, including severe trials, dissensions caused by angry and judgmental words, and abuse of the poor by the wealthy
- **Emphases:** practical faith on the part of believers; joy and patience in the midst of trials; the nature of true (Christian) wisdom; attitudes of the rich toward the poor; abuse and proper use of the tongue

OVERVIEW OF JAMES

Traditionally James has been read as a more or less random collection of ethical instructions for believers in general. But there is probably more order to it than first meets the eye. The main concerns are mapped out in 1:2–18, which basically takes the form of consolation to believers in exile: Trials may serve to test for the good (vv. 2–4, 12) or tempt toward evil (vv. 13–15); wisdom is God's good gift for enduring and profiting from trials (vv. 5–8, 16–18); in God's eyes the low and high position of poor and rich are reversed (vv. 9–11).

The next section (1:19–2:26) is in three parts, held together by James's concern that his hearers put their faith into practice—at the very practical level of one's speech and of caring for the poor. He begins by denouncing community dissension, insisting that people actually do what the word says, not just talk about it (1:19–25). This is applied specifically to the tongue and to caring for the poor (vv. 26–27) and then to wrong attitudes toward the rich and the poor (2:1–13). He concludes the section where he began, by insisting that faith must be accompanied by deeds appropriate to faith (vv. 14–26).

The next section (3:1–4:12) returns to the matter of dissension within the believing communities. He starts with the perennial problem child—the tongue (3:1–12; cf. 1:26), which in this case is aimed at their teachers in particular. Returning to the theme of true wisdom, which leads to peace (3:13–18; cf. 1:5–8), James then attacks their quarrels head-on (4:1–12).

Related to the way that the first mention of wisdom (1:5–8) is followed by a blessing of the poor and warnings to the rich, here in reverse order there is a twofold word to the rich (4:13–17; 5:1–6) and a call to patience on the part of the suffering poor (5:7–11). The letter concludes with a warning against oaths (v. 12), a call to prayer—especially prayer for the sick (vv. 13–18)—and correction of the wayward (vv. 19–20).

SPECIFIC ADVICE FOR READING JAMES

James is admittedly difficult to read through, because of its many starts and stops, twists and turns. But along with seeing the threads that hold things together, which we noted above, several other matters should help you to read this letter with better understanding.

First, in terms of content, you will find the letter to have a variety of kinds of material in it, all of it directed specifically at Christian behavior, rather than propounding Christian doctrine. Included are a goodly number of sayings or aphorisms that look like Old Testament wisdom on the one hand and the teachings of Jesus on the other. That is, much as the Synoptic Gospels often present the teaching of Jesus in the form of sayings—which at times ring with echoes of Jewish wisdom—so with James. This is found both in his emphasis on wisdom as such and in the frequent aphoristic nature of so much that he says. In this vein you should also look for his frequent echoes of the teachings of Jesus (e.g., 1:5–6; 2:8; 5:9, 12). As with all Jewish wisdom (see the introduction to the Old Testament Writings, p. 120), the concern is not doctrinal or logical, but practical; the test of its truthfulness has to do with how it works out in the reality of everyday life.

Second, in terms of form, you will find a kind of sermonic quality to James. As you read, note the various rhetorical devices he employs, especially some that reflect the Greco-Roman diatribe (see "Specific Advice for Reading Romans," p. 319)—direct address ("my [dear] brothers and sisters" 14*x*), rhetorical questions (e.g., Jas 2:3–7, 14, 21; 3:11–12, 13; 4:1, 5), and the use of an imagined interlocutor (2:18–20; 4:12, 13, 15). Thus James's use of the Wisdom tradition is not proverbial but sermonic; he hopes to persuade and thus to facilitate change in the way God's people live in community with one another.

Third, don't fall into the habit, which is easy in this case, of reading James as though it were addressed to individual believers about their one-on-one relationship with God and others. Nothing could be further from James's own concerns. From the outset his passion is with life within the believing community. While it is true that each must assume his or her individual responsibility to make the community healthy, the concern is not with personal piety as much as it is with healthy communities. To miss this point will cause you to miss what drives this letter from beginning to end.

Finally, you need to read the sections about the rich and poor with care (1:9–11, 27; 2:1–13; 4:13–5:6), since it is not easy to tell whether both groups are members of the believing community. In any case, James is decidedly—as is the whole of Scripture—on the side of the poor. The rich are consistently censured and judged, not because of their wealth per se, but because it has caused them to live without taking God into account and thus to abuse the lowly ones for whom God cares.

A WALK THROUGH JAMES

☐ 1:1–18 *Salutation and Introduction to the Themes*

Here James introduces most of his major concerns. Note how, after a letter-type salutation (v. 1), he jumps immediately into the issue of trials, urging joy because trials develop perseverance and lead to maturity (vv. 2–4; anticipating 5:7–11). Next he urges prayer for wisdom (1:5; anticipating 3:13–18), insisting that prayer must be accompanied by faith to be effective (1:6–8; anticipating 5:13–18). That leads to the major concern about the poor and rich, offering hope to the former and warning the latter (1:9–11; anticipating 1:27–2:13; 4:13–5:6); here note the echoes of Isaiah 40:6–8, which is also expressed in a context of comfort for exiles. Returning to the matter of trials and testing, he notes that they can lead beyond testing to *temptation* (only one Greek word for both ideas), for which God is not to be blamed (Jas 1:12–15), concluding that God instead gives only good gifts, especially "birth through the word of truth" (vv. 16–18).

☐ 1:19–2:26 *Putting the Faith into Practice*

As you read this section, think about what gives it a measure of cohesion. Starting with anger and the tongue, James moves next to urge that his readers live out the word they hear, especially regarding the tongue and caring for the poor (1:19–27). To care for the poor means to show no favoritism toward the rich; to do so is sin, and to do otherwise—to lack mercy—means to come under judgment (2:1–13). Finally, he attacks those who understand faith as mere verbal assent to doctrines believed; to speak about faith without tangibly caring for the poor—that is, faith without action—is to be dead (vv. 14–26).

☐ 3:1–4:12 *Dissension in the Community*

You may wish to go back and reread 1:19–27 before you read this section. Here James turns to the large issue of dissension in the believing communities, beginning with what has become the classic exposition of the use and abuse of the tongue (3:1–12); the tongue is "a restless evil, full of deadly poison" (v. 8). Can you relate? Similar to the preceding admonition against "faith without deeds," here he is concerned about the same tongue being used to praise God and curse others.

This in turn leads directly to a return to the theme of wisdom (3:13–18), contrasting godly wisdom with what is false and insisting on true wisdom as being pure and peace-loving.

Note that these two matters (the tongue and wisdom) together serve to introduce the crucial issue of quarreling within the believing community (4:1–12). In turn, James exposes its sinful roots (vv. 1–3), its worldliness (vv. 4–5), and the need for humility (vv. 6–10), returning at the end to the abuse of the tongue in judging one another (vv. 11–12).

☐ 4:13–5:11 *To the Rich and the Poor*

Note that this is the third time James takes up the issue of the rich and the poor, suggesting that it is a major concern. Although we cannot be sure, he seems to speak first to wealthy believers, who treat their business in a worldly fashion (4:13–17). This is followed by a harsh denunciation of wealthy farmers (apparently unbelievers), who abuse their workers by underpaying them (5:1–6).

Finally, returning to the issue of trials, probably in this case to the suffering poor, he once more urges perseverance (vv. 7–11; cf. 1:3).

□ 5:12–20 *Concluding Exhortations*

The concluding exhortations seem somewhat more loosely connected to what has preceded. He begins with oaths (v. 12), clearly echoing the teaching of Jesus (Matt 5:33–37); he then turns to prayer and faith (Jas 5:13–18; cf. 1:6–8), especially showing concern for the poor (the "sick" in this case). He concludes with a blessing on those who restore the wanderer (5:19–20). Note the lack of any letter-type conclusion.

James is the New Testament counterpart of the Jewish Wisdom tradition, now in light of the teachings of Jesus. Although James is sometimes read in contrast to Paul, both James and Paul are, in fact, absolutely together at the crucial point made by James throughout his letter, namely, that the first thing one does with one's faith is to live by it (cf. Gal 5:6).

1 Peter

ORIENTING DATA FOR 1 PETER

- **Content:** a letter of encouragement to Christians undergoing suffering, instructing them how to respond Christianly to their persecutors and urging them to live lives worthy of their calling
- **Author:** the apostle Peter; written by Silas (5:12), the sometime companion of Paul
- **Date:** ca. A.D. 64–65 from Rome (5:13, Babylon was used by both Jews and Christians to refer to Rome as a place of exile)
- **Recipients:** mostly Gentile believers (1:14, 18; 2:9–10; 4:3–4) in the five provinces in the northwest quadrant of Asia Minor (modern Turkey), referred to—with a play on the Jewish Diaspora—as strangers (= exiles) in the world
- **Occasion:** probably concern over an outbreak of local persecution that some newer believers (2:2–3) were experiencing as a direct result of their faith in Christ
- **Emphases:** suffering for the sake of righteousness should not surprise us; believers should submit to unjust suffering the way Christ did; Christ suffered on our behalf to free us from sin; God's people should live righteously at all times, but especially in the face of hostility; our hope for the future is based on the certainty of Christ's resurrection

OVERVIEW OF 1 PETER

Peter's primary concern is for truly Christian living in the context of hostility and suffering. The letter moves forward in a kind of elliptical way, embracing first one and then the other of these concerns, returning to them over and over again along the way. At the same time these concerns are placed within the context of Christ's suffering and resurrection, his suffering offering a pattern for believers as well as saving them, his resurrection giving them hope in the midst of present suffering.

The opening thanksgiving (1:3–12) sets forth the themes: salvation, hope for the future, suffering, genuine faith (= faithful living). The rest of the letter falls into three parts (1:13–2:10; 2:11–4:11; 4:12–5:11), signaled by the address "dear friends" in 2:11 and 4:12 (and the doxology in 4:11). Part 1 is a call to holy living, with emphasis on their life together as the people of God. Using all kinds of images from the Old Testament, Peter reassures them that they are God's people by election, whose lives together are to give evidence that they are God's children and thus declare God's praises.

Part 2 focuses primarily on their being God's people for the sake of the pagan world (2:12)—those responsible for their suffering. He begins (2:11–3:7) by urging Christlike submission in specific institutional settings (pagan government [2:13–17]; pagan masters [2:18–25]; pagan husbands [3:1–6]) in which believers may expect to suffer. He then generalizes this appeal to all believers (3:8–4:6), specifically when facing suffering for doing good; again, Christ's death and resurrection serve as the basis for holiness and hope. He concludes by speaking once more to their life together as God's people (4:7–11).

In part 3 he puts their suffering into a theological context, while urging the elders to lead the others in properly Christian responses to undeserved suffering, as well as in their relationships to one another.

SPECIFIC ADVICE FOR READING 1 PETER

The special vocabulary of 1 Peter tells much of the story and should be watched for as you read. These words are especially important: suffering (11*x*); *anastrophē* ("way of life, behavior" 6*x* [1:15, 18; 2:12; 3:1, 2, 16]); God (39*x*); Christ (22*x*); Spirit/spiritual (8*x*); God's will (4*x*); election/calling (10*x*); save/salvation (6*x*); and hope (5*x*)—along with a number of other words that point to the future (inheritance, glory, etc.), plus a large vocabulary reminding them that they are God's people, living as "foreigners" or "strangers" or those in exile in the present world.

What propels the letter from beginning to end is their suffering. Peter's concern is that they understand their suffering in the larger context of God's saving purposes. Thus the strong emphasis on the work of the Triune God. God, the author of salvation, has both chosen and called them to be his people in the world. Suffering may therefore be understood as in keeping with God's higher purposes (his will); yet Christ's death and resurrection have made their final salvation altogether certain so that they live in hope. Note that Peter—significantly—always refers to Christ's redeeming work in terms of his suffering (rather than "dying") for us, which at the same time also serves as the example to be followed (2:21–24; 3:15–18)—all of which is enabled by the Spirit (1:2; 2:5; 4:14). All of this is said over and over again, with obvious interest in encouraging and reassuring them.

At the same time Peter is greatly concerned about the way they live, both their conduct as a people together and the way they respond to suffering. First, he repeatedly reminds them that they are a pilgrim people—strangers and foreigners here, whose inheritance is in heaven—and that they should live the life of heaven in their sojourn on earth. Second, by living in this way they will serve as God's priestly people for the sake of the pagans who are hostile to them so that they "may be won over" (3:1). Thus his readers are to fulfill their calling where Israel failed—to be a blessing to the nations. In the end there is not a thing in this letter that does not have these ends in mind. Be looking for them as you read.

You also need to have a sense of the first-century household in order to appreciate what is urged in 2:18–3:7. In ways that are hardly understandable to Western cultures over the past several centuries, in the first-century Greco-Roman household the male head of the house was the absolute "lord and master." In most such households, if he cared at all for things religious (and religion was a part of their way of life, whether taken seriously or not), then it was customary for the entire household (wife, children, household slaves) to adopt the religion of the householder. Peter is speaking into this context, where some household slaves and wives have gotten out of line on this matter by becoming followers of Christ, whereas when he speaks in a secondary way to the husband in 3:7 he assumes that he and his household have all followed Christ.

A WALK THROUGH 1 PETER

□ 1:1–2 *Salutation*

This salutation is theologically compact. Watch for Peter's emphases: their election, their being "strangers in the world," and the saving work of the Triune God.

☐ 1:3–12 *A Berakah (Blessing of God)*

In keeping with the Jewish imagery and emphasis throughout, Peter begins with a *berakah* ("blessed be God"; cf. Eph 1:3), first with an emphasis on their sure future (vv. 3–5) before turning to their sufferings (v. 6), which have refining value (v. 7), pointing again to the future, this time with focus on Christ (vv. 8–9). This end-time salvation brought through Christ was prophesied by, but not available to, the prophets—nor to angels (vv. 10–12). After reading this section through and identifying these characteristics, you may want to go back and read it again to get a sense of its majesty.

☐ 1:13–2:10 *The Call to Holy Living As God's People*

With emphasis on God's call and character (1:15–17) and Christ's redeeming work (vv. 18–21), Peter begins by reminding them that God's call was to a holy way of life, especially in their communal relationships (1:22–2:3). God's goal is a "spiritual house" (house of the Spirit = temple), where a holy people offer "spiritual sacrifices" (2:4–8). Note how he concludes (vv. 9–10): By using language from Exodus 19:5–6 and Hosea 1:9 and 2:23, he reassures these Gentile believers that they are the new-covenant continuation of the people of God.

☐ 2:11–3:7 *The Call Particularized in Various Pagan Settings*

After an opening exhortation to "live ... good lives among the pagans" (2:11–12), he urges them to submit "for the Lord's sake"—first, all of them toward the governing authorities (vv. 13–17) and, second, the Christian household slaves (the Greek word is very specific) to their pagan masters (2:18–25), especially when treated unjustly. Here he appeals to the suffering and redemptive work of Christ with all kinds of echoes from Isaiah 53:3–6 (you may wish to pause and read the Isaiah passage, and then look for the echoes in 1 Peter).

Finally, he appeals to Christian wives of pagan husbands (3:1–6)—these wives have very little to say in such a household, but their manner of life must reflect Christ—concluding (v. 7) with a brief word to Christian husbands about their relationship with their wives.

☐ 3:8–4:11 *The Call Generalized—in the Face of Hostility*

Next Peter generalizes, beginning again with communal relationships (3:8–12), before focusing on how to respond to undeserved suffering

(vv. 13–17), appealing to Christ's suffering, his proclamation (of triumph) to "the imprisoned spirits" (probably fallen angels), and his resurrection (vv. 18–22).

Note that, as in 2:18–25, Christ's suffering again serves as a pattern, this time for putting sin behind them (4:1–6). The concluding exhortations (vv. 7–11) once more have to do with life together as God's people, set in the context of "the end"—with God's praise through Jesus Christ as the goal.

□ 4:12–5:11 *Conclusion: Suffering, Hope, and Christian Conduct*

Addressing the issue of their suffering one final time, Peter now (4:12–19) puts it into theological perspective (God's sovereignty and their rejoicing over the privilege of participating in Christ's sufferings and thus bearing his name). With a variety of echoes from 2:24–25 (regarding Christ) and appealing to his own role, in 5:1–4 Peter urges the elders to lead the people by their example in these matters (a very important "therefore" is not translated in 5:1 in the TNIV) before appealing one final time to their communal life (v. 5) and to their suffering while they await the "eternal glory in Christ" (vv. 6–11).

□ 5:12–14 *Final Greetings*

The letter concludes with a very brief note about its purpose, concise words of greeting, and a final wish of peace.

Since most of the New Testament books are concerned with how the people of God live in their relationships with one another, it is important to the biblical story to have one that focuses especially on our being like Christ (repeating his story, as it were) in our response to suffering that comes as a result of pagan hostility.

2 Peter

ORIENTING DATA FOR 2 PETER

- **Content:** a "farewell speech" sent as a letter, urging Christian growth and perseverance in light of some false teachers who both deny the second coming of Christ and live boldly in sin
- **Author:** the apostle Peter, although questioned both in the early church and by most New Testament scholars; possibly a disciple who wrote a kind of "testament of Peter" for the church
- **Date:** ca. A.D. 64 (if by Peter); later if by a disciple
- **Recipients:** an unknown but specific group of believers
- **Occasion:** a desire to establish the readers in their own faith and godly living, while warning them of the false teachers and their way of life
- **Emphases:** concern that God's people grow in and exhibit godliness; the sure judgment on the false teachers for their ungodly living; the certainty of the Lord's coming, despite the scoffing of the false teachers

OVERVIEW OF 2 PETER

The letter is in four parts that focus on godly living in light of the certainty of the Lord's coming, against the backdrop of those who deny the latter, with its concomitant judgments, and who thus live like pagans. Part 1 (1:3–11) is an exhortation to growth in godliness, thus confirming their "calling and election" (v. 10) so as to "receive a rich welcome into the eternal kingdom" (v. 11).

Part 2 (1:12–21) is Peter's testament about the "coming of our Lord Jesus Christ" (v. 16), an event that both the transfiguration (vv. 16–18), which Peter witnessed, and the reliable word of prophecy (vv. 19–21) argue for.

All of this is set (in part 3) in the context of the greed and licentiousness of the false teachers, whose condemnation is certain (2:1–22). The main thrust of this section is to reaffirm the certainty of divine judgment on those who reject God by rejecting holy living; thus several Old Testament examples are brought forward by way of illustration. You may want to read Jude 4–18 alongside this passage, since it reflects similar concerns and uses some of the same examples from the Old Testament and Jewish apocalyptic. These teachers "promise freedom" but are themselves "slaves of depravity" (2 Pet 2:19), who would finally have been better off never having followed Christ than to have followed and then rejected him (vv. 20–22).

The false teaching itself is exposed and argued against in 3:1–18 (part 4). Against those who deny the second coming (vv. 3–4) is the certainty of God's word, and thus the certainty of coming judgment, and a biblical view both of "time" and of God's patience (vv. 5–10); the conclusion urges readiness, in obvious contrast to the recklessness of the false teachers (vv. 11–18).

SPECIFIC ADVICE FOR READING 2 PETER

Watch for the two (interlocking) concerns that drive 2 Peter from beginning to end: (1) the false teachers as such and (2) their denial of the second coming of Christ. You will find the description of them in chapter 2 especially vivid. Besides their immorality (licentiousness, sexual immorality, disavowal of authority), note that they are especially scored for their greed (2:3, 14–15) and the exploitation of the unsuspecting and unstable (2:3, 14, 18–19). And the twin pictures of their rejection of Christ are especially graphic—a dog returning to its vomit, a washed sow returning to wallow in the mud (v. 22). Note also how those on the other side, who eagerly await the coming of our Lord, are exhorted to "holy and godly" living (3:11–12).

Regarding the certainty of the coming of Christ, which will include inevitable judgment on those who reject him by the way they live, be watching for the emphasis on the sure word of prophecy, both Old Testament and apostolic. This is the point of 1:16–18 and 1:19–21, where the transfiguration of Christ itself was a prophetic foretaste of the future, and where true prophecy is completely reliable. The coming of the "false prophets" is also prophesied (2:1), while the final exhortation (ch. 3) begins by reminding the readers once more of the sure word of the "holy prophets" and the "apostles," with emphasis on the reliability of God's word—that the same word that brought the created world into being is preserving it for the day of judgment.

A WALK THROUGH 2 PETER

□ 1:1–2 *Salutation*

The salutation emphasizes both the "righteousness" that comes from God and the "knowledge" of God and of Jesus our Lord. You should make a mental note that these emphases go together and anticipate much that follows.

□ 1:3–11 *The Themes Stated: Godliness and the Eternal Kingdom*

As you read this section, think about how it sets out the major concerns: (1) God's power is available for all that is necessary for "a godly life" (vv. 3–4); (2) growth in godliness must be intentional (vv. 5–7); (3) without these qualities of godliness one cannot be an effective believer (vv. 8–9); and (4) the readers are thus urged to "make every effort to confirm your calling and election" (v. 10), with entrance into the eternal kingdom in view (v. 11).

□ 1:12–21 *Peter's Last Testament*

Note now how Peter's testament (vv. 12–15) leads to an affirmation of the coming of Jesus, which is assured first by the transfiguration, which Peter witnessed (vv. 16–18), and second by the reliable word of prophecy, which has its origin, not in human will, but in God through the Holy Spirit (vv. 19–21).

□ 2:1–22 *The Indictment of the False Teachers*

Following the emphasis on the trustworthiness of the prophets is the prophetic word of Peter about the coming of the false teachers, whose evil purposes and final condemnation are asserted at the beginning (vv. 1–3). What follows is so full of striking language and images that you will need to watch carefully for its "logic." First, the judgment on the false teachers and the rescue of the righteous are contrasted by means of Old Testament examples (vv. 4–9), concluding (v. 10a) with the two specific reasons for their condemnation, namely, living for "the flesh" ("follow the corrupt desire of the sinful nature") and despising authority.

These reasons are then elaborated with a series of images (vv. 10b–18a) that concludes by condemning the false teachers for destroying others as well (vv. 18b–19). Finally (vv. 20–22), they are condemned for having turned their backs on Christ and returning to the "corruption of the world."

☐ 3:1–10 *The Nature of the False Teaching: Denial of the Lord's Coming*

This final section lies at the heart of things. It begins, you will notice, with another reference to prophecy, recalling now both the Old Testament prophets and the apostolic predictions about such false teachers (vv. 1–4). Their scoffing, based on the lack of past judgment (nothing has changed since creation!), is responded to first by a reminder of the certainty of God's sovereign word (vv. 5–7; note that creation began with water and ends in fire) and second by appealing to God's forbearance (vv. 8–10; note how v. 8 echoes the reliable word of Ps 90:4).

☐ 3:11–18 *Exhortation and Conclusion*

The preceding warnings against the false teaching are now applied to the readers' situation by way of warning and exhortation (vv. 11–15a); note that after the judgment by fire comes the new heaven and new earth prophesied by Isaiah (Isa 65:17). This is followed by an appeal to similar kinds of things said by Paul about patience and salvation (2 Pet 3:15b–16), suggesting that some of the false teaching came about by a distortion of Paul's teaching. The letter concludes on the note with which it began—a warning and an exhortation to grow in grace.

As Peter's last will and testament, 2 Peter is critical to the biblical story, declaring the certainty of the Lord's coming and thus pointing the way toward the final book in the story, the revelation Jesus gave to John.

1 John

ORIENTING DATA FOR 1 JOHN

- **Content:** a treatise that offers assurance to some specific believers, encouraging their loyalty to Christian faith and practice—in response to some false prophets who have left the community
- **Author:** the same author who wrote 2 and 3 John, who there calls himself "the elder"; a solid historical tradition equated him with the apostle John
- **Date:** unknown; probably toward the end of the first Christian century (late 80s, early 90s).
- **Recipients:** a Christian community (or communities) well known to the author (whom he calls "dear children" and "dear friends"; the false prophets defected "from us," 2:19); it has traditionally been thought to be located in or around Ephesus
- **Occasion:** the defection of the false prophets and their followers, who have called into question the orthodoxy—both teaching and practice—of those who have remained loyal to what goes back to "the beginning"
- **Emphases:** that Jesus who came in the flesh is the Son of God; that Jesus showed God's love for us through his incarnation and crucifixion; that true believers love one another as God loved them in Christ; that God's children do not habitually sin, but when we do sin, we receive forgiveness; that believers can have full confidence in the God who loves them; that by trusting in Christ we now have eternal life

OVERVIEW OF 1 JOHN

You can experience some real ambivalence in reading 1 John. On the one hand, John's writing style is very simple, with a very limited and basic vocabulary (so much so that this is usually the first book beginning Greek students learn to read). It also has a large number of memorable—as well as some profound—moments. On the other hand, you may experience real difficulty trying to follow John's train of thought. Not only is it hard at times to see how some ideas connect with others, but certain, obviously significant, themes are repeated several times along the way.

Although, like most of Paul's letters, the aim of 1 John is to persuade, it nonetheless does not come in the form of a letter (notice that there is no salutation or final greeting). Most likely this is because John is writing to communities where he has direct oversight. What he writes includes teaching that "you have heard from the beginning" (2:24) about "the Word of life" who "was from the beginning" (1:1; cf. 2:13).

The primary concerns are three: the Incarnation; love for the brothers and sisters, especially those in need; and the relationship between sin and being God's children. The first two of these are the more urgent and are expressed together in 3:23: "This is his command: to believe in the name of his Son, Jesus Christ, and to love one another."

The Incarnation is touched on in 1:1–4 and 2:20–25, then specifically taken up in 4:1–6 and 5:1–12. The saving significance of Christ's death—the ultimate expression of God's love for us—is tied directly to one's belief that he "came in the flesh."

The concern about believers' loving one another is spoken to in a preliminary way in 2:7–11, then specifically in 3:11–24 and 4:7–21. The obvious tie between these two themes is that God's love for us, which we in turn are to have for one another, is fully revealed in the Incarnation, when the Son of God died for us (see 2:5–6; 3:16; 4:8–12).

The concern about sin is tied to the theme "Who are the true children of God?" This issue is first taken up in 1:5–2:2; it is picked up again in 2:28–3:10 and forms the concluding matter in 5:13–21. God's true children do not continue to live in sin, but neither are they sinlessly perfect; what matters is whether their obedience expresses itself in love for the brothers and sisters. The true children of God have already been given eternal life (= entered into the life of God, and thus are tasting the life of the age to come).

SPECIFIC ADVICE FOR READING 1 JOHN

As you read, be especially on the lookout for what John says about the false prophets, since they are the key to everything. Note that they have recently left the community (2:19), but only after trying to lead the whole church astray (2:26; 3:7; 4:1). These prophets apparently considered their teaching to come from the Spirit (cf. 4:1), which is why John urges that the believers' own anointing of the Spirit is sufficient for them (2:20, 27; 3:24). Indeed, in a marvelous wordplay on the language of "anointing" (*chrisma*), he calls the false prophets "antichrists" (*antichristos* = against the Anointed One). There has been much speculation about who these false prophets are, or what heresy they represent, but in the end these things cannot be known for certain, except that they deny the Incarnation, fail to love those in need, and (perhaps) argue that they are sinless.

The wonder of this little treatise is how much John can say, and say so profoundly, while using a notably limited vocabulary. But it is the very repetition of words, plus the use of stark contrasts, that is so effective. His special vocabulary tells the whole story: To remain/continue/abide (24*x*) in the truth (9*x*) means to believe in (9*x*) or confess (5*x*) the Son (22*x*), to whom the Father (14*x*) and Spirit (8*x*) bear witness (12*x*); it means further to be born of God (10*x*), so as to walk (5*x*) in the light (6*x*), to hear (14*x*) and to know (40*x*) God, to keep (7*x*) the commandment (14*x*) to love (46*x*) the brothers and sisters (15*x*), and thus to have life (13*x*), which is from the beginning (8*x*), and finally to overcome (6*x*) the world. All of this is in contrast to the lie (7*x*), deceit (4*x*), denying Christ (3*x*), having a false spirit (4*x*), thus being antichrist (4*x*), walking in darkness (6*x*), hating (5*x*) one's brothers and sisters but loving the world (23*x*), thus being in sin (27*x*), which leads to death (6*x*).

In putting all of this together for the reading of 1 John, it may help you to think in terms of a musical composition rather than a Pauline argument. A prelude anticipates the first theme, then the next two main themes are struck, or at least hinted at, followed by an interlude and then another prelude—this time to the major theme of the false prophets and their denial of the Incarnation. With all the major themes now in place, John works them over two more times each, adding and clarifying as he builds with powerful crescendo to the finale.

A WALK THROUGH 1 JOHN

☐ 1:1–4 *Prelude: The First Theme Struck*

Life is ours through the Word of life, whom the author (already emphasizing the reality of the Incarnation) and others "have seen with our eyes . . . and our hands have touched."

☐ 1:5–2:2 *Second Theme: On Sin and Forgiveness*

Note the two matters emphasized here—that walking in the light (and thus in the truth) means to be in Christian fellowship through Christ's continual purification of sin and that those who deny they sin do not walk in the light.

☐ 2:3–11 *Third Theme: On Love and Hatred*

Now you will find three matters emphasized: (1) Walking in truth (light) means to be obedient to Christ's commands; (2) his command is the old one—that we love one another; and (3) failure to love is to hate and thus to walk in darkness (by implication, thus to live in sin, despite denying that one sins).

☐ 2:12–14 *Interlude: Some Reasons for Writing*

Notice that all of the reasons given for writing are intended to reassure his readers that they are the true children of God: Their sins are forgiven; they know Christ and the Father; they are strong and have overcome the evil one.

☐ 2:15–17 *Prelude to the Warning: Do Not Love the World*

Love has to do with the brothers and sisters, not the things of the world. Note that this second prelude sets the stage not only for the warning that follows, but anticipates 4:1–6, where the "false prophets" are set squarely in the world.

☐ 2:18–27 *The Warning: On Denying the Son (First Theme Again)*

Here you find John's primary reason for writing. By their leaving, the deceivers have obviously shaken up those who remain loyal. Along with the emphasis on the Incarnation, everything you find here was written to reassure the first readers that they have the true anointing of the Spirit (but John does *not* mean that people with the Spirit do not need teaching!).

☐ 2:28–3:10 *Second Theme Repeated: On Sin and Being the Children of God*

As this theme is elaborated, you can now make better sense of 1:5–2:2. At issue is the relationship between sin and being God's children.

John begins by assuring them that they are the latter, before dealing with the issue of sin. Since this immediately follows the defection of the false prophets, it seems very likely that they are teaching that the true children of God are sinless.

☐ 3:11–24 *Third Theme Repeated: On Love and Hatred*

Again, it is not accidental that the discussion of sin(lessness) is followed by the truest evidence of being God's children, namely, loving each other as Christ loved us; while the "sinless" ones in fact live in the worst kind of sin: Not loving the brothers and sisters is equal to hating them. Note especially how verses 16–18 reflect the heart of the gospel while also echoing the heart of the law (Exod 22:21–27).

☐ 4:1–6 *First Theme Repeated: On Denying the Incarnation*

Now you are back to the first theme. Here in particular the major teaching of the false prophets is exposed. The clear evidence that they do not speak by the Spirit is their denial of Christ's incarnation; this is the "spirit" of the antichrist.

☐ 4:7–21 *Third Theme Wrapped Up, and Tied to the First*

In coming back to the theme of loving one another, John now ties it directly to God's love for us as manifested in Christ's incarnation; his death effected God's atonement for us. Combined with 5:6–8, this passage suggests most strongly that in denying the Incarnation, the false prophets are also denying the saving significance of the cross.

☐ 5:1–12 *First Theme Wrapped Up, Now Tied to the Third and Second*

The true children of God are those who believe that Jesus is the Messiah (including his incarnation and atonement). They are also those who love the other "children of God." Verses 6–8 give us the best hints about the heresy itself: The false teachers apparently believe something significant happened to Christ at his baptism (thus he came "by water") but that his death was not something God was involved in (John thus insists he came by water *and blood*). The true Spirit bears witness both to Christ's incarnation and his atonement. Those who believe this have eternal life.

☐ 5:13–21 *The Finale: The Second Theme Tied to the First*

After some words of confidence based on their believing what has been said up to now, John returns to the theme on which it all began—the issue of sin and who are the true children of God, who thus have eternal life. They need to flee idolatry—a final stroke against the false prophets.

After working through 1 John in this way, you can now also better appreciate the special emphases in John's telling of the story of Christ in his Gospel; it should also make the reading of 2 John make good sense. The whole biblical story stands or falls on God's love being manifested by his entry into our world of flesh and blood and dying for us in order to redeem us.

2 John

ORIENTING DATA FOR 2 JOHN

- **Content:** "the elder" warns against false teachers who deny the incarnation of Christ
- **Author:** see 1 John
- **Date:** see 1 John
- **Recipients:** the "lady chosen by God" is either a single, local congregation or a woman who hosts a house church; "her children" are the members of the believing community
- **Occasion:** John is concerned that after the defection of the false prophets from his community, they might spread their teaching in another community of faith
- **Emphases:** see 1 John

OVERVIEW OF 2 JOHN

What happens today when someone is disfellowshipped from a local church? Most often they simply go down the street to another church, usually without accountability on the part of the leadership of either community—the one they left or the one that receives them. In the elder's situation there are no other churches down the street for them to go to. But since those who have been disfellowshipped are "prophets," they can be expected to go from town to town, bent on convincing others of their "insights." These churches need to be warned.

Thus 2 John, a sort of miniature 1 John, presses the latter's primary themes—love and the Incarnation. But while 1 John was written to assure the elder's own community that they, not the false prophets, walk in the truth, this letter warns a house church in another town that these deceivers are on the loose. Notice also that 2 John 10–11 anticipate the concern over hospitality that will be raised in 3 John. Indeed, 2 and

3 John should probably be read together in order to see the two sides to hospitality that will be discussed in 3 John.

SPECIFIC ADVICE FOR READING 2 JOHN

Second and 3 John are both the size of ordinary letters in the Greco-Roman world, written on a single sheet of papyrus. Note how both letters close with a notice about John's wanting to talk with the recipients "face to face" (which probably indicates that he was running out of space on his piece of paper).

Given its brevity, you should especially note significant repeated words, both *where* they occur and *how often.* In fact, you may wish to do this for yourself before you read further, using different colored pens for the different words.

Did you note in verses 1–6 the repetition of *truth* (5*x*), its companion *walk* (3*x*), the associated word *love* (5*x*), and love's companion *command(ment)* (4*x*)? In verses 7–11, "the truth" is now *the teaching* (3*x*), which has to do with "Jesus Christ as coming in the flesh" and thus with his being the true Son of the Father. Several words refer to those who reject this teaching: *deceivers* (2*x*), *antichrist, anyone, them*, etc. This exercise pretty well tells the story about this letter. For the teaching itself, review the comments on 1 John, pages 412–13.

A WALK THROUGH 2 JOHN

☐ 1–3

These verses form the address and greeting. Written to the "lady ... and to her children," John's emphasis is on true believers (the writer, the lady and her children, and many others) as those who "know the truth." Note how the greeting (v. 3) anticipates both sections of the letter that follows ("Jesus Christ, the Father's Son" and "in truth and love").

☐ 4–6

These verses urge that "we love one another"; this is what it means to "walk in the truth" and thus "walk in obedience to [God's] commands."

☐ 7–11

These verses warn against the "many deceivers, who ... have gone out into the world." The content of their deception is a denial of the

Incarnation; the content of the warning is for "the lady" to deny hospitality to such people, for "anyone who welcomes them shares in their wicked work."

□ 12–13

The urgency of this warning is made clear by the fact that this brief and hurried note must be written and sent off before the elder can find time to visit and say these things personally and at length.

As a miniature 1 John, this short letter reinforces the role of the Incarnation and of love in the biblical story.

3 John

ORIENTING DATA FOR 3 JOHN

- **Content:** to borrow the words of New Testament scholar Archibald M. Hunter, 3 John is all about "the Elder, who wrote it; Gaius, who received it; Diotrephes, who provoked it; and Demetrius, who carried it"
- **Author:** the same elder who wrote 2 John (see 1 John)
- **Date:** probably in the A.D. 90s
- **Recipient:** Gaius, a beloved friend of the elder who lives in another town; other believers are to be greeted by name (v. 14)
- **Occasion:** an earlier letter to the church had been scorned by Diotrephes, who also refused hospitality to the elder's friend(s) and disfellowshipped those who would do so; consequently John writes to Gaius, urging him to welcome Demetrius
- **Emphases:** the obligations of Christian hospitality, especially toward approved itinerant ministers

OVERVIEW OF 3 JOHN

This is the shortest letter in the New Testament and thus the shortest book in the Bible (it is twenty-five Greek words shorter than 2 John). Along with Philemon, it is a personal letter; unlike Philemon, it is a private letter as well.

At issue is Christian hospitality, as evidence that one is "walking in the truth." The recipient, Gaius, perhaps a convert of John (v. 4), is a dear friend (vv. 1, 2, 5, 11; "dear friend" translates the Greek word *agapētos,* "beloved"). Along with the truth of the gospel (vv. 3–4), Gaius and the elder share the practice of Christian hospitality toward approved itinerants (vv. 5–8, 11–12).

Sandwiched between Gaius's two responses of hospitality toward strangers is the opposite example of Diotrephes, who has a twofold problem: (1) He is self-assertive in terms of leadership in the church (KJV, "he loveth to have the preeminence"!), and (2) his way of asserting himself is to reject both a letter from the elder and the approved itinerants who were being commended to the church in that letter. In light of 1 and 2 John, one is tempted to see Diotrephes as also on the false teachers' side of things, although doctrinal issues as such are not mentioned in this case. But in light of 2 John 10–11, hospitality toward strangers is not automatic; they must be approved as those who walk in the truth.

SPECIFIC ADVICE FOR READING 3 JOHN

This letter may seem strange to a North American culture, where itinerant ministers are usually *invited* to the church and put up in motels or hotels. But in some ways you might find the original recipients' culture more to your liking. In the first century, hospitality toward strangers was considered a virtue, and accommodations were often linked to a temple or synagogue. This practice became heart and soul for the earliest Christians. Thus if you were on the move, you could expect to receive hospitality within a local church community anywhere in the known world, a fact that runs throughout the New Testament. We find it in Jesus' sending out the twelve and the seventy-two (Luke 9:4–5; 10:5–8); it is mentioned by Paul as an expression of love (Rom 12:13) and is urged as a form of Christian conduct in Hebrews 13:2. By the very nature of things, such hospitality was usually expected of a householder, who was also the leader of the church (1 Tim 3:2), but it could also be the responsibility of any others who had sizable households (1 Tim 5:10).

Together 2 and 3 John help us see how closely connected a householder, hospitality in her or his house, and the church that meets in the house were in the first-century church. Strangers who claimed to be bearers of the good news about Jesus Christ needed to have letters of commendation (such as 3 John is for Demetrius) in order to be given Christian hospitality in the home that housed a church community. But even when the itinerants were well known (e.g., Titus in 2 Cor 8:16–24), they often carried a letter of commendation from a leader known to the community to which they were going (see Acts 15:23–29; Rom 16:1–2; cf. 2 Cor 3:1–3, where Paul is miffed at the idea that he needed such a letter in Corinth).

This cultural phenomenon is crucial to your understanding of 3 John, as well as of 2 John 10–11. In the present case, such a letter from the elder had accompanied some whom he had sent to a church; but Diotrephes had rejected it, refused hospitality, and disfellowshipped those who would like to have shown it—exactly the position the elder himself took in 2 John 10–11, indicating that the touchstone of everything is the gospel of Christ.

A WALK THROUGH 3 JOHN

After the traditional salutation (vv. 1–2), note the following:

☐ 3–8

These verses are about *Gaius, who received it,* commending him because of the good report about his faithful "walking in the truth" (vv. 3–4), in this case pointing especially to his faithfulness in showing hospitality to some strangers, who went out "for the sake of the Name" (vv. 5–8).

☐ 9–10

These verses condemn *Diotrephes, who provoked it,* regarding this issue; at the same time there is also some tension over the elder's authority.

☐ 11–12

These verses commend *Demetrius, who carried it,* urging that he be shown hospitality.

☐ 13–14

These verses conclude with words about *the Elder, who wrote it.*

Although the smallest document in the New Testament, 3 John enhances the biblical story because of the role it plays in giving us insight into Christian community and hospitality.

Jude

ORIENTING DATA FOR JUDE

- **Content:** a pastoral letter of exhortation, full of strong warning against some false teachers who have "secretly slipped in" among them
- **Author:** Jude, who modestly describes himself as "the brother of James" (thus of Jesus), but does not consider himself an apostle (v. 17)
- **Date:** unknown; probably later in the first Christian century (after A.D. 70), since the apostolic "faith" seems to be well in place (vv. 3, 17)
- **Recipients:** unknown; probably a single congregation of predominantly Jewish Christians somewhere in Palestine who were well acquainted with both the Old Testament and Jewish apocalyptic literature
- **Occasion:** the threat posed by some itinerants who have turned grace into license and who have "wormed their way in" (NEB) to the church
- **Emphases:** the certain judgment on those who live carelessly and teach others to do so; the importance of holy living; God's love for and preservation of his faithful ones

OVERVIEW OF JUDE

Jude begins and ends on the note of God's call and preservation of his people (vv. 1–2; 24–25). The body of the letter is in two parts: Verses 3–19 warn against the false teachers; verses 20–23 offer exhortations to perseverance and advice on how to help those who have been influenced by the false teachers.

The warning against the false teachers is sandwiched between descriptions of their ungodly behavior (vv. 3–4, 17–19). The meat of the sandwich (vv. 5–16) is a midrash (a kind of Jewish commentary) on some Old Testament and Jewish apocalyptic passages similar to 2 Peter 2, which offer precedents both as to the lifestyle of and God's sure judgment on the false teachers.

SPECIFIC ADVICE FOR READING JUDE

You can hardly miss the fact that the false teachers are the crucial matter. Fortunately, enough is said about them that we can piece together a picture of sorts. They have been accepted within the community as Christians (v. 4) and participate in their love feasts (v. 12). Very likely they are itinerant "prophets" (well known to us from other early Christian sources like the *Didache*), described as dreamers (v. 8) who in fact "follow mere natural instincts and do not have the Spirit" (v. 19).

Their teaching appears to be some form of libertinism: They have perverted "the grace of our God into a license for immorality" (v. 4) and follow their own evil desires (vv. 16, 18) like "unreasoning animals" (v. 10). That they "pollute their own bodies" in the "very same way" as Sodom and Gomorrah ("sexual immorality and perversion," vv. 8, 7) probably points to at least one dimension of their license. They also "reject authority and heap abuse on celestial beings" (v. 8, the latter is an indication of a Jewish Christian milieu with its reverence for angels), being "grumblers and faultfinders" (v. 16) who would divide the community (v. 19).

The fact that such people are destined by biblical decree to come under God's judgment and Jude's obvious concern for those who have been influenced by them (v. 23) indicate the seriousness of the problem.

A WALK THROUGH JUDE

☐ 1–2 *Salutation*

You may wish to compare Jude's salutation with that of James; note that neither of the Lord's brothers capitalize on that relationship in order to write with authority; they are, rather, his "servants." The salutation itself emphasizes the believers' calling and security in God.

☐ 3–4 *The Cause of the Letter*

Here you find Jude's reason for writing and the initial description of the false teachers; their denial of Christ is probably in terms of how they live rather than a theological issue.

☐ 5–7 *Three Warning Examples*

Note how the three examples of God's judgment (Israelites in the desert; angels [from Jewish apocalyptic]; Sodom and Gomorrah) serve two purposes, namely, to warn the readers and to point to the certain judgment on the false teachers.

☐ 8–10 *Second Description of the False Teachers*

Here the emphasis is on the false teachers' rejection of authority so as to go their own licentious way. The example given is from a Jewish apocalyptic work, *The Assumption of Moses* (early first century A.D.).

☐ 11–16 *Further Warning Examples*

Observe how eloquent Jude is as he now describes the false teachers—first in terms of three Old Testament examples (v. 11), and then with four examples from everyday life and nature (vv. 12–13), emphasizing their inability to make good on promises and their instability.

After citing from another Jewish apocalyptic work, *1 Enoch* (second century B.C.), as to their certain judgment (vv. 14–15), Jude concludes with a final description of their ungodly lifestyle (v. 16).

☐ 17–19 *The Apostolic Warning*

Note that Jude's final indictment of the false teachers comes from apostolic prophecy.

☐ 20–23 *A Call to Persevere and to Help Others*

These concluding exhortations indicate Jude's concern for the believers themselves. He first offers advice on how to persevere (vv. 20–21) and then urges them to help those who have been influenced by the false teachers (vv. 22–23).

☐ 24–25 *Benediction*

The emphasis in this beloved benediction is on God's preserving his people; note especially how it responds to verse 21. It is our responsibility to "keep [ourselves] in God's love," but in the end it is God's to "keep [us] from stumbling and to present [us] ... without fault."

Although very brief and focused, this letter's role in the biblical story lies with its emphasis on the importance of holy living, as well as on our perseverance and God's preservation.

The Revelation

ORIENTING DATA FOR THE REVELATION

- **Content:** a Christian prophecy cast in apocalyptic style and imagery and finally put in letter form, dealing primarily with *tribulation* (suffering) and *salvation* for God's people and God's *wrath* (judgment) on the Roman Empire
- **Author:** a man named John (1:1, 4, 9), well known to the recipients, traditionally identified as the apostle, the son of Zebedee (Matt 10:2)
- **Date:** ca. A.D. 95 (according to Irenaeus [ca. 180])
- **Recipients:** churches in the Roman province of Asia, who show a mix of fidelity and internal weaknesses
- **Occasion:** the early Christians' refusal to participate in the cult of the emperor (who was acclaimed "lord" and "savior") was putting them on a collision course with the state; John saw prophetically that it would get worse before it got better and that the churches were poorly prepared for what was about to take place, so he writes both to warn and encourage them and to announce God's judgments against Rome
- **Emphases:** despite appearances to the contrary, God is in absolute control of history; although God's people are destined for suffering in the present, God's sure salvation belongs to them; God's judgment will come on those responsible for the church's suffering; in the end (Rev 21–22) God will restore what was lost or distorted at the beginning (Gen 1–3)

OVERVIEW OF THE REVELATION

The cult of the emperor flourished in the province of Asia more than elsewhere in the empire; the result was that by the end of the first Christian century, the church in all its weaknesses was headed for a showdown with the state in all its splendor and might. By the Spirit, John sees that the martyrdom of Antipas (2:13) and John's own exile (1:9) are but a small foretaste of the great havoc that the state will wreak on the church before it is all over (see 1:9; 2:10; 3:10; 6:9–11; 7:14; 12:11, 17).

As a Christian prophet, John also sees this conflict in the larger context of the holy war—the ultimate cosmic conflict between God (and his Christ) and Satan (see 12:1–9)—in which God wins eternal salvation for his people. The people's present role is to "triumph over [Satan] by the blood of the Lamb and by the word of their testimony,... not lov[ing] their lives so much as to shrink from death" (12:11). As God has already defeated the dragon through the death and resurrection of Christ (the Messiah is caught up to heaven, 12:5), so he will judge the state for her crimes against his people.

The book plays out these themes in a variety of ways. The earlier parts (chs. 1–6) set the stage for the unfolding drama, starting with a vision of the Risen Christ, who holds the keys to everything that follows (1:12–20), while letters to selective churches represent their varied strengths and weaknesses (chs. 2–3). These are followed by a vision of the Reigning Creator God and the Redeeming Lamb (chs. 4–5), to whom alone belong all wisdom, glory, and power and before whom all heaven and earth will bow. As John weeps because no one can be found to break the seals of the scroll (which is full of God's justice and righteous judgments), he is told that the "Lion of the tribe of Judah" (5:5; see Gen 49:9–10), the "Root of David" (Isa 11:1–2, 10), has "triumphed," but the only lion John sees is God's slain Lamb (echoing the Exodus Passover [and Isa 53:7]), who has redeemed people from all the nations. Such a Conqueror can set the drama in motion by breaking the seals (Rev 6), which offer a kind of "overture" (striking all the themes) for what follows (conquest, war, famine, death [first 4 seals]—followed by many martyrdoms [seal 5], to which God responds with judgment [seal 6]). It is especially important to note that, apart from his role in the final battle (19:11–21), the only way Christ appears from here on in the narrative is as the slain Lamb; this is how his followers are expected to triumph as well (12:11).

The two interlude visions (ch. 7)—of those whom God has "sealed" from his coming judgments, but pictured in battle formation for their role in the holy war, and eventually redeemed—are then followed by the opening of the seventh seal, which unfolds as the vision of the seven trumpets (chs. 8–9). These "judgments" echo the plagues of Egypt, and like those plagues, announce temporal (and partial) judgments against their present-day Pharaoh. But as with the Egyptian Pharaoh, the plagues do not lead to repentance (9:20–21). The interlude visions between the sixth and seventh trumpets (10:1–11:14) call on the church to prophesy and bear witness to Christ, even in the face of death, while also pronouncing the certain doom of the empire, and ending with a foretaste of the final glorious reign of God and of the Lamb (11:15–19).

The remaining visions (chs. 12–22) offer explanations for and apocalyptic descriptions of the final doom of the empire. Chapters 12–14 thus give the theological and historical reasons for both the suffering and the judgment. The doom of Rome itself is portrayed in the vision of the seven bowls (chs. 15–16), which echo the trumpet plagues—but now without opportunity to repent. The whole then concludes as the (original) "tale of two cities," represented by two women (the prostitute [Rome] and the bride of the Lamb), in which the city that represents enmity against God and his people is judged (chs. 17–18). This is set against the backdrop of God's final salvation and judgment (chs. 19–20) and of the final glory of the bride as the city of God, the new Jerusalem that comes down out of heaven (chs. 21–22).

SPECIFIC ADVICE FOR READING THE REVELATION

You may easily find yourself in the company of most contemporary Christians, for whom the Revelation is difficult to read, mostly because we are so unfamiliar with John's medium of communication—apocalyptic literature with its bizarre imagery. Thus, along with knowing about the historical context and the way John works out his overall design (noted above), two other items will greatly aid your reading of this marvelous book—(1) to take seriously John's own designation of his book as "the words of this prophecy" (1:3) and (2) to have some sense of how apocalyptic imagery works, even if many of the details remain a bit obscure.

By calling his work "the words of this prophecy," John is deliberately following in the train of the great prophets of the Old Testament, in several ways: (1) He speaks as one who knows himself to be under the inspiration of the Spirit (1:10; 2:7; etc.). (2) He positions himself between some recent past events and what is about to happen in the near future. (3) He sets all forms of earthly salvation and judgment against the backdrop of God's final end-time judgments (see *How to 1*, p. 201) so that the fall of Rome is to be seen not as the end itself but against the backdrop of the final events of the end.

And (4) most important for good reading, John sees everything in terms of the *fulfillment* of the Old Testament. He has over 250 specific echoes of or allusions to the Old Testament so that every significant moment in his "story" is imaged almost exclusively in Old Testament language. This begins with the picture of Christ (1:12–18, with its extraordinary collage from Dan 7:9; 10:6; Ezek 43:2; et al.), climaxing in Revelation 5:5–6, where the "Lion of the tribe of Judah" (Gen 49:9), the "Root of David" (Isa 11:1), turns out to be a slain Lamb (from the Passover and sacrificial system). The church is imaged in the language of Israel in every possible way, beginning in Revelation 1:6, with its echoes of Exodus 19:6; its sins are expressed in terms of Israel's failures (Balaam/Jezebel), and its redemption in Revelation 7 is pictured first as a remnant of the twelve tribes and second as a fulfillment of the Abrahamic covenant, thus including the nations. So also the judgment against Rome (e.g., 14:8; 18:1–24) is expressed in the language of the prophetic judgments against Babylon (Isa 13–14; 21:1–10; 47; Jer 50–51), so much so that Rome is simply called "Babylon." The climax of the fulfillment is found in Revelation 22:1–5, with its restoration of Eden and total overturning of the curse. It is hard to imagine a more fitting way for the biblical story to end!

About John's use of apocalyptic imagery, you need to be aware of the following (for more details, see *How to 1*, pp. 255–56): (1) The imagery of apocalyptic is primarily that of *fantasy*—a beast with seven heads and ten horns; a woman clothed with the sun. (2) John himself interprets the most important images (Christ, 1:17–18; the church, 1:20; Satan, 12:9; Rome, 17:9, 18), which give us our essential clues to the rest. (3) Some of his images are well known and fixed—a beast coming out of the sea represents a (usually evil) empire; an earthquake represents divine judgment—while others are fluid and are used to evoke feelings as well as mental pictures. (4) Visions are to be seen as wholes and not pressed regarding all of their details, that is, the details are part of the evocative nature of the imagery, but the *whole* vision is what counts.

If you keep these various matters in mind as you read, you should be able not only to make your way through the Revelation but begin to appreciate some of its utter majesty.

A WALK THROUGH THE REVELATION

Introduction: The Historical Setting (chs. 1–3)

☐ 1:1–8 *Prologue*

Note how the prologue sets out the essential particulars: John has received a "revelation" (Greek, *apocalypsis*) from Christ about what is soon to take place, which he calls "the words of this prophecy," offering a blessing on the one who reads it aloud and on the hearers in the believing communities (1:1–3). He then casts his "revelation" in the form of a letter to the seven churches, with appropriate greetings and a doxology—to Christ!

☐ 1:9–3:22 *The Historical Setting*

Here you are introduced to the three primary "dramatis personae" (John, Christ, the church). John situates himself in his exile as their fellow sufferer, before giving the details of his receiving the revelation (1:9–11); he will be present as the "I" who sees and hears all that follows. Then he portrays Christ as Lord of the church (1:12–16, using a collage of echoes from Dan 7:13; 10:5–6; Ezek 43:2) and Lord of history (Rev 1:17–20; note how language for God from Isa 48:12 is appropriated by the Risen Christ!).

Finally Christ addresses the seven churches (Rev 2–3), revealing his knowledge of their present situation, usually exhorting them in some way, while urging those with ears to hear what is said, and promising eschatological rewards to those who are victors in the coming strife. The conditions of the churches are a mixed bag (some strengths and some weaknesses). All is said in light of "the hour of trial that is going to come upon the whole world" (3:10).

Introductory Visions: The Scene in Heaven and on Earth (4:1–8:5)

☐ 4:1–5:14 *A Vision of the Heavenly Throne*

Before the awful conditions on earth are unveiled, John is shown first the incomparable and eternal majesty of God the Creator (ch. 4). This is responded to by the vision of God's Lion, the slain Lamb, who through his death has triumphed over the dragon in the holy war (see ch. 12) and who, because of his redemptive work, is worshiped along with God and is deemed worthy to unveil God's righteous judgments (ch. 5).

Don't go too quickly past these visions; all the rest must be seen in their light. You may wish to read Ezekiel 1 and Isaiah 6:1–3 for the Old Testament background to much of what is said in Revelation 4, and Genesis 49:8–12 and Isaiah 11:1–11 for Revelation 5. What John is offering is the perspective of heaven (where there is constant praise and worship of God and the Lamb), from which his readers are to view the gruesome situation on earth. This is made clear by his including the opening of the seven seals (6:1–8:5) within the framework of this vision, as 6:1, 3, 5, 7, and 9 make clear.

□ 6:1–8:5 *The Opening of the Seven Seals*

Although part of the preceding vision, the account of the seven seals also begins a series of three visions (seals, trumpets, bowls), all of which have the same structure—a series of four, a series of two, an interlude of two visions, and a seventh.

In this first vision, the four horsemen (adapted from Zech 1; 6) represent conquest, war, famine, and death (= the empire against God's people). The series of two (fifth and sixth seals) also prepares the way for the rest by asking the two key questions: (1) The martyrs cry out, "How long?" and are told it will get worse before it gets better (Rev 6:10–11), and (2) those receiving God's judgment cry out (echoing Mal 3:2), "Who can stand [the day of God's wrath]?" (Rev 6:17). Thus John is given an overall prelude of the judgments that follow.

The immediate reply to this last question is the interlude. The ones who can stand are those who are "sealed" by God (Rev 7:1–8) and the multitudes who have come out of the great suffering—the redeemed of the Lord (7:9–17). As you read, note that the picture of the people of God in 7:1–8 echoes Israel's encampment in battle formation in Numbers 2, thus anticipating their own role in the holy war. This in turn leads to the next picture of their final rest in the presence of God, which echoes Isaiah 25:8; 48:10–13.

The opening of the seventh seal then marks the unveiling of the seven angels with trumpets (Rev 8:1–5). The silence is for effect; note that the judgments about to be revealed are in direct response to the prayers of the saints (6:10).

Preliminary (Temporal) Judgments on the Empire (8:6–11:19)

This first set of woes announces temporal, partial judgments while also anticipating the final one (chs. 16; 18). That is made clear by the fact that the first four are clear adaptations of the Egyptian plagues, which were temporal, not final judgments on Egypt, and the repeated motif of one-third.

☐ 8:6–9:21 *The Judgments of the Seven Trumpets*

Note how this series of four (8:6–13) picks up the picture of God's wrath from the sixth seal, but now as trumpets (warning judgments). Watch how John adapts three of the plagues against Egypt to fit Rome, who derives its power and wealth from the sea: hail (#7; Exod 9:13–35); river into blood, split into two parts—sea and freshwater (#1; Exod 7:14–24); darkness (#9; Exod 10:21–29).

The series of two woes (the third is withheld until Rev 18) pictures the judgments in more historical terms, feeding first on Roman fears of the barbarian hordes (9:1–12; men with long hair), but pictured in terms of Joel's locust plague (Joel 1:6; 2:1–5). This is represented second as a great and decisive battle (Rev 9:13–19). But even though the judgments are of temporal and partial nature, they do not lead to repentance (9:20–21).

☐ 10:1–11:19 *The Two Interlude Visions*

These two visions bring us back to John and the church. The first confirms John in his prophetic task (notice especially the echoes of Ezek 2:9–3:3 in Rev 10:9–11). But note that it begins with a mighty angel standing with one foot on the land and another on the sea, thus marking these off as belonging to God, not to Satan and his beasts (see 13:1, 11).

The second points to the prophetic role of the church, to carry out the expected end-time witness of Elijah and Moses (see 11:6), even though it means martyrdoms (vv. 7–10). But instead of the third woe (anticipated in 8:13; 9:12; 11:14), the seventh trumpet introduces an anticipatory picture of the end itself—but as already present: A song of triumph celebrates the consummation of the kingdom of God (11:15–19; note that the one "who was, and is, and is to come" [4:8] is now "the One who is and who was" [11:17]; what "is to come" is pictured has having come).

Conflict between the Church and the Evil Powers (12:1–14:20)

These three chapters form the absolute center of the book—not only literally in the overall design of the narrative, but as the theological perspective (ch. 12) and historical reasons (ch. 13) for everything, while chapter 14 prepares the way for the rest of the book.

☐ 12:1–17 *War in Heaven and Its Aftermath*

Note how the two visions of chapter 12 offer the theological key to the book. In his coming and ascension (12:5, the whole story is recalled by picturing the beginning and end), Christ has defeated the dragon (pictured as war in heaven in vv. 7–11), who now goes off to wreak havoc on Christ's people.

Thus "salvation" has *already* come; Satan has already been cast down, so "rejoice, you heavens." But the end is *not yet,* so "woe to the earth." Knowing that his time is limited, Satan will pursue the Messiah's people (thus pointing to ch. 13), who will overcome him through Christ's death and their own bearing witness to it, even to the point of death.

☐ 13:1–18 *The Beasts out of the Sea and the Earth*

This vision sets out the historical context for their suffering—prophesying how Satan will pursue them (economic restrictions and martyrdom)—which will take place because of their rejection of emperor worship.

The beast from the sea is an adaptation of Daniel's fourth beast from the sea (Dan 7:2, 7–8, 23–25). Pictured is Rome in all its apparently invincible might (note how in Rev 13:4 the people parody the Divine Warrior hymn from Exod 15:11) as it makes war against God's people (Rev 13:7)—which will lead to many martyrdoms (v. 10, echoing Jer 15:2). Note: the "fatal wound" that has been healed (Rev 13:3, 12) alludes to the year A.D. 69, when at the death of Nero the world expected Rome to collapse as it went through three emperors in succession. The fact that it didn't is what made it seem invincible.

The beast from the earth represents the priesthood of the emperor cult that flourished in the province of Asia. Note how those who do not bear the mark of the first beast (666 is a play on the name of Nero) are isolated economically.

□ 14:1–20 *Outcome of the Holy War: Vindication and Judgment*

This series of visions then sets the stage for the final visions, picturing first the redeemed martyrs as firstfruits standing on eschatological Mount Zion (vv. 1–5), and then the fall of Rome in the language of Old Testament prophetic judgments—especially those against Babylon (which theme will be carried on to the end). The collection of brief vignettes (vv. 6–13) thus prepares the way for the rest of the book, as do the twin visions of harvesting the earth and trampling the winepress (vv. 14–20), which point to the future harvest of God's people and the judgment of Rome.

The Seven Bowls: God's Judgment against "Babylon" (15:1–16:21)

This third and final set of judgments (see chs. 6; 8–9) specifically singles out God's judgments against Rome.

□ 15:1–8 *The Prelude*

Note how this prelude to the judgment starts with John back in heaven (cf. chs. 4–6), while the martyrs sing the song of Moses and the Lamb—an exquisite collage of passages from all over the Old Testament (see the TNIV note on 15:3–4). Note also how the setting (vv. 5–8) picks up the imagery from 11:19.

□ 16:1–21 *Babylon Is Judged*

Watch how these woes echo the trumpets, but now without the "one-third" qualifier. As with the first four trumpets, the first four bowls are adaptations of the Egyptian plagues; note how the third one (water into blood) receives an immediate response in terms of the *lex talionis* (eye for eye). Here the set of two continues this motif. The interlude in this case (vv. 15–16) is noticeably brief and enigmatic (a call to readiness and a reference to Armageddon), while the final bowl of wrath repeats the earthquake from the sixth seal, at the same time continuing the plague motif (hail).

Wrap-Up: The (Original) Tale of Two Cities (17:1–22:21)

Using the powerful and evocative images of the two cities as two contrasting women—Rome as an opulent harlot; the church as the bride of Christ—John now places the judgment of Rome against the backdrop of God's final judgments and salvation. Note especially how the two are introduced (17:3; 21:9–10) and concluded (19:9–10; 22:7–9) in similar fashion and that the one (the fall of Rome) is seen in the "desert" (17:3) and the other (the new Jerusalem) on a "mountain great and high" (21:10).

□ 17:1–19:10 *God Judges the Harlot for Economic Oppression*

Note how this initial picture of Rome as an expensive prostitute sitting on the beast (ch. 17) echoes several such pictures of Tyre and Babylon in the prophets (Isa 23:15–18; Jer 51:6–7). Note also that the interpretations in Rev 17:9 and 17:18 make it clear who Babylon really is.

John then proceeds to sing a funeral dirge over her (18:1–3—talk about prophetic boldness!), followed by a call to God's people to escape from "Babylon" (18:4–8; cf. Isa 48:20; 52:11; Jer 51:45; etc.) and the resultant mourning by those who participated in her sins (the "kings of the earth" [provincial governors], merchants, merchant marine; Rev 18:9–24). Here at last is the third woe (see 8:12; 11:14), which itself takes the form of three woes (18:10, 16, 19). Here is the one place where John generally abandons the apocalyptic mode for a prophetic one, especially denouncing Rome's economic policies by which it grew enormously wealthy off the backs of the poor. Note how the immediate response to her doom is rejoicing in heaven (v. 20; cf. 12:12a), while another angel announces the finality of her doom (18:21–23) with echoes from Isaiah 25:10, ending once more on the ultimate reason for her doom—the killing of the martyrs (Rev 18:24).

And now watch as the threefold "Woe" is responded to with a threefold "Hallelujah" in heaven (19:1, 3, 6). And so John returns to the scene in heaven (from ch. 4), where the wedding supper of the Lamb and his bride, the church, is envisioned (19:1–10).

□ 19:11–20:15 *The Last Battle*

The interlude between the "destiny" of the two cities brings conclusion to the theme of the holy war, both in John and in the Bible as a whole. This picture forms the final (eschatological) backdrop against which the judgment of Rome itself is to be understood. Christ is thus pictured as the Divine Warrior who takes on the beast, the prophet, and Satan himself (19:11–20:15); note especially how this "unholy trinity" is one by one thrown into the lake of fire (19:20; 20:10).

Observe how John pictures a separation between the final demise of the two beasts and that of Satan (20:7–10). This suggests, along with the scene in verses 1–6, where the martyrs are pictured as secure and presently reigning with Christ, that Satan still has a further time after the overthrow of Rome. The final event is the judgment of those who have followed him (vv. 11–15).

☐ 21:1–22:11 *The New Jerusalem: The Bride of the Lamb*

Structurally 21:1–8 belongs to the "last battle": note how it anticipates the city of God (described in the vision that begins in vv. 9–10), but also concludes (v. 8) with a note about those who have been judged in the "second death." Notice especially how it begins with language from Isaiah 65:17–19, with its "new heaven and new earth."

Thus John's final vision pictures the city of God, a new Jerusalem, coming down to earth, where there is a restoration of Eden and a reversal of the effects of the Fall (Rev 21:2–22:6). Watch for two things: (1) The city echoes language and ideas from Ezekiel's vision of the eschatological *temple*, where Yahweh's glory returns to the temple (Ezek 40:1–43:12), and (2) the city itself *is* the temple precisely because it is the place of God's own dwelling (Rev 21:3–4, 11, 22–23; 22:3–5). And note finally how much of 22:1–5 echoes Eden restored, also using imagery from Ezekiel 47:1–12.

☐ 22:12–21 *Epilogue*

You can recognize this as a true epilogue in the sense that it echoes many themes from the prologue. Thus, as a fitting conclusion to his vision that has taken the form of a letter, John both exhorts and invites his readers—and us—to participate in God's great future through the coming of Christ.

It is hard to imagine the biblical story ending in a more significant way. Here is the final wrap-up of the story, not only in the vision of the restored paradise in 22:1–5 but as the climax of the story of God's saving his people and of his judgment on those who reject him. John gathers up all the main strands from the Old Testament and places them in the context of the New, with Christ and his salvation of God's people as the centerpiece of the whole.

Glossary of Terms

The following terms are used on a regular basis in this book. Because some of them reflect technical language (allowing us the economy of one word rather than many), we have tried to isolate most of this vocabulary (plus some other technical language referring to pagan deities) and explain it here.

acrostic: Poetry in which each new section or verse begins with a succeeding letter of the alphabet.

agonist(s): In literature the major character(s) in the plot who are involved in a contest or struggle.

anathema: Something or someone placed under God's curse—or the curse itself. Thus, *anathema* can refer to something that is to be avoided as especially ungodly or repugnant.

Asherah: A Canaanite mother-fertility goddess often worshiped by the Israelites when they fell into idolatry. She was regarded as the sex partner of Baal and was worshiped for her supposed power to make animals and crops fertile. Most references to her in the OT are to her idol, a large pole presumably bearing her likeness. Asherah and Ashtoreth (see below) were so similar in the belief system of Canaanite polytheism that they are sometimes referred to interchangeably (Judg 2:13, "served Baal and the Ashtoreths"; Judg 3:7, "served the Baals and the Asherahs").

Ashtoreth: A Canaanite mother-fertility goddess similar to and sometimes considered the same as Asherah (above). Because her name in Greek was *Astarte,* it is usually assumed that the Hebrew form of the name may be the result of scribes' using the vowels (o and e) from the Hebrew word for "shame" to give her name a distorted sound in the biblical text. In some localities, distinctions between Ashtoreth and Asherah were made; in others they apparently were not, since it was the habit of polytheistic syncretism often to blur or interchange the distinctions between gods, with every location free to do its own thing with regard to worship and theology.

Baal: The chief male Canaanite fertility god—or the idol that represented him. Baal was sometimes called "the cloud rider" by the Canaanites because they thought that he controlled the weather, especially the rain, which was the key to agricultural productivity.

canon (canonical): The official collection of books that make up the Bible (or one of its Testaments). A canonical writing is one that is part of the Bible. Works judged not canonical were those that were considered not to "fit" within Scripture. "Canonical" is sometimes used to refer to the *order* of the books within the canon.

chiasm (chiastic): A literary device that follows an AB BA pattern (e.g., "food for the stomach; the stomach for food") of any length (e.g., ABCDCBA), which served the purposes of memory in an oral culture (where most people could not read but had sharp memories for what they heard read to them). This may happen in sentences, paragraphs, or large sections of books. We sometimes use the language of "framing device" or "bookending" or "concentric pattern" to refer to this phenomenon when we are dealing with larger sections of text.

concentric: See chiastic

conflict stories: Stories in the Gospels in which someone presents a challenge to or a criticism of Jesus, and he uses the occasion to provide a moment of instruction.

covenant: A formal legal-contractual arrangement in which both parties have obligations and responsibilities to one another. In the great biblical covenants, God's obligation is blessing and mercy to those who keep covenant with him; the obligation of his people is obedience, especially the obedience as expressed in loving God and neighbor.

cycle: A story pattern or theme that is repeated for emphasis or effect.

Deuteronomic: Notably consistent with and/or actually based on the theology or vocabulary contained in the book of Deuteronomy.

Diaspora: A NT Greek term used to describe believing Jews living outside Palestine in ancient times—especially NT times, although its beginnings go back to the Babylonian exile (when the majority of exiles did not return to Judah) and the self-imposed exile in Egypt recorded in Jeremiah 41:16–45:5. Also called *the dispersion*. In Acts 15:21, James refers to the importance of the Diaspora for the spread of the gospel when he says, "For the law of Moses has been preached in every city from the earliest times. . . ."

discourse: A relatively lengthy and formal speech or written communication on a subject or a group of related subjects.

disfellowship: To remove someone from membership, attendance, and social contact with other believers in a church in order to correct a serious sin and restore the sinner. Such a severe action was undertaken because the sin endangered the church's own life and witness in the community.

Divine Warrior: A description of God in his role as the leader of the holy war (see below), a great fighter on behalf of his people (see, e.g., Exod 15:3; Isa 42:13; Jer 20:11).

doxology: A statement of praise to or about God, usually near or at the end of a biblical book or major portion thereof.

eschatological: Of or about the end times or last days, derived from the Greek word *eschaton,* which means "end."

exilic: Referring to the time during the Babylonian exile, which began in 586 B.C. and was officially over with the decree of Cyrus in 539 B.C.

fertility god: Any of the many Canaanite gods and goddesses, all of whom were seen as having the power to help people's crops and cattle be more fertile in exchange for being given food offerings. (Ancient pagan belief held that the one thing the gods couldn't do was to feed themselves!) See also *Baal* and *Asherah/Ashtoreth.*

Greeks: At a few points in the NT this term is used to refer to non-Hebrew (or Aramaic)-speaking Jews. Sometimes in Paul it also becomes a "stand-in" word for Gentiles.

Hellenists (Hellenistic): People who spoke Greek or followed Greek ways to some degree, even though they might otherwise be Jewish.

hermeneutics: Principles of interpretation, often used with reference to how biblical passages function for a later time and in new circumstances.

holy war: God's special battle against evil and those who manifest evil (very often in the form of idolatry)—a battle God fights on behalf of the righteous but allows his people to participate in. Because of God's omnipotence, there is no question who will ultimately win the war, but because of his great patience in waiting for evil people to turn to him, the war is not yet concluded.

horizontal: In OT law, describing the relationships and obligations of humans to each other; see *vertical.*

idolatry (idolatrous): A system that was inherently polytheistic, syncretistic, and (usually) pantheistic and that was present in virtually all ancient nonbiblical religions. Idolatrous practice relied on the belief that the gods could be influenced by offerings made in the presence of their idols, since the idols "manifested" the gods, including their nature and power; the idol was sometimes understood in both OT and NT to be the locus of demons or demonic power.

Incarnation (incarnate): God's becoming human in the person of Jesus of Nazareth.

messiahship: The position and/or action of fulfilling the OT expectations for God's special anointed servant-leader of Israel.

metanarrative: The great overall, overarching story of the Bible as a whole; the grand narrative of God's redemption of a people for himself, told progressively throughout the Bible.

monarchy: The period of time when Israel and/or Judah had a king, i.e., ca. 1050 B.C.–586 B.C.

motif: An important idea or theme that constitutes one of the concerns of a book or passage.

oracle: A particular revelation from God; often used synonymously with "prophecy" or "revelation," when these refer to a *specific* message from God to a prophet.

panel: A distinct subsection of a narrative, containing a group of stories sharing a theme or topic.

passion: When used about Jesus, this refers specifically to his suffering and death.

Pharisaism (Pharisaic): The attitude that righteousness before God was related to obeying every OT law to the letter, including the Pharisees' own (often legalistic) extensions and extrapolations of those laws; and the attitude that only people who did so could be accepted as good Jews.

Pentateuch: The first five books of the Old Testament; also known as the "(Five) Books of Moses."

polytheism (polytheistic): The belief that there are many gods and goddesses, each with his or her own specialties and each potentially worthy of worship for what he or she could do better than any of the others. The whole ancient world was polytheistic except for those who kept covenant with Israel's God.

postexilic: The time after 539 B.C., i.e., after the Babylonian exile, which began in 586 B.C. and was officially over with the decree of Cyrus in 539.

preexilic: Before the Babylonian exile began, i.e., before 586 B.C.

Presence: God's special empowering manifestation of himself among humans whereby he gives a discernible sense of his greatness, holiness, support, approachability, etc. In OT times first the tabernacle and then the Jerusalem temple was especially often the locus of his Presence; in NT times it is primarily the Spirit in the church, but also in the individual.

proselyte: A Gentile who converted to Judaism and therefore practiced Jewish law, including especially circumcision, and was accepted into the Jewish community.

protagonist: The main character, main mover, or hero in a story or event.

restoration: The reestablishment of Israel as a people under God after the Babylonian exile.

refrain: A wording, topic, or idea that an author uses repeatedly for clarity or effect.

revelation: God's "unveiling" of himself so as to be "seen"/understood by people; sometimes used to refer to his imparting his truth to people.

sanctions: The part of the covenant that provided incentives to keep it, in the form of blessings (benefits from God) and curses (miseries of various sorts as punishments for disobedience).

sanctuary: A place where God specially manifests his Presence and where God is appropriately worshiped by his people.

Septuagint (septuagintal): The ancient Greek translation of the Old Testament, produced in the third and second centuries B.C. in Alexandria, Egypt. It was the Bible of most New Testament Christians, and it has had enormous influence, including on the order of the books in our English Bibles and in the NT sometimes on the wording itself.

Speculative Wisdom: The process of trying to think through what life and its choices really are all about. Asking and answering questions and responding to assertions—whether in dialogue or monologue format—are common in Speculative Wisdom literature.

syncretism (syncretistic): The sharing and blending of religious beliefs. When the Israelites continued to worship Yahweh as their national god but also worshiped Baal as a fertility God, or when they worshiped Yahweh via golden calf-idols, they were practicing syncretism.

theological (theology): Describing God, his truth, and his relationship to his world; also describing the particular way a given Bible writer conveys his part of the whole of God's truth.

theophany (theophanic): An appearance of God in some form. Although "no one has ever seen God" (1 John 4:12), God has "appeared" in the sense of specially manifesting his presence through angels (Judg 13:22), the incarnate Christ (John 1:18), storms (Ezek 1), etc.

tradition: Shared beliefs and/or practices passed on from one generation to another.

vertical: In OT law, describing the relationships and obligations of people to God; see *horizontal.*

vision: In prophetic literature, a special type of revelation in which what is seen helps orient the prophet to what will be said. What is described as "seen" in a vision is almost always simple, and normally it does not convey a message in itself, apart from the words of explanation that follow.

Appendix: A Chronological Listing of the Biblical Books

This appendix is for those who might wish to read the biblical books in a chronological order. Some of this is guesswork, of course, especially in the case of the Old Testament works, since some books (e.g., Joel) are not easily dated. Our list is related primarily to their *content*, not to *date of composition*—although even in this case some exceptions are made: We have put 1–2 Chronicles before Malachi and Ezra-Nehemiah, and the Gospel of John with 1–3 John and the Revelation. Moreover, bear in mind that some books overlap each other in ways that a simple chronological listing cannot fully represent (e.g., Daniel and Ezekiel). The OT books that cover various times or contain few specific chronological clues have been grouped separately at the end of the OT list.

- ☐ Genesis
- ☐ Exodus
- ☐ Leviticus
- ☐ Numbers
- ☐ Deuteronomy
- ☐ Joshua
- ☐ Judges
- ☐ Ruth
- ☐ 1–2 Samuel
- ☐ 1–2 Kings
- ☐ Jonah
- ☐ Amos
- ☐ Hosea
- ☐ Isaiah
- ☐ Micah
- ☐ Zephaniah
- ☐ Nahum
- ☐ Habakkuk
- ☐ Joel
- ☐ Jeremiah
- ☐ Ezekiel
- ☐ Obadiah
- ☐ Lamentations
- ☐ Daniel
- ☐ Haggai
- ☐ Zechariah
- ☐ Esther
- ☐ 1–2 Chronicles
- ☐ Malachi
- ☐ Ezra- Nehemiah

- ☐ Job
- ☐ Proverbs
- ☐ Ecclesiastes

- ☐ Song of Songs
- ☐ Psalms

- ☐ Mark
- ☐ Matthew
- ☐ Luke
- ☐ Acts
- ☐ 1 Thessalonians
- ☐ 2 Thessalonians
- ☐ James
- ☐ 1 Corinthians
- ☐ 2 Corinthians
- ☐ Galatians
- ☐ Romans
- ☐ Colossians
- ☐ Philemon
- ☐ Ephesians
- ☐ Philippians
- ☐ 1 Timothy
- ☐ Titus
- ☐ 2 Timothy
- ☐ 1 Peter
- ☐ 2 Peter
- ☐ Jude
- ☐ Hebrews
- ☐ 1 John
- ☐ 2 John
- ☐ Gospel of John
- ☐ 3 John
- ☐ The Revelation

ZONDERVAN®
.com